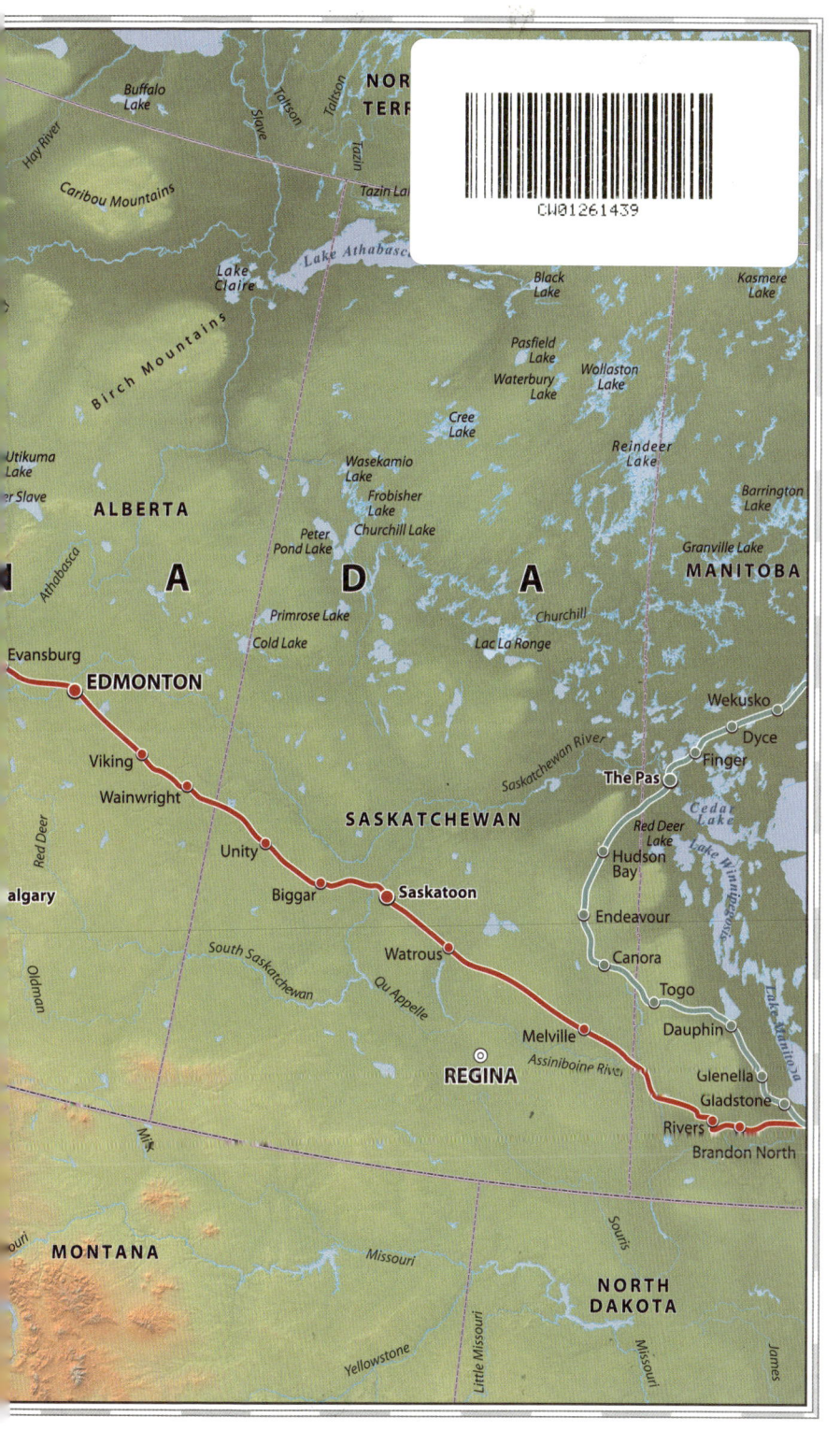

CANADA
by Train

WAY·OF·THE·RAIL
PUBLISHING

Bernards Township Library
32 South Maple Avenue
Basking Ridge, NJ 07920

Discover more at: *www.wayoftherail.com*

CANADA
by Train

So immense is the beauty of Canada that coming face to face with its vast lands, rich forests and natural landscapes can be an overwhelming experience. The best way to take in the beauty and wonder of this majestic nation is to enjoy it piece by piece, vista after vista. Thankfully, there is VIA Rail, which preserves and sustains the best way to explore Canada – by train.

Riding the train is coasting through the rich history that binds Canada with its rail tracks. Since 1885, when the first rail company, the Canadian Pacific Railway, built miles and miles of tracks across the nation, passenger rail service continues to transport not only Canadians but travelers around the world in an enriching and entertaining mode. Through the looking glass, one can bear witness to the majestic hands of nature that carved Canada's beauty evident whichever way one turns – the great Rockies, the rolling plains, the strong river currents, the icy terrains, the shining cityscapes and so much more.

Embark on a voyage of discovery that will allow you to experience Canada at its most magnificent. No matter what the season, a trip aboard VIA Rail promises a truly unique perspective of the many facets of this country, keeping the great tradition of train travel alive. Through the windows of our legendary train, the romance of one of the world's greatest journeys lives on. See the people, the places and the things that make Canada unique — up close by train. Travel VIA Rail and experience Canada today.

About the Authors

Chris Hanus — Born in the Philippines, Chris grew up in Vancouver, British Columbia, where the charm of train travel has always lured him. His colourful career with VIA Rail spans ten years, starting in 1997 when he first worked as an Activity Coordinator aboard the Canadian. His productive stint with the Crown Corporation culminated in January 2008, where he held the position of Product Specialist for the company's Marketing Planning Department.

Over the years, Chris mastered the fine details of the railway system, amassing a cornucopia of railroad facts and personal insights into life aboard the trains. He has extensively traversed Canada aboard VIA Rail and on some train services in North America, covering some 500,000 kilometres (over 300,000 miles!), and still counting.

Chris established Way of The Rail Publishing in 2002, in response to the growing demand for printed guides on railway journeys across Canada. He published the Railway Map Guide to British Columbia and Canadian Rockies, a pioneer in travel publication, and largely contributed to the development of the latest and comprehensive *Canada by Train* Guidebook.

John Shaske — John, the founder and president of John Steel Rail Tours, discovered his passion for trains when he was just four years old. His family often travelled between Edmonton and Vancouver on the Canadian National Railway, and John learned a great deal about trains during those trips. This was also when he decided to become an engineer. Years later, however, when John enrolled in the University of British Columbia, he chose a degree in Pharmacology instead.

Fortunately, some dreams never die. In the winter of 1981 John was asked to guide a B.C. Rail trip to Lillooet. The trip sealed John's fate — he was hooked on train travel forever. For years, John studied every aspect of the rail business and worked in railroading. His efforts culminated in 1990, when he founded John Steel Rail Tours. Today, the company is famous all over the world and John is rightly regarded as a Canadian rail expert.

ABOUT THIS BOOK | 5

CANADA by Train

Publisher: Chris Hanus
Editors: Carmela Jocelyn Tarroja, Herminio S. Beltran Jr.
Contributors: Thulasi Srikanthan, Liane Cherrett, Mandy Morgan
Design & Illustrations: Triay Design
Picture Research: Analiza Beltran
Cartography: Compare Infobase Limited
Photographers: Margaret Kitson, Suzanne Ingeborg, George Triay, N. Matsumoto

U.S. Distribution:
Atlas Books Distribution
30 Amberwood Parkway
Ashland, OH 44805
Tel: (301) 459-3366
Fax: (419)-281-6883
Order Tel: 1-800-266-5564
Email: orders@AtlasBooks.com
www.atlasbooksdistribution.com

CANADIAN Distribution:
Sandhill Book Marketing Ltd.
#99-1270 Ellis Street,
Cannery Row Building
Kelowna, BC
V1Y 1Z4 CANADA
Tel: (250) 763-1406
Fax: (250) 763-4051
Order Tel: 1-800-667-3848
Email: info@sandhillbooks.com
www.sandhillbooks.com

Published in Canada by:
WAY OF THE RAIL PUBLISHING
All rights reserved. No part of this publication may be reproduced, stored in a retrieval system or transmitted, in any form or by any means without prior permission of the copyright holder, WAY OF THE RAIL PUBLISHING.

Help Improve Our Guides
At WAY OF THE RAIL PUBLISHING, we deeply care about our readers. However, we cannot accept responsibility for any consequence arising from the use of our guides. We make every effort to ensure that our guidebooks are up-to-date when each edition goes to print. If you find that the information given in our guide is no longer current, please let us know. We welcome any comments about our guides, and we will make every effort to incorporate our readers' suggestions and make our guides as practical and useful as possible.

To thank you for your suggestions and feedback, we will send a free copy of our guide to readers whose information or ideas are incorporated in the next edition. Please send contributions to the Publishing Manager, WAY OF THE RAIL PUBLISHING, P.O. Box 4498–349 West Georgia Street, Vancouver, BC V6B 3Z8 Canada.

Custom Book Publishing:
Our train travel guides and maps are a valuable resource for any business. Customized maps and guides are ideal for business travelers, conference organizers, and tour operators. In addition, the high quality and practical nature of our products are guaranteed to make them a treasured gift for your employees or business associates.

WAY OF THE RAIL PUBLISHING will be glad to customize all its titles according to your specifications. We can personalize our guidebooks and maps by adding your corporate logo, a specially-designed cover, or by altering the information contained in the guide to suit your particular needs.

For more information regarding purchasing books in bulk at great discounts or customizing books, please contact Special Marketing, WAY OF THE RAIL PUBLISHING, 4498 – 349 West Georgia Street, Vancouver, BC V6B 3Z8 Canada.

National Library of Canada Cataloguing in Publication Data
ISBN:
978-0-9730897-5-2

Introduction

How To Use This Guide

▬▬▬▬▬ THE GET TO KNOW CANADA chapter, with a green bar at the top of each page, covers a comprehensive introduction of Canada, its government, people, regions, wildlife, economy and what it has become today as a First World Nation.

▬▬▬▬▬ THE HISTORICAL ROOTS OF CANADA'S RAILWAY chapter, with a purple bar at the top of each page, covers a rich historical account of the beginning of the Canadian rail system - the people, places and things that made possible the formation of what is now the Crown Corporation passenger train service.

▬▬▬▬▬ THE TRAIN CLASSES & SERVICES chapter, with a red bar at the top of each page, gives complete details on the different classes of accommodations and perks of a particular train class that will suit your preference and budget.

▬▬▬▬▬ THE RAIL TRAVEL TIPS chapter, with a limegreen bar at the top of each page, is a treasure trove of practical advice on train travel to relax the nerves. It includes quick references from booking to boarding, as well as life-saving reminders you need to know to get the most out of your train journey.

▬▬▬▬▬ THE CANADIAN RAILWAY 101 chapter, with an orange bar at the top of each page, provides added information on the technical workings of the railway system and how its smart features help run the course of lands and lives. It also has a supplementary onboard fitness handbook – the Railway Yoga.

▬▬▬▬▬ THE ROUTE GUIDE chapter, with a blue bar at the top of each page, gives a comprehensive description of the routes your train is traversing. Each region is vividly described and you are given exciting "previews" of the amazing journey that lies ahead through valuable mile-by-mile route guides.

▬▬▬▬▬ THE APPENDIX chapter with a grey bar at the top of each page, serves as instant information finder for easy retrieval of rail references. The listings are grouped according to topics and include Timetable, itinerary guides, tour operator partners, travel agents and a compilation of commonly used railway lingo.

ABOUT THIS BOOK | 7

Added Features
Your *Canada by Train* Guidebook contains enjoyable features for a more enriching experience.

COLOUR CODING - The pages of your travel guide has coloured bars on top to identify each chapter, making it easier for readers to look up topics and locate information. This colour coding system also serves as a guide in marking and following routes, completely listed on the book's back flap.

PHOTOGRAPHS - A visual feast that provides travelers not just the eye-catching glimpse of the magnificent views but an impressive foresight of life on board captured in snapshots.

EDITORIAL BOXES - Spot the star icon on your travel guide and gain useful information to enhance your travel, and learn bits of trivia about a celebrated person, a fascinating object or a remarkable place which you are most likely to encounter along the train tracks.

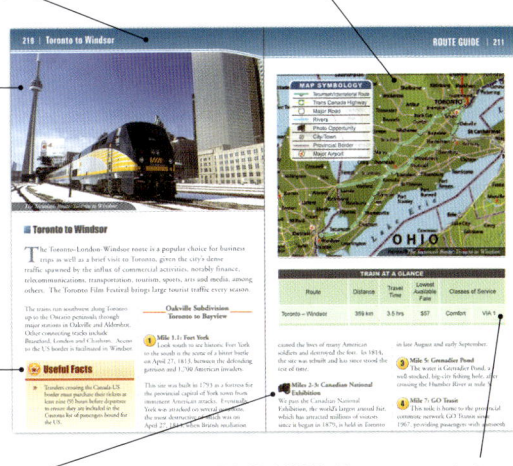

CAMERA ICONS - Can't afford to miss those photos of a lifetime? The camera icons on your travel guide mark the perfect spots for photo opportunities, with sample snapshots of mesmerizing backdrops to guide you in capturing those happy holiday moments.

DETAILED MAPS - A handy companion that gives travelers visual orientation of an entire region for easy appreciation of the journey.

TRAIN AT A GLANCE - Every segment of VIA Rail routes featured in the travel guide is accompanied by a table of basic details which passengers can thumb through for quick reference. This table lists down the route, distance, travel time, lowest available fare and classes of service available for that train line.

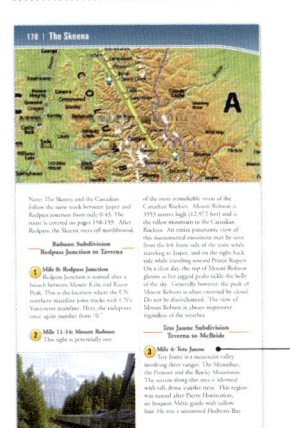

235 LOCATING YOUR POSITION - Watch for mileposts along side the track to locate your position in your subdivision. Mileposts are located at every mile alongside the tracks. Numbers increase from east to west and south to north. Numbers go back to zero at the beginning of every subdivision. Mileposts indicate the location of the train enabling passengers to anticipate points of interest. These signs can be along either side of the track. They are usually rectangular white boards with black numbers on them.

MILE-BY-MILE ROUTE GUIDES - A welcome feature that gives travelers hints on what exciting landmarks to expect along the way, including a brief history and fascinating trivia.

8 | **Introduction**

Contents

Get to Know Canada

Government and Politics **12-17**
Arts and Cultures **18-19**
Global Economic Model **20-21**
Multiculturalism **22-27**
Natural Regions **28-29**
Wildlife **30-35**
A Brief History of Canada **36-39**

Historical Roots of Canada's Railway

The Great Canadian Links **42-49**
The Nation that the Railway Built ... **50-55**
Legendary Moments **56-59**
Chronology **60-65**

Train Classes and Services

Classes of Service **68-74**
Types of Railcars **74-83**
Accommodation and
Seat Configuration **84-95**

Train Travel Tips

Fares and Reservations **98-99**
Pre-Boarding Checklist **100-101**
Safety Measures Onboard **102**
Baggage Policy **102-103**
The Train – Your Home
Away From Home **104-111**
Onboard and Overnight **112-113**
Travel Setbacks **114-115**

Canadian Railway 101

The Development of the Standard
Rail Gauge System **118-119**
A Railway Full of Freight Cars **120-123**
Smart Features **124-125**
Signs & Symbols Along the Way ... **126-127**
The Railway Yoga **128-137**

Route Guide

Western Canada **140-191**
  The Canadian **142-167**
  The Skeena **168-181**
  The Malahat **182-189**
  Snow Train to Jasper **190-191**

Prairies and Central Arctic **192-193**
  The Hudson Bay **194-199**

Ontario and Québec **200-245**
  Montréal to Toronto **202-207**
  Toronto to Ottawa **208-209**
  Toronto to Windsor **210-215**
  Toronto to Sarnia **216-219**
  Toronto to Niagara Falls **220-223**
  Montréal to Ottawa **224-227**
  Montréal to Québec City **228-229**
  The Chaleur **230-235**
  The Saguenay **236-241**
  The Abitibi **242-243**
  The Lake Superior **244-245**

Atlantic Canada **246-261**
  The Ocean **248-261**

Appendix

Timetable **263-301**
Suggested Itineraries **302-307**
Travel Tour Operators **308-309**
Overseas Travel Agents **310-311**
Railway Lingo **312-315**

Index and Acknowledgements

Index **316-319**
Acknowledgements **320**

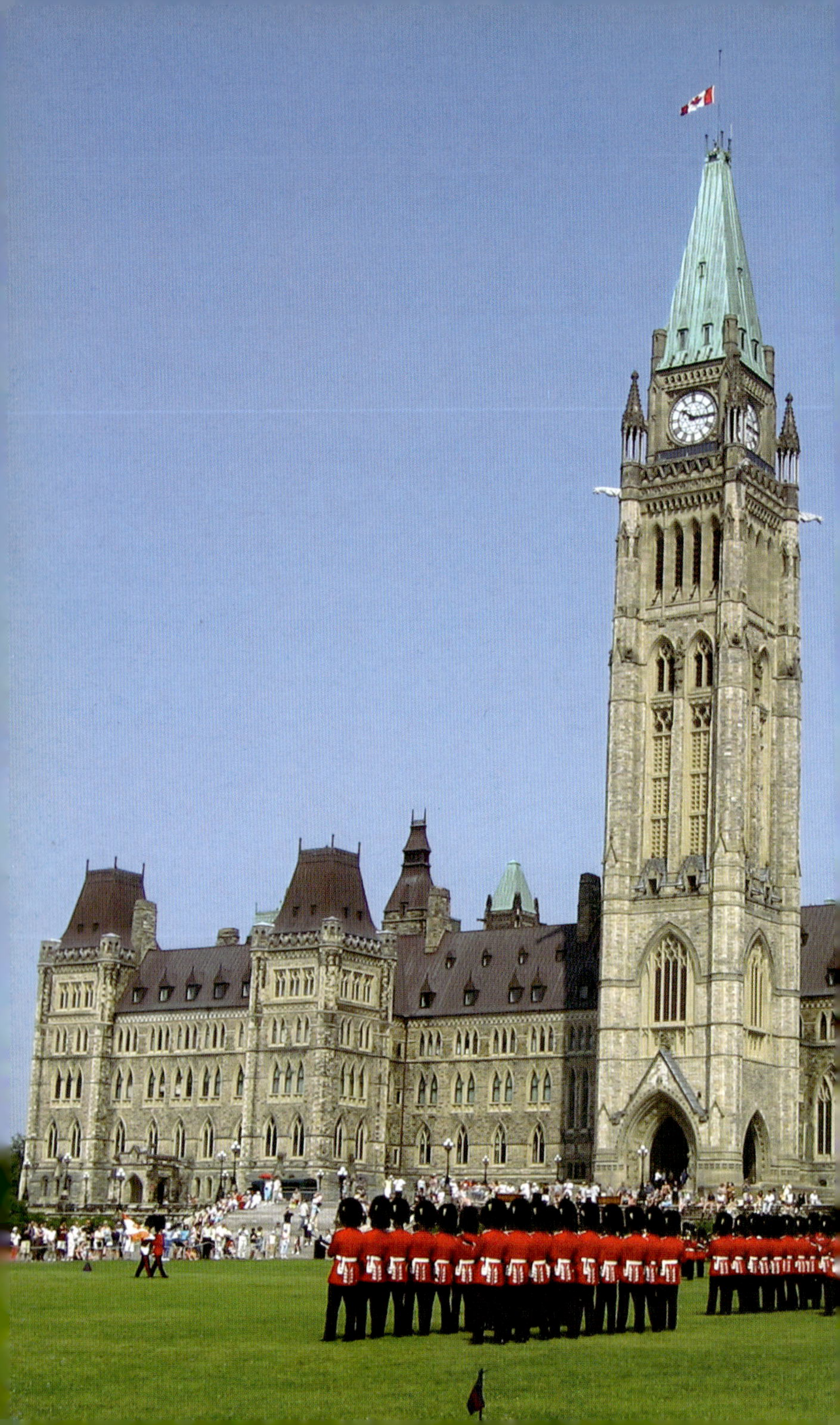

GET TO KNOW CANADA

Government and Politics 12-17

Arts and Cultures 18-19

Global Economic Model 20-21

Multiculturalism 22-27

Natural Regions 28-29

Wildlife 30-35

A Brief History of Canada 36-39

Government and Politics

Canada is the second largest country in the world and the biggest nation in the continent of North America. The name Canada is derived from an Iroquoian-Indian term "konata" which means village or community, the kind of organized settlement which existed in the lowlands long before the Europeans arrived in the 15th century.

Geographical and Political Components

Canada is officially composed of ten provinces and three territories. These are Alberta, British Columbia, Manitoba, New Brunswick, Newfoundland, Nova Scotia, Ontario, Prince Edward Island, Québec and Saskatchewan. Its three territories are in the North namely, Northwest Territories, Nunavut and Yukon Territory. Majority of Canada's population resides in the Southern part due to its close proximity to the borders of the United States, while large tracks of lands in the Northern areas are sparingly populated and mostly serves as protected home for Canadian aborigines.

Although most of Canada borders the United States of America, Canada takes pride in its unique and independent culture. Because of Canada's historical ties with Britain, Canada inherited a similar parliamentary system. Today, Queen Elizabeth II resumes her position as the Head of State. The Queen persists to be the leading lady of the Canadian Mint as her image is portrayed on the $20 dollar bills and her profile is inscribed on Canadian coins. She does not have a strong influence on Canada's political field per se, but her presence symbolizes Canada's loyalty as a Commonwealth country. In addition to similarities with the British form of government, Canada uses the metric system, and adheres to the rules of British grammar and spelling as the standard for language.

The fact that Canada is a bilingual country proves to be one of her unique attributes. English and French are equally the official languages of the nation. While visiting the province of Québec, where French is the official language, it is wise to carry a pocket English-French dictionary when traveling outside of Montréal, Québec's most metropolitan city. Québec maintains an indigenous culture as shown in its traditions and festivals. This province brims with several of Canada's most renowned musicians, authours and filmmakers. No doubt, Québec is heralded as the pulse of Canadian arts.

Canada's government is a federation, meaning the powers and responsibilities are divided between the federal government and the ten provincial and three territorial governments.

The federal government takes care of issues and concerns that affect the entire nation; foremost of these are national

GET TO KNOW CANADA | 13

The House of Commons.

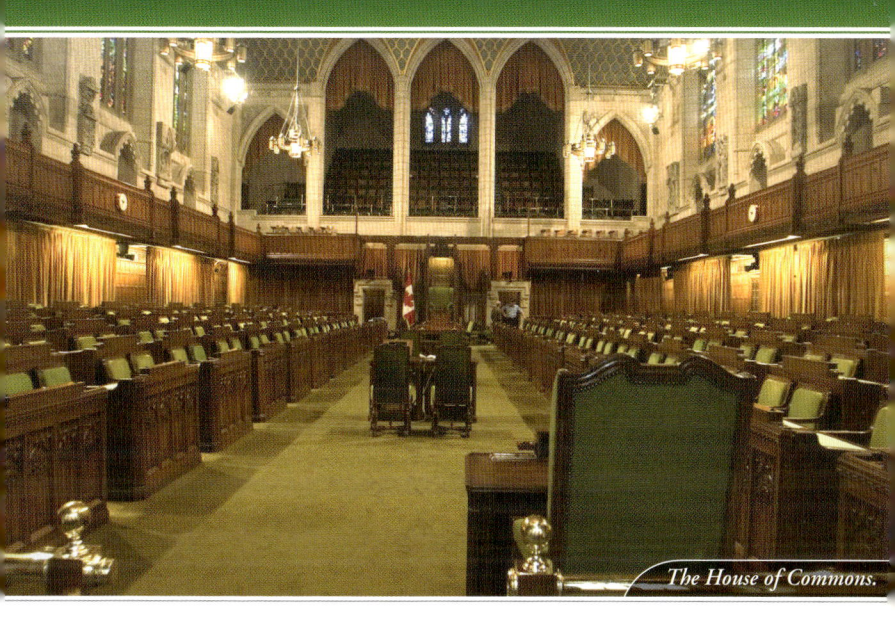

defence, foreign policy, citizenship, criminal law, banking and the postal system. The provincial and territorial governments implement the system and laws on transportation, education and health care, while some laws like environmental protection are shared with the federal government.

On the other hand, administration of laws that directly concerns the community such as peace and order, safety, cleanliness, garbage disposal, and other community environmental programs are enforced by the municipal or local government.

Leadership in all three levels of government are determined by an election, participated in by all Canadian citizens eligible to vote.

Centre: Queen Elizabeth II.

The Queen, House of Commons and Senate

Canada's federation has a parliamentary system of government. The Parliament is composed of the Queen, the House of Commons and the Senate (Upper House). The seat of the Parliament is in the national capital of Ottawa.

With Her Majesty Queen Elizabeth II as Canada's titular head of state, Canada is likewise a Constitutional Monarchy. The Queen is represented in Canada by the Governor General, who serves at Her Majesty's pleasure and signs all federal laws on the Queen's behalf.

The House of Commons is the strongest political influence in the Canadian parliament and national legislature. They are elected by the people. This level is made up of 308 Members of Parliament,

Government and Politics

The Senate.

popularly known as MPs. Most MPs belong to a political party while some are independent members.

While MPs are elected, members of the Senate or the Upper House are appointed by the Governor General upon the recommendation of the Prime Minister, the highest official of the land.

The Queen through the Governor General, the House of Commons and the Senate must approve all proposed legislations before they are enacted as official laws of the land, with few exemptions.

The Prime Minister and the Cabinet

The House of Commons is composed of members of the dominant political party and assumes the lead role in forming a government. The government is either a majority government (a political party with 155 or more elected members) or a minority government (if the leading political party occupies less than 155 seats). The leader of the biggest party that forms the government becomes the Prime Minister. The party with the second highest number of seats becomes the Opposition and its leader becomes the Leader of the Opposition.

The Prime Minister is responsible in forming his official Cabinet members, chosen from the members of his political party. Each chosen member takes the role of a Cabinet Minister, with a specific responsibility like overseeing the operation of one or more federal departments or agencies, where he assumes the title of a Deputy Minister.

To successfully form a so-called "responsible government," all elected and appointed leaders, particularly the Prime Minister and his Cabinet must earn the trust and confidence of the House of Commons.

Provincial Governments

Provincial governments are formed in the provinces in the same manner they are created in the federal level. The political party with the most number of seats in the provincial legislature leads the government, and the head of this party assumes the role of the Premier of the province. The Premier appoints the members of his provincial Cabinet from the elected members of the leading party. Like the federal government, a provincial government may also be a majority or a minority government, depending on the number of seats won by the leading political bloc.

The Lieutenant Governor represents the Queen in the provinces. Unlike the federal government, the provinces do not have a counterpart Senate level. Before a provincial legislation becomes an official law, it must be approved first by the provincial legislature and the Lieutenant Governor.

Provincial governments are responsible for overseeing the implementation of civil justice, property management and the operation of the various municipal institutions. The laws on major areas like health services, agriculture, immigration, social assistance and transportation are shared with the federal government.

Territorial Governments
Being territorial domains, the Northwest, Nunavut and Yukon Territories of Canada are not sovereign units but rather, their governments are subordinate bodies with powers delegated by the Parliament. The territorial assemblies are also elected and they have the same responsibilities as the provincial governments in overseeing major areas like the environment, social assistance, health and the transport system.

Local Governments
The leaders of the local government are directly elected. The Mayor is the leader of a municipal government while the other elected members are known as councilors. They perform the tasks delegated to them by the higher levels of the government. Generally, they manage the operation of the municipalities, cities, towns and regions. Their responsibilities include police protection, water and sewage services, fire department operation, local public transportation and other services within a specific city or region.

The Rule of Majority
Canada's federal and provincial elections are held every five years, although in some instances, an election may be called earlier. This usually happens if a minority government loses the trust and confidence of the House of Commons. In this case, the Prime Minister decides to call a special election.

Some provinces set specific dates for their elections while municipal elections are held every two or three years, depending on the province. The basic requirements to be eligible to vote in a federal election include a Canadian citizenship and a minimum age of 18 years. These two basic requirements may vary in the provincial or municipal elections. The conduct of voting in all levels — federal, provincial and municipal — is done through secret ballot.

Law and Order
An organized system of laws governs the nation of Canada. There are two forms of law: civil law which deals with disagreements between people and organizations, and criminal law which deals with crime and appropriate punishment.

As in any democratic setup, no one is above the law and everyone in Canada, from the federal leaders down to the provincial, territorial and municipal levels, has the obligation to obey the laws.

The country has an independent justice system, with the Supreme Court as the highest court. Its foremost responsibilities include interpreting Canada's Constitution and setting the limits of powers of the federal and provincial governments. Under the Supreme Court are several levels of courts at the provincial and municipal levels.

Below: Royal Canadian Mounted Police.

16 | Government and Politics

Canada faces its second Québec referendum on sovereignty in 1995.

The Royal Canadian Mounted Police or the RCMP is Canada's national police force. They enforce the laws together with the Canadian courts. Ontario and Québec each have their own provincial police force, the Ontario Provincial Police and the Sureté du Québec, respectively. They provide police services, as well as the RCMP, to a few areas which do not have their own police forces.

Upholding the People's Rights

The Canadian Charter of Rights and Freedoms lays down the basic principles and values that govern Canada as an independent nation. The charter guarantees fundamental rights to everyone regardless of race, colour, religion and personal or cultural belief and ensures that the government cannot take these rights away without just cause.

The basic rights safeguarded and guaranteed by the charter include:

- Basic freedoms such as freedom of speech and peaceful assembly.
- Democratic rights (suffrage or the right to vote)
- Legal rights (representation by a lawyer or legal counsel, fair trial)
- Equality rights (protection against racism and discrimination)
- Aboriginal Peoples' rights (preservation of the indigenous culture)
- Mobility rights (freedom of movement to live and work anywhere in Canada)

Bilingual Canada

With the advent of migrants largely from Britain, Scotland and Ireland who are English speakers combined with the French migrants in Québec whose strong sense of nationalism hinges on the French language, Canada became largely a bilingual nation, with English and French as the two most widely used languages. Over the years, parliamentary discussions and legislations focused on the adoption of a bilingual nation. Formally, in 1969, Canada became officially bilingual. This official bilingualism gives its people equal rights to communicate in either English or French with the Parliament, the courts and all levels of government, and access to many opportunities in the areas of education, business and technology.

Political Parties:
A Showcase of Canadian Voices

Canada's political landscape is shaped by four dominant political parties: The Conservatives, The Liberals, The New Democratic Party (NDP) and The Bloc Québecois (BQ).

The Liberals are ardent supporters of the Free Trade, favour state intervention and, with their broadminded stance, defend controversial changes from conservative norms, such as gay marriage. They have moderate fiscal and social platforms and thus, occupy a safe position in the Canadian political sphere. The Liberal Party is especially popular in Eastern Canada.

On the contrary, the Conservative Party remains fiscally and socially conservative. It favours minimal government intervention and closer alliance with the United States. It also prioritizes Free Trade. The current Conservative Party was formed with the coalition of two conservative parties, The Alliance Party and the Progressive Conservatives. The Conservative Party is largely popular in the West.

Meanwhile, the NDP is seen to lean on the left of the political scale, what with their promotion of the rights of organized labour and their critical stance against budget cuts and shortcuts in social programs. The NDP's political agenda is popular in British Columbia and the Maritimes.

Composed of fervent French descendants of the very first Québec settlers, the BQ party is focused on gaining state sovereignty for Québec, clamoring for separation from the rest of Canada.

Diversity rally in Canada's nation capital, Ottawa.

Arts and Cultures

Showcase of Talents
Céline Dion, Sarah McLachlan, Diana Krall, Bryan Adams, Shania Twain and Avril Lavigne are just among a number of talented Canadian musicians. Recently, the Montréal and Toronto music scenes have made their mark as being the birthplace of several internationally acclaimed musicians. Some of these artists include The Arcade Fire, Stars, Social Broken Scene, Leslie Feist, K-OS and Metric.

Considering Canadian sense of humour, it's not surprising this nation has produced and continues to supply the world with our most championed comedians. John Candy, Dan Ackroyd, Martin Short, Mike Myers and Jim Carrey are just to name a few. Other esteemed Canadian actors include Denys Arcand, Molly Parker, Keanu Reeves and Michael J. Fox. The Canadian film industry cannot compete with Hollywood wages and production levels and inevitably loses most laudably recognized actors to the south.

Internationally, Canadian writers are among the most heralded and successful. Michael Ondatjee and Margaret Atwood are two of the most critically acclaimed authours in the world. Canada also produces many award-winning authours who come from different cultural backgrounds. Rohinton Mistry and Yan Martel are just two examples. All authours mentioned have been successful recipients of either international or national book awards.

Preserving Canadian Culture
American programming occupies the majority of what is broadcast on Canadian television and radio. The Canadian Radio-television and Telecommunications Commission (CRTC) was established by Parliament in 1968. It's an independent public authourity constituted under the Canadian Radio-television and Telecommunications Commission Act and reports to Parliament through the Minister of Canadian Heritage.

The organization's mandate is to determine the appropriate percentage of foreign content permitted on Canadian airwaves. This institution acts to preserve, promote and protect Canadian culture.

Right: Bagpiper at the Halifax Citadel National Historic Site.

GET TO KNOW CANADA | 19

Global Economic Model

From a largely agricultural vastland with an emerging urbanscape of chaotic migrant settlement phases, Canada today towers above the shadow of its struggling past. The economic revolution ignited by the railway and the telegraph system in the early 1800s gradually pushed a steady tide of technological advancement – the combustion engine that modernizes transportation, the assembly line that multiplies industrial production, and the advent of computer networks that linked the nation and its people to all parts of the world.

These are landmark advances that paved the way for Canada to become the economic giant that it is today. Globally, the rapid technological advancement and the opening up of international markets are vital in spurring and sustaining the economic growth of Canada.

Today, Canada operates on a so-called knowledge-based or 'smarter' economy where the results of technological innovations are largely utilized to produce automated, state-of-the-art machinery and equipment that bring about industrial progress.

Technology Without Borders
Canada is a wealthy nation that has a high standard of living. Endowed with gains from new technologies and the liberalization of global trade, Canada continues to evolve from a primarily rural nation into a high-tech powerhouse. From its small domestic market, Canada has successfully expanded multilateral trading relationships to larger, more affluent economies.

On the homefront, Canadian businesses benefited from information and communication technology advancements, enabling them to explore buyers and partners anywhere on the globe. The acquisition of new knowledge, enhanced research facilities and intensive service industries has enabled three out of four Canadians with employment. This transformation has essentially reshaped and strengthened the nation.

Today, Canada is similar to the United States in terms of high living standards, prolific production system and market-oriented policies. Stimulated by the sweeping global rehabilitation after World War II, Canada's micro-economic sectors like manufacturing, mining, and services displayed brisk growths that contributed largely to groom the nation into an industrial leader.

The Canadarm in space.

GET TO KNOW CANADA | 21

North American Free Trade Agreement
The world's most profitable trading relationship is that between Canada and the United States. The 1989 Free Trade Agreement is responsible for $1.2 billion dollars crossing the borders every day. This trading relationship exceeds more than each member of the European Union combined. The 1994 North American Free Trade Agreement (NAFTA), a treaty signed between Canada, Mexico and the United States, also contributes greatly to this lucrative partnership.

Growth Versus Unemployment
1993 marks the year where Canada's economy has continued to accrue steadily. Since then, the unemployment rate has decreased approximately 8 percent to 6 percent. However, issues such as "brain drain," the emigration of Canadian professionals going south attracted by higher paying positions and lower taxes, continue to be a concern for Canada's growth.

Oil boom in Fort McMurray, Alberta.

Multiculturalism

Canada takes pride in its sundry of ethnicities from all over the world. Unlike other countries where immigrants are encouraged to adopt the country's predominant identity, a method referred to as a 'Melting Pot,' Canada prefers to promote the 'Mosaic' method, acting to foster the preservation of diverse cultures. When walking the streets of any downtown Canadian city, the exciting scent of blended international foods triggers appetites while the traveler marvels at districts festooned with vivacious colour. This reflects Canada's array of ethnicity.

Predecessors of Modern Canadians

First Nations, Métis and Inuit are the three recognized aboriginal people in Canada. Approximately one million First Nations reside in Canada. Majority or 75 percent of this population identify themselves as Aboriginals (such as Woodland Cree, Ojibway, Menominee and Saulteaux), 20 percent as Métis and 5 percent as Inuit.

Métis are also referred to as Bois-Brûlé or mixed-bloods born of mixed marriages between the aboriginals and French, Scottish or English migrants. Inuit, on the other hand, are indigenous people with the same culture predominantly living in the Canadian Arctic. About 60 percent of the Aboriginal people reside on reserve land, and they currently occupy 900 out of the 2,370 reservations where the residents are allowed by the government to exercise self-rule.

First Nations advocate self-government, which they uphold as their foremost right under the Charter of Rights and Freedom. The federal government gives value to First Nation autonomy by providing them with support and freedom to practice their original culture and practices long embraced by their forefathers before they were trampled upon during the dark period of colonialism.

Canada's showcase of First Nation support is found in the Nunavut Territory, an icy territory in the northernmost part covering over 349,650 sq km. In 1999, the federal government granted the Inuit this official homeland, the name of which aptly means "Our Land." In this territory, the Inuit's culture is successfully preserved, and their native language Inuit is proclaimed the second official language.

The First Migrants
The Canadian population data of 2007 showed that about 14 million Canadians trace their ethnic origin as English (6 million), Scottish (4.2 million) or Irish (3.8 million).

In 1497, the Italian explorer John Cabot was commissioned by the British Government to explore previously uncharted territories. In this mission, he discovered Newfoundland, an original province of Canada. Although Cabot was credited with this "discovery," the First Nations had inhabited the major parts of North America for several hundred years even before Cabot's historical quest. It was not until a century later that Britain explored and took advantage of the vast potential and richness of the New World, or the Americas. From thereon, British settlements were built, sustained largely by trade and agriculture.

A large influx of immigrants from the British Isles followed, with the hope to alleviate their previous living conditions. Majority of them were Irish settlers who fled from the Potato Famine in Ireland between the years 1845 and 1849. More European settlers journeyed into Canada after the government decreed the distribution of free land in the western part to populate the provinces and commence progress.

As history shows, the British, Irish and Scottish migrants had major roles and

Left: Inuit building an igloo.

Portrait of Jacques Cartier.

profound impact in building what we know today as Canada. This is largely true of Britain, whose laws and traditions reverberate with the rich colonial heritage of Canada.

**French Canadians:
Quest for Independence**
French Canadians make up more than 20 percent of Canada's population.

As early as the 16th century, the French had been fishing off the coast of Newfoundland, way before the French government commissioned the Italian Mercenary Giovanni de Verrazano in 1524 to discover the coastlines of the New World. He came upon a fertile land south from Newfoundland and named it Acadia.

In 1834, the French navigator Jacques Cartier set out in search of the Asian route and found himself on the shores of Acadia where he erected a lofty

Cross, providing this small settlement with French sovereignty. Soon after, missionaries, fur traders and farmers immigrated to this area establishing the colony of New France.

Tension between France and England made its way to North America in the mid-18th century, spurring the Seven Years War (1756 to 1763) where French settlers were forced to become English subjects. Despite this, the French persisted to preserve their language and religion. For centuries onwards, the French culture flourished and greatly fostered a strong sense of independence. This lingering display of nationalism survived till now, as Québec nationalists passionately advocate for Québec to be granted a self-determined and independent state . Today, the Bloc Québecois (BQ) political party is a strong advocate of a sovereign Québec state.

Chinese railway workers, 1884.

Chinese Canadians: The Sino Settlers

About 5 percent of Canadian population identify themselves with Chinese descent. They constitute the largest visible minority group in Canada.

The first Chinese settlers to arrive into Canada reached the shores of the Pacific Ocean in the mid-18th century and were unfortunately captured and deported to Mexico. In 1858, the first permanent Chinese settlers arrived from San Francisco as gold miners. The settlers worked in British Columbian mines and contributed greatly to the grueling task of constructing the Canadian railway.

Asian settlers were unjustly discriminated against by the government, working long hours with lower wages under dangerous working conditions like explosions for mountain passes. They do not have the right to vote and unlike other immigrants to Canada, they were required to pay a head tax upon entrance into the country. Of course, this has all changed as Canada takes pride in accepting an abundance of diverse cultures. In 2006, Canada formally apologized for the tax imposed on Chinese settlers.

Recently, affluent Chinese families in prosperous Hong Kong migrated to Canada after Britain turned over this former colony to China in 1997, as they do not want to adhere to strict Chinese principles.

Today, each Canadian metropolis boasts of a vivacious Chinatown characterized by busy streets alive with distinct night markets, vermillion lantern ornaments, and teaming with eclectic Chinese food and inviting teahouses.

Italian Canadians: Grazie Molto, Canada

Approximately 4 percent of the national population identify their ethnicity as Italian.

In the 19th century, the so-called Resurgence or Italian Unification, where the different states of the Italian peninsula were unified, prompted many Italians to go to Canada to escape the prevailing social turmoil, lured by news of profitable prospects in New World. Most immigrants ended up working in

GET TO KNOW CANADA | 25

Italian bistro in Montréal.

the forests, mines and railways of Canada. After World War II, more Italians escaped from the chaos in Europe and made their way to Canada.

In most major Canadian cities, Italian districts are alive with aromatic coffee houses, delicious delis and first-rate billiard halls. During world soccer matches where Italy plays an elimination game, Italians fill the atmosphere with impassioned cries of triumph or defeat in Italian districts like in the Greater Toronto Area, Greater Montreal Area, Vancouver and many areas in Ontario.

German Canadians: Escaping the Wrath of Wars

Approximately 2.7 million citizens identify themselves as Germans in Canada. The turn of the 19th century marked a multitude of German settlers in Canada, escaping the threats of German socio-political paranoia at that time. This initial wave of German migration continued after World War I and World War II.

Unlike the French nationalists, the German settlers have largely integrated themselves into the English-speaking majority. Although there are now a few large German enclaves, this does not mean there are no more German communities. Proof is the existence of the Amish community in Ontario. The Amish, a German religious branch of the

German immigrants from Hambourg

Multiculturalism

Ukraininan immigrants.

Mennonite Church, practice austere living and this strong German tie is still strongly observed until today. German culture is also found in communities such as the Waterloo in Ontario and in places like Lunenburg, Kitchener and Nova Scotia.

Ukrainian Canadians: The Prairie Settlers

The Ukrainian community in Canada is estimated at over one million strong, or 3.6 percent of the total Canadian population.

The first Ukrainian immigrants arrived in the country in the late 1890s due to lingering Soviet economic and social instability, and founded the Edna-Star Settlement, the first and largest Ukrainian block settlement. They initially immigrated to the prairies of Alberta, Saskatchewan and Manitoba, built their distinct churches that echo their Ukrainian heritage, and toiled in the fertile Canadian lands bringing with them their agricultural practices.

Indo-Canadians: Enriching the Cultural Mosaic

Data from Statistics Canada show at least 700, 000 people from East India reside in Canada. The Sikh soldiers were the first Indian immigrants to arrive in Canada as members of the British Army. They are followers of India's predominant Sikh religion based in Punjab. Like the Chinese, Indian immigrants were subjected to discrimination like racism and were refused to land ashore upon arrival in Canada.

Today, East Indians are encouraged to practice their diverse and bountiful faiths. It is always easy to find a charming and savvy Indian restaurant in any Canadian city, especially in Indo-Canadian centres like the Greater Vancouver Area, the Greater Toronto Area and in the growing Chinese communities in Calgary, Edmonton and Montréal.

Indian immigrants at Frank Station. Alberta, 1903.

GET TO KNOW CANADA | 27

I AM CANADA

Natural Regions

Next to Russia, Canada is the second largest country in the world, covering 9,976,140 sq km. For most of Canada's history, this nation has remained isolated from battling wars in other parts of the world. With the lack of development in the frozen Canadian north, approximately 80 percent of Canada's population lives within 300 km of the U.S. border.

Canada borders only with the United States and is bounded on the north by the Arctic Ocean, on the west by the Pacific Ocean, and on the east by the Atlantic Ocean and its associated bodies of water, including Baffin Bay and the Labrador Sea.

River systems are bountiful in Canada, coming from places such as The Great Lakes, Lake Winnipeg, Saskatchewan Rivers, Bear Lake and the Québec Reservoirs. Canada has an abundance of natural resources including iron ore, nickel, zinc, copper, gold, lead, molybdenum, potash, silver, fish, timber, wildlife, coal, petroleum, natural gas and hydropower.

Cordilleran Region
The Cordilleran Region covers 15.9 percent of all Canada, occupying most of British Columbia, the Yukon Territory and southwestern Alberta. This region is a complex mountain system composed of sedimentary rock and young fold mountains that extend along the Pacific coast.

The immense size and soaring height of these Canadian Rockies is one of the most remarkable sights of nature. During the summertime, folding lines of strata show how these mountains have shifted and grown throughout the millions of years. In the wintertime, this sight is especially awe-inspiring, what with mountain tips and slopes coated in fresh, crisp snow.

Interior Plains
A continuation of the Great Plains of the United States, the Interior Plains lie between the Canadian Shield and the Rocky Mountains and occupies 18.3 percent of Canada, including the wheat-producing Prairie provinces of Alberta, Manitoba and Saskatchewan. It is an area of flat land with rolling hills and accounts for nearly all of Canada's wheat production

The prairies are a perfect backdrop for a dazzling display of nighttime Northern Lights. It is also common for a traveler to view a spectacular prairie storm releasing panoramic electric waves without the obstruction of buildings or mountains.

GET TO KNOW CANADA | 29

The Appalachian Region
The Appalachian Region occupies approximately 3.4 percent of Canada. It is composed of many interesting landforms like low mountains, flat uplands, rocky cliffs and forests with a variety of vegetation and wildlife. Canada has a small region of the Appalachians; the majority of these forests are in the United States.

The Appalachian forest spreads across arable lowland areas, and blankets Québec's tallest peaks. The region offers excellent spots for forestry, coal and oil mining, and a variety of marine activities.

The Innuitian Region
The Innuitian belt stretches from the Arctic Lowlands to Ellesmere and to Axel Heiberg Islands in the far north. Composed of sedimentary and metamorphic rocks, it is rich in oil, coal and natural gas.

With height ranging from 100 metres to about 2,926m above sea level, most of this mountainous region is covered with glaciers or polar deserts while the sparse vegetation is mainly lichens and mosses. The region has a cold, dry Arctic climate.

The Canadian Shield
The Canadian Shield, also referred to as the Precambrian Shield, Laurentian Shield or the Laurentian Plateau, is the oldest land in Canada and was formed by the solidification of molten rock. It is in a U-shaped formation and the largest region extending nearly half of the country's land mass across eastern and central Canada covering over 5 million sq km.

It is rich in minerals including copper, gold, silver and nickel. Sudbury, Ontario is the town most renowned for extracting minerals.

Lowlands Region
The Great Lakes - St. Lawrence Lowlands region constitutes only 1.3 percent of Canada but is where most people live, a flat to gently rolling region extending southwest from Québec City to Lake Huron and includes all of the St. Lawrence River valley and the densely populated Ontario Peninsula.

The 3,000 km-long St. Lawrence River is Canada's gateway to the Atlantic Ocean, flowing from Kingston, Ontario and out into the Atlantic. Meantime, the Great Lakes formed 10,000 years ago during the Ice Age, consists of five members: Lake Superior, Lake Michigan, Lake Huron, Lake Erie and Lake Ontario.

Wildlife

If the traveler is a lover of wildlife, one of the most exciting aspects of visiting Canada is exploring and watching the abundance of wildlife inhabiting all parts of the country. Sables, wolves, coyotes, foxes, grizzly bears, black bears and skunks are commonly seen Canadian animals. Polar bears and arctic foxes are renowned for their white colour and are found in arctic regions. Rocky mountain goats and big horned sheep frequent the lower bases of the Rockies. The dense forests of British Columbia are inhabited by cougars, panthers, eagles and bears. If travelers are planning a trip into the wild, it is better to be well-informed on the precautions to follow in order to avoid possible dangerous and sometimes fatal situations.

The Timber Wolf

The black, white and grey-coloured timber wolf species inhabit the most isolated regions of the Boreal Forest.

The Polar Bear

Polar bears hold the title as being the largest carnivorous land animal in the world and weigh from 450 to 1,300lbs. The white coloured bear prefers his time alone, and enjoys tasty meals consisting of seals, belugas, whales, rodents and walruses.

The Loon

The loons haunting call has made it a symbol of Canadian wilderness and can be found throughout most parts of Canada. This water bird is featured on the Canadian 1$ coin, referred to as a 'Loonie.'

The Black Bear

Black bears are ubiquitous within North America. They may seem docile as they sleepily lumber along, but they can be fierce and dangerous. Black bears eat grasses, herbs, fruits and rodents.

The Elk

The elk is celebrated as the most populous animal of the Canadian Rockies and happens to be the second largest deer in the world. Although elks are smaller than moose, the male weighs almost twice as that of the female.

The Caribou

The caribou, also referred to as a reindeer outside of North America, has antlers for either sex. Traveling in herds of 10,000 or more, they migrate to the northern tundra in the springtime and travel south to the forests during wintertime.

The Eagle

The eagle, perhaps one of Canada's most respected animals, soars and circles over mountainous and densely forested areas. Canada's golden eagle is one of the rarest treasures with a wing span of up to 7 feet. Bald Eagle sightings are more frequent especially in western Canada.

Wildlife

Big Horn Sheep

Don't confuse these with the mountain goats. Big horn sheep are brown and Rocky Mountain goats are white.

The Moose

Moose are the largest deer in the world weighing from 850 to 1200 lbs, and can be up to 7 feet tall at the shoulders.

The Grizzly Bear

Aside from its voracious appetite for fish, this bear is mostly vegetarian and enjoys spending time scavenging for food. The grizzly bear is a fatal animal and must be avoided within close proximity.

The Beaver

The beaver is Canada's national animal. Their most intriguing features include their flat tails that enable them to swim quickly, and their very large jutting front teeth, used to saw the wood to build their dams. Beavers inhabit rivers and lakes, and are proudly portrayed on the Canadian nickel.

The Orca

The Orca, commonly referred to as a Killer Whale, loves to devour fish, seals, dolphins and whales. They travel in pods and are found in the waters of Canada's west coast. Keep in mind, there are no records of any human fatalities, but it would not be wise to hang on to one's tail for a ride.

The Mountain Goat

Mountain goats have white fur, double-bearded chin and narrow head with black horns rising in a backward curve. They travel in herds and frequent the base of the Rockies, especially in British Columbia. Despite weighing about 150 to 300 pounds, this animal is sure-footed and agile due to its hooves with cushioned skid-proof pads for better grip.

The Cougar

The cougar, one of Canada's most feared predator, is found in Alberta, British Columbia and the north. They stealthily stalk their prey and pounce and destroy when they find the moment suitable.

Face to Face with Canada's Wild Side

The following guidelines will help protect both the traveler and the wildlife when exploring Canada's wilds.

1 Feeding wildlife animals is strongly prohibited. Animals being accustomed to being fed will expect this treatment from visitors, and will become a nuisance, and possibly a danger. Although it is tempting to offer a crumb to a squirrel or a bird, this practice establishes a dangerous dependency on unnatural food sources. Likewise, some of the foods offered are very harmful, especially to animals that hibernate.

2 Throw leftover food and garbage in designated trash bins. Animals may accidentally eat packaging and food wraps and may result in serious consequence. Bears, for instance, frequent campgrounds and townsites if accustomed to easily obtainable food or garbage. Travelers should place all garbage in the animal-proof receptacles provided. Store food in the trunk of your vehicle.

3 Do not get too close to wildlife. Most wildlife animals are untamed and dangerous. Be cautious and take photographs from a distance. Use a telephoto lens if you have one.

4 Do not disturb natural conditions of wildlife groupings or families. Keep away from natural wildlife groupings, for instance, a mother nursing its offspring. Mothers are especially protective of their young and may feel threatened with an outside interference, both animals and human.

5 Reduce speed limit especially when traveling at night. Pay special attention when driving to areas frequented by animals. Do not expect animals to get out of the way of your vehicle. Be prepared to stop instead.

6 Avoid wildlife during mating season. This period usually falls on September to November. It is best to avoid animals like sheep, goat, elk and moose because their behaviours are highly erratic and volatile during these times. Leave them alone and find other subjects instead.

7 Do not immediately approach bears. Bears are fickle, they may be sweet one moment and violent the next. As such, it is better to take precaution when encountering them. If on a road, sit still and avoid catching the animal's attention. Report your sighting immediately to a park officer.

GET TO KNOW CANADA | 35

A Brief History of Canada

Canada's historical past, though brief compared to the voluminous documents in archives of other nations, remains undeniably rich and eventful. After the various waves of foreign settlers struggling to integrate their own culture and way of life into their new environment, the Dominion of Canada was finally founded in 1867. Canadians are fascinated with their past and have exerted efforts to trace the original cultural footprints of their ancestors, now preserved through the many historical sites around the country.

First Nations: The Native Pride
Before the waves of immigrants from Europe, Britain and Asia, Canada had thriving, organized communities peopled by First Nation Canadians who lived mostly in the Northern part about 10,000 to 30,000 years before discovery missions landed on the Canadian shores. There is an estimated 50 diverse cultures that existed in Canada before European settlement. First Nations are composed of various tribes with their own way of life, religious beliefs and practices. However, they are united by a common spiritual belief – that Divine characteristics reside in all creatures, and every object must be regarded with respect. But their natural way of living swiftly changed when the Europeans established settlements.

The First Nation people contributed largely to the establishment of an organized system imposed on them by English and French colonizers. After the Europeans fostered an organized method for trade, the natives were subsequently marginalized, their lands stolen, and were assimilated into British culture. Their indigenous way of life was invaded by foreigners and their natural protective habitat destroyed. Thousands of First Nation inhabitants perished due to the outbreak of diseases like measles and small pox.

Recognizing their rights as original Canadians in whose veins run the blood of Canadian ancestors, there is a strong advocacy since two decades ago to protect First Nation descendants and their homelands. A national representative of the First Nations in Canada is known as the Assembly of First Nations.

Fiery French Empire
The French settled in the lowlands near the St. Lawrence River when they first arrived in Canada over 400 years ago. The area was already known by its Iroquis name Kanata, or Canada when New France or Québec was founded in 1608. People who lived in New France

Top: Newfoundland and Canadian Government delegation signing the agreement admitting Newfoundland to Confederation.

soon became known as Canadiens. They developed their own culture and way of life as seen in their church, state, military and commercial institutions.

Over time, the French settlers had deeply immersed themselves as North Americans without losing their fiery nationalism. When the British conquered Canada in 1760, the French numbering about 60,000 was a force to reckon with, organizing military blockades as seen in the Rebellion of 1837, all the way to more recent history, the separatist crisis of the early 1970s.

The Early Years

Shortly after the defeat of France in 1760, Britain flashed its domination over Canada with the its flag waving over newly controlled areas, from Hudson Bay in the north all the way to Florida in the south. But despite British dominance, they enforced a liberal policy and allowed French to be used as a principal language while the Roman Catholic religion remained a unifying facet amid colonialism. With these, the distinctive identity of the Canadiens was never lost and continued to flourish.

It was not until 15 years later when the most threatening challenge to Canada's independence came, during the American Revolution. Thirteen of the old American colonies (more popularly Virginia, Massachusetts, and Pennsylvania) rebelled against the oppressive colonial policy of Britain. In the armed conflict that ensued between 1775 and 1783, the American rebel colonies strongly pressured Canada to strengthen their cause by becoming the 14th colony in revolt. Despite a military invasion of Canada, the French resisted and Canada remained independent as it is today.

The Great American Breakaway

The United Empire Loyalists, the settlers in America who favoured British rule, also revolted against America's independence. They immigrated to Canada and settled in the North. These Loyalists together with the immigrants from the British Isles joined forces and helped build English Canada. Then, in 1792, Canada was divided into two colonies, Upper Canada (Ontario) and Lower Canada (Québec). The remaining northern colonies which did not join the Revolution (Nova Scotia, the new colony of New Brunswick, and especially Canada) became a refuge for the United Empire Loyalists and the hundreds of refugees from the American Revolution of 1783. The communities they formed provided the foundation for the development of English Canada.

Over time, migrants from Britain increased and the population grew accordingly. Thus, English Canada grew and expanded around the old French colony. This development led to the lingering linguistic divide, French and English, which remains today.

Confederation

The road to confederation was long and arduous. The fear of American dominance and the potential for economic benefits urged the idea of unification forward. Britain's relaxed approach to keep an eye on Canada also led to the confederation movement.

Confederation came to pass in 1867 after consultation with the maritime colonies. The decision was not supported in many regions of Canada, but it was made nonetheless. Ontario, Québec, Nova Scotia and New Brunswick became unified as Canada.

Since 1867, the nation continued to grow when in the 1870s, the government purchased the interior of Canada from Rupert's Land, a large portion of North America previously controlled by the Hudson's Bay Company. With this, Alberta, Saskatchewan and Manitoba became Canadian provinces. British Columbia was also initiated as a Canadian province during this time with the promise of a transcontinental railroad that would link them to the rest of the country. It was not until 1949, where Newfoundland joined the confederation after much opposition. The union of all the old colonies was finally completed. With their combined land areas, Canada became the second largest country in the world, covering a landmass of just under 10 million square kilometres.

The Golden Years

Canada's road to prosperity commenced with the remarkable recovery of world economic conditions after 1896. This combined with the vast progress in the domestic scene, primarily the large-scale production of wheat on the newly settled prairie provinces, the development of hydroelectric power and the intensive exploration of mineral and forest resources on the Shield. All these developments dramatically stimulated Canadian economy, paving the way for future growth.

Whereas Canada was predominantly agrarian in the 19th century, it became increasingly industrialized and urbanized in the 20th century. A census conducted in 1911 revealed that more Canadians lived in cities than in rural areas.

In the years that followed, manufacturing of textiles, steel, and electrical products grew as cities expanded. From 4.32 million inhabitants in 1881, the population of Canada ballooned to 18.23 million in 1961. Between those periods, urban growth was pegged from 23 percent to 70 percent. In 2007, Canada's population was pegged at 33,390,141.

The Quest for Independence

Even though Canada maintained strong links to the monarchy for most of its young life, it was in 1931 that subordination to Britain was legally dispelled. Participating as an independent force in both world wars also helped foster a sense of national pride and identity among Canadians.

Diversity

In the latter part of the 20th century, Canada quickly evolved into a multicultural mosaic. During the period of the initial confederation, more than 90 percent of the population was either French or English. Currently, this number totals less than 50 percent. A shift in immigration policies in the mid-1900s contributed to Canada's increased diversity. Entrance into the country was not restricted to Britain,

America or Northern Europe; all ethnicities were welcomed equally.

Canada Today
The divide between the English and the French proves to be a highly contentious issue as the threat of possible separation persists. The influx of English influence integrated into French culture is seen as a threat to the integrity of their language and culture.

The debate between the government and the First Nations people remains to be a concern in Canadian politics. Treaties promising land to the First Nations were signed and overtime dishonoured. Land is a disputable concern in Canada because some of the land promised to the First Nations have been developed. This circumstance is a reoccurring concern raised to the Supreme Court of Canada.

In conclusion, modern Canada stands as a democratic nation encouraging the voices of differing groups to lament or celebrate their concerns and diversity. Ultimately, it is a challenge for the government to appease and satisfy all concerns. However, Canada is a fortunate nation in that it encourages all citizens to vote without discrimination.

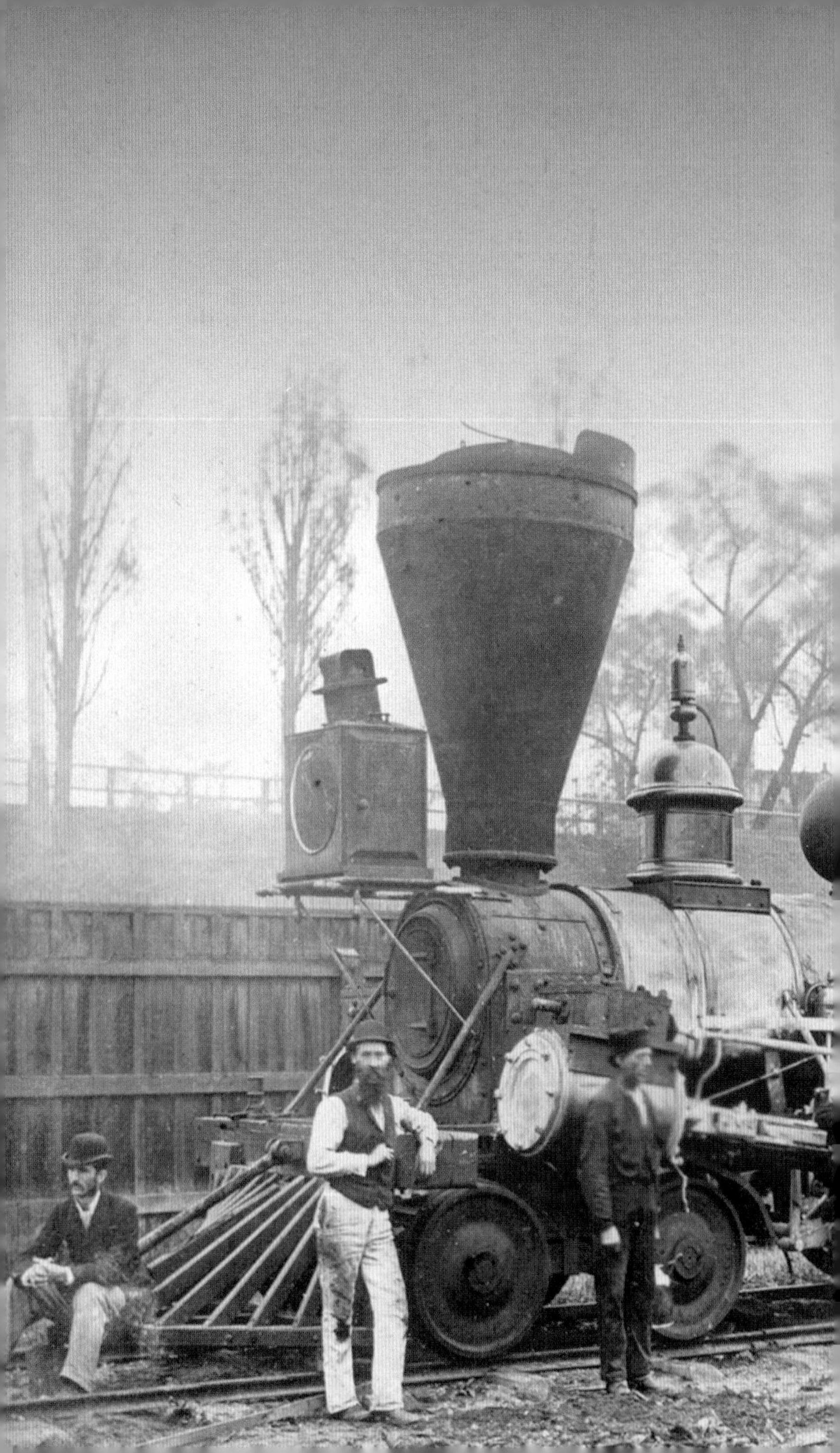

THE HISTORICAL ROOTS OF CANADA'S RAILWAY

The Great Canadian Links **42-49**

The Nation That The Railway Built **50-55**

Legendry Moments **56-59**

Chronology **60-65**

The Great Canadian Links

Construction of Canadian National Railway near Beynon, Alberta.

The Great Canadian Links

Since the 18th century, an organized railway network has been critical for any newly formed country raring to grow and prove itself to other nations. Before the advent of modern engineering feats like superhighways, quays and airport-runways, carving a railway system was the most pressing task to accomplish, the best way to unite a nation and usher it into progress.

Laying the Tracks of History

Settlers were challenged when they came to Canada and attempted to build an infrastructure enabling transportation from one place to another. Before the introduction of the first British North American passenger train, settlers were inclined to take long arduous trips to reach a desired destination. The unyielding weather of Canadian winters and challenging landscapes made it difficult for many settlers to succeed. Traveling by foot, wagon, coach and sleigh were some forms of transportation used. Each year the pathways that were built were flooded, forcing travelers to trudge through sloughs of mud. Wagon wheels could not withstand the constant beatings of new planks and logs and broke down often. This condition greatly discouraged travel for resettlement, trade, business and leisure. The seemingly hopeless situation forced self-subsistence among the pioneering settlers who had to contend with crude trading within the literally small domestic market of their communities.

Eventually, improvements were made and the roads were 'macadamized' with layers of crushed pebbles, tar and asphalt.

Years before the cities of Montréal and Toronto were connected through rail tracks by the Grand Trunk Railway, travelers had to endure a grueling 36 hours on stagecoach to travel between these major locations, weather permitting.

HISTORICAL ROOTS OF CANADA'S RAILWAY | 43

Remote areas such as British Columbia and Newfoundland were virtually impossible to reach.

In 1836, Canada's first public railway was opened by the Champlain and Saint Lawrence Railroad company. With rails of wood and iron straps, it journeyed between La prairie and Saint-Jean, Québec.

After the inauguration of the first railway in Québec in 1836, most Canadians swiftly recognized the potential benefits for having a railway pass through their towns. The men of those families suffering from poverty would be provided with employment. People realized a potential profit by exchanging goods. These possibilities raised the eyebrows of politicians who rapidly made it an integral priority to not only unify regions and towns but also build a larger, more economical powerhouse of a nation. Eventually, railway construction earned a great deal of public and political attention.

The railway race was on and, for some, the dream of a complete railway proved to be over-ambitious. Far from the ideals of a national rail network with seamless links across towns and regions, there were huge capital and massive labour requirements coupled with natural elements which derailed construction plans that those poor railway companies had no way but to default financially. Many rail entrepreneurs fell into the hole of debt and defeat. Railways were forced into bankruptcy, or scooped into the hands of larger companies.

Excessive expectations from all directions – investors, builders, politicians and the public – contributed to the great railway disaster that plagued the industry in the 19th century. Over-the-top enterprise promotions shrouded the reality of impossible feats and unrealistic promises. Nobody wanted to be excluded from the benefits the railway offered, and the race for lucrative profits consequently saturated the market. Towns competed for station stops as a means to immediately accrue the economic state of the inhabitants. Governments providing economic assistance to companies lost their investments because the firms could not generate enough profit to pay their debts. More notably, chaos and confusion ensued with too many cooks spoiling the broth, so to speak. So many companies received permission to construct rail lines within the same areas, as many as 40 at a time.

Just as the first Great War was underway, four independent railway competitors survived the railway rush: Canadian Pacific Railway (CPR), The Canadian Northern Railway, (CNoR), The Grand Trunk Railway (GTR) and the Grand Trunk Pacific(GTP). Although these railway companies survived the over-zealous race for independence, the constant competition left them ultimately exhausted with dwindling funds. The

Pre-Confederation Grand Trunk sleeping car

latter three coasted along the fine line of bankruptcy because of the imminence of war, the feuding for decreased resources and competition for government assistance. When World War I broke, immediate action by the federal government was instilled to improve the miserable state of the Canadian railway. The CNoR, GTP and GTR formed a coalition creating the Canadian National Railway (CN) in 1923.

A decline in railway passenger travel ensued because of the competition of other modern modes of transportation. Automobiles were ubiquitous in the 1930s and destinations were more accessible because of improved paved roads. Airlines provided public travel in the 1940s and '50s. Travelers found it more expedient to journey by air because it was a luxury and many times faster. Consequently, ridership markedly declined to the point that the passenger component of rail companies was no longer viable. In the 1960s several passenger train companies collapsed as international travel became more desirable. Major passenger routes were dropped one after the other. CPR, for instance, insisted on discontinuing its remaining transcontinental route, the Canadian. But the government did not heed, and instead sought a way out to save the legacy and functionality of passenger rail. In 1978, CPR and CN amalgamated together to form VIA Rail, Canada's only current transcontinental passenger rail line.

Grand Trunk Railway (GTR) In 1852, the Canadian government officially declared its plan to have a railway built between Montréal in Québec and Toronto in Ontario. With this intention already in mind, the GTR railway group jumped on this opportunity and ambitiously commenced the construction of this railway.

The goal of the GTR was to build a chief railway between the two major points, with smaller surrounding routes coming and going from the mainline along the way. During the latter months of 1856, the GTR built a railway successfully extending all the way to Sarnia, and also triumphantly built a railway south of the border, operating between Portland, Maine in the U.S., and Sarnia, Ontario.

The expansion of the railway and minimal rail traffic spurred a serious debt for over hundreds of thousands of pounds. Sir Edward William Watkin, a famous English railway manager, was recruited from London by GTR to help mitigate the company's financial state. He successfully convinced the Canadian government to appropriate legislation to assist in reorganizing the financial mess of GTR. The railway was rescued from bankruptcy; however, the government continued to accrue serious amounts of debt.

The GTR rebounded to a lucrative position, continuing to buy up other suffering railways. In order to remain in

Building Grand Trunk Pacific railway track bed, Assiniboine Valley, Manitoba.

the railway enterprise, GTR remained in competition with other rivaling rail companies. The GTR formed the Grand Trunk Pacific Railway Company (GTPR) to compete against the Canadian Pacific and the Canadian Northern Railway. This subsequently led to financial tragedy and GTR consequently declared bankruptcy. Unable to repay debts, the federal government took over GTR in May 1920 and thereafter, became the GTPR in July of the same year. Seeing that Canadian railways were becoming nothing short of a disaster, the Canadian federal government took charge in 1923 by amalgamating GTR with Canadian National Railways, which in the years to follow became Canada's current Canadian National (CN).

Grand Trunk Pacific (GTP)

The 1890s proved to be an ambitious decade for Grand Trunk Railway as it branched out westward. The GTR's manager, Charles Melville Hays, proposed that the railway stretch pass all preconceived destinations and proceed all the way to the north west coast of British Columbia's Prince Rupert. He argued that this vision could seize some of Canadian Pacific Railway's (CPR) grain market and tap into the natural resources from regions north of CPR's routes. Prince Rupert was a convenient destination because it was closer to Asia than CPR's terminus in Vancouver. Inevitably, Mr. Hays projected the possibility of an increase in trade between Asian countries and the GTR.

In 1903, Mr. Hays' dream was realized and he was appointed the first president of the Grand Trunk Pacific Railway (GTP). Sadly, two years before the line would see completion, Mr. Hays died in

Dining staff and porter, Grand Trunk Pacific Railway, 1914.

the unforeseeable sinking of the Titanic. The GTP failed to be as prosperous as Mr. Hays originally envisioned. Because of low volumes of traffic control, this line was abandoned and became a major contributor to the national railway's catastrophe since before World War I. Canadian National Railways purchased this unused line in 1920.

Canadian Pacific Railway (CPR)

The CPR played a key role in the development of Western Canada, building the nation's first transcontinental railway from 1881 to 1885 that connected eastern Canada and British Columbia, which entered the confederation in 1871 upon the condition of a national railway link to be completed in 10 years.

Former Canada Prime Minister John A. Macdonald from the Conservative Party was considered as the man responsible for the unification of Canada from the east to the west coast. He relentlessly attempted to convince the British North American

The Great Canadian Links

Construction train on Stoney Creek bridge, British Columbia.

colonies to amalgamate. After droves of immigrants settled into western America, Macdonald foresaw the potential threat for Western Canada to be staked as American territory. He convinced the British Parliament with this ominous reality and succeeded with solidifying the British North American Act (BNA). By this time, some Americans considered a railway imperative to the unification of the nation because it would fortify the country economically as already there was interest in land north of the 49th parallel. Macdonald took charge immediately and suggested the construction of a railway linking the established eastern Canada to the undiscovered west. Macdonald found it advantageous, geographically and politically.

For most, John A. Macdonald's vision seemed entirely ludicrous. Canada did not have the funds to financially see this overly ambitious project through. Building a railway over uncharted mountainous territories was far from reality. However, British Columbia assented to the grand plan of a national railway under the condition of joining the confederation. Renowned engineer and surveyor Sandford Fleming was delegated the man in charge after the infamous Pacific Scandal involving rail construction bribes that led to the impeachment of John A. Macdonald in 1873. Regardless of these trials, the last spike was driven into the ground at Craigellachie, British Columbia in 1885.

CPR was also largely responsible for the influx of immigrants especially in the western prairies traversing the tracks they built, through CPR agents which lured immigrants with a cheap package of ship voyage, rail ticket, and land once they relocated.

Sir William Van Horne, CPR's first president, denominated the Canadian Pacific. CPR later grew into Canada's most gargantuan transportation corporation with the purchase of luxurious hotels, fleets of cruise ships and airlines. CPR went international, promoting Canada's wealth in tourism and discovery. Like the CNR, CPR's passenger unit was badly affected by its automotive and air competition, removing it entirely as a core business segment when its transcontinental train, the Dominion, was dropped in 1966. In 1978, CPR's passenger service became what is now known as VIA Rail. CPR freights continue to circulate the tracks. It also operates three commuter rail services under contract – TransLink in Vancouver, GO Transit in Milton-Toronto, and AMT in Montréal.

Canadian Northern Railway Company (CNoR) The Canadian Northern Railway Company was established in 1899 by William MacKenzie and Donald Mann, two experienced railway entrepreneurs. In 1886, both men collaborated together and purchased the Manitoba Lake Railway and Canal Co., offering service in northern Manitoba. The men continued to push for rail lines into the west. By 1902, rail routes were laid between Edmonton and Hudson Bay. In following years, routes between Quebéc and Nova

HISTORICAL ROOTS OF CANADA'S RAILWAY

Scotia, and Toronto to Hudson Bay by Sudbury were established. In 1915, a rail link was made between Edmonton and Vancouver, founding a transcontinental rail route binding the far-reaching east and west coast together.

CNoR withstood the competition between the other leading railways and successfully surmounted all impending obstacles. After World War II, the railway went in the red and was consequently sold to Canadian National Railways becoming a principal constituent.

Canadian National Railways (CNR)

The Canadian National Railways (CNR) was created by the federal government in December 1918 to serve as the umbrella firm of acquired cash-strapped rail companies, along with government-owned railways.

The reality of an imminent World War threatened the life for Canada's flooding railway systems. Strangely, the railways continued to expand despite all of the ominous signs foreshadowing a collapse. The poor grain market, fewer immigrants, freight competition and decreased government loans were the impending indications that the railways were going to fold. Thanks to a strong national conviction that holds dear the nation's history with the thousands of track miles laid. Focus on the railway's economic plights were arrested and redirected on the mobilization of soldiers and war products at a reduced price.

The first railway to go was the CnoR which the government took control of in September 1918, and was subsequently combined to CNR. The GTP collapsed and was also scooped up in May 1920 by Canada's new power-engine railway corporation, leading to an arbitration against GTR officials opposed to rail nationalization. In 1923, GTR was eventually absorbed into the CNR. In April 1978, CNR passenger service amalgamated with CPR passenger unit to form VIA Rail, Canada's only coast-to-coast passenger train service.

Sir William Cornelius Van Horne (1843-1915)

William Cornelius Van Horne, the first president of the Canadian Pacific Railway, started his colourful train career by accepting a position for the CPR at the mere age of 14 years.

Initially a ticket agent, Mr. Van Horne worked his way up through various positions until, at the age of 28, he became the superintendent of the railway.

Van Horne was a lively eccentric heralded for his skills as a geologist, mind reader, caricaturist, violinist and practical joker.

People scoffed at Van Horne's determination to lay down 800 kilometres of track during the first season of building the railway. This insistent visionary laid 832km! Under Van Horne's management, CPR was able to accomplish massive engineering feats for Canada that were instrumental in shaping the nation's history. These include the Lethbridge Viaduct, the longest railway bridge in Canada, and the Connaught Tunnel, the longest railway tunnel in the Western hemisphere.

The Great Canadian Links

The Birth of VIA Rail Canada

The 17th to the 18th centuries were nostalgic, colourful periods in the history of Canada's railway system, strongly linked to the history of the nation itself. The magnanimous effort to build a national rail network was also an endeavor to build a nation of united people. In the 20th century, fast-paced modernity stabbed at the heart of the rail industry and proved no match for the innovations of the times, notably the automobile and airplane. What were once thriving tracks rich in passenger tales were given up for sale, debt repayment, or wanton abandonment to the hands of the federal government. Eventually, the standard of passenger service declined steadily and the reality of inflation prompted the federal government to promote a service train for passengers only.

Essentially, the government recognized the demand for a passenger train, and identified the loss of interest as a reflection of disappearing Canadian history. In 1978, the government founded VIA Rail, a train service focusing entirely on the interest of the passenger.

The government believed that costs can be balanced and a level of service can be upgraded. Severing ties with the freight systems was first and foremost, the ultimate goal. VIA Rail purchased locomotives and passenger cars from the freights and built trains entirely separate from freight influence. In time, the Corporation acquired train crews, maintenance services and access to the tracks from the freight companies. VIA Rail is Canada's first devoted passenger rail service and continues to run today, continually innovating and faithfully transporting not only Canadians but a cornucopia of people in the most magnificent places in Canada and beyond.

VIA Rail in the 21st Century

2007 In October 2007, Canadian transport Minister Lawrence Cannon announces fresh funding amounting to $691.9 million, the largest capital investment in VIA Rail's history. The funding will be spread over a period of five years, to be used in the company's compliance to reduce gas emission, refurbishing of locomotives and passenger cars, increasing capacity and upgrading of service quality, among others. The capital infusion is part of the government's $33 billion allotment to fund the Building Canada infrastructure program. Things are really looking up!

The 21st century. At the dawn of the third millennium, VIA Rail is clearly an essential entity: in addition to being a viable business, it continuously innovates. And above all, it has convinced millions of people that trains are "the more human way to travel."

2006 A first in North America, VIA Rail made Wi-Fi (wireless Internet access) service available to passengers, initially in the Québec City-Windsor corridor and thereafter, in many stations along the route.

HISTORICAL ROOTS OF CANADA'S RAILWAY | 49

2005 The Easterly class dubbed A Maritime Learning Experience is launched aboard the Ocean route between Montreal and Halifax.

2004 Renaissance trains continue to provide top-rate service to passengers on the Eastern Canada routes.

2003 A new funding package is issued by Transport Minister David Collenette. These funds are responsible for boosting inter-city passenger rail services, and ensuring that VIA Rail's present-day infrastructure and services offered are prolonged into the future. The year also marks the 25th Anniversary of VIA Rail as an independent Crown Corporation.

2002 The first Renaissance car is used aboard The Enterprise, the overnight train between Montreal and Toronto.

2001 VIA Rail adopts a new organizational structure: Strategy, Operations, Control. Launching of its new corporate news magazine, VIA Destinations.

2000 A $402 million investment over a five-year period is announced by the federal government in a bid to invigorate the Canadian passenger rail service and for the nation to comply with environment-friendly agreements, specifically the Kyoto Protocol. The fund enables the company to upgrade its infrastructures and stations and improve safety measures. They include the acquisition of new rolling stock and new Renaissance cars that reduce greenhouse gas emission.

VIA Rail Canada

50 | The Nation That The Railway Built

Driving the last spike on the Canadian Pacific Railway, Craigellachie, British Columbia.

■ The Nation That The Railway Built

In 1871, Sir John A. Macdonald saw his vision of connecting Canada by rail crucial in order to fortify the nation economically, and to save western regions from American control. Macdonald declared, "Until this great work is completed, our Dominion is little more than a geographical expression." Macdonald faced many obstacles including impeachment in 1973 for being a participant in a large political scandal involving rail contracts. Other stumbling blocks included finding routes that crosses uncharted mountains and rugged terrains, back-breaking constructions of bridges and tunnels, and cultural issues with aborigines.

Nonetheless, Macdonald overcame these challenges, was re-elected into office in 1878, and successfully saw his 'national dream' realized. The completion of the Canadian Pacific Railway (CPR) was the last rail line built to link the west and east coast of Canada together. The completion of CPR tracks in British Columbia in 1885 convinced the region to join the confederation. Canada was unified. This event appointed Macdonald as one of the most important men in Canadian history.

Groundwork for Economic Transformation
The integration of the railway system in Canada strongly improved the economy. Every track laid acted as a binding force that unites the many social, cultural and economic specks of the growing nation.

It enabled assimilation among people, and most importantly, transporting goods became efficient, cheap and reliable.

Fast travel between destinations marked an increase in commercial farming which later opened up markets. The railway contributed to Canada moving away from being a primarily rural nation into an industrialized developed country. Employment became bountiful because of the need for train crew and construction workers. Construction of rail stations was a sure stamp of progress for the lucky community. As such, not only was the rail a business matter, it also became a fierce political issue.

Successful railway companies operated mainlines with smaller resource lines connecting to them. The smaller 'feeding' or 'spur' lines were related to specific industries. The aggrandizement of Canada's railway was challenging because everybody wanted a share in its profit-making promise. The railway business became an over-saturated market. Between 1836 and 1986, over two thousand companies were permitted by the government to construct rail lines and only a selected few succeeded. Insufficient traffic, building costs and indebtedness to the government were reasons for railway companies to fold. Most enterprises went belly-up resulting in bankruptcy or being incorporated by larger companies.

Accelerating the Nation's Pace

Passenger train travel became the most efficient, reliable and speedy mode of land transportation. Journeys that normally took several weeks were made in a few days. Initially, passenger train travel was not overly comfortable. The cars comprised flat hard benches without

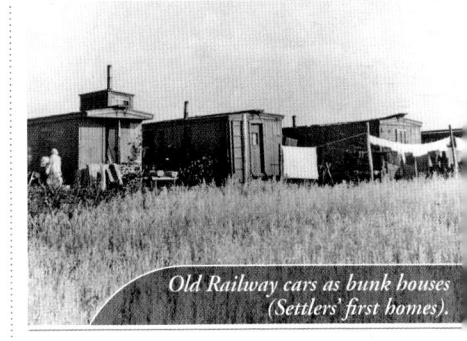

Old Railway cars as bunk houses (Settlers' first homes).

privacy or washrooms. Train travel was precarious during winter months because of blizzards and possible derailments. In time, the conditions improved affording the passenger with a reliable and comfortable journey. However, the invention of automobiles, paved roads and air travel decreased the demand of passenger rail significantly.

The railway benefited many with employment, prosperity and travel. But there was a downside - The Métis and First Nations were affected negatively, however. Towns and tracks self-righteously ploughed over their communities, and they were consequently uprooted from their traditional land and had no recourse but be assimilated.

Rolling the Stock to Urban Growth

The railway was a prosperous component spurring Canada into an industrialized nation. The railway is a significant factor in attracting immigrants to populate arid vast lands, and strengthened the nation's fort in the northern parts from threat of occupation by the United States, its sole neighbor. The first immigrants were able to reach Canada in a few days aboard the train's Colonist cars, equipped with sleeping and kitchen facilities. They established settlements, toiled on the lands and spurred livelihoods and

52 | The Nation That The Railway Built

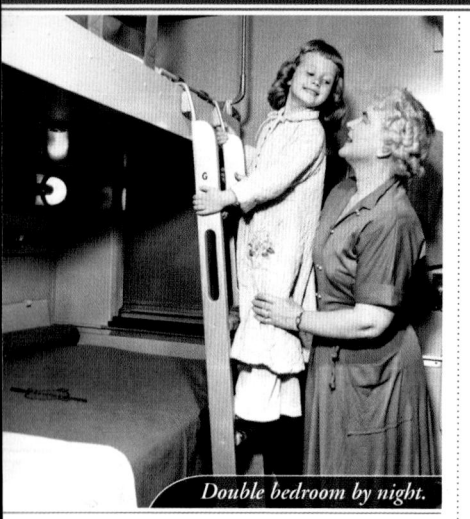

Double bedroom by night.

industries that are the foundation of present-day Canadian economy.

Canadians benefited from train travel because it increased employment, travel speed and the opening up of markets. Resources such as coal, timber and wheat were easily mobilized expanding commercial activity. Areas holding resources attracted the railway and were quickly converted into booming towns. The railway also brought prosperity to normally smaller communities. For instance, large manufacturers in Québec and Ontario easily obtained the rich raw materials they need from direct producers in the west. Labour, resources and production were stirred as the railway budged.

Linking Communication Points

Most of North America set their clocks according to the position of the sun in the late 1880s. Canada is so vast a nation of this continent that there is marked time difference among its geographical divisions. The growth of the railway demanded on-time performance. This plight proved to be difficult because it was impossible to determine the time between destinations. Sir Sandford Fleming, who worked for a decade in mapping a northern path for the rail and the man responsible for seeing the successful completion of Canada's transcontinental railway, had a solution. He proposed that the world be divided into 24 segments. These segments were considered time zones measured against the time set in Greenwich, England. The result of this innovation is known to us today as 'standard time' (GTE). With this, time variations can be synchronized on land, air or sea. And history accorded Fleming the title "Father of Standard Time."

An important mode of communication then, the telegraphs, helped with the operations of the trains. With the advent of telegraphing, engineers were able to provide and receive important information pertaining to dangers, delays or derailments, accelerating freight and passenger travel as well as ongoing track constructions. In the same way, the continuously extending railways prompted more telegraph points en route. Train lines were able to use this rapid mode of communication only if telegraph lines were put up alongside the tracks.

Needless to say, more and more people benefited from a system that was the predecessor of wire, cable and other modern means of communication. Much later, in 1932, rail passengers enjoyed the installation of a rail-based radio network across Canada, which gave birth to the Canadian Broadcasting Corporation.

Process Standardization for Safety

Multiple track gauges were used in Canada's railway network and created problems. Rail companies used narrow gauges with tracks at approximately 42" apart, and others used broad gauges with tracks built approximately 5'6" apart. Diverse track sizes kept competitors off the tracks, including American rail trains. Narrow tracks, usually cheaply made, could not withstand the weight required for transporting goods. In the 1880s, a standard gauge was established at 4'8.5", enabling a smoother, more efficient railway operation. All lines were converted and restructured to fit the "standard gauge."

The advanced invention of diesel trains eventually replaced the arduous steam-powered trains. This mode of train operation demonstrated to be more cost-efficient and reliable. The downfall of this conversion was that several jobs were lost. Firemen used to maintain the fires for the production of steam were no longer in demand. The government felt that Prince Edward Island, Canada's smallest province, was the best location to test the diesel trains. In 1950, PEI converted its railway network into diesel, and was impressed by its efficiency. Soon after, the rest of Canada adopted this method. Today, modern electric-powered trains are harnessed by the company.

Riding the Wheels of Destiny

Immigration recruitment campaigns were implemented by the government to attract European settlers to the west. This mass crusade distributed books and brochures all over the world enticing immigrants to make their way west. Rallies and demonstrations were organized by the government promoting the benefits and advantages of living in western Canada.

To facilitate Western settlement, the government granted CPR 25 million acres of land, which it sold at a low price of 2.50 per acre and up, along with complete transport fare via ship and train. This strategy shot two birds with one stone – forming its immigration force in the west and earning high revenues for its own rail company. Between 1886 and 1914 droves of immigrants traveled to the west via the Canadian Pacific Railway (CPR). Approximately three million people settled in the west. The CPR saw the benefit of people migrating to the west and also pitched immigrant recruitment crusades. New settlers were privileged to ride in the 'colonist cars' for the leg of their journey, equipped with sleeping quarters and kitchen facility.

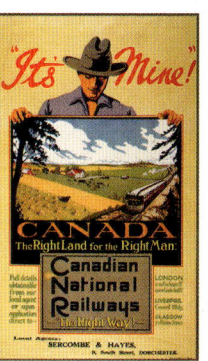

Inside the Pullman sleeping car by day.

54 | The Nation That The Railway Built

Fortifying National Security
Canada's railways has always served the nation in times of war, beginning in the Northwest rebellion in Saskatchewan in 1885 where Cornelius Van Horne mobilized troops in Winnipeg via trains, some incomplete sections of the tracks notwithstanding. With the civil war thwarted by early troop arrival, the government saw the need for a national railway to fortify national security and infused fresh funding into CPR.

When the First World War broke out in 1914, passengers were not encouraged to ride the trains, as they were primarily used to mobilize Canadian soldiers, artillery and supplies. This was a leading issue responsible for sending most Canadian railways in the red. Nonetheless, the railway companies were devoted to transporting the troops. The railways lost what little passenger business they had to inflation. The government sensed a ruinous end for the railways and realized a solution. Despite the inflation, the government's transport rates were low, spurring the railways deeper into debt.

Before the Canadian Northern Railway (CNoR) and the Grand Trunk Pacific Railway (GTP) reached the ultimate bottom, the Canadian government saved them from bankruptcy by assimilating them with Canadian Government railways. This amalgamation procured the Canadian National Railway (CNR).

Lures of the Coached Life
After the hysteria of the railway race, the remaining companies saw a market for tourism. Train companies realized the possibility for providing luxurious trips for affluent travelers. Train travel became the craze, and once again, train companies engaged in competition. Brochures were made and distributed with alluring images and enticing captions.

For the Niagara Gorge Railroad Company, "The Most Magnificent Scenic Route in the World" was the pitch line used to lure wealthy tourists to bear witness to Canada's most acclaimed

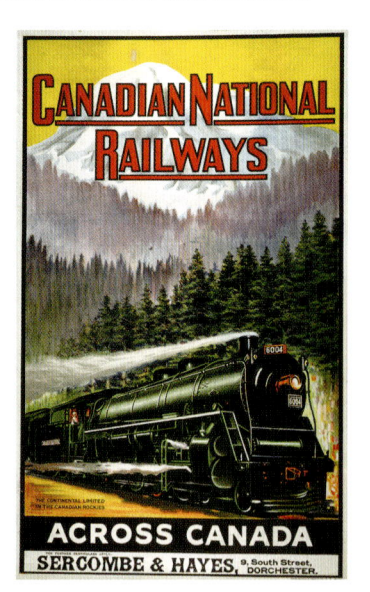

Top left: A Canadian National Railways conductor reassures a young immigrant.

tourist destinations. Publications of brochures, books and broadsheets were distributed internationally. Captivating images of sublime nature covered most brochures with small details of history and points of interest. And with the new money created by the rapidly growing economy, the tourism market proved to be a smart point to focus on.

Servers bringing food to passengers in the dining car.

an end to the unfair treatment. In 1935, they went on strike.

The unemployed men often snuck onto the trains to travel the nation desperately looking for work. This practice was referred to as "riding the rails" or "riding the rod." A few men stealthily hopped onto the train heading to the nation's capital, Ottawa, with the intention to rally against the government. Unfortunately, this expedition known as the "On to Ottawa Trek" failed because all dissenters were met by the RCMP in Regina. Violent riots marred these infamous treks.

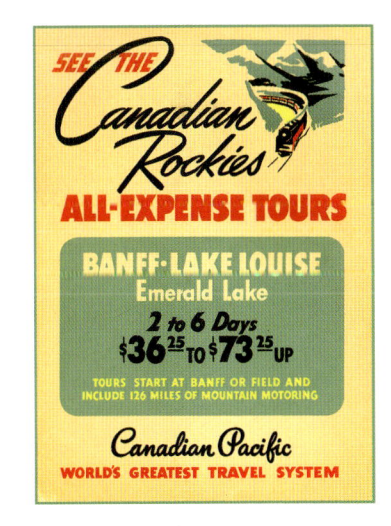

Riding the Rods

Reeling from the ruins of the destructive war, the Great Depression hit Northern America between 1929 to 1939, and affected Canada. Makeshift camps were erected by the government of Prime Minister Richard Bedford Bennett to distribute work and provide food and shelter for increasing numbers of unemployed citizens. Men complained that the camps were unlivable and no efforts were being made by the government to get them work.

With chaos and resentment growing, the Relief Camp Worker's Union was organized in British Columbia aimed at overthrowing the government and put

Legendary Moments

In 1836, Canada's first public railway was opened by the Champlain and Saint Lawrence Railroad Company. With rails of wood and iron straps, it journeyed between La Prairie and Saint-Jean, Québec.

On June 28, 1886, Canada's first transcontinental train departed from Montréal's Dalhousie station at 8 pm and arrived in July 4, 1886 in Port Moody at noon. This historic train is composed of two first-class coaches, one second-class coach, two immigrant sleepers, two sleeping cars, two baggage cars, a mail car and a diner car.

This CPR train was the first successful train to make this journey. Approximately, 12,000 men, 300 dog-sled teams and 5,000 horses participated in building the largest railway in the world back then.

Traipsing the Wilds Within

Instead of slogging a northern trail following the Saskatchewan River Valley to cross the Rockies, the CPR turned to a southern, more direct route to the Selkirk Mountains via the Kicking Horse Pass. This was deemed closer to the U.S. boarder and will guard against American encroachment. However, it was not sure yet if a route existed in the area.

CPR commissioned a surveyor named Major Albert Bowman Rogers to find two adequate routes through the Rockies and Selkirk in exchange for a $5,000 fee, and the honour of having the pass he would find named after him.

Rogers took in the challenge and devoted his time in discovering the two possibilities for a train route going through the Rockies. Rogers sent his 21-year old nephew Albert through Kicking Horse Pass, while he traveled through Howse Pass. Both terrains proved difficult. A search party was organized for Albert when he failed to return to camp. He was found emaciated and exhausted, but he also found a route through the Rockies. With this pronouncement, the elder Rogers discontinued his expedition through Howse Pass and immediately announced a potential train route through the Rockies via the Kicking Horse Pass. This landmark eventually became the home to Canada's first mountain tracks. Rogers' plight was not complete without finding a route through the Selkirk Mountains. After a labourious pilgrimage through the unyielding mountains, Rogers declared the discovery of a pass on July 24, 1882. The CPR commemorated his success by naming his discovery "Rogers Pass."

The name for Kicking Horse Pass came from Dr. James Hector who was kicked in the chest by a packhorse. The doctor claimed to have been knocked unconscious for some time. After discovering the pass, he named it Kicking Horse Pass in memory of his exciting run-

Left: Major Albert B. Rogers.

HISTORICAL ROOTS OF CANADA'S RAILWAY | 57

Snowshed construction, Selkirks, B.C.

in with a bad-tempered horse, and the name stuck until today.

A Labour Wonder
It is unfathomable to analyze the success of rail builders who constructed the railway through the mountains. Unyielding winters, precarious heights, and fatigue were elements the men battled with in order to complete the lines. Van Horne was ridiculed when he declared his goal to lay 800 km of track in the first year of construction. Nobody expected the project would span 842 km.

The rail workers, or "navvies," climbed up 5,000 feet, hiked into uncharted territories and perilously blasted mountainsides to construct train tunnels. With back-breaking toil and dangerous working conditions, no doubt there were several fatalities along the way. Many of the navvies were European and Asian immigrants who left behind their families for meager wages that they sent back home. Few managed to send decent earnings while some unfortunately never made it home alive.

With the overwhelming labour, manpower, capital and great plans painstakingly laid down to the ground steel after steel, the CPR rail line was an extraordinary accomplishment that far exceeded the expectations of engineering skills at that time. The sight of British Columbia's 325-foot wooden trestle bridge demonstrates the immensity of their achievements.

The Last Spike to Greatness
Simultaneously, construction of Canada's first transcontinental rail line commenced in the east and the west. The rail workers intended to link up and complete the job somewhere in the middle of the nation. On November 3, 1885, the last spike of the lake Superior section was sledged in Jackfish, Ontario. Finally, on November 7, 1885 the historical last spike was hammered into the ground in Craigellachie, British Columbia. With Macdonald's vision, Van Horne's determination and the workers' perseverance, the railway was successfully completed six years ahead of schedule.

The Last Spike.

Noble Trains of Troops
The Northwest Rebellion broke out in Saskatchewan with the uprising of Métis and First Nations. The government agreed the military was needed to mitigate this dilemma. There was a problem. The troops had no quick way of getting to the centre of turmoil. Cornelius Van Horne,

Legendary Moments

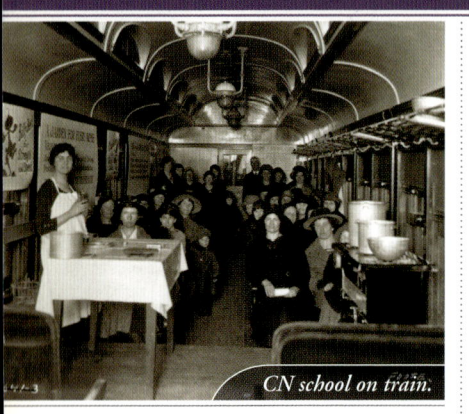

CN school on train.

president of the Canadian Pacific Railway (CPR), proposed to the government that the soldiers be transported by train. Deep inside, he secretly wanted the government to acknowledge the benefits of having a transcontinental railway and invigorate CPR's coffers with new funding. Van Horne promised the government that the troops could get there within 10 days. There was a serious problem however. A combination of 86 miles of track was incomplete north of Lake Superior.

The boys hopped on the first train leaving Toronto on March 30, 1885. There were other trains to follow. The first opening in the tracks was at Dog Lake. The troops were gathered into horse-led sleighs and were continuously toppled over. The winter conditions were severe. Nonetheless, the troops boarded their next train at Birch Lake. Unfortunately, the train carried open cars providing no relief from the cold. Frostbite was a serious threat.

The men met their next gap at Port Munro and were subsequently forced to tread across the frozen plains of Lake Superior. One soldier lamented, "I can tell you I'll never forget that march …we dared not stop an instant as we were in great danger of being frozen, although the sun was taking the skin off our faces. One man of our company went mad and one of the regulars went blind from snow glare."

The last breach in the rail line proved to be the most difficult for the troops. They were required to lug their stumbling and cold feet over a 10-mile stretch of melting ice. The cold wet leaked through the seams of their boots and many collapsed from absolute exhaustion. The last train greeted them at the terminus ready to transport them to the rebellion.

Approximately 8,000 troops successfully made it to the frontlines of the rebellion within nine days and the rebellion was quickly thwarted. As Van Horne had secretly hoped, the federal government recognized the need to have a national rail network and issued the money required to finish the great undertaking of the Canadian Pacific Railway.

School Trains

School for children living in isolated regions of Northern Ontario during the 1920s up until 1960s was in a train. Once a month, a school on wheels pulled into remote towns staying for approximately one week. The school comprised one rail car, half of the car was the teacher's home and the other half was the classroom. The car was supplied with texts, books, blackboards and maps for all levels of education. Mostly, the school-on-wheels served children of railway workers, trappers, miners or farmers.

Hobos

The trains were flooded with hobos during the Great Depression of the late '20s to early '30s. Desperately looking for work, vagrant men threw caution to the wind by hopping on and off the

HISTORICAL ROOTS OF CANADA'S RAILWAY | 59

Their Majesties King George VI and Queen Elizabeth on board the royal train.

trains at various destinations. Hobos generally rode the tops or insides of freights, considering the lack of security aboard. Often, boards would be laid across the brakes and men would ride the bottom exterior of the train. This was highly dangerous and illegal. Inevitably, some of these hobos were killed on their dangerous journey.

Funeral Trains
In Canada, it is customary to carry deceased national leaders by train to commemorate the legacies they have left behind, playing a key role by leading a solemn memorial 'march' onboard.

Winston Churchill and Abraham Lincoln are two such leaders who were carried by train to their final stopping place. In August 1979, Canada's Prime Minister John Diefenbaker's funeral train led a long procession through the prairies from Ottawa to Saskatoon. Likewise, thousands of Canadians paid tribute for Canada's well-loved Prime Minister Pierre Eliot Trudeau as his funeral train traveled from Ottawa to Montréal in 2000.

Royal Tours
The British Royalty has been riding the rails since 1860. A memorable Royal train tour was made by King George V and Queen Elizabeth who went around Canada by rail in 1939 to promote the alliance between Canada and Britain just before the Second World War. The event marked the first time that the reigning British monarch visited the country.

The tour began with King George V and Queen Elizabeth II arriving into Wolf's Cove in Québec and setting off on the Empress of Canada. This train comprised five Canadian Pacific (CPR) cars, five Canadian National (CNR) cars and two specialty cars. The CPR and CNR shared honours and delicate responsibilities of transporting the royal couple across Canada, the CNR traveled in the East and CPR took over for the western leg of the journey.

The voyage took 44 days stretching across a distance of 3,224 miles. All other rail traffic was thwarted except for a specialty train carrying the press and officials running approximately one hour behind the Empress. The locomotives used to carry the King and Queen were adorned in royal crowns and denominated as Royal Hudsons. Other Royal tours preceding this tour was the Duke of York in 1901 and the Duke of Connaught in 1906.

Chronology

1836 Canada's first railway is up and running! A 23km run between La Prairie on the St. Lawrence River near Montréal and Saint-Jean on the Richelieu is successfully completed by the Champlain and Saint Lawrence Railroad Company.

1850 The government permits approximately 40 businesses with the opportunity to build rail lines. Only six lay tracks because of the fierce competition.

1851 In Québec and Ontario, the 5'6 gauge is declared as the standard gauge; whereas in 1870, the 4'8 ½ resumes the standard gauge.

1853 The successful formation of the Grand Trunk Railway, an important mainline traveling between Toronto and Montréal, with smaller lines joining the mainline.

1853 The Great Western Railway inaugurates lines running between Windsor and Niagara Falls. Building, leasing and buying alternative railways in Southern Ontario, this railway is acclaimed as the first Canadian system.

1854 Introduction of the Bytown and Prescott Railway between Prescott and Bytown. First railway service to Ottawa as Bytown is renamed Ottawa in 1855. The railway becomes the Ottawa and Prescott Railway Company, now belonging to Canadian Pacific.

1855 First railway suspension bridge constructed by the Great Western Railway. Boasting of its 250-metre lenght, this structure is acclaimed as the engineering masterpiece of the period.

1855 The opening of the Montréal to Toronto line, by the Grand Trunk Railway, a cause for an exciting celebration.

1856 Inauguration of the Grand Trunk Railway is celebrated in Montréal.

1859 In preparation for a visit from the reigning Prince of Wales, Albert Edward (son of Queen Victoria and later crowned as Britain's King Edward VII), the first sleeping car is constructed at the Brantford shops of the Buffalo and Lake Huron railway.

1860 Grand Trunk inaugurates its route between Montréal and Rivière du Loup.

1863 The New Vancouver Coal Mining Company opens the first railway in Western Canada. This is done to transport ballast and coal in the Nanaimo region on Vancouver Island.

1867 Unification of Canada is confirmed, making Ontario, Québec, Nova Scotia and New Brunswick one nation. Conditions for this confederation included a railway connecting Nova Scotia with the St. Lawrence within close proximity to Québec, and the development of Canadian Pacific Railway to geographically link Canada from coast to coast.

1869 Canada buys the three prairie provinces from the Hudson's Bay Company. At this time, this land was referred to as Prince Rupert's Land.

1870 Manitoba enters the confederation.

HISTORICAL ROOTS OF CANADA'S RAILWAY | 61

The first locomotive to cross North Saskatchewan River to Edmonton.

1871 British Columbia joins confederation under the condition of having a railway built to connect to the rest of Canada. They demand this one request or else B.C. becomes part of the United States.

1873 When Prince Edward Island runs out of money to build an independent rail line, they join the confederation.

1882 William Cornelius Van Horne is inaugurated the first General Manager of the Canadian Pacific railway. In the summer of 1882, he swiftly lays 480 miles of track traversing the prairies.

1883 Railways inherit a standardized system of keeping time using hour-wide time zones.

1885 The Second Northwest Rebellion breaks out and Van Horne mobilizes Canadian troops to the area of conflict by train. This demonstrates to the government that the projected transcontinental railway has advantages. Van Horne receives the funding by the government to complete the Canadian Pacific Railway line.

1885 The last spike is driven in the ground to complete the Canadian Pacific Railway (CPR) line. With 4,666 km, this rail line becomes the longest in the world. Canada's East and Canada's West are linked by a transcontinental railway.

1885 The first successful voyage across Canada is complete. Taking only 139 hours, the CPR transcontinental arrives in Port Moody covering almost 3,000 km from Montréal.

1887 The CP line is elongated 12.2 miles along the Burrard Inlet to

The Grand Trunk Railway Last Spike: Fort Fraser, BC, 1914.

Vancouver, pulled by the Port Moody-based locomotive No. 374. This locomotive can be seen on display and in excellent condition at the Vancouver Drake Street Roundhouse Community Centre.

1899 With the amalgamation of the Winnipeg Great Northern Railway, Lake Manitoba Railway and Canal Company, The Canadian Northern Railway is founded.

1903 The National Transcontinental Railway Act is passed. Agreement for the National Transcontinental Railway to build a line from Moncton, New Brunswick to Winnipeg, Manitoba, and for the Grand Trunk Pacific Railway (GTP) to build a line between Winnipeg, Manitoba and Prince Rupert, British Columbia is solidified by the government.

1905 The Canadian Northern lines traverses the Prairies to Edmonton. Alberta and Saskatchewan joined confederation.

1909 Canadian Pacific finishes the Kicking Horse grade relocation on the main line between Hector and Field, British Columbia.

1912 The body of Mr. Charles Melville Hays, President of the Grand Trunk (GTR) and Grand Trunk Pacific Railways (GTP) arrives in Halifax by the Mackay-Bennett Steamship. He is killed in the tragic sinking of the Titanic. A special GTR train transports the body from Halifax to Montréal. GTR offices closed for staff members to attend Mr. Hays' funeral at Mount Royal Cemetrey.

HISTORICAL ROOTS OF CANADA'S RAILWAY | 63

1914 WW1 commences, and most Canadian railways are on the brink of bankruptcy due to over-saturation and over-expansion.

1914 The Grand Trunk Railway main line is completed between Winnipeg, Melville, Edmonton, Jasper and Prince Rupert. Ninety-three miles west of Prince George marks the spot where the last spike is driven.

1915 The Canadian Northern Railway completes its transcontinental main line from Vancouver to Québec. The line travels through Edmonton, North Battleford, Dauphin, Winnipeg, Fort Frances, Capreol, Ottawa, Hawkesbury and Montréal.

1922 The Canadian National Railway becomes an enterprise.

1923 The Canadian government combined the CNoR, GTP and GTR with Canadian Government Railways to found The Canadian National Rail (CNR). The government absorbs the rail companies before they file for bankruptcy. The CNR becomes Canada's most lucrative and powerful railway system.

1923 CNR makes radio broadcasts.

1926 Remote and isolated areas in Northern Ontario are visited by Canada's first traveling school train. The train arrives into small communities for a week at a time. The train car is converted into a fully functioning classroom supplied with blackboards and texts for all levels of education.

1929 Hudson Bay Railway completes its run in Churchill, Manitoba.

1930s The accessibility of buses and automobiles creates a significant decline in passenger rail service.

1933 Canadian government purchases CN's broadcasting rights and sells them to the Canadian Radio Broadcasting Commission (CRBC).

1939 King George VI and Queen Elizabeth set off from Wolf's Cove on a 44-day tour aboard The Empress.

1943 Canadian National opens Central Station in Montréal

1949 Newfoundland joins the Confederation becoming Canada's tenth province. CN purchases Newfoundland's railway. The system operates on a narrow gauge and has to be converted to the standard gauge.

1950s The popularity of international air travel contributes to the dwindling of passenger train travel.

1953 Budd Rail Diesel Cars (BRDC) or simply Budd Cars are introduced into the Canadian system. The cars are nicknamed "Dayliners" by CP and "Railiners" by CN.

1955 The new passenger train is introduced. Stainless steel cars with 360-degree observatory domes and sleepers are set to travel across the country between Montréal and Vancouver. The line "the Canadian" is coined.

1956 The Pacific Great Eastern Railway completes the line between North Vancouver and Prince George, B.C.

1960s Many railways fold up.

1967 Ontario, under an operating agreement with CN, opens "GO transit" between Pickering, Toronto, Oakville and Hamilton.

1972 National Railway no longer uses Morse code for telegramming.

1972 Pacific Great Eastern Railway changes its name to British Columbia Railway.

1976 CN erects the world's tallest man-made structure in Toronto: The CN tour. CN creates VIA Rail to be Canada's passenger train service.

1978 CPR and CN combine their passenger train services to form VIA Rail. VIA Rail becomes a Crown corporation.

1979 Prime Minister John Diefenbaker's body is carried on a funeral train from Ottawa to its final destination in Saskatoon.

1981 VIA Rail cuts close to 20 percent of its services.

1982 VIA Rail publishes two acclaimed, scenic rail guides by a conductor veteran, Bill Coo. A must-have book for train buffs.

1984 VIA Rail Transports Her Majesty Queen Elizabeth on her Royal Train. Likewise, Pope John Paul II is welcomed aboard the Pontifical Train.

1988 CN abandons the completion of Newfoundland's railway.

1989 CN abandons the completion of Prince Edward Island's railway.

1990 Fifty percent of VIA Rail's passenger service is cut. VIA Rail runs one route across Canada. The transcontinental train runs on the CN line going through Toronto, Winnipeg, Saskatoon, Edmonton, Jasper, Kamloops and Vancouver.

1990 The Great Canadian Railtour Company purchases and privatizes the daytime tourist train Rocky Mountaineer.

1992 Silver & Blue Class by VIA Rail is offered providing high-class accommodation, premium service and delectable meals while traveling across Canada.

1995 West Coast Express, one of Vancouver's commuter service runs over CP rail between Vancouver and Mission, British Columbia.

1995 To raise future funds for the railway, CN puts lists shares on the TSE and the NYSE and walks with a $2.2 billion sell-off.

1996 The Rocky Mountaineer hauls longest passenger train in Canada's history. Three GP40 locomotives lug 34 cars from Vancouver to Kamloops.

1998 Operation over the former CP line between Sicamous and Kelowna is taken over by the Okanagan Valley Railway.

1999 RailAmerica Inc. takes over the operation of the Esquimalt and Nanaimo Railway from CP. Now, as E&N Railway Company, it also purchases the line between Port Alberni and Nanaimo, leasing the section between Victoria and Nanaimo.

2000 The sleek and improved Renaissance I car is put on the track and

HISTORICAL ROOTS OF CANADA'S RAILWAY | 65

Snow Train ribbon-cutting ceremony with VIA Rail President Paul Côté.

promises the beginning of passenger rail upgrades throughout Canada. Federal government contracts $402 million in capital funding.

2002 Eighty-eight years of passenger seizes between North Vancouver and Prince George, British Columbia. The rail's run of the Prospector Cariboo is replaced by two 20-seat "rail shuttle vehicles."

2003 The second modernized sleeper car is welcomed on the tracks. The Renaissance II is an elaborate sleeper car polished with utmost class. Transport Minister announces $692.5 million in new funding for VIA Rail.

2003 CN absorbs the publicly-owned BC Rail Ltd. for $1 billion. CN owns the rights to travel over BC Rail's roadbed under renewable 60-year leases. CN picks up shares becoming Canada's third largest railway.

2005 Inauguration of the Easterly class on board the Ocean. A route traveling the perimetre of the East Coast and Maritimes, providing an environment of learning, relaxation and tourism.

2006 Inauguration of the Whistler Mountaineer that offers a scenic three-hour train trip between North Vancouverand Whistler.

2007 Inauguration of the Snow Train Express, a new seasonal weekend departure from Edmonton to Jasper using VIA Rail's Panorama (fully-domed) cars. In October, the government announces a much-anticipated new round of funding.

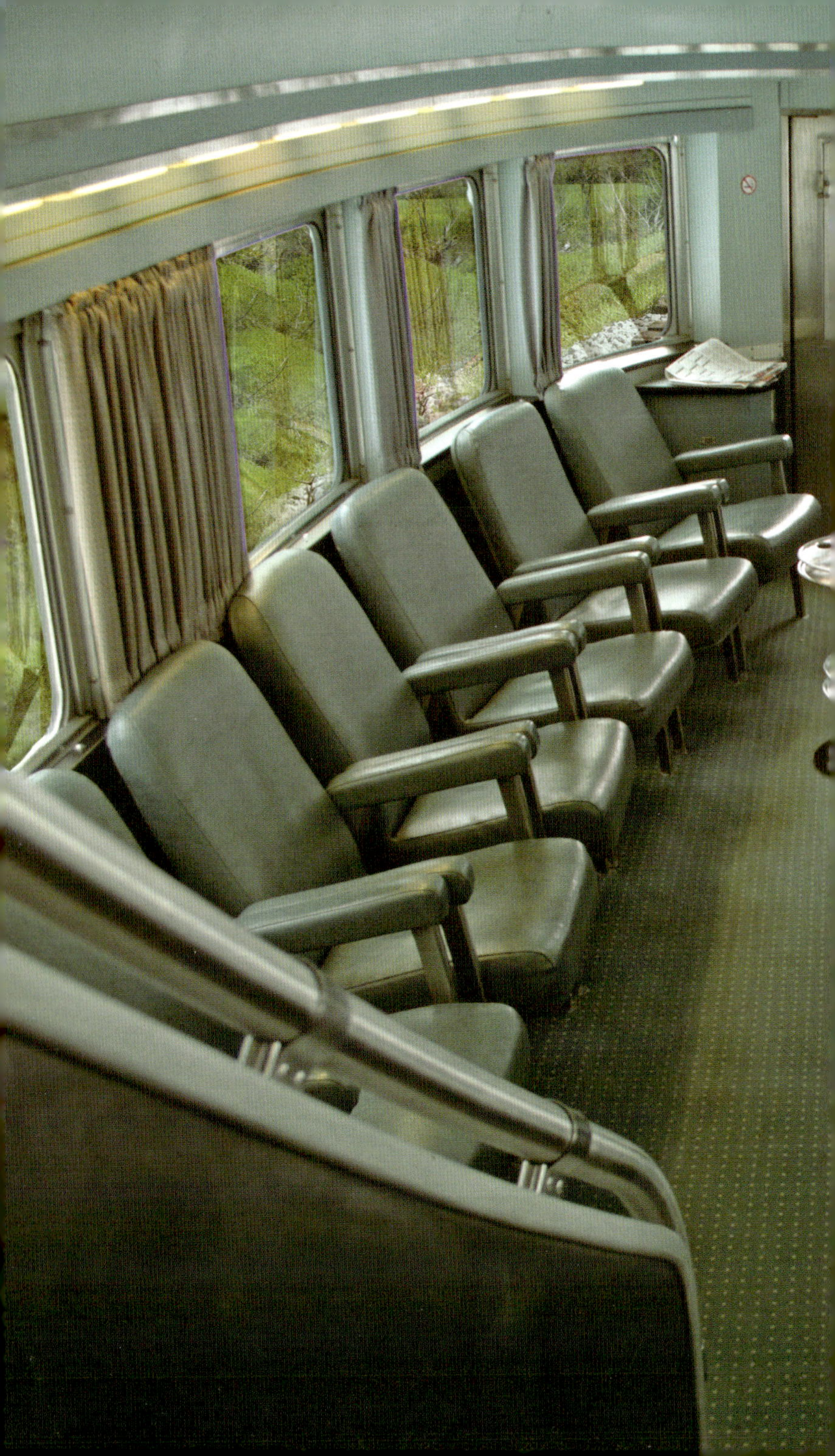

TRAIN CLASSES & SERVICES

Classes of Service **68-74**

Types of Railcars **74-83**

Accommodation & Seat Configuration... **84-95**

68 | Classes of Service

Comfort Class
The most economical service on board all of VIA Rail's services. It provides passengers with comfortable, reclining, stretch-out seats, panoramic windows, and access to snacks and refreshments at a supplementary cost. On most overnight services, pillows and blankets are available from onboard staff upon request.

Travelers of Comfort Class are not provided with specially-prepared meals, but there is take-out service. If the passenger does not want to risk an allergic episode by using this facility, it may be wise to bring a personal supply of food.

Comfort Sleeper Class
Overnight passengers can expect a private and relaxing place to retire in at the end of the day with the Comfort Sleeper Class. There are varied choices catering to every budget and sleeping preference.

BERTH – For a practical value, one can have a choice of an upper or lower berth, which is draped with heavy curtains at night to ensure privacy. They have access to the public shower facility and are provided with shower kits and thick, fresh towels.

SINGLE BEDROOM – The single bedroom is ideal for a traveler out for some time of solitude or needing some quick work updates with its own electrical outlet and a private washroom equipped with toilet, mirror and sink. By day, the bed is transformed into a relaxing seat.

DOUBLE BEDROOM – The double bedroom makes for a homey suite for couples with its private washroom, closet, armchairs, a table and an electrical outlet. For group travelers, two bedrooms can be cleverly combined into one spacious suite.

TRAIN CLASSES & SERVICES | 69

VIA 1

Long-haul trips either for business or leisure can be a stressful activity. That is why, for the sophisticated trekker, there is no other way to travel but through first class. VIA Rail offers an optimum traveling accommodation known as VIA 1 that caters to the demands of the meticulous traveler.

First introduced in 1980 in the Québec City Windsor Corridor, VIA 1 offers premium services and amenities for passengers on a journey from Windsor, Toronto, Ottawa, Montréal or Québec City. A VIA 1 ticket is your pass to a luxurious and pampered journey with its spacious and upholstered lounge seats, providing you with ease and flexibility of movement. You can also look forward to a sumptuous three-course meal and elaborate wine choices served in a fine-dining ambience.

Panorama Lounge

The Panorama lounge is the exclusive waiting room for VIA 1 passengers in the major urban stations of Toronto, Ottawa, Dorval, Montreal and Québec City as well as Kingston or London. For those entraining in the Dorval Station, VIA 1 rail tickets must be picked up right in the station before getting access into the Panorama lounge. Lounge attendants will take care of the baggage, advice priority boarding call and guide passengers upon entraining. Inside, the passengers can pep up their travel mood with a refreshing complimentary soft drink and browse on an array of the day's newspapers and magazines.

Business and Leisure-Friendly Features

In VIA 1, passengers have the privilege to choose the seat they want to occupy for the duration of their journey. This class offers the highest level of comfort and ease of travel for its passengers, beginning with large upholstered seats that can be reclined at various angles to relieve the body from stiffness. The footrest can be stretched further for a more spacious legroom. After hours squeezing work and leisure onboard, the seat's soft headrest is perfect for a much-needed power nap.

VIA 1 is popular among business travelers with its work-friendly features. Each seat instantly transforms into a mobile office cubicle with built-in power outlets and fold-up trays that hold laptops and other electronic gadgets. With this, one can work away unperturbed as the scenic vista rolls by. In VIA 1, passengers are protected from the discomfort of glaring sunlight that hits glass windows, thanks to the Light, Rapid and Comfortable (LRC) type of cars used in this class. LRC cars have window glasses that protect the eyes from harsh sunlight making VIA 1 truly the mobile businessman's best choice.

Classes of Service

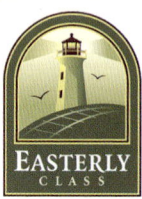

Easterly Class
A combination of Tourism and Learning – Welcome to the sea! The Easterly class guarantees a superb experience for travelers wanting to see the Canadian East Coast. This part of Canada, referred to as the Maritimes, is the most relevant birthing grounds for Canadian history as we know it today.

The Easterly class features an outgoing Learning Coordinator who is responsible for informing the passengers with the historical backdrop to the captivating islands. The Learning Coordinator enlightens the passengers with entertaining presentations encouraging the guests to participate. The passenger is endowed with a more personable understanding of the Maritimes, as the train parallels the perimetre of the Atlantic. The superior sights of the russet coloured cliffs, charming warm communities, verdant lush hills and circling gulls make the Easterly experience memorable. Guests are provided with snug sleeping accommodations, generous fresh breakfasts, three-course hot-meals and unlimited refreshments. Enjoy the sights of true Canadian sea-side living!

Some of the privileges of traveling Easterly class are:

• **Special Touches** – For an Easterly passenger, several perks are included. Shower kits including, soap, shampoo and body lotion are placed in the rooms as well as a welcome-aboard basket before the passenger boards. Twenty-four-hour coffee and tea service is provided for the passengers along with fresh fruit and biscuits. On board, entertainment services are available including newspapers, magazines, films, puzzles and board games. All Easterly class passengers enjoy priority serving and check baggage service. The Panorama lounge is accessible for those boarding from Montréal.

• **Sleeper Cars:** A Cozy Comfort – Renaissance car may request a room with a private shower (there will be a price difference). All bedrooms are equipped with private washrooms and shower amenities. By day, relax into the comfortable chairs while watching for sea-life from a private large window. By night, nestle into the snug bed provided for you by the service attendant.

• **Park Car:** Lounge and Observation Deck – At the very tail-end of the train is the Park car. Unique with its elegant design, this hospitable car provides bar-service and refreshments. Home to the Easterly Learning Coordinator, the Park car is the epicentre for socializing and meeting fellow travelers. Take some binoculars up to the 360-degree observatory and revel in the immensity of the Atlantic.

Dining Car: Guaranteed Decadence!

TRAIN CLASSES & SERVICES | 71

The charming dining car is certainly the meeting place for travelers on the train. Passengers are required to sit with other guests; a first-rate way to meet intriguing people from around the world. Decorated with Maritime elegance, the diner serves exquisite meals form morning, noon to evening. Revel in the delicious three-course provided for at dinnertime while engaging in memorable conversation. Please be advised that lunch meals are à la carte.

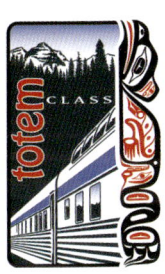

Totem Class
During the peak season, (mid-May to late September), passengers who enjoy an unconventional route of travel can reserve a seat in the Skeena's Totem class. This run is potentially VIA Rail's most renowned route for unparalleled beauty and mountain exposure. While enjoying the remote landscapes of peaks scraping beneath the skies, passengers can enjoy a delicious meal provided by VIA Rail's friendly staff. A trip to the 360-degree panoramic observatory in the Park Car is ideal for pointing out bears and other forest creatures.

Romance by Rail
Perfect for lovers young and old, VIA Rail's Romance by Rail is a luxurious feature comprising the conversion of two bedrooms into a double-bed with 'his' and 'her' private washrooms and sinks. Upon boarding, the couple will walk into a room ornamented with fresh flowers, and two flutes for the champagne chilling on ice anticipating to be cracked open. Lovers can sprawl on the queen-size bed adorned with lofty pillows and comfortable down dressings. Watch the country pass, honour each other's company and enjoy breakfast in bed!

Romance by Rail is available year-round on the Canadian between Toronto and Jasper, and between Jasper and Vancouver, in Silver & Blue class.

- Toronto-Jasper-Vancouver (the Canadian), Silver & Blue class

- Montréal-Percé-Gaspé (the Chaleur), Comfort sleeper class

Classes of Service

Silver & Blue

Rail travel luxury at its best, the acclaimed Silver & Blue class is exclusively available on the historic Toronto-Vancouver transcontinental route, the Canadian, and is hailed as the best way to see the majestic Canadian Rockies. The amenities and service aboard this elite class is akin to four-star hotel accommodation, complete with a welcome reception of wine, fruits and flowers. Superior lodging awaits every traveler, while access to viewing cars and stylish lounges afford the lucky ones with a bevy of choices to roam around in style.

Some of the privileges of traveling Silver & Blue are:

- **Exclusive Use of The Park Car** – Equipped with a 1950s round bar, passengers can enjoy an afternoon beverage sitting with others in the semi-circled bullet. The Mural Lounge is another charming attribute of the Park Car, revealing a large painting created by one of many renowned Canadian artists. The Mural Lounge is an ideal place to watch a film or play a game of cards. Directly above the Mural Lounge is the observatory provided for passengers wanting a panoramic 360-degree view of the dignified Rockies. Attendants prepare a continental breakfast comprising freshly baked muffins, fruit and juices for the enjoyment of the guests and a 24-hour tea and coffee service is provided in the back seating area. Those passengers wishing to purchase souvenirs can ask the Park Car attendant for assistance. Supplied with daily newspapers and other assorted magazines, the Park Car makes an excellent reading destination. No doubt, the refurbished 1950 Art Deco Park Car is a favourite feature.

- **"Bon Voyage" Reception** – The passenger is greeted by friendly VIA Rail personnel upon boarding and continues to be treated with courteous service. Champagne and hors d'oeuvres are served upon departure from Vancouver, Jasper and Toronto.

- **Activity Car** – The Skyline car is the entertainment centre aboard the Canadian, supplied with an Activity Coordinator who ensures ultimate service for the guests. The Activity Coordinator is a charismatic leader in charge of creating an interactive environment for the passengers to engage in fun and collaborative activities. Karaoke, Name that Tune, Trivia, Scrabble and Cribbage Get-Together are events organized for the guests' pleasure. Skyline cars have

TRAIN CLASSES & SERVICES | 73

empty tables free for passengers to play board games, card games and puzzles. An entertainment system is also provided for watching films and playing video games. Ask the Activity Coordinator for selections and feel free to make requests. Supplied with a full bar, guests can enjoy an afternoon aperitif while watching the seas of wheat sway from the 360-degree observatory dome. Supplied with daily papers and magazines, the Skyline car makes an enjoyable reading setting.

- **Magnificent Meals** – Silver & Blue class fare includes all meals and soft drinks aboard the Canadian. The Silver & Blue dining car is a bedazzling replication of a 1950's Art Deco hotel dining room. All diners aboard the Canadian are named after Canada's most prized and elegant hotels. The room is adorned with soft pink linens, fresh flowers, and porcelain settings in the daytime. Passengers are welcome to come in for breakfast at 6:30 a.m. By night, this room is quickly transformed into an inviting elegant dining room. The chairs and tables are dressed in navy linen, wine glasses are polished, the tables are set for a four-course meal, and the attendants are prepared to deliver the guests a memorable meal.

The meals freshly prepared onboard the Canadian are generous and utterly delectable. All VIA Rail chefs are required to be nationally certified chefs before employment. The cuisine is inspired by local regions set between Toronto and the West Coast. Generous portions of traditional breakfast are served aboard followed with a tasty lunch comprising unique options. All dinner meals commence with a hot soup, followed by a freshly-prepared crisp salad. Passengers choose between four flavoursome entrées for dinner, and are then offered a desert from a sundry of options. While savouring a delicious meal, guests zigzag through the Rocky Mountains, enjoying the awe-inspiring sights of Mount Robson and Pyramid Falls.

- **Activities and Menus for Children** – Games, activities, video games and movies are organized in the Activity Skyline cars from 7:30a.m. until 10a.m. This perk is exclusively available in Silver & Blue class. Children's menus are available in the dining car.

- Silver & Blue Lounge – Silver & Blue lounges are available in the Vancouver and Toronto stations. After picking up tickets, passengers are welcome to take a seat and enjoy a pre-boarding celebratory refreshment. During peak season, travelers in Vancouver enjoy a live-music venue while anticipating first-call boarding.

- **Alcoholic Drink** Service – Several bars are distributed throughout the train providing the passenger with a selection of Canadian wines, micro-brewery beers, cocktails, scotch and liqueurs. Legal serving hours are between 11:00a.m. until 11:30p.m. Certain bottles of VQA wines are also available for purchase in the diner at meal times. Alcohol not purchased on the train cannot be consumed in the bars.

74 | Classes of Service / Types of Railcars

Note that there are designated times for passengers to drink alcohol depending on the laws of whichever province the train is traveling through. The service attendant will inform you should there be a prohibition in alcohol intake where your train is.

• Accommodation – Lodging aboard the Silver & Blue class is nothing short from restful and comfortable. Passengers are given the choice between spending the night in a berth, single bedroom, double bedroom or triple bedroom. By day, the room is a welcoming private space for passengers to quietly sit and admire the scenery. Supplied with shower amenities and storage area, guests are free to hunker down and relax. The attendant converts the sitting areas into cozy, warm sleeping quarters by evening where beds are dressed with snug down quilts and plump pillows. Attendants embellish the sleepy mood by dimming the lights and placing a bottle of water and chocolate on the bed. If passengers are having trouble falling asleep, they can simply open the blinds and watch the soft display of stars or watch the moon get sucked into nighttime rivers only to reappear again.

Types of Railcars

HEP 1 Cars

The Silver & Blue class deploys a type of stainless steel cars called the Head End Power (HEP 1) car, which is used in long-haul trains like the Canadian, the prairie-rich route of Hudson Bay and the Gaspé routes connecting to Montréal. The HEP 1 cars were a legacy from the steam-heated passenger locomotives that were the pride of the early train companies. VIA Rail acquired them and were thoroughly modernized by the famous Budd Manufacturing Company of Philadelphia. VIA Rail's present fleet of HEP 1 cars boasts of more pleasing car details and higher aesthetic value inside and out. More importantly, they are more reliable, safe and comfortable to match the needs and demands of today's passengers.

COACH CAR

Car Type	Passenger Car
Series	8100
Weight	51,691 kgs (113,960 lbs)
Length	25.9 m (85 ft)
Height	3.6 m (11 ft 9 3/4 in)
Width	3 m (9 ft 8 in)
Seating Capacity	62
Fleet	34

TRAIN CLASSES & SERVICES | 75

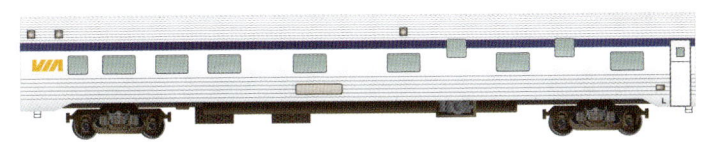

CHATEAU CAR

Car Type	Sleeping Car
Series	8200
Weight	55,320 kg (121,960 lbs)
Length	25.9 m (85 ft)
Height	3.6 m (11 ft 9 3/4 in)
Width	3 m (9 ft 8 in)
Sleeping Capacity	23
Fleet	29

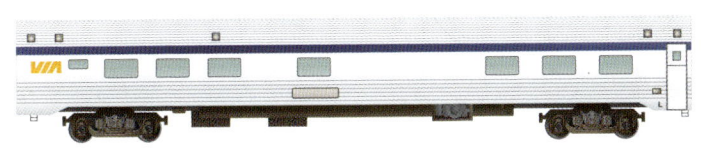

MANOR CAR

Car Type	Sleeping Car
Series	8300
Weight	55,828 kgs (123,080 lbs)
Length	25.9 m (85 ft)
Height	3.6 m (11 ft 9 3/4 in)
Width	3 m (9 ft 10 in)
Sleeping Capacity	24
Fleet	40

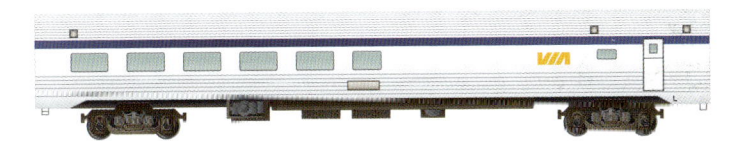

DINER CAR

Car Type	Dining Car
Series	8400
Weight	55,293 kgs (121,900 lbs)
Length	25.9 m (85 ft)
Height	3.6 m (11 ft 9 3/4 in)
Width	3 m (9 ft 10 in)
Seating Capacity	48
Fleet	13

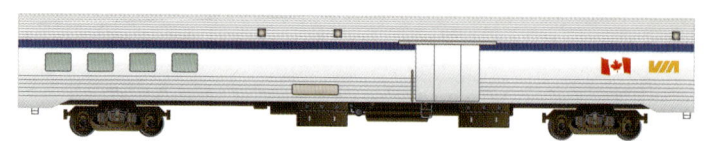

Types of Railcars

BAGGAGE CAR

Car Type	Baggage Car
Series	8600
Weight	44,225 kgs (97,500 lbs)
Length	25.9 m (85 ft)
Height	3.6 m (11 ft 9 3/4 in)
Width	3 m (9 ft 10 in)
Fleet	22

SKYLINE CAR

Car Type	Activity/Bar &Observatory
Series	8500
Weight	55,883 kgs (123,200 lbs)
Length	25.9 m (85 ft)
Height	4.3 m (14 ft)
Width	3 m (9 ft 10 in)
Seating Capacity	62
Fleet	13

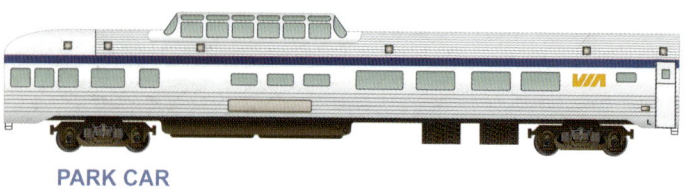

PARK CAR

Car Type	Sleeping Car/Lounge/Bar & Observatory
Series	8700
Weight	60,391 kgs (133,140 lbs)
Length	25.9 m (85 ft)
Height	4.3 m (14 ft)
Width	3 m (9 ft 10 in)
Seating Capacity	34
Sleeping Capacity	9
Fleet	12

TRAIN CLASSES & SERVICES | 77

HEP 2 Cars

It has always been the goal of VIA Rail to deploy only the best and modern fleet of cars for the safety and convenience of its passengers. The acquisition of Head End Power (HEP) 2 cars in 1996 is a realization of this vision and part of VIA Rail's modernization program of its corridor services.

The electric-powered HEP 2 cars have better safety controls and enhanced passenger comfort with more functional seat design, improved luggage compartment and more pleasing interiors. Naturally, they were utilized in first class trains and popular corridor routes. The entry of the HEP 2 cars saw the end of the last of the steam-powered rolling stocks that were the legacy of the old railway companies.

COACH CAR

Car Type	Passenger Car
Series	4100
Weight	54.432 kgs (120,000 lbs)
Length	25.19 m (82 ft., 4 in.)
Height	4.17 m (13 ft. 8 in.)
Width	3.15 m (10 ft., 4in.)
Seating Capacity	72
Fleet	23

VIA 1 CAR

Car Type	Passenger Car
Series	4000
Weight	54.432 kgs (120,000 lbs)
Length	25.19 m (82 ft., 4 in.)
Height	4.17 m (13 ft. 8 in.)
Width	3.15 m (10 ft., 4in.)
Seating Capacity	56
Fleet	10

Types of Railcars

Renaissance Cars

The diesel and electric-powered Renaissance cars joined the VIA Rail fleet in 2002, servicing the Corridor and Ocean routes. This new state-of-the-art fleet primarily hosts overnight passengers that can afford to pay for luxurious business class amenities. Renaissance cars accelerate travel time at a speed of over 175 km/h.

Inside, there are ample baggage cars for big luggage and plush dining cars for a more enjoyable mealtime. The sleeping cars boast of comfortable bedrooms with their own private shower and toilet, a cozy lounge area, power outlets and other exclusive amenities. The enhanced car design also includes areas for wheelchairs and fully accessible suites for disabled passengers. The Renaissance fleet paved the way for the phase-out of decades-old locomotives.

COACH CAR

Car Type	Passenger Car
Series	7200
Weight	51,000 kgs (112,440 lbs)
Length	23.0 m (75½ ft)
Height	--
Width	--
Seating Capacity	50
Fleet	33

VIA 1 CAR

Car Type	Passenger Car
Series	7100
Weight	51,000 kgs (112,440 lbs)
Length	23.0 m (75½ ft)
Height	--
Width	--
Seating Capacity	50
Fleet	14

TRAIN CLASSES & SERVICES | 79

SERVICE CAR

Car Type	Lounge Car
Series	7300
Weight	55,000 kgs (121,250 lbs)
Length	23.0 m (75½ ft)
Height	--
Width	--
Seating Capacity	12
Fleet	20

SLEEPER CAR

Car Type	Sleeping Car
Series	7500
Weight	55,500 kgs (122,360 lbs)
Length	23.0 m (75½ ft)
Height	--
Width	--
Sleeping Capacity	20
Fleet	47

DINING CAR

Car Type	Dining Car
Series	7400
Weight	55,000 kgs (121,250 lbs)
Length	23.0 m (75½ ft)
Height	--
Width	--
Seating Capacity	48
Fleet	13

Types of Railcars

BAGGAGE CAR

Car Type	Baggage Car
Series	7000
Weight	55,000 kgs (121,250 lbs)
Length	23.0 m (75½ ft)
Height	--
Width	--
Fleet	12

Panorama Car

Panorama cars are fully glass-enclosed cars perfect for a full view of the varied Canadian landscapes. VIA Rail acquired its Panorama cars from the luxury cruise train Whistler Northwind in 2002. They feature three single-level domes that afford passengers with an enjoyable 360-degree sweep of the sceneries outside, in the comforts of well-appointed interiors.

Today, VIA Rail's Panorama cars services the Jasper-Prince Rupert route of the Skeena from mid-May to mid-September; and the Edmonton-Jasper route of the seasonal Snow Train to Jasper from end-November to end-March. Clearly, there is no other way to get refreshing glimpses of snow-capped mountains and bear witness to the majestic Rockies along these routes than on the Panorama car viewing deck.

PANORAMA CAR

Car Type	Passenger Car
Series	1700
Weight	--
Length	26 m (85 ft.)
Height:	3.7 m (12 ft., 11 in)
Width	--
Seating Capacity	72
Fleet	3

TRAIN CLASSES & SERVICES | 81

LRC Cars

VIA Rail's long-term success in providing reliable passenger train service is largely due to the tested endurance of its Light, Rapid, Comfortable (LRC) cars. Considered as the swiftest trains in Canada, the diesel-powered, lightweight LRCs are capable of accelerating speed of up to 208 km/h due to its active tilt technology designed to increase speed.

The first LRC train was ordered in 1977 from Bombardier Transportation, the rail equipment division of the world-renowned Bombardier Group. The first LRC fleet consisted of 10 units and went into service in 1981 servicing Toronto to Sarnia. Today's LRC cars are used on short inter-city destinations in Ontario and Québec.

VIA Rail has two (2) series of LRC cars built by Bombardier.

LRC COACH

Car Type	Passenger Car
Series	3300
Weight	47,628 kgs (105,000 lbs)
Length	25.11 m (82 ft., 4 in.)
Height	3.66 m (12 ft.)
Width	3.2 m (10 ft., 5 5/8 in.)
Seating Capacity	72
Fleet	72

LRC VIA 1

Car Type	Passenger Car
Series	3400
Weight	47,628 kgs (105,000 lbs)
Length	25.11 m (82 ft., 4 in.)
Height	3.66 m (12 ft.)
Width	3.2 m (10 ft., 5 5/8 in.)
Seating Capacity	56
Fleet	26

82 | Types of Railcars

RDC Cars

VIA Rail's fleet of Rail Diesel Cars (RDC) originated from self-contained cars designed by the Budd Company of Philadelphia. Powered by multiple diesel bus engines, the first RDC cars were patterned after the military tanks used in World War II. They can be used either as a single unit or as an entire train.

Today's RDC trains are the predecessors of modern bi-directional rail cars. They can advance on either end without having to turn around. The seats are mounted on parallel sides, with passengers facing each other. VIA Rail's present fleet of RDC cars are much improved, with better engine designs and refurbished interiors enjoyed by passengers traveling along the scenic Malahat and Lake Superior routes.

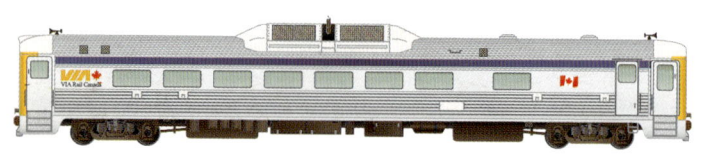

RDC 1

Car Type	Passenger Car
Series	6100
Weight	61,235 kgs (135,000 lbs)
Length	26 m (85 ft.)
Height	4.5 m (14 ft., 8 in)
Width	3.48 m (10 ft.)
Seating Capacity	88
Fleet	3

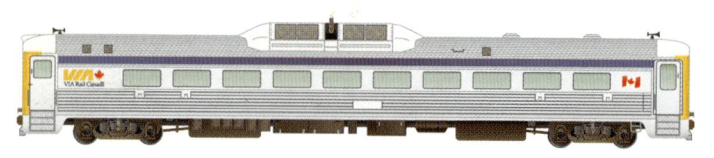

RDC 2

Car Type	Passenger Car
Series	6200
Weight	61,235 kgs (135,000 lbs)
Length	26 m (85 ft.)
Height	4.5 m (14 ft., 8 in)
Width	3.48 m (10 ft.)
Seating Capacity	71
Fleet	3

TRAIN CLASSES & SERVICES | 83

Glenfraser Car

The height of luxury accommodation, the Glenfraser car is a specialty lounge car designed for exclusive receptions onboard. Originally a coach car of VIA Rail, it was sold to Okanagan Wine Train and later purchased and refurbished by BC Rail as the lounge service for its luxury rail, the Whistler Northwind. When this class was dropped, VIA Rail bought back its former car from BC Rail, along with three new Panorama cars.

Today, the Glenfraser car is available for charter as part of VIA Rail's acclaimed PRIVA custom car service. With elegantly upholstered banquettes, polished stand-up bar, full picture windows and other features of a private club, the discerning well-heeled traveler will surely be at home in the Glenfraser car.

Locomotive Engines - F40PH-2D

The General Motors F40PH-2D model is a 16-cylinder, 3000 horsepower, diesel-electric locomotive intended for passenger service. This model provides a top speed of 145 km/h (90 MPH). The locomotive provides electric heating, air conditioning, and cab lighting for the entire train.

Locomotive Engines - P42-DC

The General Electric P42-DC model is a 16-cylinder, 4250 horsepower, diesel-electric locomotive designed specifically for passenger service. This model provides a top speed of 177 km/h (110 MPH). The locomotive provides electric heating, air conditioning, and cab lighting for the entire train.

Accommodation & Seat Configuration

HEP 1 Cars (Stainless Steel)

Sleeping Cars
VIA Rail trains are customized with a variety of sleeping accommodations with its Sleeper cars, catered to the needs and preferences of an individual or group travelers on long-haul, overnight trips.

Manor Car
The Manor sleeping cars are equipped with various levels of accommodations. Each car is named after a famous Canadian personality of British descent. It has four single bedrooms, six double bedrooms and four berths (two lower and two upper). Single bedrooms are on a convenient level with the floor on the Manor cars, unlike in the staggered locations in the Chateau cars where passengers ascend to their rooms.

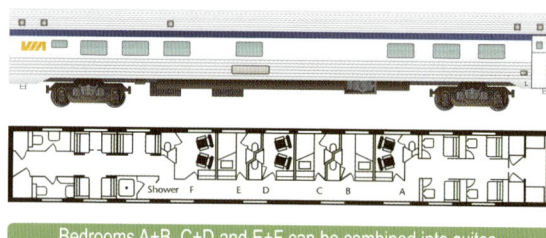

Bedrooms A+B, C+D and E+F can be combined into suites.

Chateau Car
The Chateau cars have eight single bedrooms, three double bedrooms, a drawing room and four berths (two lower and two upper). Each car is named after famous Canadian historical figures of French descent. The Chateau car provides economical sleeping accommodation with semblance to the classic Pullman sleeping car service. Smaller bedrooms may be combined to form a more spacious suite.

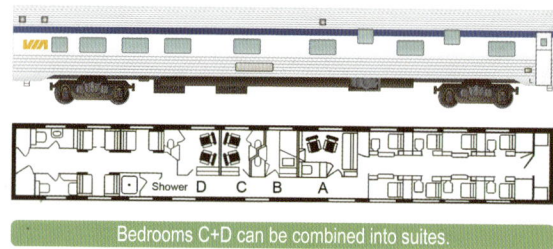

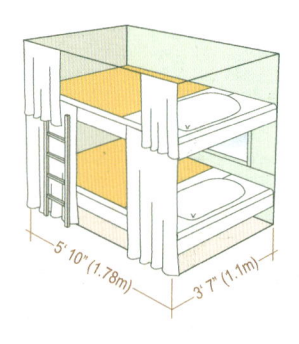

Bedrooms C+D can be combined into suites.

Berths
Not only are these means of accommodation the most economical, berths are absolutely the most comfortable beds on the train. By day, the berths are two double adjacent seats located beside a spacious window. By night, enjoy the attendant perform train

5' 10" (1.78m) 3' 7" (1.1m)

acrobats, and watch your section transform into a snug and quiet sleeping quarters. Curtains are provided for the privacy of the passenger. Washroom and shower facilities are conveniently nearby. The train attendants issue shower kits before bedtime. The passenger can save a few dollars by reserving the top bunk because it does not have a window.

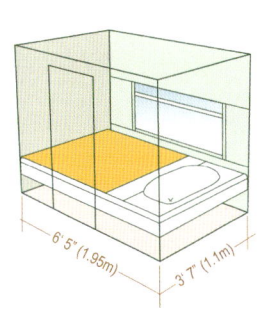

Single Bedroom (Roomette)
A private room for one person, although rather less spacious, features a small loveseat, a picture window, power outlet, call button, concealed toilet and vanity. By night, it converts into a cozy bedroom. The door locks from the inside and the shower is located down the hall.

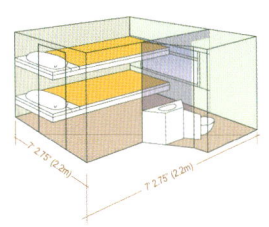

Double Bedroom
The double bedroom is a personalized private space supplied with two restful armchairs, a walk-in private washroom, a small closet, fan, double bunks, electrical outlet, shower amenities, sink and three-tiered mirror. Bedrooms are perfect refuge areas for afternoon naps and private time.

By day, two comfortable armchairs are erected tilted towards the large window. By night, the service attendant collapses these chairs and pulls down two comfortable bunks adorned with goose down quilts. Another double bedroom feature is the ability to ensuite two side-by-side bedrooms.

Accommodation & Seat Configuration

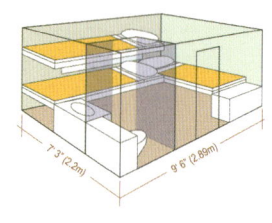

Triple Bedroom (Drawing Room)

The most elabourate room on board is the Drawing room. This lofty train accommodation sleeps three, and includes a lay-down comfortable sofa. Like the double bedrooms, the Drawing room is also equipped with two armrest chairs, shower amenities, three-tiered mirror, walk-in private washroom, sink, electrical outlet and fan. The couch folds down into a bed, and after the armchairs are collapsed, the attendant pulls down bunk beds. Enjoy a restful sleep in the most spacious compartment on the train. The Drawing room is only available in the Park car or Chateau car.

Park Car

The Park car, named after a Canadian national or provincial park, is located at the very end of the train. Supplied with a bar, the Park Car is an exquisite place to meet new friends while sipping on a refreshing aperitif in the reputable Mural lounge. Marvel at the scenic landscapes from the panoramic view provided by the dome car section of the Park car's upper level. Accommodation is also available in this car, three bedrooms and a drawing room with a bed.

Bullet Lounge

Scenic Dome

TRAIN CLASSES & SERVICES | 87

Dining Car
Seats 48, the traditional room, renowned for its tasteful decor of sort art-deco, is the gathering place for exquisite meals, all-Canadian wine and unforgettable conversation.

First class dining rooms are reputable for generously portioned gourmet meals made-to-order by on-board nationally certified chef. The passenger is informed with the details concerning meal times and reservations shortly after boarding.
Bon apetit!

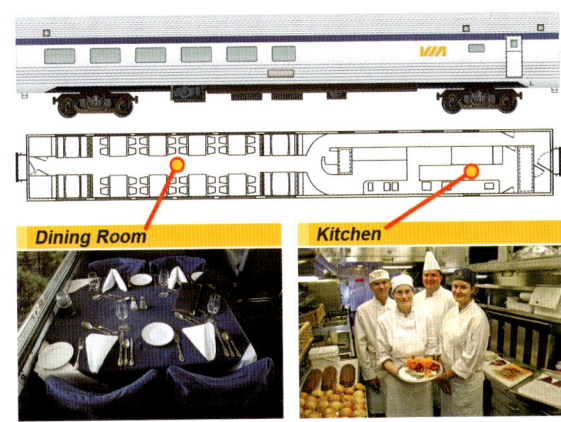

Coach Car
The following diagrams describe HEP 1 Coach cars interiors:

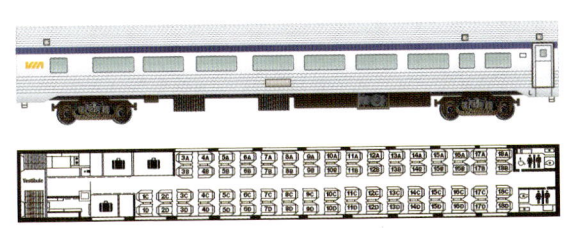

- Blinds
- Foot and leg rest
- Large picture window
- Swivel seats with reclining backs
- Folding and retractable food tray on the back of each seat
- Overhead storage compartments
- Individually controlled reading lights
- Spacious seats with an agreeable legroom space, and a convenient headrest.
- Accessible washroom
- Wheelchair tie-down device
- Seating capacity: 62

Accommodation & Seat Configuration

Shower Facility
With the exception of the Park car, all stainless steel cars have a clean, well-maintained and modern shower facility with a change room. Shower kits with all the necessary amenities are located in the bedrooms. Passengers traveling in berths can request one from the service attendant. Do not hesitate to bring your personal robes and suitable footwear for walking back to your room. Those lodging in the Park Car are welcome to use the shower facilities in the next car. Showers are available in sleeping service cars only.

HEP 2 Cars

Coach Car
The following diagrams describe HEP 2 Coach cars interiors:

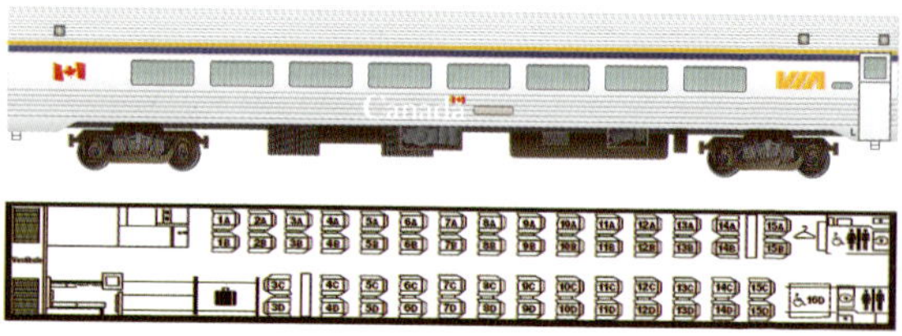

- Overhead storage compartments
- Foot and leg rest
- Large picture window
- Seats with adjustable reclining backs and retractable food trays housed in the side-arms.
- Swivel seats with reclining backs
- Blinds
- Individually controlled reading lights
- Spacious seats with an agreeable legroom space, and a convenient headrest.
- Accessible washroom
- Wheelchair tie-down device
- Seating capacity: 72

VIA 1 Car
HEP 2 VIA 1 cars offer all the benefits of the HEP 2 coach car. But in addition, VIA 1 passengers have a power outlet for their portable computer or other personal entertainment device.

The following diagrams describe HEP 2 VIA 1 cars interior

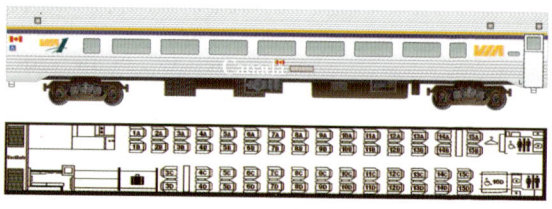

TRAIN CLASSES & SERVICES | 89

- Overhead storage compartments
- Foot and leg rest
- Large picture window
- Seats with adjustable reclining backs and retractable food trays housed in the side-arms
- Swivel seats with reclining backs
- Blinds
- Individually controlled reading lights
- Spacious seats with an agreeable legroom space, and a convenient headrest
- Accessible washroom
- Wheelchair tie-down device
- Seating capacity: 56

Renaissance Cars

Sleeping Car

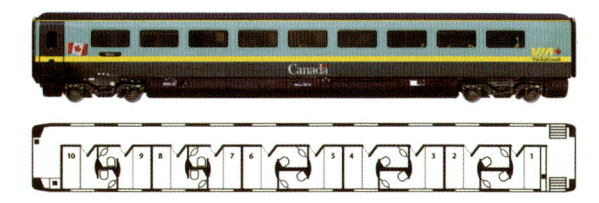

Renaissance bedrooms sleep two adults comfortably. The Renaissance bedroom can be accommodated for three people if a child of 11 or younger is traveling with the passengers, or if one adult is traveling with two children. Please note that occupancy for three guests is restricted for families with children only and that this request must be made to VIA Rail ticket agents. Please be advised, there are still only two beds. Renaissance sleepers may run seasonally; it is wise for the passenger to inquire as to when these premium sleepers are in service.

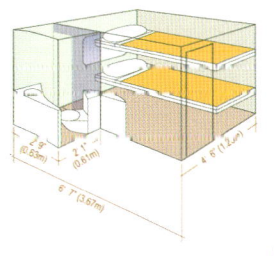

Standard Double Bedroom

These highly modernized sleek cars, feature bedrooms with a sink, mirror, wardrobe, private washroom and couch. Passengers hold a key to their room guaranteeing security of their possessions. This enables the guests to freely roam the train and visit fellow travelers in the luxurious Renaissance lounge. At night the comfortable couch converts into two cozy inviting bunk beds. Naturally, guests are ensured with a restful sleep.

90 | Accommodation & Seat Configuration

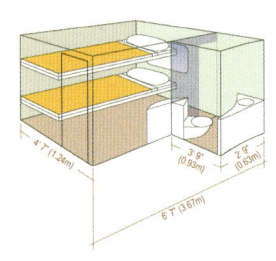

Deluxe Double Bedrooms

The Renaissance Deluxe Bedrooms replicate the Renaissance bedrooms. The addition of a private shower and a blow dryer are extra amenities allowing guests to feel more at home. Enjoy the extra time for perfect preening, and show up for dinner bedazzled by your exquisite good looks!

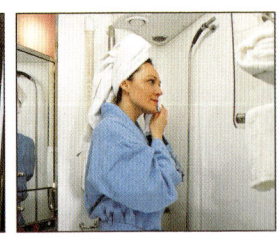

Coach Car

The following diagrams describe Renaissance Coach cars interiors:

- A window with an individual pull-down blind rests beside each seat
- Roomy reclining seats featuring a headrest, a large fold-out tray and a footrest enabling the passenger to stretch out comfortably
- Accessible washroom
- Wheelchair tie-down device
- 6 seats facing backward
- 42 seats facing forward
- Limited space available for carry-on baggage
- Baggage may be checked on trains where bag gage service is available
- Seating capacity: 50

TRAIN CLASSES & SERVICES | 91

VIA 1 Car
The following diagrams describe Renaissance VIA 1 car interiors:

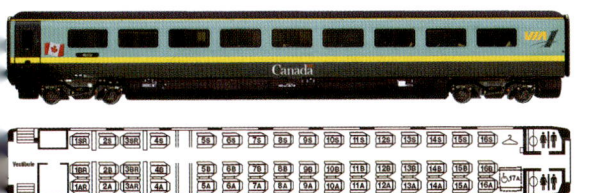

- A window with an individual pull-down blind rests beside each seat.
- Roomy reclining seats featuring a headrest, a large fold-out tray and a footrest enabling the passenger to stretch out comfortably.
- Accessible washroom
- Wheelchair tie-down device
- 6 seats facing backward
- 42 seats facing forward
- Limited space available for carry-on baggage
- Baggage may be checked on trains where bag gage service is available
- Seating capacity: 50

Dining Car
The following diagrams describe Renaissance Dining cars interiors:

Each Renaissance dining car has 48 places. On one side, there are 32 seats (eight tables for four), and on the other, there are 16 seats in tables for two along the wall of the car.

Accommodation & Seat Configuration

Service Car

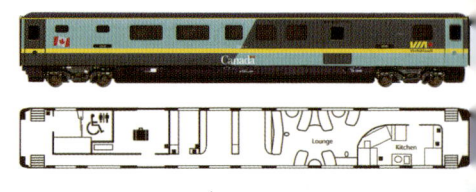

The Renaissance Service car has a number of integral features making it comfortable for the passengers. Beautifully lighted and open in design, the Renaissance Service car offers the perfect setting for a lounge: a casual atmosphere in an elegant layout that makes it easy to meet other passengers and engage in conversation. A take-out counter offers refreshments and snacks, to take back to your accommodation or to savour on the spot. For travelers with reduced mobility, this car is equipped with an accessible suite. The service car contains two lounge areas (sitting and standing), a galley, an accessible suite, a baggage compartment and a communication room. The passenger lounge features semi-circular seating adjacent to the galley and two raised counters for the convenience of standing passengers.

LRC Cars

Coach Car

The following diagrams show the typical interior of LRC Coach Car in VIA Corridor trains

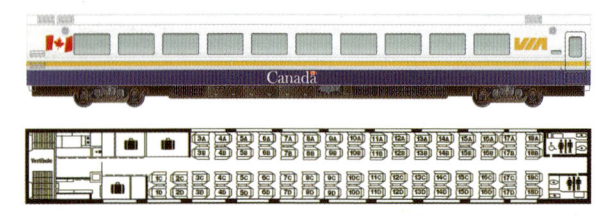

- Spacious seats with an agreeable legroom space, and a convenient headrest
- Overhead bins used for carry-on baggage
- Changing table
- Accessible washroom
- Seating arrangement may vary
- Seating capacity: 72

TRAIN CLASSES & SERVICES | 93

VIA 1 Car
The following diagrams show typical interior of LRC VIA 1 Car in VIA Corridor trains:

LRC VIA 1 cars offer all the benefits of the LRC coach car. But in addition, VIA 1 passengers have a power outlet for their portable computer or other personal entertainment device.

- Spacious seats with an agreeable legroom space, and a convenient headrest
- Overhead bins used for carry-on baggage
- Changing table
- Accessible washroom
- Wheelchair tie-down device
- Power outlets located between each seat
- Seating capacity: 56

Panorama Car

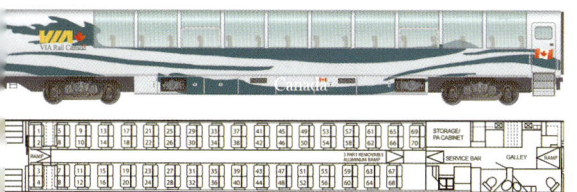

Panorama Car
The following diagrams show Panorama cars interiors:

- Fully-enclosed glass dome
- Individually controlled reading lights
- Foot and leg rest
- Folding and retractable food tray on the back of each seat
- Swivel seats with reclining backs
- Blinds
- Spacious seats with an agreeable legroom space, and a convenient headrest
- Accessible washroom
- Wheelchair tie-down device

94 | Accommodation & Seat Configuration

RDC

RDC
The following diagrams show RDC interiors:

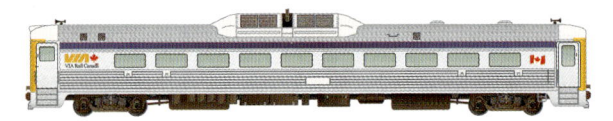

- Spacious seats with an agreeable legroom space and a convenient headrest
- Overhead bins used for carry-on baggage
- Accessible washroom
- Swivel seats with reclining backs
- Large picture window

Glen Fraser Car

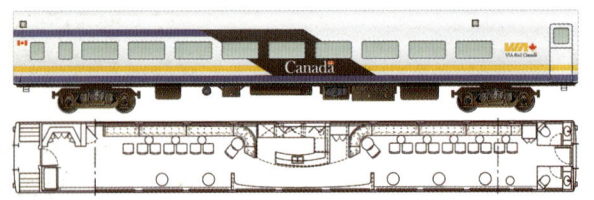

Glen Fraser Car
The following diagrams show Glen Fraser Car interiors:

The Glenfraser car is a specialty lounge car designed for exclusive receptions onboard. With elegantly upholstered banquettes, polished stand-up bar, full picture windows and other features of a private club, the discerning well-heeled traveler will surely be at home in the Glenfraser car.

TRAIN CLASSES & SERVICES | 95

09:09
56 MONTREAL
42 OTTAWA
97 NEW YORK
60 MONTREAL
73 WINDSOR
44 OTTAWA
46 OTTAWA

TRAIN TRAVEL TIPS

Fares and Reservations **98-99**

Pre-Boarding Checklist **100-101**

Safety Measures Onboard **102**

Baggage Policy **102-103**

The Train – Your Home Away
From Home **104-111**

Onboard and Overnight **112-113**

Travel Setbacks **114-115**

Fares and Reservations

Booking your tickets over the Internet. Visit *www.viarail.ca*.

Booking and Reserving Tickets

Alternative modes of reserving your tickets are as follows:

- Purchase tickets over the telephone by calling 1-888-VIA-RAIL toll free from any location in Canada or the U.S.

- Purchase tickets at a station ticket office. Try telephoning the station beforehand because smaller stations may not sell tickets or have any VIA Rail personnel on duty.

- Use a VIA Rail self-service ticketing kiosk available at the following stations: Dorval, Followfield, Kingston, London, Montreal, Oshawa, Ottawa, Québec City, Sainte-Foy, Toronto and Windsor.

- Travelers from either Canada or the U.S can purchase tickets with travel agents.

- International travelers may purchase tickets with one of VIA Rail's general sales agents. Names and addresses are listed in the appendix.

- Individuals with speech or hearing impairments may communicate by (TTY: 1-800-268-9503).

VIA Rail self-service ticketing kiosk.

Getting your Ticket – On the Spot!

Via Rail offers self-service ticketing kiosks at most stations in the Windsor-Québec City Corridor. Fast, and easy to use!

1. Print a ticket from Internet purchases.
2. Print tickets from purchases made with a travel agency.
3. Pay and print a ticket with a phone reservation.
4. Book, pay and print a ticket on the spot.

Ticket Replacement, Exchange and Refund

Often travel plans change. It is necessary to inform VIA Rail with any changes in your train travel itinerary. In order to be reimbursed with an exchange or refund, tickets must be presented to a ticket agent with receipt coupons. A refund can be issued for an unused or partially unused tickets if the ticket holder brings the ticket into a VIA Rail ticket office. A canceled cheque used by the financial institution to purchase the original tickets must be shown to a VIA Rail representative in order to acquire a refund in full. If this quest proves impossible, and the passenger is unable to acquire the copy, a request must be completed for a refund. Eventually, reimbursement will be issued by mail.

Those who purchase tickets from a travel agent will be refunded by the agency. Be aware that certain conditions may apply failing to reimburse the passenger with a refund in full.

TRAIN TRAVEL TIPS | 99

Only under specific conditions can a lost or stolen ticket be reimbursed. In most cases, VIA Rail does not refund lost or stolen tickets. Contact VIA Rail for more information.

Advance Purchase Discount

It is highly recommended to book accommodations in advance because vacancy tends to fill up rapidly during peak seasons. Fares will vary on the date and time you travel. Discounts are issued for those travelers who book a ticket five days in advance. Advance discounts are offered for all VIA Rail travel including Comfort, and Sleeper classes. Remember, you must book five days in advance to acquire the discount. Exceptions may apply to specific bargains. Please contact a VIA Rail representative for further details.

Canrailpass

Unlimited travel in Canada is the most affordable way. Tickets should be obtained as soon as applicable because during the peak-seasons reserved space for rail passes are limited.

- 12 days of unlimited travel in the Comfort class during a 30-day period. Tickets will be issued each time the traveler entrains as long as the pass is shown to a ticket agent.

- This pass is valid for all VIA Rail destinations.

- Stops can be made along the way within the 30-day period.

- Three additional days can be purchased in advance during the 30-day period, providing passengers with 13, 14 or 15 unlimited travel days.

First Class: If a specific accommodation does not suit the needs of a passenger, an upgrade to first class can be done by paying a surcharge when obtaining the ticket with the Canrailpass at any VIA Rail ticket office. Passengers over the age of 60, children (aged two to 11), students (aged two to 17), and students (aged 18 and over) with an ISIC card are eligible for special discounts.

North America Rail Pass

The North American Rail Pass enables the passenger to participate in 30 days of unlimited and exciting travel with both VIA Rail and Amtrak, America's passenger train. The discovery of the majestic Rockies, The Southern States, New York and Halifax can be part of the unlimited itinerary. The North American Rail Pass provides:

- 30 days of unlimited travel on a 45,000-kilometre rail network-(the distance around the equator).

- Direct access to over 900 cities and communities in Canada and the U.S.

Student Discounts

Students are always provided a discount with VIA Rail in both Comfort class, and first class. Students over the age of 18 must display their ISIC card in order to be issued a bargained fare. Please be aware that at VIA Rail, the only valid student identification is the ISIC card. Student fares are available for all trains and destinations year-round. Because a student's journey is a whimsical experience.

Pre-Boarding Checklist

The Service Manager oversees customer service onboard, ready and waiting at the station platform to welcome guests. Passengers can direct any concern, request or boarding assistance they may require to the Service Manager or to any of the train attendants.

They can also be asked queries on train schedules, arrival and departure times and direction the train is going. These friendly VIA Rail representatives gladly direct the passengers to their traveling car and make them feel at home.

Important Things to Tell your Ticket Agents and Boarding Crew

Trains on short-distance routes do not guarantee reserved seats for its passengers since they run often one after the other. In case a passenger is unable to board, another one is sure to arrive a few minutes after.

Inform your ticket agent right away if you are with a companion, a group or your family in Comfort class, as there is no guarantee that you will be assigned adjacent seats without a prior request to be seated together. Coordinate with the station official at the gate for a special seating request before you board. Families are accorded priority boarding in all stations. A train attendant will check the validity of the tickets in first class before boarding. Once cleared, passengers will be given full assistance all the way to their private rooms, where they can be assured of first-rate services from the energetic and friendly train crew.

Check-In Time

It is advisable to pick up your tickets at the station and check in your luggage at least one hour before your scheduled departure. Passengers requiring special assistance like the disabled, elderly on a wheelchair or walker or those with medical conditions are advised to come to the station much earlier so that unhurried and proper assistance can be administered. In all instances, it is best to call VIA Rail first for information on what time your particular station opens prior to boarding.

Special Needs

Passengers who need assistance with their personal needs (eating, medical care, personal hygiene) are required to be accompanied by an escort capable of providing such care. The escort travels free, so long as assistance is provided for the VIA Rail attendants when moving the passenger about on board, and when entraining and detraining the train. Before boarding, a document must be provided attesting the passenger cannot travel alone. A medical certificate or an

Passenger check-in at Montréal station.

identification card issued by a recognized organization will suffice.

Passengers who require medication must make sure not to forget it with their checked baggage. A sufficient supply of disposable syringes must be carried by diabetic passengers because the trains do not supply these. On advance notice and where trains have the appropriate equipment, VIA Rail will accommodate customers who have medications that requires storage at cool temperatures. For more information, consult a VIA Rail agent.

Pack Smart and Travel Light
Whether you are in for a brief travel or a long distance journey, it is always best to pack light. Ensure that important items are included in your bags before your final zip and lock. For safety and security, all bags should bear tags with the passenger's name, address and contact numbers. Valuables, documents, prescription medicines, toiletries and other personal items must be included in your carry-on bags, along with maps and a good book which may come in handy.

Large, heavy items and clothing articles can be put inside a big luggage for check-in. Two overnight bags should be adequate for long-haul trips. Remember that spaces inside the trains are limited and the less you park in your room, the more comfortable you will be. Your train attendants will also thank you for being sensitive.

Priority Boarding
Most stations first board the passengers in Sleeper class (Silver & Blue, Easterly, etc.) and in VIA 1.

Live entertainment in the Silver and Blue lounge at Vancouver station.

Those traveling with children, pregnant women, seniors, people with disabilities and passengers with restricted mobility can also expect priority boarding. If you require any assistance, please inform the VIA Rail ticket agent upon purchasing your ticket. Guaranteed that once your need has been acknowledged, a VIA Rail attendant will assist you with immediate care.

The Final Checklist
Before final packing, make a last-minute check of all the things you will need on a day-to-day basis. Shower kits containing soap, shampoo and body lotion are complimentary in overnight trains.

Personal effects like toothbrush and toothpaste, a razor and shaving cream for men and feminine hygiene supplies for women can also be requested as complimentary supplies. Note that only the Silver & Blue class aboard the long-haul Canadian route is equipped with a hairdryer and ironing board.

Safety Measures Onboard

At VIA Rail, safety is regarded as a serious matter and accorded top priority. As such, all VIA Rail employees must pass rigorous training and possess a certification in CPR and emergency response procedures so that they can respond immediately during emergency.

Passengers must also ensure their own safety onboard. On rainy or snowy days, grip the bars tightly when walking on the vestibules to avoid slip-and-fall accidents. Note where the emergency exits are located, like the one nearest your seat. Before the train leaves, an attendant will demonstrate the emergency exit procedures in case of urgent situations. A passenger will be taught how to open and close the vestibule doors.

Safeguarding Your Possessions

Passengers are expected to take care and safeguard their belongings inside the train. This responsibility cannot be passed on to service attendants. Before entraining, take note of the number of bags and luggage you have, and the valuables inside. For peace of mind, leave large sums of cash and valuables in your home. If you have to bring them along, keep them secure and close by, especially on overnight trips. For first class passengers, bedrooms lock only from the inside so make sure they are bolted right before going out. Renaissance sleeping cars lock from both inside and out.

Passengers will be glad to know that stealing is a very rare occurrence on VIA Rail trains. Still, everyone is advised to carry valuables and tickets with them at all times. Check thoroughly before detraining to be sure no item is missing from your bags or left behind on the seats or rooms. VIA Rail employees cannot be held liable for any missing or stolen item.

Reporting Lost or Stolen Item

If a passenger lost a personal item or has reason to believe it was stolen in the train, report the incident immediately by calling 1-888-VIA-RAIL. The staff will exhaust all means to find items reported missing. Again, the company cannot be held responsible for lost, stolen or damaged articles.

Baggage Policy

Baggage policy flyers are available for download at www.viarail.ca/pdf/en_baggage.pdf. Passengers on the train are entitled to bring up to six items of baggage free of charge.

This is possible only if the train has a baggage car. The baggage car, located behind the engines, is a long empty car perfect for storing items such as baggage, animals and outdoor equipment. Most long-haul trains include baggage cars except for southern Québec and southern Ontario (consult the train appendix A pages 278 – 299). In this case, only two items of baggage are permitted on board. Accommodation on the train is limited to smaller living quarters. Be advised

TRAIN TRAVEL TIPS | 103

that lugging large suitcases into your seats, sections or rooms can be extremely uncomfortable for the passengers and VIA Rail service attendants. It is recommended that passengers check in large and heavy baggage with VIA Rail personnel and comfortably enter the train with smaller bags carrying necessities.

Pets

Pets are prohibited from roaming around in passenger cars; they and are put back into the 'doghouse' in the baggage car. Only service animals for visually- or hearing- impaired customers are permitted in passenger cars. Without a baggage car, animals are unable to travel the trains. Cats, dogs and small rodents are the only animals permitted to travel aboard the train so long as their cage permits enough room for the animal to stand. Some baggage cars, like the Renaissance baggage car, do not accommodate animals during the summer months because of insufficient ventilation. The summer season runs from May 1st until September 30th. The owner of the animal must be traveling on the train, and can only visit with the permission and company of the Service Manager.

Cages may be purchased at most major VIA Rail stations. If the condition of the cage supplied by the passenger appears to be unsafe or inadequate, a new cage will be required for the pet to travel on the train.

Carry-on Baggage

Carry-on baggage must not exceed 23 kg (50lbs) or measure more than 66 x 46 x 23 cm (26 x 18 x 9in).

Baggage that goes beyond these measurements must be checked in the baggage car. Passengers should be aware whether or not their specific train is actually carrying a baggage car because specific trains do not possess such a car. Depending on your destination, a passenger can take up to six items of baggage without being charged. Be prepared that a surcharge of $15 will be required if any train item exceeds the standard measurements and goes beyond four feet.

VIA Rail may refuse to accept baggage weighing more than 32 kg (70lb) or longer than 180 cm (six feet). Outdoor sporting equipment does not apply to these regulations. These include canoes, bicycles, tents, traps, snowshoes and other outdoor equipment.

Baggage Inspection

VIA Rail reserves the right to inspect all baggage on board to ensure safety for all personnel traveling on the train. Police officers with dogs are often seen on the premises shortly before boarding. Do not be alarmed. VIA Rail uses police dogs as a measure of security.

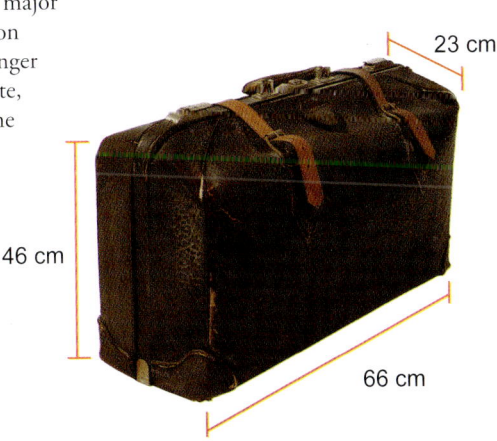

The Train – Your Home Away From Home

Traveling is one of the many joys of being free, enabling one to get to know both the world and one's self. All modes of travel ushers us to the gateway of a lifetime experience, but few, such as a leisurely train travel or a gentle ocean cruise, really afford one with the sweet pleasure to breathe in the wonders of a new surrounding.

However, a train tour and an ocean cruise are two very different ways to travel and give two distinct experiences. A cruise ship, especially luxury liners, have activities geared on group entertainment with many opportunities to participate in ship-initiated socializing. Onboard amusement itinerary fills up the entire cruise period, led by the ship captain who also commands the winds of mingling and merrymaking.

Meantime, traveling by train gives one the option to enjoy the wonderful sights and sounds in quiet privacy. As train travel offers a wider opportunity for dramatic backdrops, passengers may naturally want to treat those moments as their own personal experience. Hence, entertainment onboard is sparely scheduled and only as appropriate. After their private time, passengers can share their experiences among the throngs of passengers in designated areas for socializing.

Your Friendly VIA Rail Crew
Every VIA Rail train is manned by a group of amiable, hardworking, and energetic staff who underwent rigorous training to ensure a safe, comfortable and satisfying journey for all. All of them meet stringent qualifications and skills assessment before they are deployed to various posts onboard.

Leading the pack are two locomotive engineers who operate the engines and ensure a smooth journey from the point of departure to the final stop. Passengers have the engineers to thank for a trouble-free, on-time arrival to their destinations.

At the forefront of passenger satisfaction is the Service Manager, who leads a group of train attendants in ensuring that the travelers' needs are well taken-care of and makes certain that all aboard are having a pleasant journey. Should there be a concern regarding the level and quality of service or safety, the Service Manager is sure to attend to it right away.

Another group of dedicated and diligent staff can be found in the dining areas, where they eagerly serve nourishing and delectable meals to hungry guests. The dining room's host is called the Service Coordinator, who hands out an array of

The engineer plans for smooth operations.

TRAIN TRAVEL TIPS | 105

drinks in the bar, all the while ensuring that high-quality service is accorded to all.

Passengers can anticipate a comfortable time onboard, courtesy of service attendants who take care of their needs. Attendants prepare the seats and arrange the headrest, footrest and recliners to passenger preference. They check comfort level, tidy up the space and attend to special requests. In overnight trains, they amazingly transform seats into comfy beds. They also prepare the bedrooms of first class passengers, ensuring that sleeping amenities are well in place for a good night's rest. Aside from the main crew, other VIA Rail staff are also assigned on board according to the route and service class of the train.

Special Stops
This is one of VIA Rail's intriguing and traditional features. The passenger can request for the train to stop on demand. This feature is ideal for hunting, camping, hiking and canoeing. A ticket must be purchased with the request for the special stop 48 hours before departure. Welcome to Canada's true wild! Please note that this service is available on these trains only:

- Jasper- Prince Rupert (The Skeena)
- Montréal- Jonquière (The Saguenay)
- Montréal- Senneterre (The Abitibi)
- Sudbury-White River (The Lake Superior)
- Toronto-Winnipeg-Jasper-Vancouver (The Canadian)
- Winnipeg-Churchill (The Hudson Bay)

Please be aware that if the train is severely delayed, VIA Rail may refuse a special stop.

VIA personnel helps passenger load his bicycle into the baggage car.

English and French Are Welcome
A pre-requisite before being hired in VIA Rail is fluency in both English and French, the two official languages of Canada. Both languages are used in any station of VIA Rail. So whether you're French- or English-speaking, you're assured of the best passenger service and will have no language barrier problems onboard.

Strictly No Smoking Policy
Canadian laws strictly enforce a No Smoking policy anywhere on the VIA Rail trains and their premises, including the vestibules. This is in compliance with the Non-Smokers' Health Act which safeguards non-smokers against the health hazards caused by second-hand smoke. Train attendants impose necessary action if there is a violation, whether or not the offender is aware of this policy or not. Passengers are advised to report to any train attendant anyone who violates this policy.

A VIA Rail representative issues a warning to a first-time offender. If a passenger insists on smoking, the Service Manager has the right to evict him or her from the train. A police report will

The Train – Your Home Away From Home

Anticipating the next photo opportunity.

be filed and the offender will have to pay the corresponding fine from $50 to $100. VIA Rail will not issue a refund or replacement for the offender's ticket. To prevent embarrassment and inconvenience, talk to a service attendant for a smoke break at the next major stop, and you will be assisted with safe detraining and entraining.

Power Access

Electrical gadgets like laptops, IPods and power chargers are musts to carry along nowadays. VIA Rail trains are equipped with 110-voltage electrical outlets for the convenience of passengers. In VIA 1 class, individual power outlets are installed in each seat, complete with a fold-down table for laptops or wireless portable devices. In Comfort class, power outlets are available in front of the baggage coach. Passengers are advised to take care of their electronic and digital devices. Train employees cannot be held liable for missing or stolen belongings.

Guides to Taking Amazing Photos Onboard

Needless to say, a journey onboard VIA Rail offers one of the richest and most diverse photo opportunities to anyone. Whether on your seat, in the privacy of your room or in the viewing domes, the large picture windows vividly capture images of the wonders of the world rolling by! Make sure you have ample rolls of film or digital memory cards. Of course, don't forget your trusted camera!

The glass-domed Panorama cars are the perfect spot to take pictures, especially when traveling along the Rocky Mountains. The windows of the Skyline cars and the back windows of the Park cars are also great to capture the gently sloping sceneries on film, and both cars offer 360-degree views. Sunlight hitting glass windows can create a bit of trouble, so it is advised to take photos at a 45-degree angle to avoid overly bright exposures.

On most long haul trains, VIA Rail provides complimentary route guides that includes the landmarks along the way. Passengers can browse the images featured and take photo-taking cues from there. Anticipating a point of interest is easy through a reference called "mile markers" planted along the routes. They measure the distance traveled and provide hints on how far yet an anticipated scenery is.

What to Wear:
Fashion Aboard the Train

Dinners aboard the cozy lounges are opportunities to be fashionable, so a chic evening dress for her and an elegant dinner jacket for him may come in handy for a romantic night. Viewing domes like the Panorama cars and the Skyline cars may be chilly, so don't forget a warm sweater or a jacket. Bathrobes and slippers are necessary for shower. Overall, pack and wear sensible outfits while onboard for optimum travel comfort.

Onboard Games and Entertainment

Overnight trains offer a host of activities and games to entertain passengers and encourage a warm and fun atmosphere. In the Silver & Blue class of the Canadian, there is a Skyline car called the Activity car, with spacious tables where passengers can spend a lazy afternoon playing board games, cards, puzzles or a Sony Playstation. Adults can simply enjoy an afternoon aperitif here. An Activity Coordinator motivates passengers to mingle by facilitating popular group games like "Scrabble tournaments" and "name that tune" and conducting fun activities like wine-tasting and karaoke match. The Activity car also has an entertainment system where film showings are held.

On the Easterly class, a route that combines tourism and learning, a Learning Coordinator serves as the master of ceremonies in a fun-filled itinerary while traversing the Canadian East Coast. This energetic and lively staff narrates the historical background of the Maritimes, presents entertaining videos, leads group games and encourages passenger participation for a truly engaging train ride with more than just a glimpse of the seaside.

Exclusive Train Merchandise

Passengers can purchase a variety of train merchandise stamped with the VIA Rail logo to serve as travel mementos. These include mugs, spoons, pins and clocks as well as books and videos. An array of quality clothing items, from polo shirts, t-shirts, sports shirts, sweatshirts and vests, to caps and hats are also available. These can be bought in the souvenir boutiques conveniently located in the Activity cars and Park cars. They can also be purchased by placing orders through e-mail.

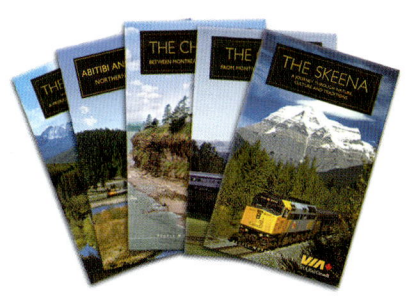

Handy Guide to Routes and Landmarks

On long haul trains, VIA Rail passengers are given a complimentary route guide that serves as quick reference for information like distance covered and points of interest along the way. A comprehensive map is also included, with brief descriptions of towns covered by the route, travel highlights and tips on the best location onboard for the best view of these sceneries. The rail-issued guide makes sightseeing easier for a truly exciting journey.

Public Address System

A Public Address or P.A. System is installed in VIA Rail trains for instant mass communication onboard. With this, important information are clearly and easily conveyed to passengers, including nearby points of interests and historical sites. For instance, Manitoba-bound travelers will be delighted to know that the biggest bottle of Coke in the world can be seen just 30 metres away. Passengers aboard the Canadian will appreciate that Mount Robson, the tallest mountain in the Canadian Rockies

The Train – Your Home Away From Home

is the next important spot after passing the Redpass Junction. The P.A. System is also crucial in informing fellow passengers about a lost or found item.

Fees and Purchases

Some items can be purchased onboard like souvenirs, snacks, soft drinks, alcoholic beverages and personal kits, among others. For any purchase, VIA Rail accepts payments either in U.S. dollar or traveler's checks and all major credit cards.

Passenger Conduct While Onboard

- Be sensitive of your fellow passengers by maintaining cleanliness and orderliness of common areas, especially the general washroom. The same goes to your private washroom. In doing so, service attendants will be more inspired to give the best service.

- Access to some areas like the Dome car can be quite limited. Do not monopolize viewing lounges by hugging on to them for too long. Be considerate and let others enjoy the same breath-taking experience by graciously giving way to them once you are done enjoying the views yourself.

- The Dining rooms are nice places in which to meet and chat with other passengers. Just make sure you don't linger too long. Ask your new friend if it is okay to carry on the acquaintance in the Dome car or other common areas. This gives the staff ample time to prepare the table for the next batch of diners. If you are among the last ones, remember that your dining crew may be waiting for you to vacate the area so they too can partake of much-needed meal.

- Adults should always keep an eye on children traveling with them. This is especially true in trains where the vestibules can pose dangers to kids. Children are prohibited from running inside the train, and parents or guardians are expected to supervise in their kids' behavior while onboard.

- Show respect for your fellow passenger at all times. Don't put your feet up on chairs, stools or benches.

- Be quiet when passing by areas adjacent to sleeping cars so as not to disturb passengers that may be sleeping or napping inside.

- Address train staff by their proper title and position. Refrain from calling the staff assisting in your baggage as "porter;" this is now obsolete and demeaning. Rather, refer to them as Car or Service Attendants. Likewise, the dining crew should not be addressed as "waiters" or "waitresses." Use Servers or Service Attendants instead. To make it easy, why not address them by their first names? It's a lot cooler and friendlier.

Left: Onboard crew gets an opportunity to sit down and enjoy breakfast.

TRAIN TRAVEL TIPS | 109

TIPPING GUIDELINE

Position	Amount
Station Attendant	$2.00 per bag
Meal Car Attendant	$2.00 per meal
Dining Car Attendant Breakfast	$2.00 per person
Dining Car Attendant Lunch	$3.00 per person
Dining Car Attendant Dinner	$4.00 per person
Activity Coordinator	$2.00 per person/day
Learning Coordinator	$2.00 per person/day
Bar Attendant	Same as bar lounge in hotel
Sleeping Car Attendant	$5.00 per person/night (consider extra for special service)

Tipping: Graciously Thanking Your Train Crew

A customary tip is a show of gratitude for excellent service and prompt attention accorded to a customer. In North America, tipping is expected in any service establishment. Your VIA Rail crew will feel rewarded for their hard work if they are accorded proper tipping rate. Tips can be given with discretion after each service, or as a cumulative sum at the end of the trip.

Attendants in first class sleeping cars do their best to put guests at ease and comfort. A decent tip for them is at $5 per passenger per night. Increase the amount if a special request like room service was accomplished. In Comfort class, tipping may be unnecessary except for special services like meal take-outs and luggage handling. A $2 tip per night is fair enough. Dining attendants are the ones that should be given a fair tip in consideration of their hard work and the nature of their jobs. A standard rate of $2 per dining crew after every meal is expected. The total daily tips are divided among the dining attendants, cooks, chefs, servers and the Service Coordinator. Likewise, the Learning Coordinator in the Easterly class, the Activity Coordinator in the Silver & Blue class cars and the lounge attendants also welcome tips. VIA Rail staff observes proper tipping etiquette and will not personally solicit or demand tips from passengers. A staff reported to do so will be penalized by VIA Rail.

The Heart of the Train: The Park Car

One of VIA Rail's admired facilities, the Park car, is located at the rear of the train and named in homage to one of the famous national parks of Canada. It is an exclusive section designed for optimum pleasure of first class passengers. Its three salons have distinct flair and attraction.

The upper level offers the best view of all. The 360-degree observation deck affords taking professional-quality photos, capturing the details of mesmerizing nature, like the graceful fall of the leaves of autumn. Below the viewing dome is the Mural Lounge that hails Canadian artistry by featuring a centrepiece painting

The Train – Your Home Away From Home

by a renowned Canadian painter. The elegantly upholstered seats are perfect for intimate dining and conversation. Rounding up the place is the Bullet Lounge with its 1950-style circular bar, perfect for an afternoon chat. Those who can afford it can reserve any of the Park car's three double bedrooms and one triple bedroom.

Seating Coach-style
Coach cars are an economical means to travel in Comfort class. There are no specific seat assignments and passengers may choose a convenient spot on a first board-first sit basis. The spacious armchairs face the direction the train is traveling while other sections can be rotated, ideal for families and group travelers. After collecting your ticket, a paper with your destination written on it will be posted above your seat to confirm that place for you. Do not confuse the seating confirmation by switching places. If you need to change your seat, inform a service attendant who will help you settle in a better location.

TRAIN TRAVEL TIPS | 111

Recliners that Lull

Coach cars have spacious reclining seats that make for a comfortable travel with their soft headrests and ample legroom. Passengers can easily fall asleep as they would in a horizontal cot. Middle coach seats are a safe distance away from washroom foot traffic and are ideal spots for snatching ample winks.

Top left: First class passengers enjoying themselves at the comfort of Park car's Bullet Lounge.

Above: Students in the quadruple seating arrangement traveling in the Comfort class.

Onboard and Overnight

Overnight travelers can expect a comfortable bed at the end of the day, as well as replenished quarters and clean seats in the morning, thanks to service attendants who deftly transform them into fresh, welcoming accommodations every day.

Beds are made during dinnertime, or earlier upon request. The seats are folded down, covered with a clean mattress and laden with fluffed pillows. Thick, soft blankets are ready to warm the body on a usually cold night onboard. Hypoallergenic blankets are available upon request. For optimum pampering, a bottle of fresh water and chocolates are placed on the bed. Lastly, the reading light will be on to soften the mood. Imagine a bedroom this inviting while on a train!

In the mornings, beds are folded back into seats, washroom amenities are replenished and everything is tidied up while the passengers are out for breakfast. Upon returning, they will find their bedrooms fresh and unsoiled from last night's slumber. Attendants must make up at least 34 beds every morning, quite a lot! Please allow them enough time to thoroughly attend to your room.

Maximizing Your Space
Private quarters and even common areas inside trains are naturally small and look tight. Do not fret, for this is just what it seems. You will be surprised that everything can comfortably fit in. Maximize the space of your room by packing light. A carry-on bag with your valuables and personal effects and a small yet compact luggage will fit snugly in your private compartment for days of journeying. Remember that your seats are deftly transformed into beds at night and back into day couch the next morning. Should you feel claustrophobic inside or you want a larger space, seek out the help of the Service Manager for a possible change that may suit you.

Easy Freshening Up Onboard
Overnight passengers can freshen up with an invigorating shower anytime while onboard. Those in the Renaissance cars have accommodations equipped with a private shower, while those in the Sleeper cars have access to a full-sized shower room and a change room. Shower kits containing soap, shampoo and lotion are given by attendants to passengers on berth sections while these are included in the amenities in the private rooms. Be ready with your bathrobe and sleepers

Car attendant making up lower berth.

TRAIN TRAVEL TIPS | 113

Room service: Breakfast in bed.

to wear between the shower room and your quarter. After your turn, extend courtesy by cleaning up and readying the shower for the next user. Train attendants regularly sanitize and maintain order of the shower rooms. The shower is shut off on schedule to refill water.

Room Service
VIA Rail offers Room Service; just inform the service attendant ahead of time. Hot beverages like coffee or tea can be brought into your room upon request. Note that alcoholic beverage bought outside of the train prior to boarding must be strictly consumed only in your private bedrooms, and in moderation. Inform an attendant should you need ice and glasses inside your room.

Getting a Squeaky-Free Slumber
Noises like rattling, squeaking and grinding can be quite annoying especially for a weary traveler. These small noises are normal part of the train locomotion and should not be a cause for worry. Most noises are easy to track down and stopped.

Rattling sounds are caused by the constant moving and vibrating of locomotive parts. It can be warded off by wedging a piece of cloth or tissue paper into cracks. Check for unsecured hangers in the rooms since they rattle noisily. Plug the washroom sinks because the clatter of wheels turning over the tracks can seep through the hole. Crushing and grinding sounds emanate under the train, caused by friction when the centre-casting comes in contact with the train wheels.

Onboard noises should be tolerable. If there is an unusually loud, persisting noise, inform a train attendant to check on the source right away. For sensitive ears, the personal amenity kit includes earplugs for a more comfortable sleep.

Travel Setbacks

VIA Rail values the time of passengers and enforces punctuality when it comes to train schedules. All trains are likely to be on time especially in the major stations, and no train ever leaves earlier than scheduled. Short-distanced trains may be briefly impeded by route connections with incoming trains, while most long-haul trains share tracks with other railway companies and may be shortly halted.

Causes of delay include freights that broke down across the route, damaged tracks or extreme weather. They are unlikely situations and VIA Rail ensures the train will arrive as soon as possible. Should there be an anticipated delay, call the 1-888-VIA-RAIL hotline for an updated schedule. Some small far-off stations may not have washroom facilities, so passengers must be ready in the remote possibility of being stuck in long delays.

Avoiding Inconvenience of Tardy Trains

To avoid inconvenience, an allowance for slight delay must be considered. Standby passengers as well as relatives or friends who will pick up their kin from the station are advised to confirm arrival schedules by calling the 1-888-VIA-RAIL hotline. This is especially important for passengers who need to catch an early or night train to spare them the agony of missed appointments.

Late Stops in Major Stations

Late trains arriving in major stations take a brief stop and prompt departure to avoid further delay. Service attendants will swiftly usher passengers to detrain and will prepare the train for its next journey immediately. Platforms need to be cleared for orderly detraining and entraining. Passengers on longer destinations can step out for a breath of fresh air or a brief exercise but must be ready as soon as the announcement to entrain is given.

Missing Connecting Trips

As in any mode of transport, delayed arrivals can be frustrating and troublesome. Those with connecting trips either on a plane, a train or a cruise will have to struggle with a mangled travel itinerary. One can only imagine the extent that missed appointments or absence in planned activities may cost the poor passenger.

A road trip may face a lot of undue obstacles on the way particularly impediments relating to weather and forces of nature. These instances are out of VIA Rail's control. At the very least, the company will compensate passengers holding "guaranteed tickets." However, nothing will compensate for wasted time and lost opportunities on missed connections. If a passenger fears that a connecting trip will be missed, talk to the Service Manager for travel advice and possible options. To avoid hassles, passengers with multiple scheduled trips should plan an itinerary that allows for a full day before embarking on a major travel connection. This is applicable on all modes of transport – bus, train, plane or ship.

TRAIN TRAVEL TIPS | 115

Station stop in Jasper, Alberta.

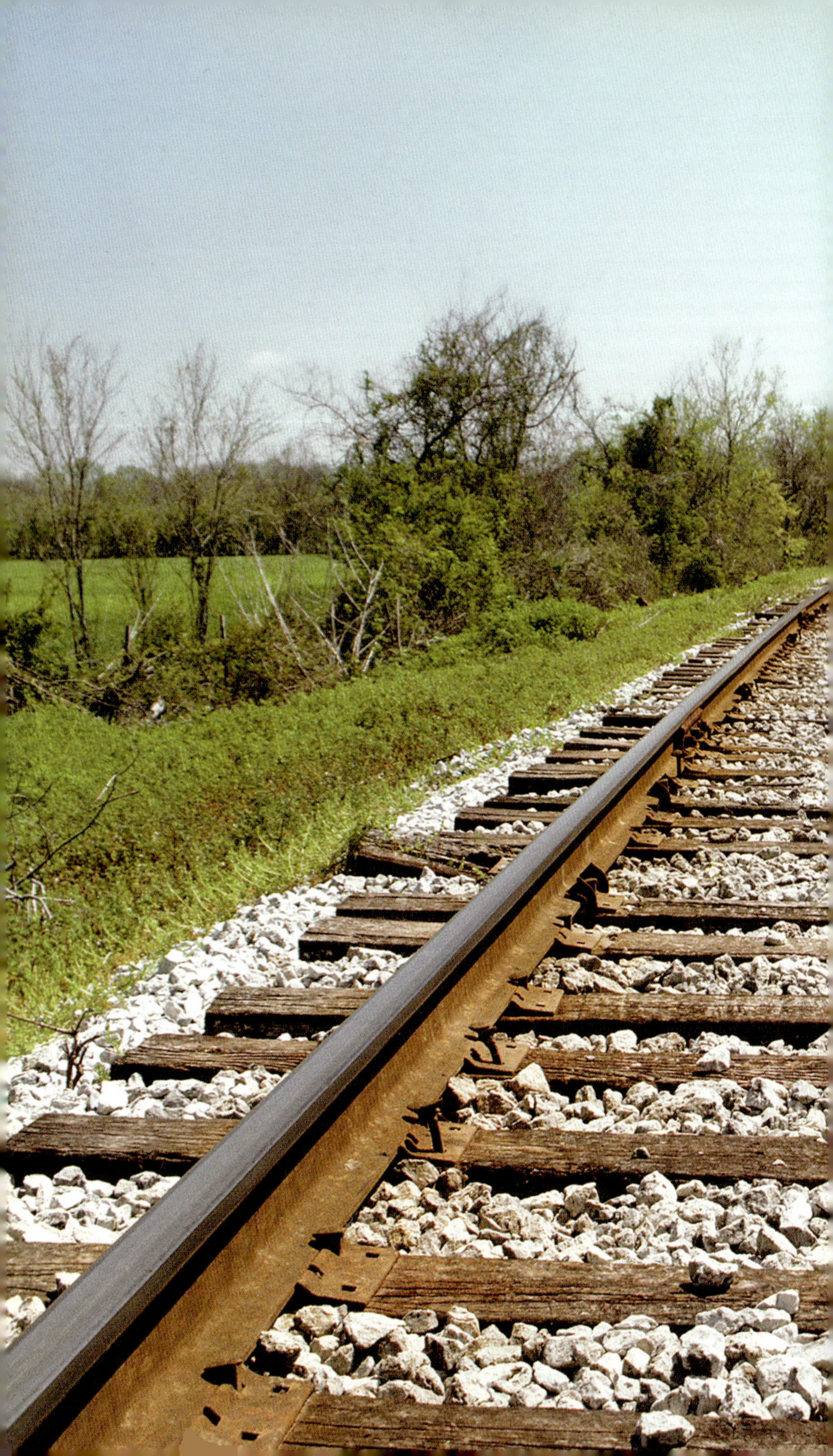

CANADIAN RAILWAY 101

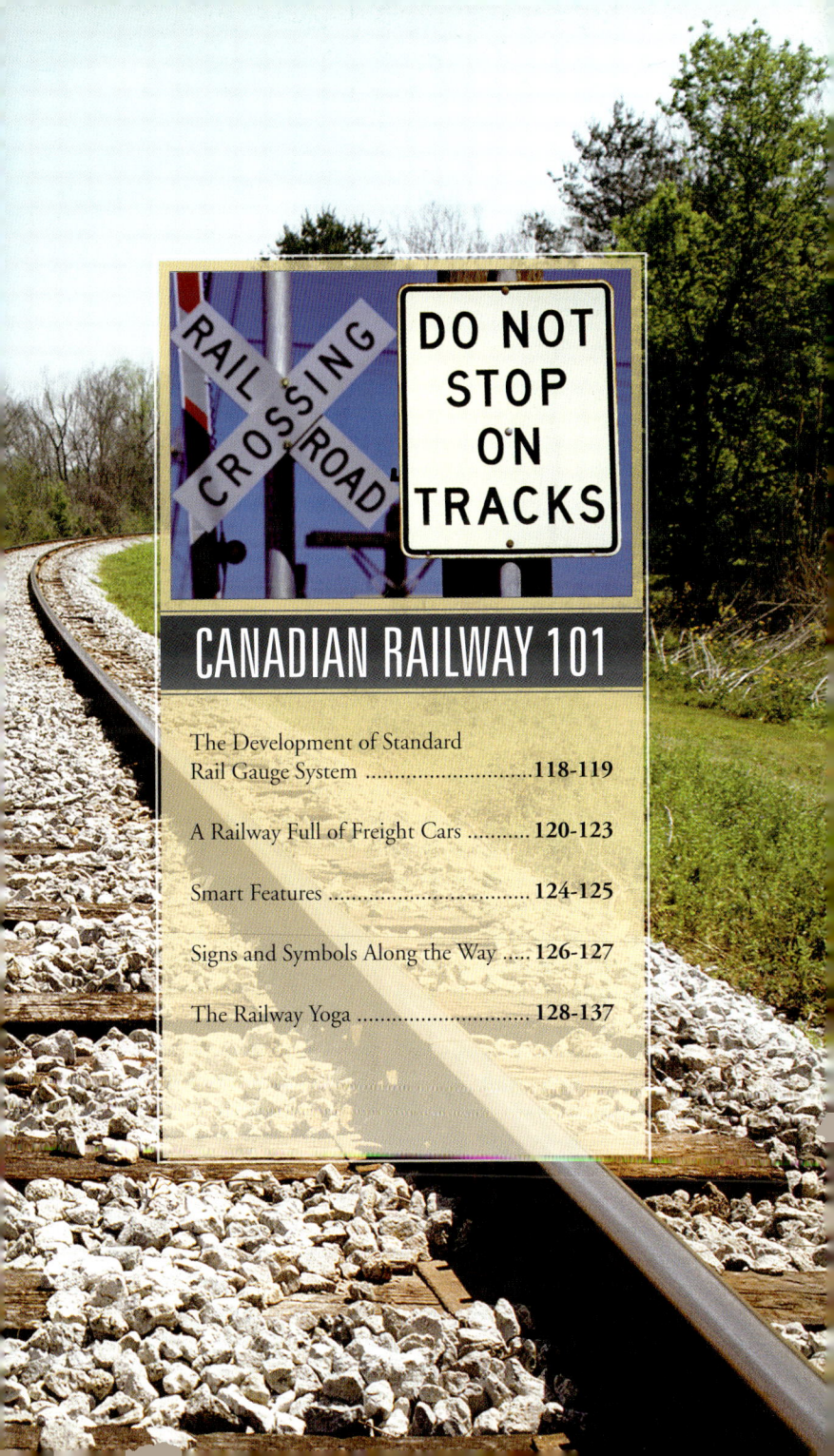

The Development of Standard
Rail Gauge System 118-119

A Railway Full of Freight Cars 120-123

Smart Features 124-125

Signs and Symbols Along the Way 126-127

The Railway Yoga 128-137

The Development of Standard Rail Gauge System

Canada's standard railroad gauge emulated that of Britain's. The Canadian railway was initially conceptualized and engineered by British settlers. The first railway to move between two major cities was built by George Stephenson who designed the Stockton & Darlington Railway in 1825. He used a gauge of 4 feet, 8 inches, common for English roadways at that time.

This measurement was also used because of his familiarity with a mine tramway using the same proportions in Newcastle. For the run between Liverpool and Manchester, Stephenson increased the size of the gauge by one-half inch. It is suspected that lateral play to the flanges was increased, resulting in a smoother operation. Most steam engines throughout Britain, North America and Western Europe used the standard gauge.

Archeological excavations disclosed that this gauge had been used for centuries prior to the innovation of the railway. Late 1870 excavations in Pompeii revealed that Romans used a similar gauge for the ruts on their chariots and carts. Rumour has it that Julius Caesar systemized ruts for his war chariots. Walton E. Evans, an American engineer, was determined to prove this postulation and set out to measure the ruts of the antiquated chariots. He converted the measurement into inches and found that the ruts from centre to centre were about 4 feet, 9 inches. This became the custom gauge for the Romans and it subsequently spread into Western Europe. Evidence revealed that the current standard gauge evolved from the established gauge of the Roman Empire.

British railway historian, Charles E. Lee, suspected that the Romans acquired their gauge by the distance between two chariot wheels being roughly equal to the maximum weight that a Roman horse could pull. The gauge of the railway was not formed to cater to horses. Human beings are the most relevant reason for today's standard gauge. Considering the average size of human beings, a gauge of 4 feet, 8.5 inches is not far off. This gauge permits passengers to sit beside each other comfortably on both sides of the train. It created for a compact yet appropriate space for travelers to feel comfortable in.

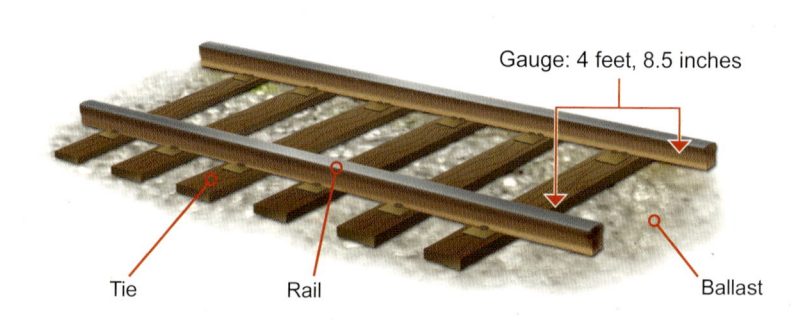

Gauge: 4 feet, 8.5 inches

Tie   Rail   Ballast

CANADIAN RAILWAY 101 | **119**

A Railway Full of Freight Cars

Freight trains are the primary transport device carrying goods and resources across Canada. During a Canadian train journey, passengers will witness dozens of seemingly endless freights. Freight trains carry commodities to be either imported or exported. Ore, sulfur, lumber, grain, automobiles and coal are products commonly carried.

Freight traffic in the west is particularly busy because the trains transport goods destined for the Pacific Rim.

The advanced diesel locomotives hold enough power to carry freights up to two miles long. Usually, their size exceeds the length of siding tracks enabling trains to pass each other. Inevitably, the mammoth freights are given priority and passenger trains must wait on siding tracks until it is clear to continue.

Automobile Car
A train car that carries automobiles.

Box Car
The most common car found on freight trains. This car has two sliding doors on either side enclosing cargo that cannot be exposed to the elements.

CANADIAN RAILWAY 101 | 121

Caboose
Cabooses are located at the very tail-end of freight trains. Traditionally, the caboose was used as an observatory for engineers to detect any potential dangers on the tracks. Crew members were able to detect overheated journal bearings that cause derailments. Currently, cabooses are obsolete and have been replaced with automatic detectors on the side of the tracks.

Centre Beam Car
A common car used for transporting lumber, timber and pulpwood.

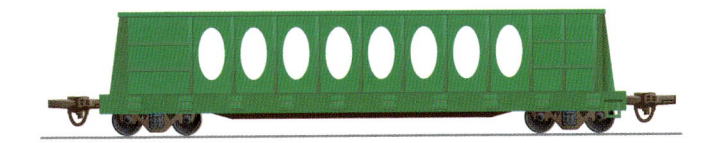

Flatcar
A freight car without tops or sides used to transport commodities that do not require protection from weather.

122 | A Railway Full of Freight Cars

Tank Car
A freight car specifically used for transporting liquids and chemicals.

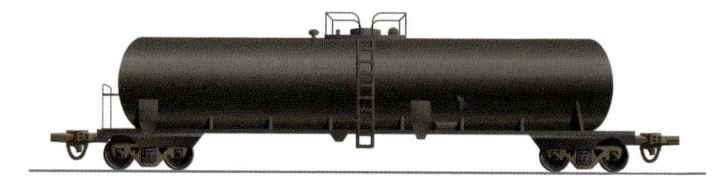

Refrigerator Car
A closed car with refrigeration and insulation. Perfect for keeping materials cool during the summertime. Cars carrying produce during winter months are slightly heated so the fresh products do not freeze.

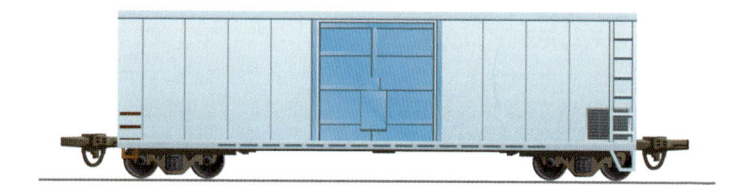

Cylindrical Hopper Car
Covered hoppers are normally used for a specific type of service to avoid cross-contamination of the products. Products carried range from grains, cement and a variety of powdered chemicals.

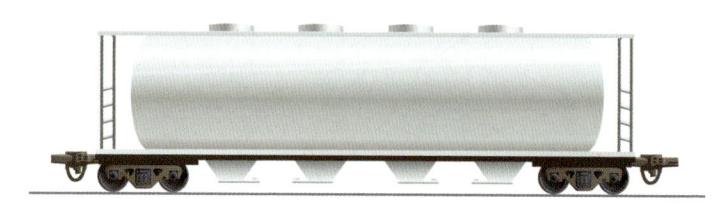

Gondola Car
A freight car with an open top and low sides. Ideal for carrying products that may be exposed to the weather.

Hopper Car
Similar to Gondola cars except that they have sloped sides and ends. This allows materials to be dumped out through passages in the car's bottom. Ideal for transporting grain and coal.

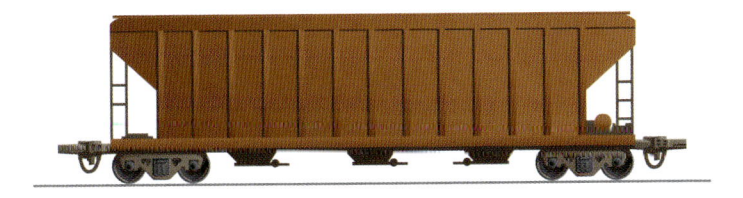

Smart Features

Interpretation of Railway Signal Lights – Just as roads have lights to direct traffic, trains also have lights to command traffic. Road traffic-lights were actually adopted from the railway.

Block
A train block is anywhere between three and six miles. Traffic lights indicate whether a train can enter or not and at what speed the train can travel. Generally, only one train is permitted to move through a block at one time. Often, when the train stops, it is waiting for another train to pass through the block.

Trains require a longer distance to make a complete stop because they are extremely heavy. Typically, a train safely comes to a complete stop after slowing down for approximately one mile. Railway traffic lights position yellow lights to be displayed before red lights.

Green Signal
Green lights inform engineers that the tracks are clear for the next two blocks.

Red Signal
Red signals mean that the next block is occupied or a train traffic controller wants to stop the train to permit another train to pass. Red signals may also suggest a danger. Examples include, damage to the track, obstruction on the track, or an improper switch set in the tracks ahead.

Yellow Signal
Yellow signs indicate that the next block is clear, but the following block is occupied or unsafe to enter. The next signal will most probably be red indicating that the engineers have one block to stop the train.

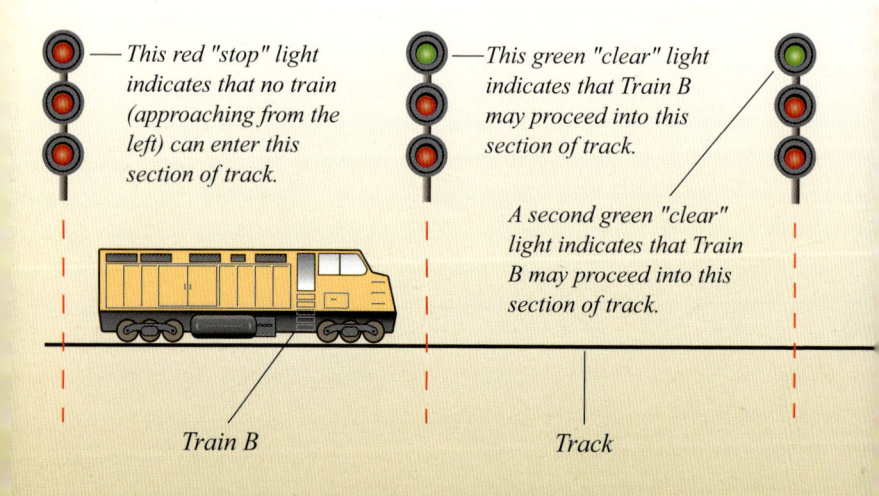

This red "stop" light indicates that no train (approaching from the left) can enter this section of track.

This green "clear" light indicates that Train B may proceed into this section of track.

A second green "clear" light indicates that Train B may proceed into this section of track.

Train B

Track

Determining the Speed of the Train

It is possible to find out the approximate speed by computing how long it takes to travel between two mileposts.

SPEED TABLE					
Time per Mile	**MPH**	**Time per Mile**	**MPH**	**Time per Mile**	**MPH**
0 min. 36 sec	100	0 min. 52 sec	69	1 min. 30 sec	40
0 min. 38 sec	95	0 min. 54 sec	67	0 min. 35 sec	38
0 min. 39 sec	92	0 min. 55 sec	65	0 min. 40 sec	36
0 min. 40 sec	90	0 min. 57 sec	63	0 min. 45 sec	34
0 min. 41 sec	88	0 min. 58 sec	62	2 min. 0 sec	30
0 min. 42 sec	86	0 min. 59 sec	61	2 min. 10 sec	28
0 min. 43 sec	84	1 min. 0 sec	60	2 min. 20 sec	26
0 min. 44 sec	82	1 min. 5 sec	55	2 min. 30 sec	24
0 min. 45 sec	80	1 min. 10 sec	51	2 min. 50 sec	21
0 min. 46 sec	78	1 min. 15 sec	48	3 min. 0 sec	20
0 min. 48 sec	75	1 min. 20 sec	45	3 min. 30 sec	17
0 min. 50 sec	72	1 min. 25 sec	42	4 min. 0 sec	15

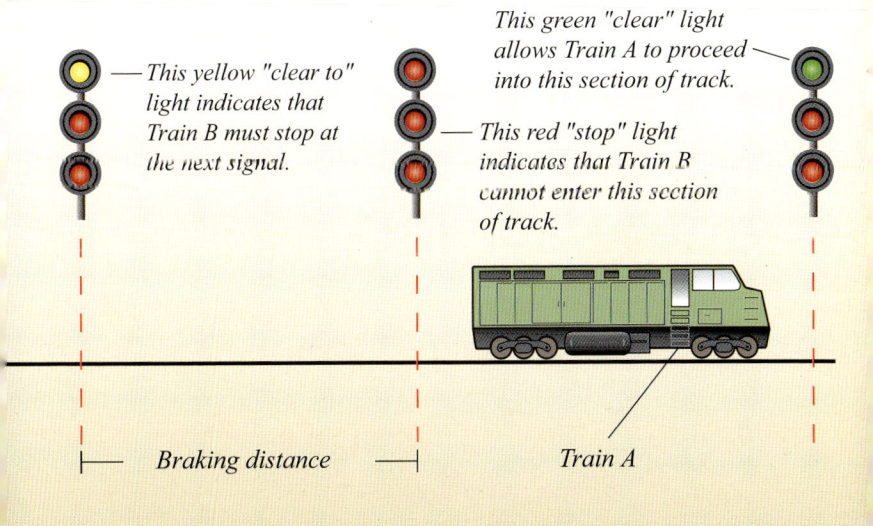

This yellow "clear to" light indicates that Train B must stop at the next signal.

This green "clear" light allows Train A to proceed into this section of track.

This red "stop" light indicates that Train B cannot enter this section of track.

Braking distance

Train A

Signs and Symbols Along The Way

Mileposts
Mileposts are located at every mile alongside the tracks. Numbers increase from east to west and south to north. Numbers go back to zero at the beginning of every subdivision. Mileposts indicate the location of the train enabling passengers to anticipate points of interest.

Speed Limit Signs
Train speed limit signs comprise two numbers. The number on the top is the speed limit for passenger trains and the one on the bottom is the speed limit for freight trains.

Derail Signs
These signs warn of a switch that automatically stops the train from rolling forward. The switch is a metal instrument of a bright orange or yellow colour. These signs are seen along sidings, which are shorter tracks located beside main tracks. They prevent trains from accidentally moving onto the tracks where another train may be passing. Essentially, derail signs prevent major accidents.

Flanger Boards
These signs warn snowplow operators of obstacles hidden by snow.

Whistle Prohibited

Whistle Tunnel 1,000 feet

Block Begin

Block End

Begin Avalanche Zone

Avalanche Zone End

CANADIAN RAILWAY 101 | 127

Hot Box Detector Signs

Signs informing engineers that a safety device is coming up on the tracks. Hot box detectors notify engineers of car axles that may be too hot. These instruments help prevent derailments and track damage.

Windsock

Windsocks indicate what direction the wind is blowing and how strong the wind is traveling. Windsocks are also useful just in case there is a chemical spillage.

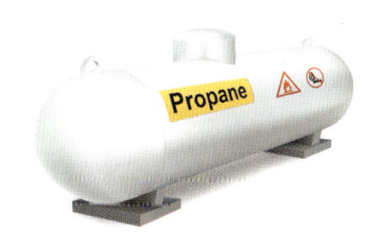

Propane Tanks

A switch heater used to melt ice from track switches. It warms the switches preventing malfunction.

Station Name Boards

Names of sidings, junctions and stations are often displayed alongside the tracks. Signs can be either of a white background with black lettering or a black background with white lettering. Along CNR routes, signs have a yellow background with black lettering.

Whistle Posts

Signs posted before blind corners, tunnels and sharp turns permitting the engineers to blow the whistle to warn any animals or people along the tracks.

Slide Detectors

Wire fences along the sides of steep hills act as a slide-detection system. The wires will break when there is a slide and signals will be sent to the engineer warning of an impediment on the tracks up ahead.

The Railway Yoga

What? Exercise on a train? And yoga at that! I'm supposed to be enjoying the trip, right? What about the breath-taking sceneries, the romance of looking outside and passing the world by? I just cannot afford to miss all that and have my quiet peace disturbed…

Well, think again. On second thought, it is for your better enjoyment of the trip that yoga exercise should be part of your time onboard. It is not hard as it seems, and only takes a few minutes of your time, right there on your seat.

Exercise gives the body a different kind of high. After a few concentrated efforts on stretching, pulling, and rhythmic breathing, your body will definitely feel more agile, lighter and on the go to enjoy all there is to experience onboard – minus the cramps and the aching backs.

The Railway Yoga is a series of exercises to help relieve discomforts caused by long travel. The exercises were developed by **Liane Cherrett**, a yoga instructor who teaches the workout in her school in Winnepeg called Source Yoga Studios. Having worked in VIA Rail aboard the transcontinental route the Canadian, Liane knows the physical strain caused by traveling on long-haul trips. Following are easy step-by-step instructions on railway yoga guaranteed to bring welcome relief to tightening muscles and swollen legs onboard.

Train compartments are tight, but this is never a problem when it comes to exercise. All you need is yourself and your small space.

Mountain Pose (Tadasana)

Often, because of the hustle and the bustle of our daily routine, we neglect proper posture as the toils of the hours make us heavy and weary. Overtime, we develop a slouching posture that weighs on the heart, making us feel fatigued. A heart without undue pressure from the weight is healthy, making us feel youthful and alive. The Tadasana (derived from the word "Tada," a Sanskrit term for mountain) or Mountain Pose helps develop proper weight distribution on the feet and legs, giving relief to the spine and chest. Regular practice makes one still, steady and strong.

⭐ Benefits

On the long-term, the Mountain Pose improves posture, develops concentration, promotes stronger spine and helps maintain the youth and vitality of the legs and feet. You are sure to feel up and about walking the distances from your seat to the Park car, and have more energy for competitive fun on the Activity car!

CANADIAN RAILWAY 101 | 129

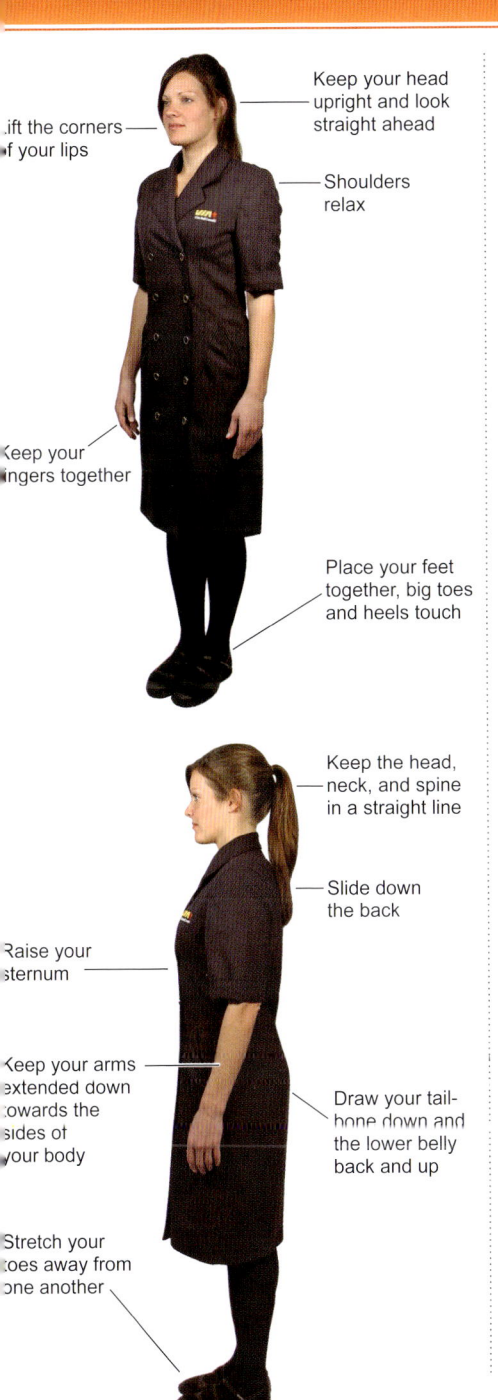

Lift the corners of your lips

Keep your head upright and look straight ahead

Shoulders relax

Keep your fingers together

Place your feet together, big toes and heels touch

Keep the head, neck, and spine in a straight line

Slide down the back

Raise your sternum

Keep your arms extended down towards the sides of your body

Draw your tailbone down and the lower belly back and up

Stretch your toes away from one another

1. Find a hard, even surface. Place your feet together, big toes and heels touch. If you struggle with balance, take your feet 2 to 3 inches apart aligning the second toe back to the centre of your heel. Lift all 10 toes off the ground and root down through the four corners of your feet evenly. Notice as the 10 toes lift, this brings energy into the feet and the legs. Keep this energy in the feet and legs as you fan the toes and place them back down on the hard surface.

2. Lift the knee caps and the quadriceps upwards. Offer the tailbone down towards your heels and simultaneously the lower contents of your belly draws back towards your spine and up towards your ribcage.

3. The shoulders gently roll back as the arms extend down towards the sides of your body. Lift the sternum and broaden your chest. Draw your chin back and down slightly as the throat remains relaxed. The ears should align over the shoulders, the shoulders align over the hips and the hips align over the heels.

4. Notice your inhalation expanding in your body and the exhalation grounding and relaxing your body. Stay here, standing tall like a mountain for 5 to 10 breaths.

The Railway Yoga

Extended Mountain Pose

Exercising should not be a contrite, forced effort. Rather, it must be enjoyed as a fun, enjoyable time in reverence to one's body. Every small movement is part of a holistic approach to wellness. The extended Mountain Pose is a flexible movement that can be done right on your seat or bed. Go lift your arms to celebrate your body, your strength, your life! You'll soon find that grasping those vestibule bars is not that hard at all!

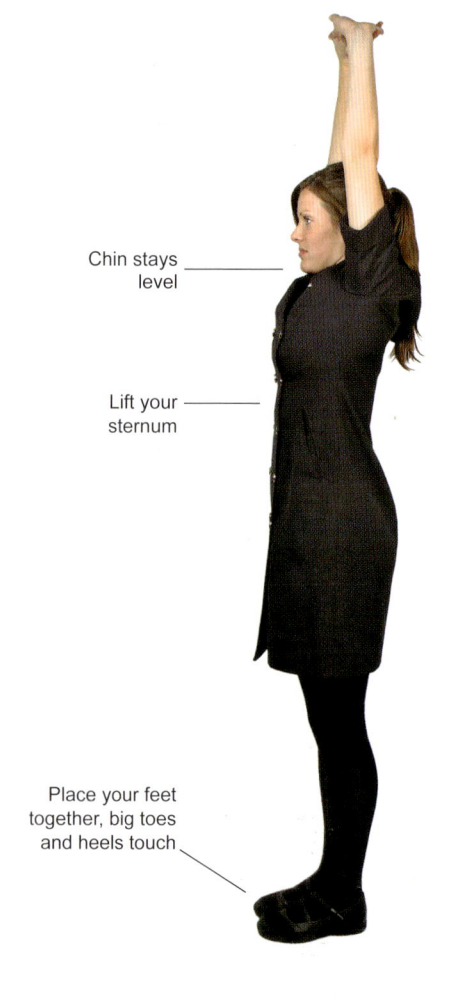

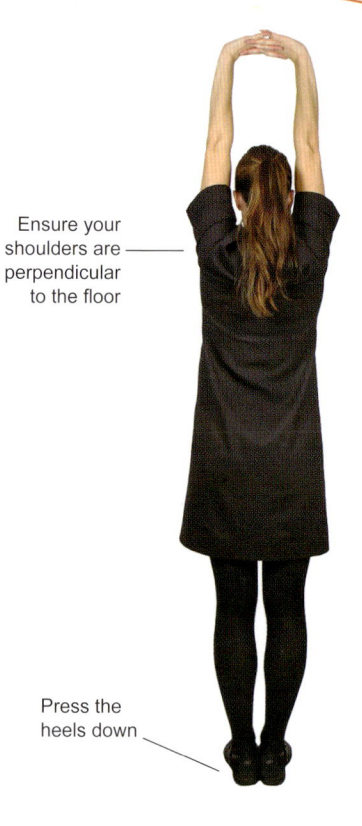

Ensure your shoulders are perpendicular to the floor

Chin stays level

Lift your sternum

Press the heels down

Place your feet together, big toes and heels touch

1 Begin in Mountain Pose.

2 Interlace your fingers and press the palms of your hands down towards the earth.

3 Connect to your breath. On the inhalation, lengthen your arms upward, pressing the palms up to the sky. Stay here, strong yet relaxed for 5 to 10 breaths.

CANADIAN RAILWAY 101 | 131

Press the palms up

Keep your head upright and look straight ahead

⭐ Benefits

Aside from the regular benefits of the Mountain Pose, the extended version gives a welcome relief from stiff neck, hard rigid shoulders and arms. On the long term, it prevents formation of elbow and finger arthritis. It also opens a freer room in the chest area for easier, full breathing. Just the way you should be when the views of the majestic Rockies leave you breathless!

132 | The Railway Yoga

Back Stretch

For most of us, slouching has become habitual which we do to get rid of that heavy feeling on the back and arms when we do usual household chores and office routine. We are not aware that by lurching our body forward, we pile as much as 15 pounds of weight on our hearts. The undue strain makes the heart weak, making us feel tired and aged. But it's never too late!

The back stretch exercise is an effective move to reverse weight pressure on the heart. Right at home or in the office, when you are standing or sitting, do this: Try slouching forward and focus the weight of the sternum on your belly button. Breathe and take notice how you feel. Then, glide the shoulders back, then down farther back and shake the sternum weight away from your system. Enjoy a deeper breath and a lighter heart!

Place your hands on your sacrum

1 Begin in Mountain Pose. Place your hands on your sacrum (the flat triangular bone between your hips), finger tips facing down.

2 To practice a backbend safely there are two things to remember: the front of the body must support the back of the body and you must go up before you go back. As the hands anchor the tailbone down, hug the abdominals towards the spine and keep lifting the chest and sternum up.

3 As you inhale, the spine lengthens and as you exhale arch back slowly. Stay here for 3 to 5 breaths.

Remember the neck is part of the spine, keep the neck extended

Stretch your toes away from one another

CANADIAN RAILWAY 101 | 133

Hug the elbows towards another

Caution

Many people will sacrifice the length in their spine so that they can go further back. Do not sacrifice alignment for a "deeper" backbend. There shouldn't be any discomfort in the lower back. If there is, chances are the abdominals are not engaged and the tailbone is not drawing down towards the earth.

Relax the throat and the face

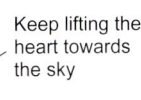

Keep lifting the heart towards the sky

⭐ Benefits

Aside from loosening tightened back muscles that corrects bad posture, the back stretch revives efficient blood flow to all parts of the body. The lungs become stronger and because of relieved weight and tension, stiff shoulders and rigid backs are invigorated. The result: an active, alert and happy you onboard and everywhere!

Place your feet together, big toes and heels touch

The Railway Yoga

Chest Opener

1 Begin in Mountain Pose or seated in a chair. Interlace your hands behind your back, extend your arms reaching the knuckles of your fingers towards the earth.

2 Inhale deeply, allowing the chest to broaden and allowing the sternum to rise up to the sky. Exhale slowly, sliding the shoulder blades down your back.

3 As you begin to relax by breathing, which you will find comfortable, you may float your arms up and away from your body. Respect your body.

4 Stay here for 5 long breaths.

Benefits

The Chest Opener offers excellent moves to relieve tension in the shoulders and chest, and strengthens and improves lung capacity. Best of all, it is an excellent fatigue-buster. Perfect for long days and nights onboard.

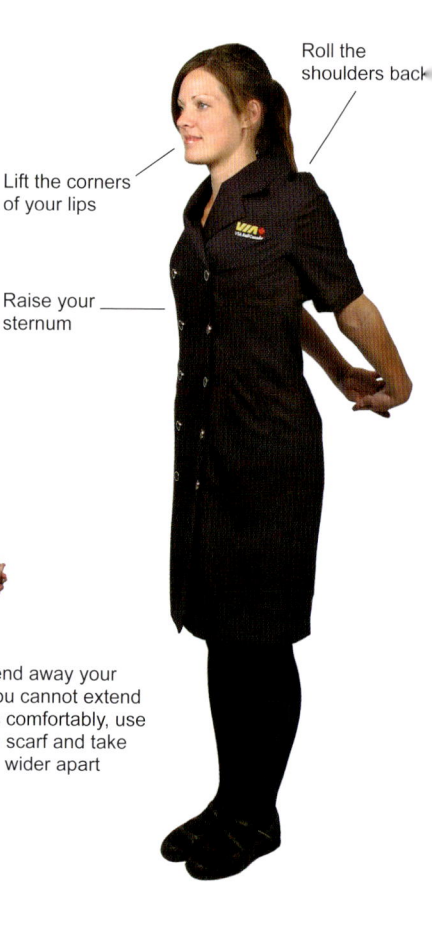

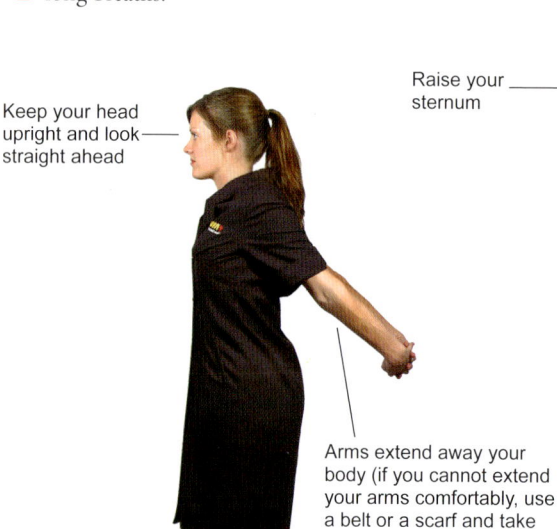

- Roll the shoulders back
- Lift the corners of your lips
- Raise your sternum
- Keep your head upright and look straight ahead
- Arms extend away your body (if you cannot extend your arms comfortably, use a belt or a scarf and take the hands wider apart
- Place your feet together, big toes and heels touch

CANADIAN RAILWAY 101 | 135

Modified Forward Bend

1 Start by sitting on the edge of your chair. Take your feet wider than hip width apart, keeping the knees at a 90 degree angle. Rest your hands over your thighs while allowing the spine to grow tall. Connect to your breath.

2 On an inhalation, the spine lengthens and on the exhalation hinges forward at the hips, placing your forearms over your thighs. On the next exhalation slowly release one hand at a time down towards the earth. Like a ripe piece of fruit, the crown of the head follows. Release any tension in the face, neck and spine. Breathe into the back of the body for 5 to 10 breaths.

3 To come out, roll up half-way to place your forearms back on your thighs. Let the head be the last thing to come up. Pause and feel the difference!

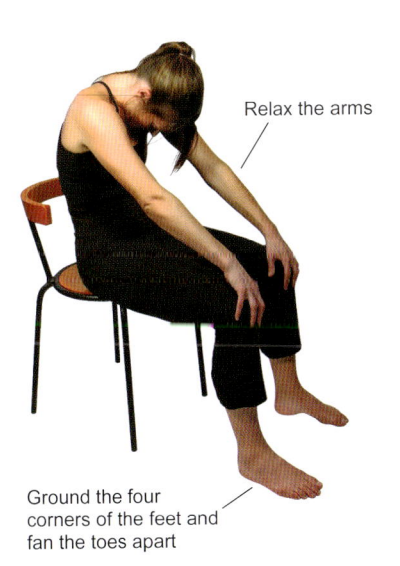

⭐ Benefits

The Modified Forward Bend relaxes the heart beat, pricks tension points on the back, and is a must for the weary traveler. It clears the head of anxiety for a calmer, more relaxed journey.

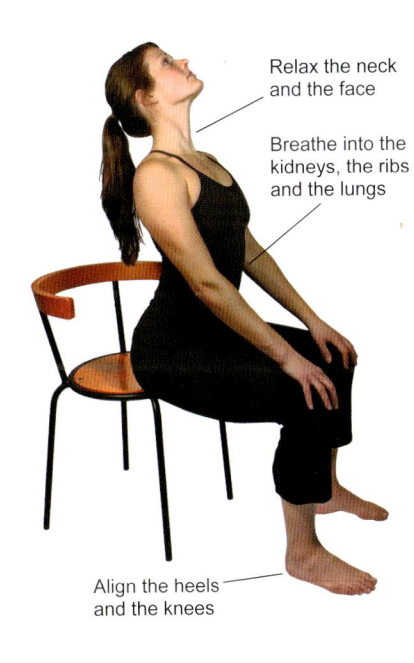

- Relax the neck and the face
- Breathe into the kidneys, the ribs and the lungs
- Align the heels and the knees
- Relax the arms
- Ground the four corners of the feet and fan the toes apart
- The crown of the head hangs down towards the earth

136 | The Railway Yoga

Twist

1 Sit on the edge of your chair with your spine erect. Place your left hand to the outer edge of your right knee and your right hand holds the outer edge of your chair.

2 As you inhale, the spine will lengthen upwards. Maintain that length and as you exhale twist to the right. Relax and take 5 long breaths. Repeat to the left side.

⭐ Benefits

The movements of the Twist tone and massage the abdominal organs like the liver, kidneys, pancreas and intestines, promoting improved metabolism functions and thereby boosting overall energy level. It also helps ease aches on the back, shoulder and neck.

- Turn your head to the right
- Take the right shoulder back
- Expand your chest
- Take the left shoulder forward
- Keep your arm extended (arm that braces the knee)

CANADIAN RAILWAY 101 | 137

Meditation

Nowhere is the art of meditation more crucial than when embarking on a long journey. Just the thought of traveling, even simply packing, is already a cause of stress. What if something goes wrong, like a long delayed trip and missing items? Here come anxiety and hypertension breaking loose. With meditation skills, these travel whammies are kept at bay, stress is curbed, and one sustains a clear, relaxed mind in the remote possibility of travel spoilers occurring.

1 Sit comfortably in your chair, allowing the spine to grow tall.

2 Close your eyes. Breathe in and out through your nose. If your mind wanders gently coax it back to your breath. It is as simple and as difficult as that!

3 Start with 5 minutes and work your way up to 10, 15 or 20 minutes. If you find it difficult to follow the breath, you may try counting the breath. Inhale for a count of 4 and exhale for a count of 4.

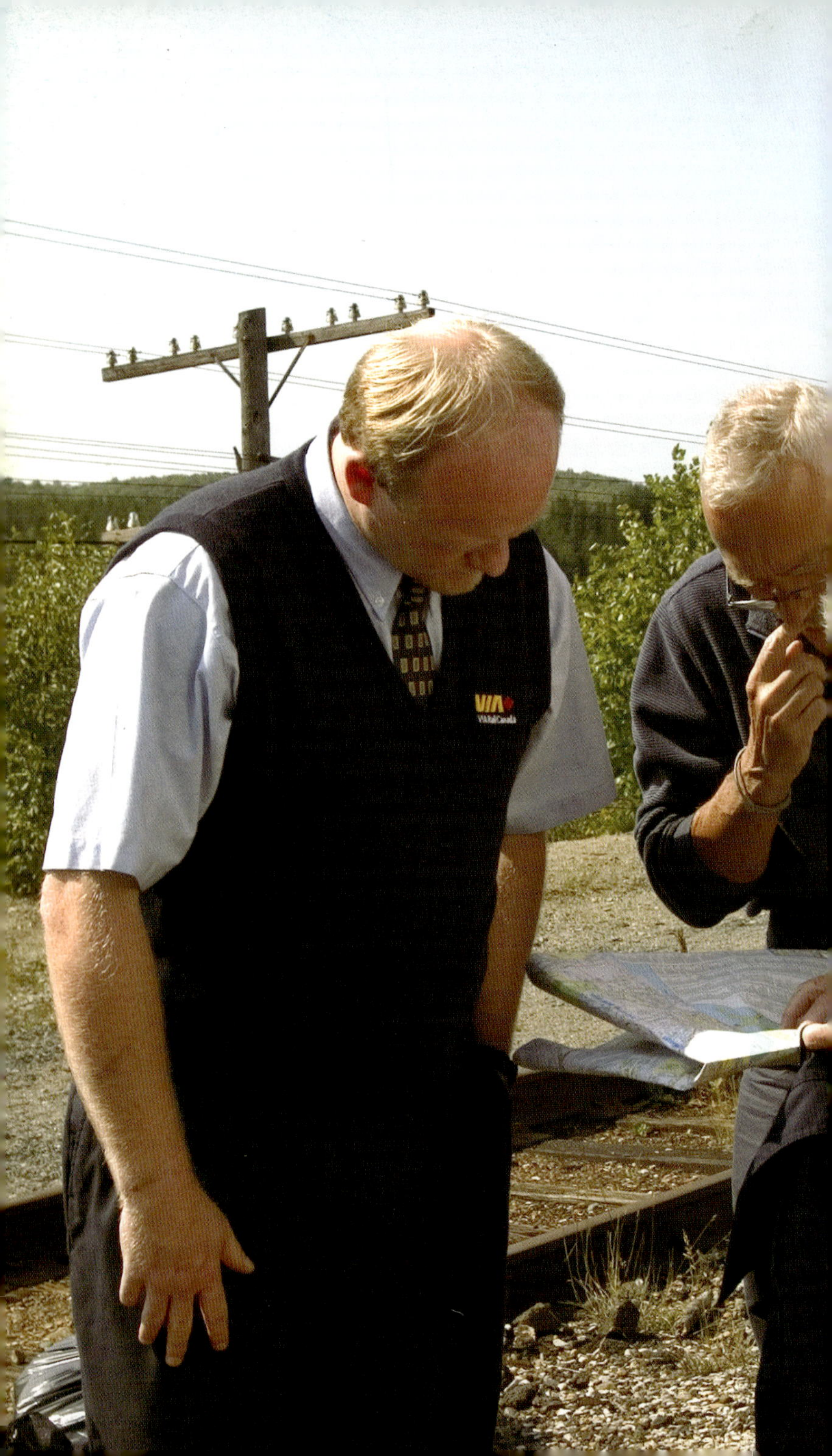
VIA

ROUTE GUIDE

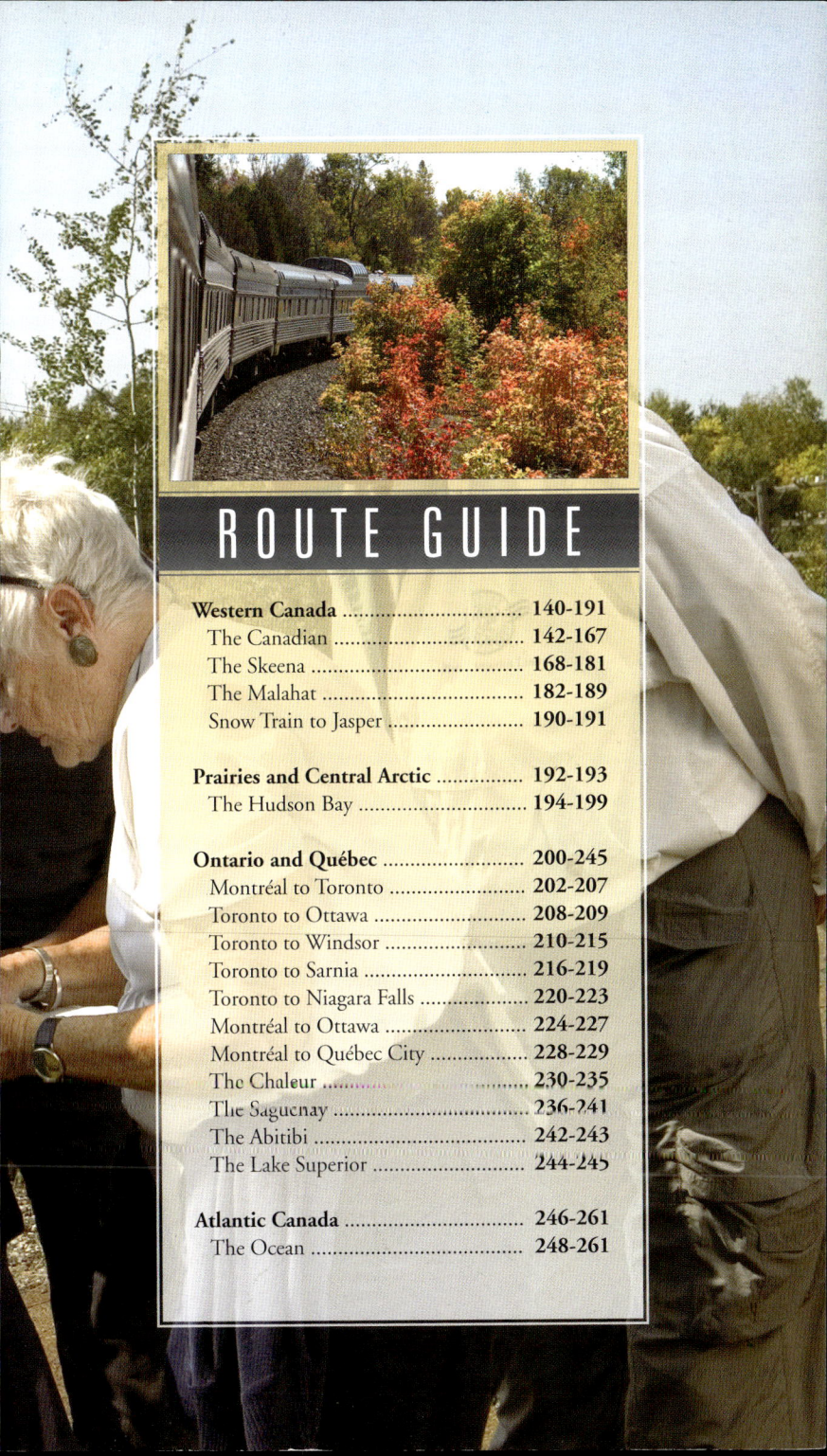

Western Canada	140-191
The Canadian	142-167
The Skeena	168-181
The Malahat	182-189
Snow Train to Jasper	190-191
Prairies and Central Arctic	192-193
The Hudson Bay	194-199
Ontario and Québec	200-245
Montréal to Toronto	202-207
Toronto to Ottawa	208-209
Toronto to Windsor	210-215
Toronto to Sarnia	216-219
Toronto to Niagara Falls	220-223
Montréal to Ottawa	224-227
Montréal to Québec City	228-229
The Chaleur	230-235
The Saguenay	236-241
The Abitibi	242-243
The Lake Superior	244-245
Atlantic Canada	246-261
The Ocean	248-261

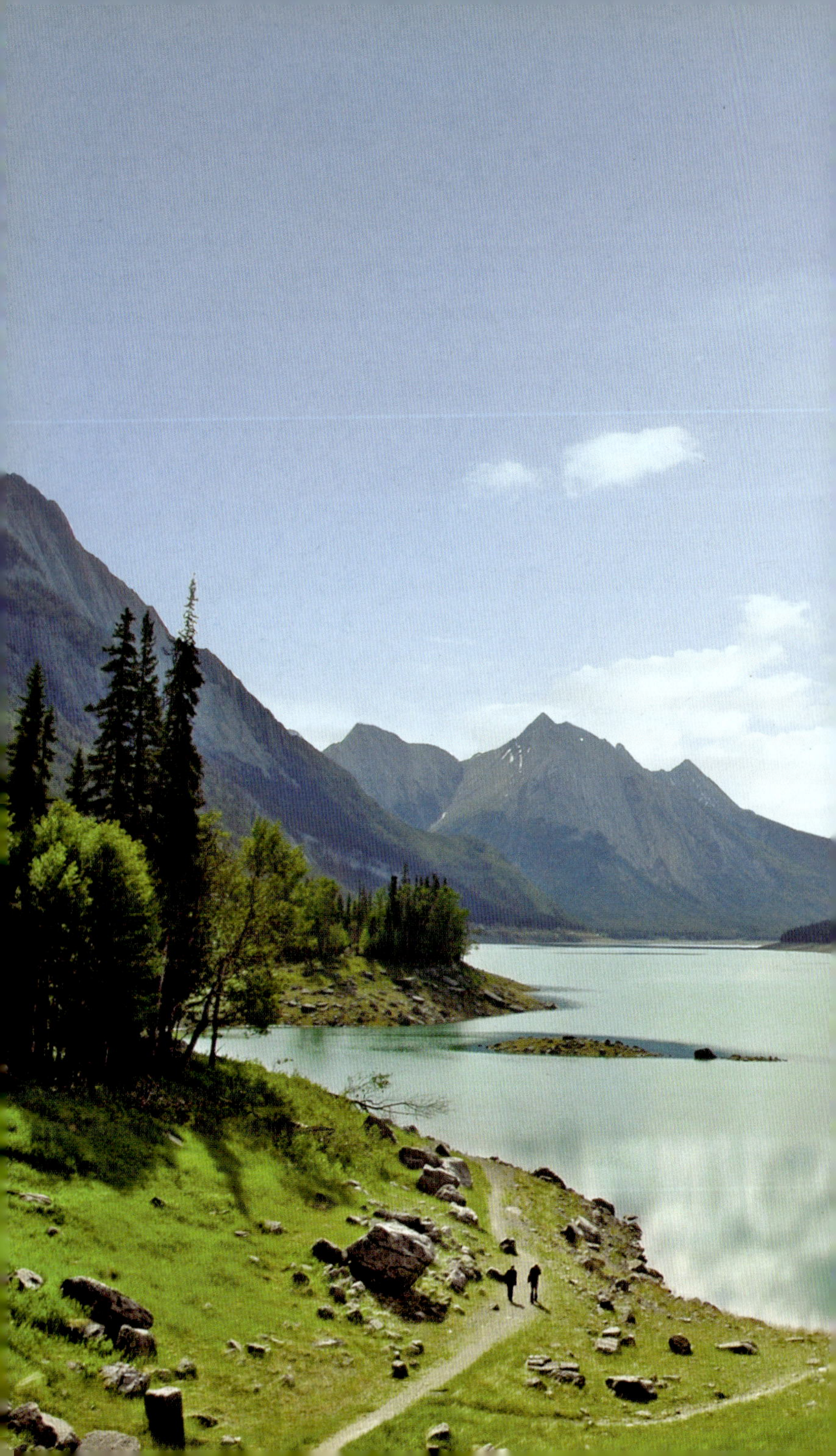

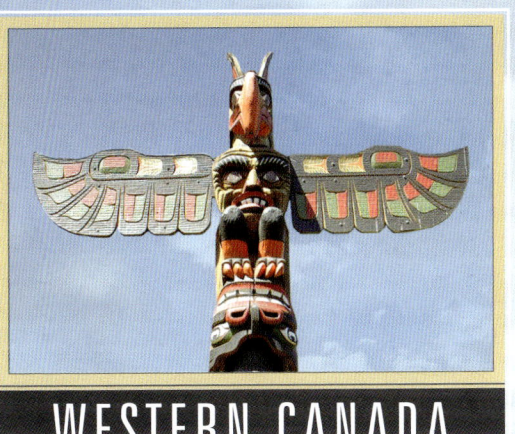

WESTERN CANADA

To bear witness to the Rockies is a goal for most ardent worldly travelers. The Canadian, VIA Rail's transcontinental flagship, travels from Vancouver to Toronto and slowly makes way through the beautiful untouched Rockies.

The Skeena, VIA Rail's daytime train adventure, explores the northern half of British Columbia, from Prince Rupert, to Prince George, and finally to Jasper, Alberta. This remote route guarantees an unyielding beauty of isolated coastal and Rocky mountainscapes.

The newest addition to the VIA Rail's western products is the Snow Train to Jasper, a seasonal winter train from Edmonton to Jasper.

Finally, jump aboard the Malahat for an adventuresome daytrip exploring Vancouver Island.

The Canadian traversing through Jasper National Park.

The Canadian

There is no finer way to discover the distinguished landscapes of Canada than jumping aboard the luxury transcontinental train Canadian. Passengers will enjoy riding the traditional steel rail cars originally built in the early 1950s. The Art-Deco stylized cars accentuate the visual aesthetics of this remarkable voyage.

The Canadian is an exciting three-day voyage passing through some of the most captivating sceneries found anywhere else in the world. The year-round land cruise carries on the classic Western transcontinental route, affording passengers with a convenient journey between the provinces of Toronto and Vancouver. The train will traverse across the placid lake areas of the east, head into soft golden wheat fields of the prairies and into the silencing beauty of the Rocky Mountains. The train passes through several pockets of distinct communities revealing small glimpses of Canadian living. The originality of the towns reflects Canada's reputation as being a mosaic of multiculturalism and diversity. The trip culminates on the coast of the Pacific, in Vancouver. Customary pauses include Sudbury Junction, Winnipeg, Saskatoon, Edmonton, Jasper and Kamloops.

ROUTE GUIDE | 143

Canadian route: Toronto to Vancouver.

TRAIN AT A GLANCE

Route	Distance	Travel Time	Lowest Available Fare	Classes of Service		
Toronto - Vancouver	4451 km	73 hrs	$428	Comfort	Silver & Blue	Romance by Rail

Travel Tips

» The Canadian operates three times weekly covering a distance of 4,451 kms and ensures daylight viewing of the resplendent Rockies. Journey time is 73 hours, or approximately three days.

» Vancouver-bound trains leave Toronto every Tuesday, Thursday and Saturday. Toronto-bound trains leave every Friday, Sunday and Tuesday. A train that leaves Vancouver on Tuesday evening will reach Toronto on Friday evening. A train that leaves Toronto on Tuesday morning will reach Vancouver on Friday morning.

» The Canadian offers passengers many ways to save – or spend – based on factors like travel class, distance covered, and the season.

» Silver & Blue is 'deluxe' first class only available on the Canadian. All meals are included.

» Romance by Rail is available year-round on the Canadian between Toronto and Jasper, and between Jasper and Vancouver, in Silver & Blue class.

The Canadian

① Mile 0: Toronto

'A Place of Meetings' is the definition of Toronto in the Huron First Nations' language. Toronto originally covered the region between Don and Humber Rivers and had been inhabited by First Nations for thousands of years before any European establishment. This area was a harmonious trading route between diverse First Nations bands. French settlers converted the area into a French trading post and shortly thereafter, it became a British port. Today, Toronto is a multicultural metropolis serving approximately five million people.

As the capital of the nation's most populous province, Toronto is the heartland of Canadian business. The image of towering skyscrapers commanding the city sky, and the bustle on the streets below justify Toronto as a prominent international city. When the train departs the downtown station, watch for the sylph-like CN tower, the tallest man-made structure in the world at one time.

Bala Subdivision
Toronto to Capreol

② Mile 16-25: The Bala Subdivision

The Bala Subdivision is a prominent stop for Toronto's GO Transit. This transit company is Canada's first public transit system to branch out of immediate downtown city districts and into interregional areas. GO Transit transports approximately 45 million passengers a year and continues to be one of North America's most effective transportation networks.

③ Mile 63: Barrie

This city of 103,710 inhabitants was officially established in 1959 and the economy progressed due to diversified manufacturing. For years before the town was incorporated, this region was a significant supply route running between Lake Ontario and Georgian Bay. Kempenfelt Bay, located close by, is an excellent location for ice-fishing.

④ Mile 63: Orillia

This region belonged to the Huron community who fished, hunted and cultivated the land before the arrival of any European establishment. Unfortunately, the people of the Huron band were expunged due to famine and uncontrollable disease. The Ojibwa subsequently settled into this region and were consequently displaced by European settlers. The Ojibwa were assimilated and forced to live in the Rama Reserve (1839).

Orillia is also the town where Stephen Leacock wrote several of his novels. Stephen Leacock (1869-1944) is one of Canada's most acclaimed and well-loved authours. Renowned for his political and economic commentaries, Leacock also wrote humourist short-stories with satirical undertones. This celebrated writer is commemorated extensively; his stories are continuously broadcast over the radio, and is listed high on the syllabus of any university course pertaining to Canadian literature.

⑤ Mile 98: Washago

"Washago" translates into "clear and sparkling water" in the Ojibway language. This peculiar town is partially located on an island and lakeshore. Washago is the

Top left: CN Tower seen from Toronto station

ROUTE GUIDE | 145

Scenic view of Perry Sound.

evidence. Peculiar rock formations protrude from the earth, revealing folds of stratum and veins of minerals. The rocks are marked by vibrant pinkish reds depending on the minerals. Most rocks comprise granite and gneiss. The Canadian Shield ranges approximately half the size of Canada's landmass and summer weather conditions are typified as being very hot with a low percentage of rainfall. The men who worked on constructing the Canadian Pacific Railway underwent several challenges as it was the most rigorous terrain to blast and manipulate.

7 Mile 262: Sudbury Junction

Heading into Sudbury Junction, the terrain changes dramatically, transforming into a barren landscape of scraggly white-bark birches, and black slag mounds.

entranceway towards the Muskokas. Lake Couchiching's shoreline is crowned with cottages for those who find liberation in fishing, canoeing and relaxing. Washago is separated into two villages, Severn and Ramara.

6 Mile 150: Parry Sound

This town was denominated after Sir William Parry, a brave Arctic explorer. Parry Sound is also the opening leading to the Thirty Thousand Islands, the largest cluster of islands in the world. The landscape swiftly shifts as the train enters the Canadian Shield, Canada's central geographical region that is over three billion years old. The Shield comprises exposed Precambrian rock developed between the time the earth's crust commenced to cool and when unicellular life progressed enough to reveal fossil

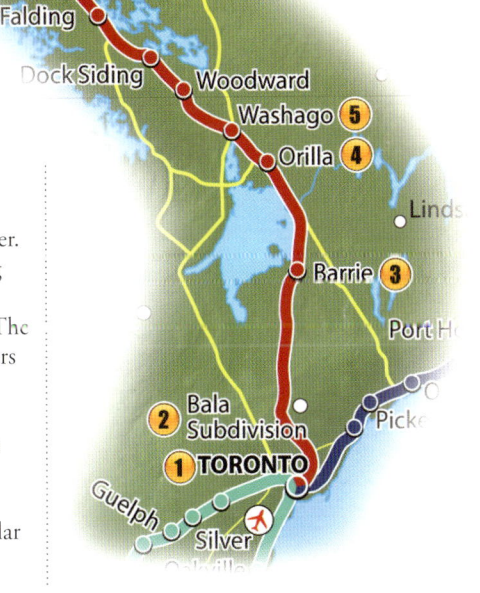

146 | The Canadian

Approximately one billion years ago, a meteorite broke through the gravity field and collided into earth creating a dip in the landscape. The indentation at Sudbury Junction is approximately 35 miles long and 15 miles wide. Upon constructing the railway, blasting revealed several valuable minerals, most notably nickel. Years of smelting resulted in the region resembling a wasteland, somewhat like the lifeless terrain on the moon. Ironically, NASA astronauts were summoned to visit Sudbury so they can better understand shatter cones, an uncommon rock formation affiliated with meteorite impacts.

8 Mile 276: Capreol
Here, the train sometimes takes a nice half-hour long break to refill water and refuel. Prescott Park displays a 12-ton meteor fragment. Try and get a peak.

Ruel Subdivision
Capreol to Hornepayne

9 Mile 1-20: Vemillion River
The train follows Vermillion River, crossing it four times.

10 Mile 20-133: Schoolhouse
The infamous train-schoolhouse traveled the track between Miles 20 and 133. The train successively visited small towns one week at a time supplied with all the necessary teaching tools. Blackboards, books, desks and writing utensils were all provided by the teacher who taught children of all ages. Take a peak at a perfect replication of one of these cars in Sloman Memorial Park in Clinton, Ontario. This area has been affectionately labeled, 'the world's longest schoolyard.'

11 Mile 86: Gogama
Like many spots within this region, Gogama became a Hudson's Bay Post after the area was used predominantly as a First Nations' trading route. This small Northeastern Ontarian town was home to the 'Wild Man of the North,' Joe Laflamme. This man was renowned for having the special ability to communicate and discourse with wild animals. Locally, he was dubbed as 'Mooseman' or 'Wolfman,' and masterfully domesticated wild animals for his own needs. Joe Laflamme apparently engaged in long-winded conversation with animals, and the beasts would willfully talk to Joe and trust his peculiar gift. Joe insisted that he understood what the animals were saying and that is why they were naturally docile with him.

12 Mile 166-189: Shenango Lake
A perfect opportunity to snap some shots of Missonga (Shenango Lake to south).

Mile 174: Photo Opportunity
The train fringes the Shiners Lake

ROUTE GUIDE | 147

to the north and Kapuskasing Lake to the south on a bend allowing an excellent view of the train and the lakes simultaneously. A perfect set up for a photograph.

destination for serious, devoted fishers. Walleye, speckled trout and northern pike are featured fish caught in nearby fishing camps. This area is admired by outdoor enthusiasts who prefer to venture into the crux of the forest and engage in some intermediate camping.

Hornepayne was incorporated as a railway town, and inevitably attracted several lumber companies which continue to foster the economy today.

13 Miles 183-257: The Chapleau Game Preserve

It is almost inconceivable, but this stretch of land is home to the largest game preserve in the world. No, Canada does not have charging elephants, hungry lions or speedy cheetahs; however, this farm does carry charging buffalo, hungry bears and speedy bobcats. The Chapleau Game Preserve is reachable by rail, gravel road, airplane or by canoe. Strict regulations banning hunting or trapping within this park are strongly enforced. The Government of Ontario's initial objective was to replenish depleting species. The area spans 7000 square miles and exhibits an abundance of animals existing in their natural habitats.

14 Mile 213.6: Trestle Rapids

Glance to the north when crossing the Greenhill River and see the Trestle Rapids.

15 Mile 296.2: Hornepayne

Hornepayne is an important

A few portions between Sioux Lookout and Toronto were originally built by the Transcontinental Railway between 1908 and 1915; however, most of the track was built by the Canadian Northern Ontario Railway.

Caramat Subdivision
Hornepayne to Armstrong

16 Mile 45.6: Canadian Northern Railway Last Spike

The Canadian passes over the exact location where the last spike was driven to complete this portion of the Canadian Northern Railway. The railway's president, Sir William Mackenzie, drove the spike on January 1, 1914. The honourable celebration to follow lasted 10 minutes due to the inhospitable cold.

148 | The Canadian

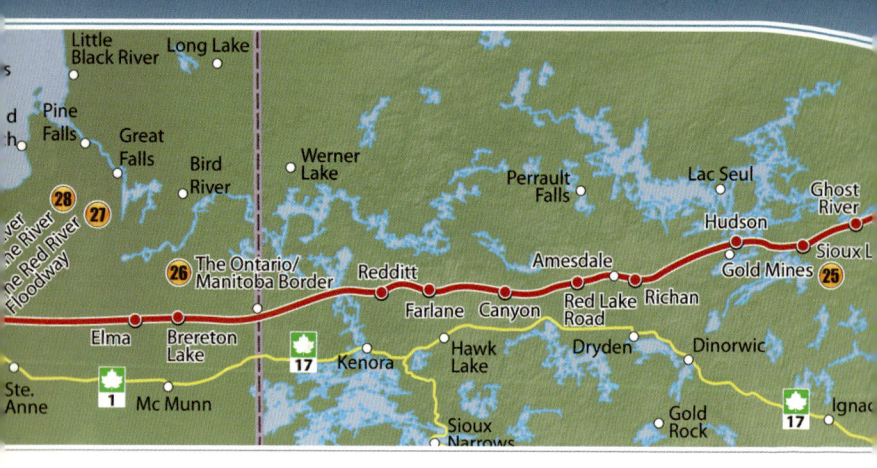

This sight is just over the Little White Otter River.

17 **Mile 100: Longlac (Long Lake)**
Longlac has a major Hudson's Bay Company trading post where First Nations and Inuit brought fur to trading posts to trade for goods. Longlac became a major canoe route for settlers eager to understand the inland terrain. These individuals were dubbed the 'Coureurs de Bois.' Instead of waiting for fur to be taken to the posts, these 'coureurs de bois' went inland to learn how to navigate through the woods from the First Nations, and to hunt and trap for themselves.

18 **Mile 131.6: Nakina**
A supply centre for the region's hunting and fishing cottages.

19 **Mile 209.9 Jackfish Creek**
The Canadian crosses the Jackfish Creek Viaduct spanning 798 feet across and skimming the water at four feet above water level.

20 **Mile 244: Armstrong**
Armstrong is the heartland for fishing enthusiasts. This region is riddled with relaxing lodges specifically designed for travelers who desire a secluded, enjoyable and peaceful fishing holiday away from the bustle of life. There are several fishing outfitters that provide lodges and outposts. Canoe tours and independent canoe voyages are spectacular when paddling in and around the pristine Wabakimi Park.

Allanwater Subdivision
Armstrong to Sioux Lookout

21 **Mile 24: Wabakimi Provincial Park**
Welcome to a wilderness haven of unspoiled Boreal forest spanning 3,444 square miles (2.3 million acres). Access to the park can be made by flying in, train or canoe. This park is home to one of the largest Boreal forest reserves in the world. It is not uncommon to see caribou, moose, eagles and bears. This expansive forest provides excellent habitats for an abundance of species. Remote fly-in lodges are ubiquitous around the area, welcoming visitors to sport fish.

22 **Mile 66-79: Fisherman's Haven**
Devoted fishers will find an array of fish to catch in these surrounding lakes: Heathcote Lake, Savant Lake and Sturgeon Lake. Walleye, northern pike and lake trout are common fish to catch.

ROUTE GUIDE | 149

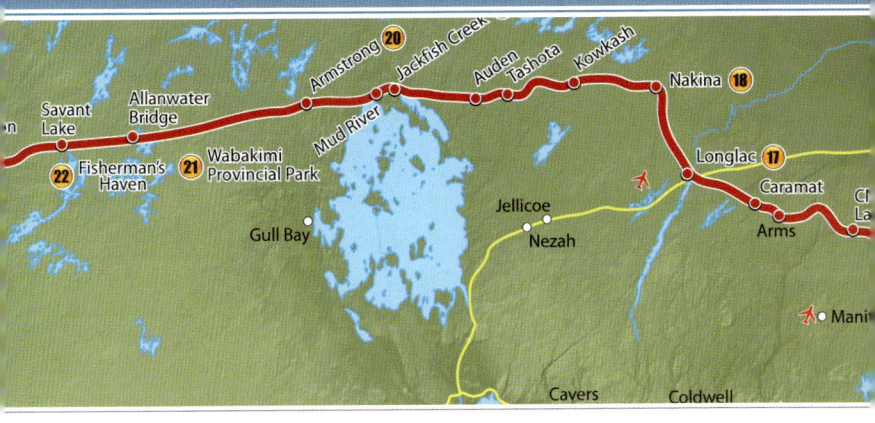

(23) Mile 133-138: Sturgeon River
The train crosses the Sturgeon River over a 458 foot bridge, and then fringes the shoreline of Abram Lake for several miles before arriving at Sioux Lookout, with its impressive mock-Tudor station. To the west across Pelican Lake lie the Sioux Mountains.

(24) Mile 138: Sioux Lookout
This was the sight where the Ojibway would stand to spot the pillaging groups of Sioux First Nations. Passengers are welcome to detrain for a moment of fresh air after breakfast.

Reddit Subdivision
Sioux Lookout to Winnipeg

(25) Mile 12.6: Gold Mines
A plaque pays homage to the early bush pilots who flew supplies during the 1926 gold rush. Fifteen mines generated $360 million in precious metal and a thousand men shared 3,500 claims.

(26) Mile 162: The Ontario/Manitoba Border
This is certainly not the region to visit if you suffer from Acarophobia, the fear of itching or insects causing itching. This area is renowned for an over-abundance of pesky flying biting pests. An estimated 16 billion eggs were located on a 15- foot rock near a waterfall and five million larvae per square metre of riverbed. Yikes! Researchers placed a small blue rug on the ground and recorded 325 black flies landing on it in one minute. Cover up and dare if you will!

(27) Mile 243.4: The Red River Floodway
Winnipeg and surrounding areas are encompassed by several river networks and are susceptible to severe flooding. The Red River Floodway was constructed after a devastating flood in the 1950s. Talented civil engineers were summoned to design a structure that would ultimately maintain the river levels and lessen the possibility of serious flooding. In 1968 the 47 km- long Red River Floodway was constructed and has successfully reduced the chances of flooding by 50 percent. The train crosses the Floodway over a 903-foot bridge.

(28) Mile 250.5: The Seine River
Fast approaching the downtown centre of Winnipeg, the train crosses the Seine River over a 368- foot bridge in St. Boniface. This quaint district is home to the largest population of French-speaking Canadians in Western Canada.

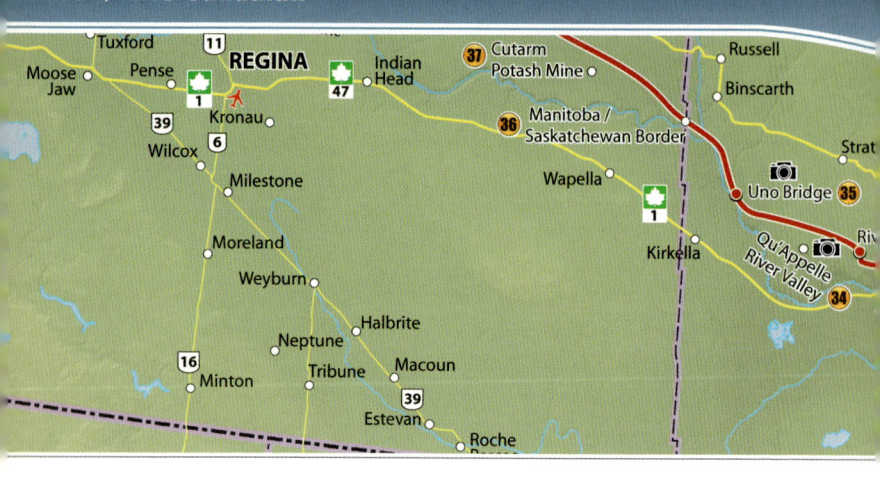

Winnipeg Union Station

Winnipeg's Union Station was built in 1911 by the same architects who designed New York City's renowned Grand Central Station.

Winnipeg is Western Canada's oldest city and the prestigious centre for business and banking. Its central geographical position was ideal for the west and east to meet, before Canada's economic heartland was moved to Toronto.

29 Mile 251: The Red River

Coming into the Winnipeg station, the Canadian crosses the Red River. The river travels from the U.S. making its way to empty into Lake Winnipeg. The Red River connects with the Assiniboine River at the 'Forks,' Winnipeg's fresh public market. The name of Red River originated from the Cree word, 'miscoupi,' meaning 'red water river.' The river acquires its red colour from the red pigmented clay found on the bottom of the riverbed.

30 Mile 252.1: Winnipeg

There is a complete crew change in Winnipeg, Manitoba's capital, traveling both to Toronto and Vancouver. The train is replenished with delicious foods, fresh water and fuel. Passengers are free to detrain here for approximately half an hour. Keep in mind that if the train is running behind schedule, station stops are brief. Forks Public Market is a good place to briefly visit before re-boarding. Providing delicious ethnic foods, fresh produce, cheese and decadent coffee drinks, the Forks is a superior place to grab delicious train snacks. Make sure to inquire with an on board VIA Rail representative about how much time you have.

Winnipeg is a multicultural mosaic of colourful and distinguished cultures. Filipino, Jamaican, Chinese, Italian, East Indian, Haitian, Ukrainian, Polish, Icelandic and Finnish are among many ethnicities gracefully represented in this city. No doubt, Winnipeg is the Canadian capital of premium cuisine.

ROUTE GUIDE | 151

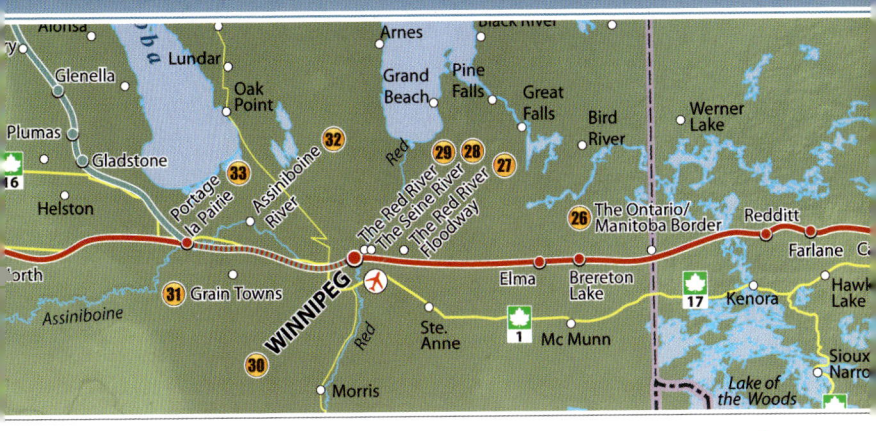

Manitobans live up to their license plate reputation as being 'friendly.' It must be all the winter sunshine as Winnipeg is the sunniest winter city in the nation, banking a good 358.2 hours of sun each winter.

Rivers Subdivision
Winnipeg to Melville

(31) Mile 0-55: Grain Towns
The succession of agricultural fields happens to be the most fertile soil in Canada. Watch for towering grain elevators bearing the name of towns close by. It is also interesting to observe that most stations in the prairie regions are on the north side of the track. This protects passengers from the whirling winter north winds.

(32) Mile 50: The Assiniboine River
The train swiftly crosses the Assiniboine River, a renowned Canadian river that carried fur traders, canoes and York boats of the Hudson's Bay Company.

(33) Mile 55: Portage La Prairie
Portage La Prairie has a long history with the fur trade. Originally, it was a rest stop for traders who had to lug their canoes between Assiniboine River and Lake Manitoba.

⭐ Wheat Boom

A century ago, Canada underwent the 'Wheat Boom,' when in the 19th-century, it took over massive agricultural production to fill the void due to abandoned rural areas in England and America as people migrated to the cities.

Droves of settlers flocked to the prairies to cultivate and export grain, turning grassy fields into prosperous fields. Grain towns were erected along the railways.

By 1930, Canada was one of the most significant grain exporters to feed the world.

(34) Mile 181: Qu'Appelle River Valley
The sky-laden prairie landscapes are interrupted as the fecund hills of the Qu'Appelle River Valley emerge in the distance. This beautiful pastoral section of the Canadian voyage is a refreshing visual venture after spending a day rolling through the flatlands. The valley was created by a tributary of the South Saskatchewan River sharply carving its way towards the Assiniboine River to the east. The Qu'Appelle River Valley is a 430 km resplendent view of rugged, fertile land resembling a prairie Eden.

152 | The Canadian

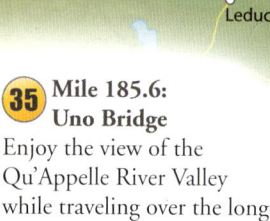

The name was originally acquired from a Cree legend. A Cree man was crossing the river and heard someone call his name and he replied, 'Who calls?', translated as 'qu'appelle' in French. His echo responded as he later discovered that it was the tremulous voice of his bride-to-be calling at the moment of her death.

'potasch,' a Dutch word referring to wood ash used by pioneers to fertilize their fields. Ninety-five percent of the world uses potash for fertilizing crops because it provides crops with essential nutrients needed to grow. Potassium is also used to make an eclectic array of glass, ceramics, drugs, synthetic rubber, soap, explosives and water-softeners.

38 Mile 280: Melville

This small grain town is proudly named after Charles Melville Hays, the president of The Grand Trunk Pacific Railroad Company who, sadly,

35 Mile 185.6: Uno Bridge

Enjoy the view of the Qu'Appelle River Valley while traveling over the longest bridge in the prairies. Uno Bridge is 1,533 feet long and crosses over the Minnewashtack Creek.

36 Mile 213: Manitoba / Saskatchewan Border

The border between Manitoba and Saskatchewan.

37 Mile 234: Cutarm Potash Mine

Look out the window and see a desert-like plateau dominating the horizon. This is the Cutarm Potash Mine. Potash is the name given for potassium compounds and materials constituting potassium. Potash originated from

drowned in the tragic sinking of the Titanic in 1912.

Watrous Subdivision
Melville to Biggar

39 Mile 129: Watrous

Watrous is home to the mystical Manitou Lake, renowned for its healing waters. Thousands of visitors come to

Left: View of Curtam Potash Mine from the Park car's scenic dome.

Manitou Lake to discover and better understand the medicinal compounds of the lake. Watrous is located at the heart of the Canadian grain belt.

Mile 189: Saskatoon
The train smoothly arrives into Saskatoon over a 457- metre long bridge over the South Saskatchewan River. By the time the Canadian slides into this prominent Canadian city, most passengers should be asleep, (unless you are kept dazzled by the spectacle of the Northern Lights seen best in Saskatchewan). This charming colonial city was established in 1882 as a temperance colony. Today, it is the Canadian crux of advanced technology and mining industries. Saskatoon holds a strong Ukrainian influence reflected in the fine architecture and the onion-domed roofs of Orthodox Ukrainian Churches. Named after a voluptuous bursting berry grown alongside the river, Saskatoon proves to be a quaint destination located in the centre of some of the flattest lands in the world.

Grain Elevator

Grain elevators allow for an efficient system of grain consolidation where trucks transport the grains to the elevators where they are graded and weighed.

There are approximately 4,500 grain elevators today after the first one was erected in Gretna, Manitoba in 1881. Grain elevators are controlled by individuals, feed dealers and cooperatives.

Grain elevators are prone to erupt in flames. Lone grain elevators are dispersed along the horizons of prairie landscapes, located on the south side of the tracks to counteract wind from spreading grain fires into town.

Railway stations and towns along the prairie heartlands are named in alphabetical order from east to west. Railway administrators used the alphabet three times in order to give each town a name.

Mile 247: Biggar
The small grain town of Biggar is renowned for its amusing repartee! A sign declaring, "New York is Big... but this is Biggar" welcomes visitors.

154 | **The Canadian**

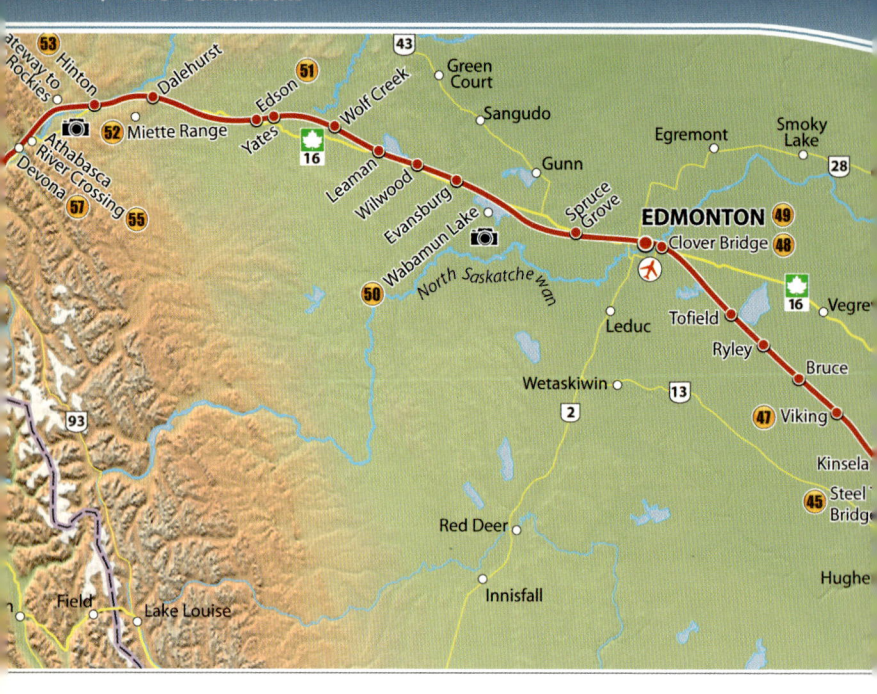

Wainwright Subdivision
Biggar to Edmonton

42 **Mile 57: Unity**
Unity is home to a major salt mine plummeting 1,127 metres below the ground.

43 **Mile 101: Time Change**
This is the location where Central Time is changed to Mountain Time. Also, the train passes the Alberta Saskatchewan border at this point.

44 **Mile 140: Wainwright**
Wainwright grew to be the largest town between Saskatoon and Edmonton after oil and gas were discovered in 1922. The town holds approximately 400 wells. During World War Two, the Bison Recovery Park established in 1909, was relocated to convert the region into a Canadian Forces Base Camp. A small number of bison were returned in 1980.

45 **Mile 149: Steel Trestle Bridge**
The Canadian soars 61 metres above the Battle River on a steel trestle bridge of 884 metres long.

46 **Mile 147: Battle River Valley**
Take a look at the mighty Battle River Valley to the north

47 **Mile 184: Viking**
Before the establishment of the town, this was considered an important region for the Plains First Nations to hunt buffalo. Afterward, the town of Viking was erected and named after the Scandinavian settlers who migrated to this region.

48 **Mile 260: Clover Bridge**
Large industrial oil refineries take up the prairies' horizons as the train crosses the 504 metre long Clover Bridge across the North Saskatchewan River and into Edmonton.

ROUTE GUIDE | 155

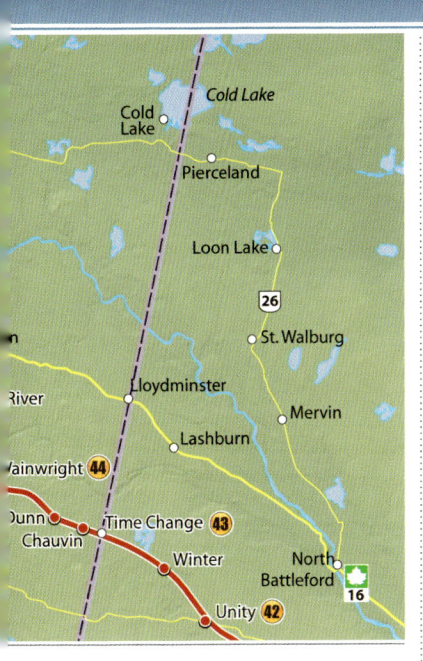

(49) Mile 266: Edmonton

Edmonton is a major stop for the Canadian to take a rest to refill and refuel before setting forth into the Rockies. Passengers are welcome to exit the train and take a refreshing stroll along the platform. Before Edmonton grew into a metropolis of 938,000 residents, Alberta's capital was considered the crossroads to the north. Explorers, surveyors, traders and gold miners were provided with the passageway to the outlying north. The discovery of oil in 1947 quickly converted this province into the wealthiest province in Canada. Edmonton and surrounding areas are the nucleus to Canada's oil industry. Approximately 2,250 wells pump for oil generating more than 10 percent of Canada's oil production.

Edmonton fringes the perimetres of North Saskatchewan River riverbanks. Edmonton possesses one of the largest malls in the world. This colossal mall holds an amusement park, indoor water park, skating rink, indoor ocean and several shopping and dining destinations. A consumers, dream!

Edson Subdivision
Edmonton to Jasper

(50) Mile 44: Wabamun Lake

Wabamun Lake is a popular summer cottage destination for excellent fishing. This serene and placid lake earned its name from the Cree word, 'mirror.'

A terrible oil spill occurred along its banks in 2005 when a freight train carrying peak oil derailed. It is estimated that approximately 560,000 litres of oil were spilt into the lake and shorelines. Forty-three CN rail cars went off the track wiping out the backyards of lovely waterfront cottages. It was an environmental emergency affecting the natural habitat of several bird and fish species. It is impossible to know the long-term repercussions of this environmental disaster; however, it is estimated that the region will take two to five years to recover.

(51) Mile 129: Edson

Edson was denominated after the General Manager of the Grand Trunk Pacific Railway, Edson J. Chamberlain. The train rolls through the foothills of the Rockies. The flora suddenly shifts from predominantly birch trees to waif-like conifers. This is the half-point between Jasper and Edmonton.

(52) Mile 150: Look – The Rocky Mountains!

The Rocky Mountains are imminently approaching! Look south and see a string of mountains. These belong to the regal Miette Range of the Rocky Mountains.

The Canadian

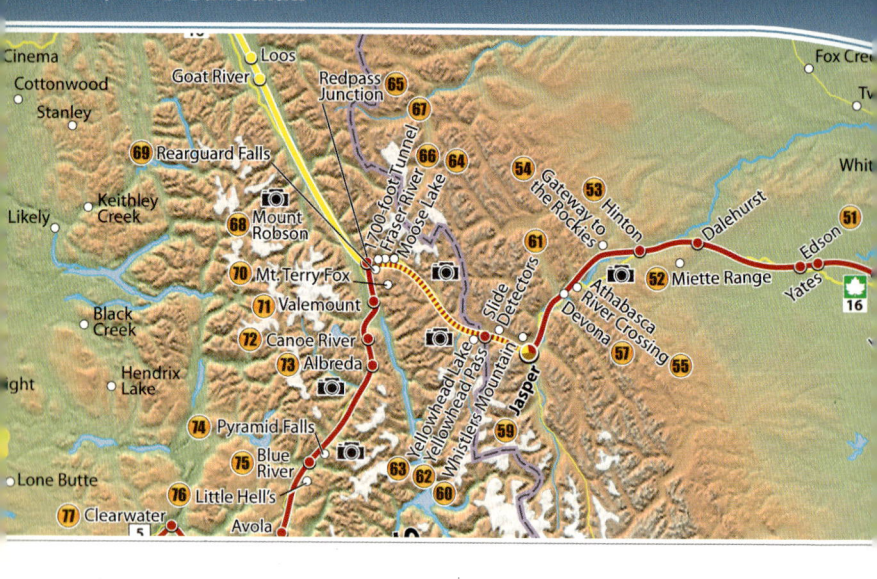

53 Mile 184: Hinton
The Canadian has climbed 3,325 above sea level and continues to ascend en route to the gargantuan peaks ahead. Hinton was established as a small little coal-mining town and now also prospers from a large lumber industry. Several cross-country skiing enthusiasts compete on the Olympic-size ski run each year.

54 Mile 189: Official Gateway to the Rockies
The Rocky Mountains were created by plate tectonics, the movement and shifting of the earth's crust. The crust is the outermost layer of the earth and measures approximately 20 km deep. Life on earth is made possible because the earth's crust protects the surface from the intense heat of the mantle, the earth's second layer. The mantle is a mass of semi-solid rock whereupon the crust floats and moves.

The constant convergence and divergence of the earth's crust resulted in the earth being pushed upward, forming mountain ranges. Secondly, the subduction of the North American Plate by the Pacific plate produced a chain of volcanoes formed from the molten rock on the ocean's floor. Approximately 150 million years ago, the uplift created the Western Cordillera Mountains. Up until 50 million years ago the Pacific Plate continued to push east, forcing the Cordillera mountain range eastward. The convergence of the two plates continually folded the rock skyward creating the noble Rockies. Lines of stratum can be seen on the mountains indicating where the folding occurred.

55 Mile 193: Athabasca River Crossing
The Canadian crosses Alberta's longest river. The Athabasca River, originating from the Columbia Ice fields, travels 12 km through Jasper National Park, up towards Fort McMurray, Alberta and is finally flushed in Lake Athabasca.

Mile 204: Photo Opportunity
The train lunges through a 735-foot tunnel beneath Disaster Point and is welcomed by the Jasper National Park on the other side. Mountain goats and big horned sheep are prominent in this area,

ROUTE GUIDE | 157

loitering along the edges of cliffs. The observer must look carefully because they are camouflaged well.

Mile 193: Photo Opportunity
Look south for an exquisite vista of the Miette Range.

57 Mile 215: Devona Siding
This is the location which gave the Jasper National Park its name. In 1817, a small trading abode was erected on Brule Lake. A Northwest Trading Company clerk, Jasper Hawes, was in charge of this small cabin and named it Jasper's House. The surrounding area and community soon became known as Jasper. In 1830, after Jasper Hawes passed away, the small post was transferred to Devona Siding where it ran until 1884. The post was abandoned and in 1927, Jasper House was proclaimed a site of national heritage.

Mile 225: Photo Opportunity
Elk sightings are common in this area. The train crosses over the Snarling River. In 1811, fur traders built the first supply post in the valley below.

59 Mile 235: Jasper
The Jasper station was originally constructed by the Canadian National Railway in 1925 for $ 30,000. This heritage station shares similar features as an old English cottage. The roofline reveals a striking resemblance to a thatched roof and the cobblestone foundation and chimney gives the station a rustic natural appearance. A gift shop selling train-related items along with freshly roasted coffee drinks are located in the station. Look to your northwest. Do you see the sleeping man on top of the mountain? A pristine vista of pyramid mountain may be seen from your northeast.

Jasper winter wonderland.

The Canadian

⭐ The Continental Divide

Aside from geographical divisions, the Yellowhead Pass also serves as an important marker for the following: Alberta-British Columbia border; exit from the Jasper National Park; and gateway to the Mt. Robson Provincial Park.

The division between Mountain and Pacific times occurs in the Yellowhead Pass.

The statuesque Victoria Cross Range can be viewed in the north while the more recent Colin Range can be seen in the east. Older mountain formations have darker hues.

Albreda Subdivision
Jasper to Blue River

60 Mile 2: Whistlers Mountain
Do not mix this Whistlers Mountain with the renowned Whistler Mountain in B.C. A visit up this exquisite local mountain on the Jasper Tramway is an excellent day excursion. The Tramway climbs an elevation of 2,285 metres. The journey provides travelers with an unparalleled vista of the Rocky Mountains stretching 80 km. Up here, travelers can listen to the silent hum of the Rockies. Spectacular!

61 Mile 6: Slide Directors
The wire fences spread across hills traveling alongside the tracks are slide-detection devices. In the event of a rockslide, these wires break, signaling engineers of an obstruction on the rails ahead. This safety measure has proven quite useful.

62 Mile 17.6: Yellowhead Pass
The train crosses through the North American Continental Divide descending to 3,700 feet above sea-level, the lowest point of the divide. The divide is a geographical division determining what direction water systems and networks will flow. The division runs from the north and south top of the Rocky Mountains. Rivers west of the mark eventually meander their way out into the Pacific Ocean. Rivers flowing east flow to be flushed out either into the Arctic or Atlantic Oceans.

63 Mile 22: Yellowhead Lake
Yellowhead Lake hugs the base of Mt. Fitzwilliam, bearing distinct lines of stratum. A stately view of Mt. Rockingham is in the background. The Yellowhead region was denominated after a Métis trapper, Pierre Hasinaton. He guided surveyors through this region and was fondly nicknamed tete-jaune, meaning 'yellow head' for his peculiar blonde hair.

64 Mile 36: Moose Lake
The placid view of Moose Lake from the train immediately puts passengers at ease. Its serene surface reflects perfectly the vista of surrounding mountains and passing clouds. Waterfalls cascade into the lake from the slopes of the verdant Selwyn Range. The vibrant turquoise hue of the water is created by the finely-ground minerals carried in the glacier runoff. The 'rock flour' stays in the water for lengthy periods of time shifting the hues in the sky's reflection.

Shores of Moose Lake.

ROUTE GUIDE | 159

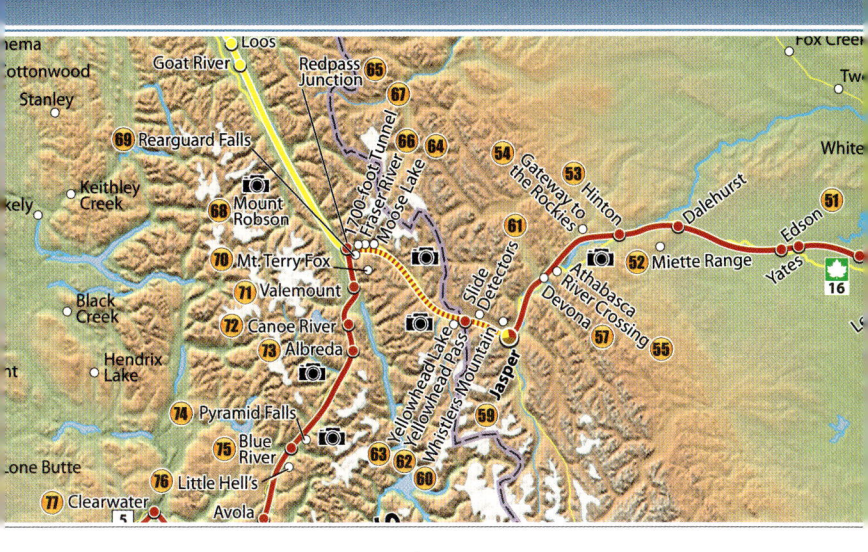

65 Mile 43: Redpass Junction
Redpass Junction marks the spot where CN's northern mainline (the Skeena) links with CN's tracks from Vancouver. The pass was named after a gap between Razor Peak and Mount Kain.

66 Mile 45: Fraser River
The Fraser River – its 850-mile journey to the Pacific Ocean. Up here in the Rockies the Fraser is extremely green and clear, quite a difference from what one sees in Greater Vancouver. Along its journey to the ocean the river picks up silt and other debris, not to mention pollutants which cloud its waters.

67 Mile 48: 1700-foot Tunnel
The train travels through a 1700-foot tunnel.

68 Mile 52: Mount Robson
Do not miss the spectacular sight of Mount Robson dominating the sky with its pristine peaks jutting through the clouds. This vista renowned for its unequaled beauty is the tallest mountain in the Canadian Rockies at 3,954 metres (12,972 ft). The plight of climbing the summit was accomplished in 1913 when Swiss guides led a group to the top. Scientific calculations predict that this sublime sky palace will erode to the same elevation as Edmonton in approximately 54 million years. Do not be disappointed if the peak is swaddled in dense clouds; this is normal due to the elevation. Catching Mount Robson on a perfectly clear day makes the Canadian journey all the more worthwhile.

Mount Robson, 14,972 ft.

160 | The Canadian

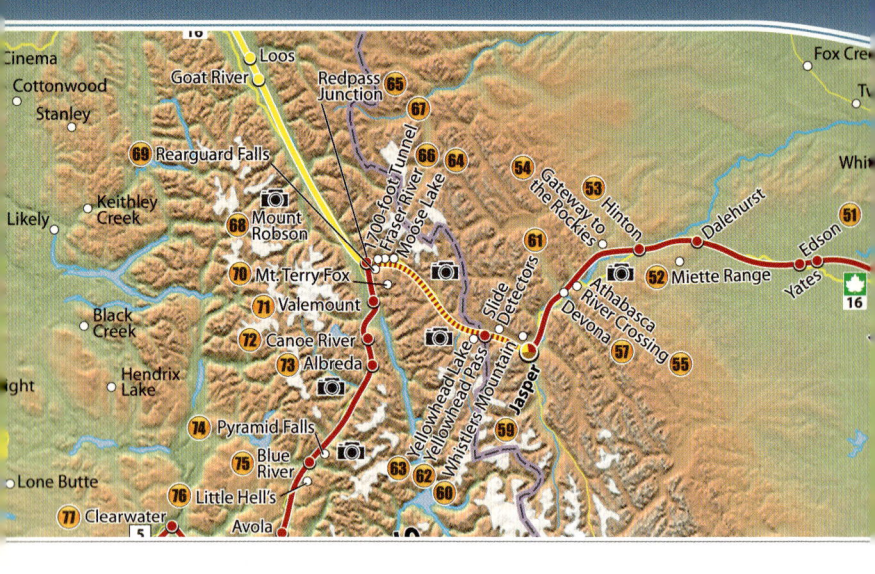

Simon Fraser

The Fraser River was named after Simon Fraser, considered the most daredevil explorer in Canadian history.

Fraser set forth on one of the most adventurous river expeditions in May 28th, 1808, embarking on a 520-mile odyssey to find a route to the Pacific. His troop surmounted treacherous rivers and canyons, one of which was the Fraser Canyon, and eventually succeeded.

The train follows the river for the most part of the journey into Vancouver, where one of British Columbia's most prestigious universities is also named after Simon Fraser.

69 Mile 54.3: Rearguard Falls
Spawning salmon do not travel up the Fraser River beyond this point, over 800 miles from the ocean.

70 Mile 73: Mt. Terry Fox
My Terry Fox can be seen on the east side of the track.

71 Mile 74: Valemount
This small lumber town of 1,200 people is encompassed by pageants of impressive mountain ranges. The tallest peaks of the Cariboo Mountains are located to the west and belong to the Premier range. Fifty years following Confederation, a succession of mountains had been put aside to be named after Canadian Prime Ministers. So far, nine out of the fifteen Canadian Prime Ministers have been honoured with their names adopted for this mountain range. The highest peak is denominated after Sir Wilfred Laurier, Canada'a first French Prime Minister. You can get a good glance at his profile on the $5 bill.

72 Mile 82.6: Canoe River
This marks the spot where a terrible train accident occurred. Jack Atherton, a railway telegrapher, was accused of causing the mishap. A former Canadian Prime Minister John Diefenbaker, while pursuing his legal career, successfully defended him. The Canoe River case was the subject one of his more famous trials during this period.

The picturesque Pyramid Falls at mile 113.

The Rocky Mountain Trench can be seen south and the Monashee Range stands majestically in the east.

73 **Mile 92: Albreda Glacier**
For a resplendent vista of the 10,000 feet high ice fields, take a look west.

74 **Mile 113: Pyramid Falls**
Pyramid Falls is one of the most spectacular sights along the Canadian route. The falls cascade down close to the train, spraying the windows with glacial mist. The train generally slows down for passengers to imbue themselves with the dazzling sight. Get your cameras ready!

75 **Mile 113: Blue River**
The nearby town is Blue River, attracting tourists to engage in winter and summer outdoor activities. This town is also home to one of B.C.'s most renowned heli-skiing outfitters in the world. Blue River provides locations for excellent fishing and outdoor activities attracting people from all over the world.

⭐ Terry Fox

Terry Fox is one of Canada's most commemorated and well-loved heroes diagnosed with bone cancer at the age of 18, resulting in the amputation of his right leg.

On April 12, 1980, Terry Fox embarked on The Marathon of Hope, beginning in St. John's Newfoundland to Thunder Bay, Ontario to raise fund for cancer cure. He devotedly ran 26 miles a day (42 km), equivalent to a marathon. Terry Fox died on June 28th, 1981 at age 22 due to cancer.

Thousands participate in the annual Terry Fox Run which to date has raised $360 million. A commemorative monument of Terry Fox stands in front of B.C. Place, B.C.'s largest sports forum.

⭐ Forest Fires

Despite immediate setbacks, forest fires are important in the balance of the ecosystem and are integral to the regeneration and cultivation of trees. The crucial importance of forest fires is evident in the following:

- Fires can burn the top organic layers of the forest bed bringing seeds into with direct contact with rich soil, which is important in coniferous forests. Humus and organic debris are exceptionally acidic and the acid leeches into the soil, making cultivation difficult. Fires burn the layer of organic waste thereby exposing mineral-rich soil.

- Black and white spruces require intense heat of the forest fires to shed their seeds. In B.C. forests, a rampant forest fire can mitigate the Mountain Pine Beetle Epidemic, a serious disease killing the pines in northern forests.

Humans are the main cause of forest fires, aside from natural causes like lightning striking fuel agents such as dry grass, brush, shrubs, small trees, woodeddebris and stumps.

Clearwater Subdivision
Blue River to Kamloops

76 Mile 8-16: Little Hell's Gate
Take a look south at 'Little Hell's Gate,' a section of violent, perilous rapids.

77 Mile 68: Clearwater
Home to the Well's Gray Provincial Park internationally acclaimed for its exciting hiking trails, mountain vistas and premium camping. Helmcken Falls, a 141-metre-long waterfall chutes down into a narrow canyon. Clearwater attracts thousands of outdoor enthusiasts yearly.

78 Mile 104-116: B.C.'s Worst Fires
The train passes through the area where B.C experienced their most devastating and destructive forest fires in 2003. Thousands were forced to flee their homes as the fire advanced incinerating whole communities. Between the towns of McLure and Barrière, more than 800 isolated fires raged through the forests and residential areas. The consequences of a serious forest fire may have effects on public health and safety, natural resources and most certainly, property.

79 Mile 124-135: Ginseng Fields
Ginseng is a relatively new crop to be cultivated in B.C. The dry interior makes for a perfect climate to grow ginseng because it reduces fungal or other diseases that impede its production. Successive fields canopied with black cloth follow alongside the North Thompson River for miles. Ginseng is an expensive product to cultivate. It requires an unconventional irrigation system unique from other traditional agricultural practices. The crops are constantly shielded from direct sunlight and takes three years to harvest. Approximately 90 percent of all B.C. produced ginseng is exported to Asia. Ginseng is used whole, powdered, and as an extract, and can be made into tea, tablets, capsules and candy.

80 Mile 135: Kamloops
Welcome to B.C.'s most populated interior city. The terrain is significantly different from the lush dense forests found in the Rockies. Small sand-coloured hills dotted with sparse conifers dominate the landscape. Lone tumbleweed carelessly crosses busy intersections and rattlesnakes and scorpions sleepily doze beneath heated rocks. Welcome to the cusp of

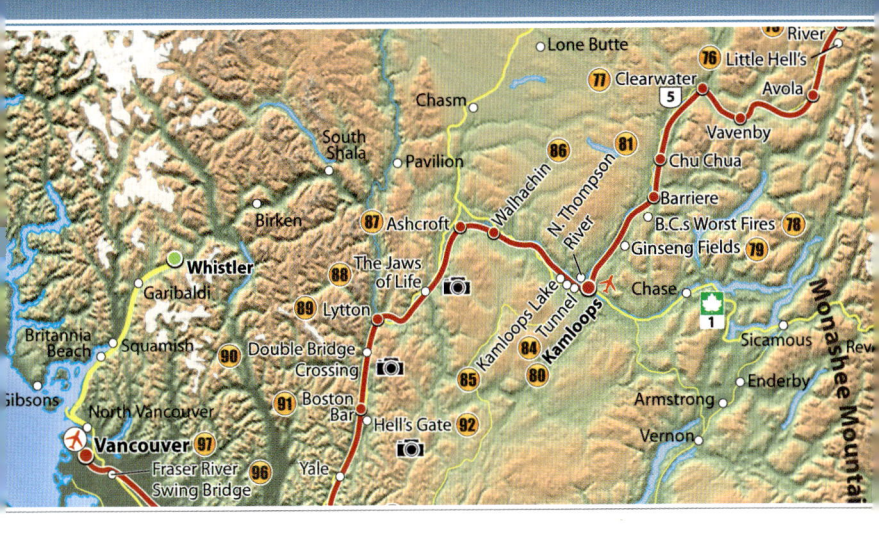

B.C.'s desert! Kamloops was initially inhabited by the Shuswap band of the Salish people who named their region 'Kahmoloops' which means 'meeting of the waters.' It was then established as a fur trading post at the junction of the North and South Thompson Rivers. There is a stop for a half-hour to refill water and refuel the train.

Ashcroft Subdivision
Kamloops to Boston Bar

81 Mile 1: North Thompson River
The train arches across a bridge spanning 1,330 feet long over the North Thompson River. This river was named after Canada's most ambitious explorer and mapmaker. As a young boy, David Thompson landed on the shores of Hudson Bay in 1784. He was hired by Northwest Company to survey and explore land. In the course of 28 years, he spanned the sources of the Mississippi, Sault Sté Marie, northeastern B.C., the westside of the Rocky Mountains and, finally, the Pacific Ocean. Thompson is a notable Canadian writer who had eloquently chronicled his journeys traveling across 55,000 miles of land.

82 Mile 9.1: Tranquille Tunnel
The train lunges through Tranquille Tunnel of 217 feet long.

83 Mile 10.2: Battle Bluff Tunnel
The train passes through Battle Bluff Tunnel of 2,831 feet long.

84 Mile 20.3: Copper Creek Tunnel
The train journeys through the 759-foot-long Copper Creek Tunnel.

85 Mile 25.7: Kamloops Lake
To the south is Kamloops Lake, with the Canadian Pacific Railway tracks on the other side.

Land irrigation at Kamloops.

164 | The Canadian

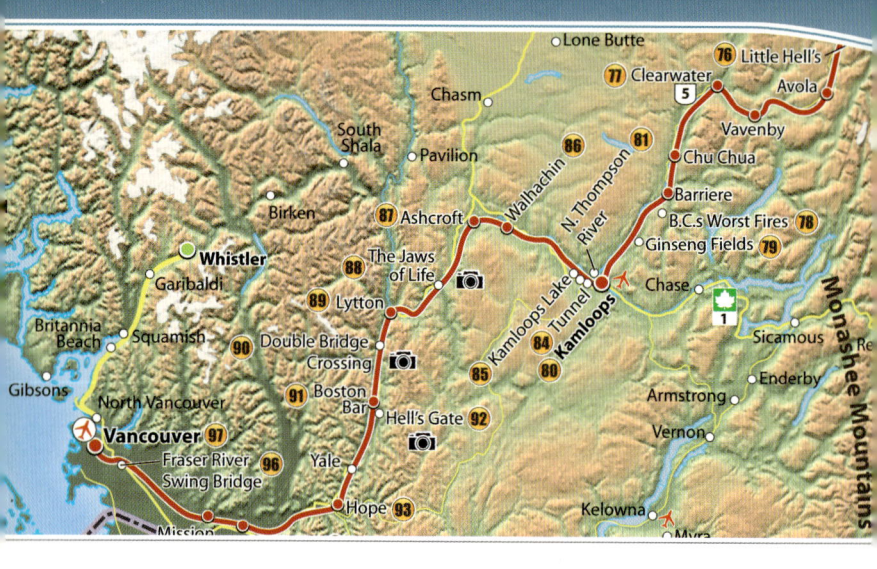

86 Mile 33: Walhachin

Walhachin was at one time a pristine small garden community between the years 1907 to 1914. Despite the difficulties of cultivating in a desert, Marquis of Anglessey planted orchards and devised a system of flumes to irrigate the gardens. Most men living in this community were summoned to return to Britain to serve in the armed forces during the war. Sadly, the men did not return and the gardens were not maintained. Currently, approximately 100 inhabitants reside in this quaint community, some are retired and others commute to and from work in Kamloops.

87 Mile 48.7: Ashcroft

Ashcroft boasts of being the driest town in Canada with an annual precipitation of seven inches per year. Ashcroft's striking desert terrain consists of undulating hills speckled with cactus and sagebrush. Sparse hoodoos, needles of rock remaining after a hill erodes, cling to the hills. Ashcroft has a very sunny and dry climate.

88 Mile 85-90: The Jaws of Life

The Thompson River is parted by the Jaws of Life where water backs up due to the narrowing walls of the canyon.

89 Mile 97: Lytton

The blue-green Thompson River and the muddy Fraser River carrying silt and sediments run alongside each other in the same channel.

90 Mile 103: An Impressive Double Bridge Crossing

This is the location of the masterful Cisco bridges. A double bridge crossing where a 812-foot-long bridge belonging to CN

Left: The blue-green Thompson river merging with Fraser river near Lytton.

ROUTE GUIDE | 165

Salmon Life Cycle

The word 'salmon' obtained its name from the Latin root 'salmo' for 'leaper.' Salmon navigate to their original spawning beds by selecting forks and streams depending on the appropriate chemical smell in the water.

Female salmon turns a vermillion red upon spawning whereas, the males develop a hook jaw. Female salmon lays approximately 4,000 eggs. Once the eggs are fertilized, both the male and the female salmon die.

The young spend close to two years in freshwater before making their journey to the great sea. Spanning about 16,000 km in the North Pacific Ocean, salmon start their migration back to the site in the river where their life started. Challenged by rapids, fishermen, bears, storm run-offs and logging, thousands make it back to start a new life cycle.

crosses the river above the 528-foot-long bridge belonging to CPR. The CP rail line changes sides of the canyon with CN.

91 Mile 125: Boston Bar
Boston Bar today was not in the same location prior to the completion of the Canadian Pacific Railway in 1885. Boston Bar was relocated to the area across the water and was replaced with the town North Bend. Initially, this area was frequented by American residents most usually from the east coast heading north to find gold. The First Nations within this region referred to the travelers as 'Boston Men.' Thus the area was named Boston Bar.

Yale Subdivision
Boston Bar to New Westminster

92 Mile 7: Hell's Gate
Hell's Gate was the most beleaguering section in constructing the Canadian National Railway in 1913. Many men lost their lives to blasting accidents and extreme conditions. The gate is a narrow passage stretching 35 metres wide (110 feet) where fast-moving water gushes through. An estimated 200 gallons of water rush through resulting in a volume twice as powerful as Niagara Falls. While railway workers blasted this passage, a rockslide was provoked, partially obstructing the Fraser River at Hell's Gate. This resulted in a drastic decline with the salmon run. Scientists and construction workers spent 30 years to repair the effects of this environmental mishap.

93 Mile 40: Hope
Originally, Fort Hope was established as a fur brigade outpost in 1848. The town then flourished significantly in 1858 with the gold rush. Now, Hope is a burgeoning town of 7,000 residents. Surrounded with the splendid panorama of the Cascade Mountain Range, Hope is a desirable

Fraser River's Hell's Gate.

The Canadian

Pacific Central Station, Vancouver, B.C.

place to live in and visit. The powerful Fraser River becomes more tranquil as it makes its transition from the whirling rapids of Fraser Canyon to Fraser Valley.

94 Mile 72: Chilliwack

Chilliwack is a growing city of 70,000 residents and is located in the crux of the Fraser Valley. Thriving fields of corn, cabbage and other vegetables are seen through this fertile stretch of farmland. Chilliwack is also home to several dairy farms, hence the successive fields of grazing cows lazily slumbering under trees. Chilliwack is the name for a local First Nations band. Translated in the Halkomelem language, Chilliwack means 'quieter water at the head.'

95 Mile 87: Mount Baker

The regal Mount Baker can be seen to the south on most clear days. Do not let the elaborate coating of fresh snow fool you. Mount Baker happens to be a young volcano at approximately 30,000 years old. Part of the Cascade Mountain Range, the volcano erupted several times between 1820 and 1870. There have been no significant rumblings since; however, Mount Baker is presently thermally active. The mountain is located just south of the Canadian U.S. border and is a popular cabin destination for Americans and Canadians alike.

96 Mile 118: Fraser River Swing Bridge

The Fraser River Swing Bridge is a tell-tale sign that the Canadian is fast approaching its terminus in Vancouver. Built in 1905, the swing bridge opens to permit larger vessels to pass through. The orange Pattulo vehicle bridge linking Surrey to New Westminster is directly above. To the west, the world's longest cable-supported transit bridge arches its way across the expansive Fraser River. Greater Vancouver is home to the longest automated rapid transit system in the world. The Skytrain moves from the core of Vancouver's downtown centre through Burnaby, New Westminster, Coquitlam and Surrey. With no engineers on board, trains are maneuvered by electricity. Averaging a speed of 45 km per hour, these environmentally friendly trains carry approximately 200,000 commuters along 49 km of track per day.

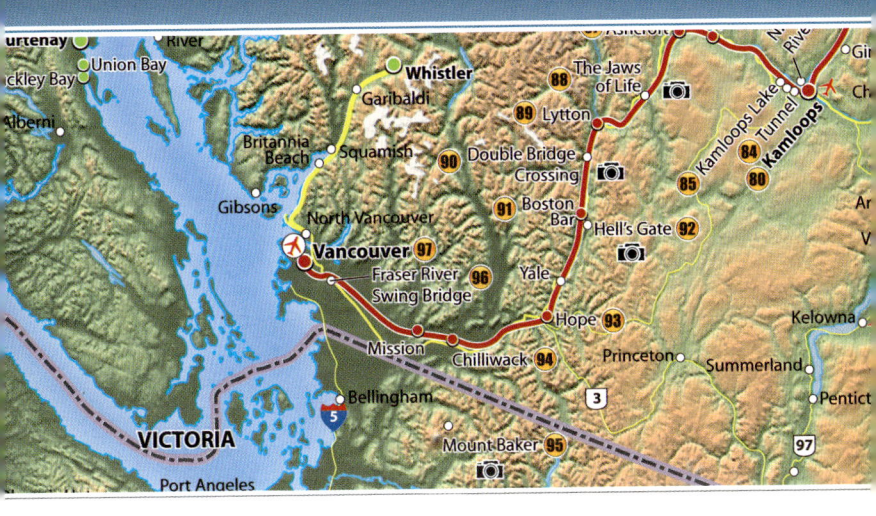

New Westminster Subdivision
New Westminster to Vancouver

97 Mile 131: Vancouver

Vancouver is a splendid city where over half of British Columbia's population resides. The perimetre of the downtown area is hugged with seawalls where residents run, walk or bicycle. The cityscape vistas are dazzling with breath-taking mountains as a backdrop. Home to the most burgeoning Chinatown in North America, Vancouver takes pride in its rich Asian cultural diversity. Take a small Aquabus that putts its way from the West End downtown area to Granville Island Public Market and watch some live performances while eating fresh delicious foods. Stanley Park is a stately feature located in Vancouver's centre. Regal conifer trees arch skyward while you take a horse and carriage around the perimetre. Vancouver is renowned for having a laid-back, West Coast feel. Enjoy the sites and get bedazzled by the beauty seething from the scenery. Vancouver will be hosting the 2010 Winter Olympics.

Billy Miner

Mission City is renowned for Canada's first train robbery, perpetrated by Billy Miner and his pack of thieves on September 10, 1910 on a CPR train. The gang bagged a whopping $7,000 of gold, $914.37 in cash and a $50,000 bond, jumped off the train, rowed the Fraser River and crossed the U.S. border by horseback.

Later on, Miner and his gang were caught by the Royal Northwest Mounted Police when they tried to rob a train outside of Kamloops. Miner was sent to the B.C. Penitentiary in New Westminster but escaped within a year.

At the age of 67, Miner was arrested for a train robbery in Georgia. Legend has it, he escaped again and then died in San Quentin at the age of 70. Billy Miner is believed to have coined popular Hollywood lines like, "Hands up" and " Goodnight boys, sorry to have bothered you." Billy Miner left his mark as a legendary gang leader.

The Skeena passing by a totem pole on its scenic journey between Jasper and Prince Rupert.

The Skeena

In the Gitskan language, the term 'Skeena' translates as 'river of mists.' Also referred to as the Rupert Rocket, the Skeena follows alongside this unspoiled river for the most part of the journey.

The Skeena is arguably the most scenic train route in North America, consisting of a two-day 1,160-kilometre (725-mile) daylight journey to Northern British Columbia's wild beauty. Make contact with native culture, experience thrilling views of magnificent mountains, plus take in all the other attractions of the region. The remote landscapes and untouched forests make for a safe habitat for bears, moose, elk and wolves. The spectacle of colossal mountain ranges coupled with vistas of pristine glacial lakes are both impressive and humbling. The Skeena passes through several picturesque towns including First Nations communities. This rail route was completed in 1914 by the Grand Trunk Pacific Railway. The intention was to have a terminus at the coastal town of Prince Rupert because it was a premium location to transport goods to Asia. Along the way, several industry towns were established specializing in forestry, agriculture, fishing and mining. Today, this is the engine route used by CN rail to transport goods like grain, timber and paper to the ports ready for exporting overseas.

ROUTE GUIDE | 169

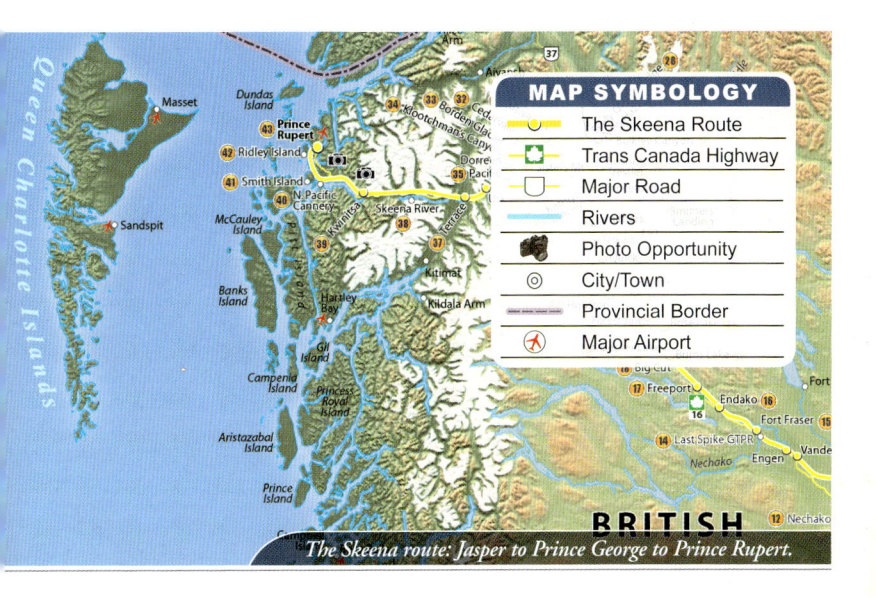

MAP SYMBOLOGY
- The Skeena Route
- Trans Canada Highway
- Major Road
- Rivers
- Photo Opportunity
- City/Town
- Provincial Border
- Major Airport

The Skeena route: Jasper to Prince George to Prince Rupert.

TRAIN AT A GLANCE

Route	Distance	Travel Time	Lowest Available Fare	Classes of Service	
Jasper - Prince George - Prince Rupert	1160 km	17.5 hrs	$106	Comfort	Totem Deluxe

⭐ Useful Facts

» The Skeena departs three times weekly (on Wednesdays, Fridays and Saturdays), year-round from Jasper, overnights in Prince George (accommodation not included) and carries on to Prince Rupert the following day.

» The schedule allows for daylight viewing of the spectacular scenery, the chance to view wildlife in their natural surroundings, and see British Columbia's northern rural communities.

» The journey time is approximately 20 hrs. One segment (8 hrs) is between Jasper, AB and Prince George, BC and the other (12 hrs) is between Prince George, BC and Prince Rupert.

» A trip aboard the Skeena easily fits into a vacation in western Canada. After Jasper, many passengers continue their journey on the Canadian. In Prince Rupert, ferries can take you to Alaska or Queen Charlotte Islands.

The Skeena

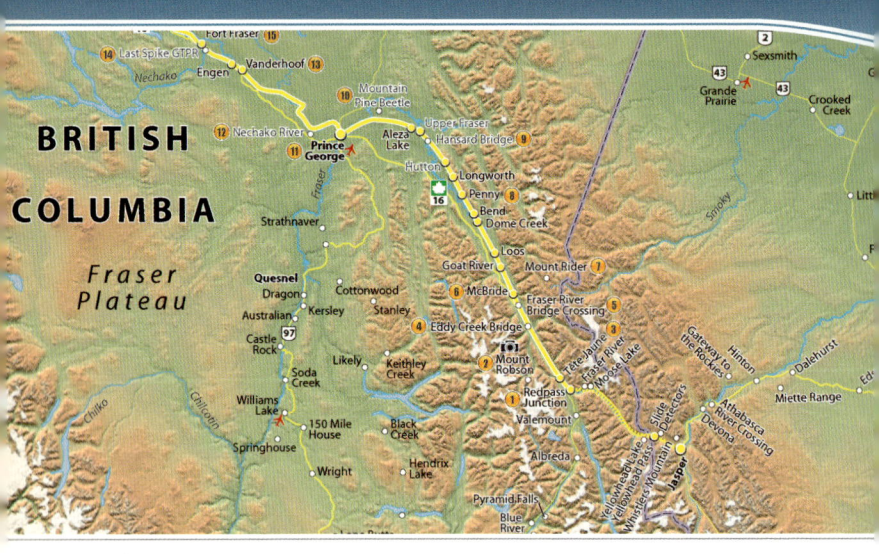

Note: The Skeena and the Canadian follow the same track between Jasper and Redpass junction from mile 0-43. The route is covered on pages 158-159. After Redpass, the Skeena veers off northbound.

Robson Subdivision
Redpass Junction to Taverna

1 Mile 0: Redpass Junction
Redpass Junction is named after a breach between Mount Kain and Razor Peak. This is the location where the CN northern mainline joins tracks with CN's Vancouver mainline. Here, the mileposts once again number from "0."

2 Mile 11-18: Mount Robson
This sight is potentially one of the most remarkable vistas of the Canadian Rockies. Mount Robson is 3,953 metres high (12,972 feet) and is the tallest mountain in the Canadian Rockies. An entire panoramic view of this monumental mountain may be seen from the left front side of the train while traveling to Jasper, and on the right back side while traveling toward Prince Rupert. On a clear day, the top of Mount Robson gleams as her jagged peaks tickle the belly of the sky. Generally, however, the peak of Mount Robson is often crowned by cloud. Do not be disenchanted. The view of Mount Robson is always impressive regardless of the weather.

Tete Jaune Subdivision
Taverna to McBride

3 Mile 4: Tête Jaune
Tête Jaune is a mountain valley involving three ranges: The Monashee, the Premier and the Rocky Mountains. The terrain along this area is adorned with tall, dense conifer trees. This region was named after Pierre Hastination, an Iroquois Métis guide with yellow hair. He was a renowned Hudson's Bay trapper

Majestic Mount Rosson.

ROUTE GUIDE | 171

responsible for navigating fur traders through uncharted territory. Tête Jaune, translated as "Yellow Head," was the name given to him by French surveyors. Yellowhead Pass and Yellowhead Highway were also named after Mr. Hastination.

4 Mile 39: Eddy Creek Bridge

The train traverses across Eddy Creek Bridge, an opportune area to take memorable photographs.

5 Mile 56.2: Fraser River Bridge Crossing

Approaching Dome Creek, the train crosses a bridge over the Fraser River. This bridge was constructed with the intention to halt all sternwheeler traffic from passing beneath it. Before the innovation of the railway, steam-powered sternwheelers were the conventional mode of transportation for transporting goods and people. When the first sternwheeler attempted to pass beneath the bridge, it failed, thus a stop was put to a very lucrative method of shipping.

McBride Station, B.C.

6 Mile 63: McBride

McBride is a small town of approximately 711 residents. This area draws multitudes of individuals who love the outdoors. McBride offers intermediate hiking and whitewater expeditions in the summertime, and heli-skiing adventures during winter. This area attracts birdwatchers who marvel at the 175 bird species within the vicinity. These include bald eagles, golden eagles and osprey. McBride is named after Sir Richard McBride who, at 33-years of age, was the youngest British Columbian premier to be elected into office.

Fraser Subdivision
McBride to Prince George

7 Mile 22: Mount Rider

The mountain peak to the north is Mount Rider (2,513 metres) named after Sir Henry Rider Haggard.

Haggard, an acclaimed British novelist, was offered by The Grand Trunk Pacific Railroad to have a mountain named to commemorate his achievements so long as the Geographical Board of Canada consented.

Upon setting foot on the prospective mountain, Haggard declared on July 16th, 1916, "I saw it. It is a wonderful and magnificent alp, some ten thousand feet high and measuring many miles around its base. Snow lies on its summit even in summer and it has deep, ripped glaciers and fir-clad ravines upon its flanks, while the crest has some resemblance to a Lion." Granted, the Geographical Board of Canada approved the request and the mountain was denominated after the prestigious novelist.

8 Mile 69.5: Penny

Penny is home to the smallest Canadian Post office in the country. This tiny community comprises approximately 20 inhabitants who enjoy a remote and peaceful lifestyle. The only way Penny receives supplies is by rail. Often, the train stops allowing passengers to detrain and explore the small post office. Inside,

172 | The Skeena

Penny resident greets the Skeena's arrival.

homemade souvenirs may be purchased, or postcards may be mailed. Also close by is a clear spring water Chinook salmon hatchery. Penny was an active sawmill establishment but those days have long since ended.

9 Mile 99.1: Hansard Bridge
This stretch of track runs parallel to the highway and when The Skeena passes over the Fraser River at Hansard Bridge, passengers may see a queue of traffic waiting for the train to cross.

10 Mile 130-146: Mountain Pine Beetle
Along the route heading towards Prince George, passengers will notice patches of red and grey pine trees. These trees are victims of the Mountain Pine Beetle (MPB) epidemic.

11 Mile 146: Prince George
Upon entering Prince George, British Columbia's largest northern city of 77,000 residents, the train crosses the Fraser River over a half-mile-long bridge. Recently, The University of Northern British Columbia (UNBC) was constructed; this being the first Canadian university was built in 25 years. The university has attracted students and professionals to Prince George and has consequently helped improve the conditions of the city. Forestry is the engine of this town's economy. Three pulp mills and 12 sawmills are where wood is processed into a product before shipment for export. These factories continue to employ hundreds of residents and supply hundreds of customers with quality products.

Nechako Subdivision
Prince George to Endako

12 Mile 0: Nechako River
For the next small leg of the journey, the train follows alongside the Nechako River. This river, actually a major tributary to the grand Fraser River, supplies electricity to a massive aluminum smelter in Kitimat.

13 Mile 69: Vanderhoof
Vanderhoof is a small oasis brimming with natural phenomena and wonder. Initially, this town of

ROUTE GUIDE | 173

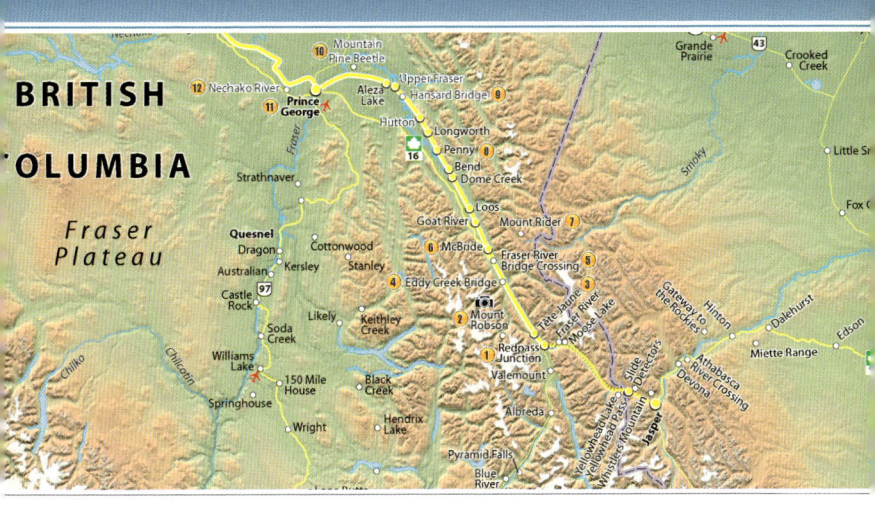

surrounding beauty was established as a retreat location for talented writers and artists. This was however marred when the industries of forestry and ranching were established. Regardless of this, Vanderhoof continues to attract aspiring artists who make a pilgrimage to this inspiring territory. Vanderhoof is also a remarkable spot for birdwatchers. This town, located in the centre of B.C. is the Swan Capital of the World. Every spring and fall, Vanderhoof is a popular pit stop for migratory birds. Take a small excursion down to Fraser Lake and bear witness to over 1,000 trumpeter swans in their makeshift habitat before departing for their migratory destination. Some other birds include Canadian geese, owls and hawks.

Mile 93.3: The Last Spike of the Grand Trunk Pacific Railway
(14) Try catching a glimpse of the commemorative plaque for driving the last spike of the Grand Trunk Pacific Railway. Inscribed on the plaque is this: "The last spike in Canada's second transcontinental railroad was driven here on April 7, 1914."

⭐ Mountain Pine Beetle

About 45 percent of the surrounding Prince George forests are currently infected with the Mountain Pine Beetle (MPB) Epidemic and the infestation continues to sprawl through the forests. It has spread from 165,000 hectares in 1999 to seven million hectares in 2004.

Unlike other conifer-beetles, the MPB attacks healthy living pine trees. Mountain beetles burrow under the bark and consume the phloem, arresting the distribution of water throughout the tree. They burrow into a healthy tree and emit a pheromone compound attracting other beetles to attack the phloem.

Perpetual freezing levels of -40 degrees can obliterate the species. But the recent rise in global temperatures adds to the proliferation of infestation.

A forest fire sweeping through the entire region is also a possible solution but that would destroy thousands of communities.

The Skeena

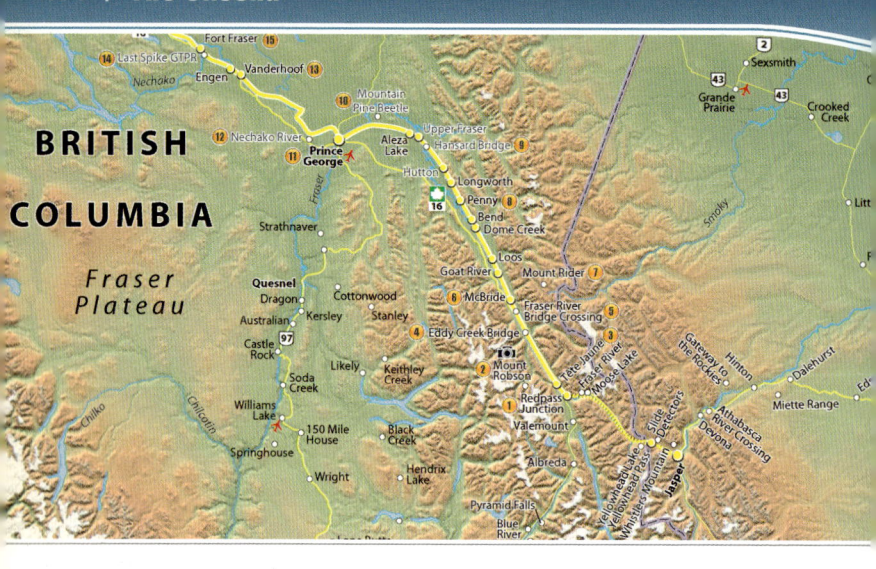

(15) Mile 94: Fort Fraser
The train veers away from Nechako River and heads alongside Fraser Lake. There's a view of Table Mountain to the north. This mountain resembles a plateau revealing million-year-old lava flows.

(16) Mile 115: Endako
Thanks to the supply of molybdenite found inside condensed quartz lodes of granite rock, Endako maintains a consistent mining economy. With the melting temperature at 2,600 degrees, molybdenum is a productive material for making highly-durable steels. Steel manufactured by molybdenum are used for products that require high temperatures. These include automobile parts, gun barrels, airplane parts, filaments of light bulbs, missiles and spacecraft.

Telkwa Subdivision
Endako to Smithers

(17) Mile 15: Freeport
This town served as former laymen headquarters since 1912 for the young men toiling to complete the Grand Trunk Pacific Railway. Legend has it that a man from Freeport, Illinois named this place after his hometown. This town was more like the frontier of the wild, wild west. Freeport earned the reputation of being rampantly hedonistic as it attracted crooked gamblers, thieves, drinkers and bootleggers. Brothels were erected and frequented by the workers. This town was home to approximately 3,000 inhabitants residing in rows of tents. Within months, gambling halls, hotels, and restaurants were established.

(18) Mile 32: Big Cut
Taking two years to construct, this section of the railway was the most grueling to complete along the Grand Trunk Pacific. A blasting accident occurred at this time, killing 30 men. Deadman's Island, located in the middle of Burns Lake, was named after the victims of the tragedy. Fifteen of the 30 men were on the island when it happened. Deadman's Island is the smallest provincial park in British Columbia.

(19) Mile 35: Burns Lake
Originally a construction camp for

Passengers shop during station stop at Smithers.

the erection of the Overland Telegraph line from Alaska to Siberia, this town currently has 1,800 residents. Burns Lake acquired its named after Micheal Byrnes, a surveyor for the Collins Telegraph Company, who passed through this area in 1866. This region is dappled with small enclaves of communities dotted along the lake's shore. Burns Lake is also home to several diverse First Nations reservations.

Mile 40.3: Decker Lake
A beautiful unspoiled lake renowned for excellent trout fishing. The lake is seven-and-a-half miles long.

Mile 51: Rose Lake
The eastern side of the lake is the headwaters for the Endako, Nechako and Fraser Rivers. The headwaters for the Bulkley and Skeena Rivers is located on the western side. This lake is internationally-acclaimed for being a proficient fishing spot. One point of the lake has been dubbed 'Millionaires Pool' because the quality of fishing here attracted celebrities like Bob Hope.

Mile 85: Houston
This small town of 3,600 inhabitants was named after a newspaper man in 1910. However, this particular newspaperman is no longer the local hero. In May 5, 1990, Warner Jarvis, an impassioned fly fisher, succeeded completing the construction of the largest fishing rod in the world. The rod was made of aluminum, and was 60 feet long and 36 inches wide at the reel. The rod was manufactured in six different local shops and 41 separate companies donated materials to see to it that this mission be realized. One of the fundraising strategies was for locals to purchase shares of the rod at $5 for one centimetre. This monolithic structure is erected at the base of Steelhead Park located on the south side of the tracks.

Mile 104: Photo Opportunity
Enjoy the parade of colossal mountain ranges as the train zigzags through the outlying landscapes of the town of Smithers. Prepare your cameras; bear and moose sightings are not uncommon.

The Skeena

Kathlyn Glacier.

Bulkley Subdivision
Smithers to Terrace

23 **Mile 4: Kathlyn Glacier**
The perfect view of Kathlyn Glacier or Hudson Bay Mountain is heralded as being the best view of a glacier in Canada traveling by train. When the ice melts, the water flows down into the cascading Twin Falls. Evelyn Peak is located to the right at 6,570 feet high.

24 **Mile 21.9: Moricetown**
This area has been a significant fishing location for the wet'suwet'en for thousands of years before the town was named after Father Adrian Morice, a French priest.

25 **Mile 28-36: Soaring Trestles**
The train shoots through the sky while traveling over the incredibly tall trestle bridges. There are three trestle bridges in succession: Boulder Creek-Mile 28.4, Porphyry Creek-Mile 31.3 and Mudflat Creek-Mile 36.1.

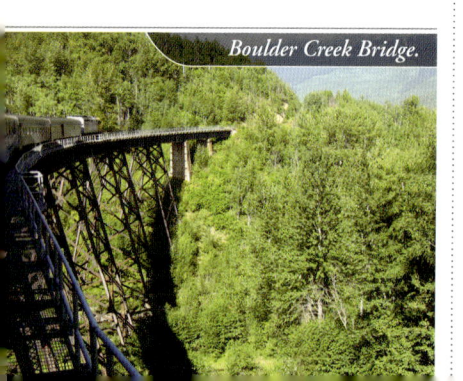

Boulder Creek Bridge.

26 **Mile 39-44: Bulkley Canyon**
This small stretch takes the train through three distinct tunnels. The first tunnel, 2,068 feet long, is the longest tunnel passed through by passenger trains traveling along CN tracks. Between the second and third tunnels passengers can catch a glimpse of Bulkley Gate. This natural display was a dike of rock close to eight feet thick and 250 feet wide. Erosion has caused the river to gush through the dike.

27 **Mile 45: New Hazelton**
Founded in 1886 by the Hudson's Bay Company, Hazleton was used as a trading post. Soon after, before the construction of the Grand Trunk Pacific Railway, Hazelton was the final destination for steamboats traveling upstream from the Skeena River. Today, Hazelton, South Hazelton and New Hazelton have 1,095 residents. New Hazelton boasts of being the Totem Pole Capital of the World!

28 **Mile 50.5: Sealy Gulch Bridge**
This bridge is 59 metres high and 275 metres long.

29 **Mile 62.2: Skeena River Crossing**
The Skeena traverses over the river that it was affectionately named after. Height, 50 metres; length, 288 metres. In Tsimshian language 'Skeena' river is translated as 'Water in the Clouds,' and in the Gitskan language it translates as 'River of Mists.'

30 **Mile 73: Kitwanga**
Kitwanga is a bygone Gitskan village with a small populace of 400 residents. 'Kitwanga' translated from Gitskan dialect, means 'People of the place of the rabbits.' A succession of totem poles can be seen looking south past the old

ROUTE GUIDE | 177

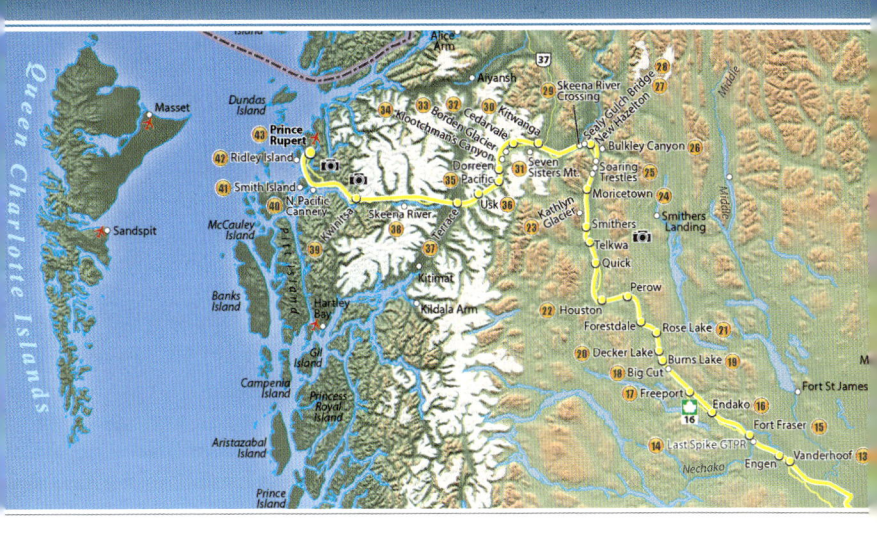

⭐ Totem Poles

Totem poles were originally pillars to support houses and attach welcoming emblems, memorials and family stories. The poles were carved from Red Cedar wood and painted with colours from natural pigments found in leaves, flowers, earth and crushed salmon eggs. First Nations painted the poles with elaborate brushes made from porcupine fur.

Totem pole-raising ceremonies are held to commemorate the life of a venerable chief. Most commonly, they reveal a family story starting from the bottom and ending at the top. Family totems such as bears, ravens, killer whales or eagles are mounted at the top of the pole. Legend has it that totem animals are closer to the spirit world.

Hudson Bay house. Some of the totem poles in this area soar up to 60 feet tall.

③① Mile 74-90: Seven Sisters Mountain
The imperial view of the Seven Sisters Mountain Range can now be seen.

③② Mile 86.1: Cedarvale
Initially, this small Native community was called 'Meekskinisht,' translated as 'foot of the mountain.' The First Nations of this region followed Christian principles stringently and the town was tagged as the 'Holy City.' The Grand Trunk Pacific Railway replaced the First Nations' name to Cedarvale, alluding to a grove of cedar trees close by.

③③ Mile 90-115: Borden Glacier
The breath-taking view of Mount Borden and Borden Glacier to the south. These mountains are part of the Bulkley Range. Nass Range can be seen to the north.

Seven Sisters Mountain.

The Skeena

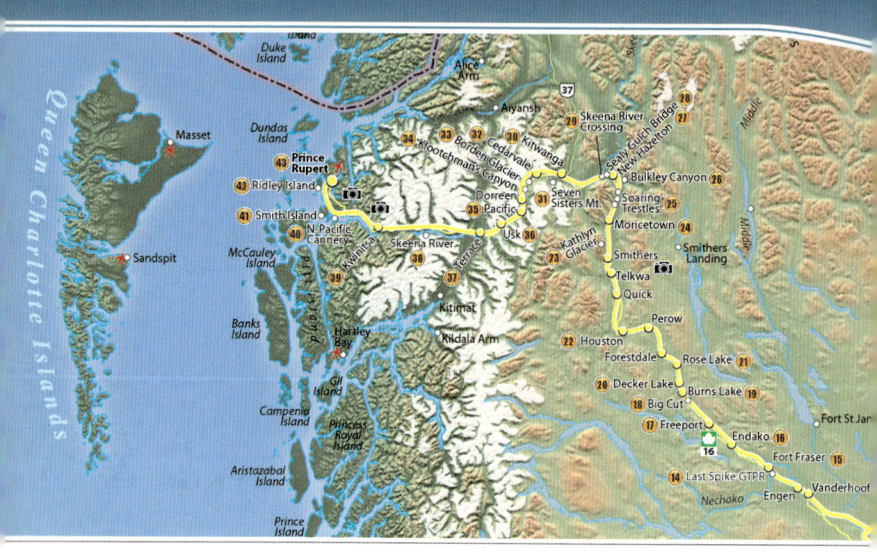

34 Mile 96-101: Klootchman's Canyon
Klootchman's Canyon. In the early trading language Chinook, 'Klootchman' means 'woman.'

35 Mile 107: Pacific
Before the 1930s, Pacific was a railway divisional point. Afterwards, it was moved to Terrace. A Terrace resident recently bought the old abandoned town of Pacific, inspiring others who yearn for a quiet life.

36 Mile 119: Usk
The Kitselas clan of the Tsimshian people inhabit this area. Their established settlements were sadly destroyed after a mudslide cleared their villages in 1935. Their name translates as 'guardians of the canyon.' For an exciting adventure, visitors can take a small trip across the Skeena River on a reaction ferry, using the might of the water to propel it. The train travels through four tunnels before it passes the Kitselas canyon.

37 Mile 131.9: Terrace
This town underwent several name changes before it officially became the town of Terrace. Initially, Terrace was denominated as Eby by the white settlers and Kitsumkalum by First Nations people. By 1905, George Little mitigated the situation by purchasing land and building a community. He inevitably called his 'dream' town Littleton. This unfortunately spurred more confusion. The Post office suggested the name be changed because there was also another 'Littletown' in the province of Ontario. The name Terrace seemed appropriate because of the vista of terraced slopes sculpted in the last Ice Age as part of the old riverbanks of the Skeena River.

Terrace station, B.C.

Skeena Subdivision
Terrace to Prince Rupert

(38) Mile 40: Skeena River
The Skeena River, after which the Skeena train route was proudly named, was initially a trading route. Bald eagles and black bears are often spotted from the train in this region. When spring commences to warm the land, melting snow cascades down the precipitous mountainsides, creating approximately 65 waterfalls. Abruptions in the river's water patterns are a tell-tale sign that the Skeena River is approaching the ocean. Old abandoned fish canneries are dotted along the river.

Mile 47: Photo Opportunity
Prepare your cameras for the view of Emanon Falls, cascading down 1,500 feet and into the Skeena River.

(39) Mile 48: Kwinitsa
The Grand Trunk Pacific Railway established approximately 400 identical train stations distributed along the route from Prince Rupert to Winnipeg. There are only four original stations today. One such station is the Kwinitsa station built in 1911. In 1985, this antiquated edifice was slowly moved down the Skeena River on a barge bound for Prince Rupert. Today, this station is erected as the Kwinitsa Station Railway Museum, informing visitors on the construction of the railway and how it served the communities.

Mile 65-70: Photo Opportunity
The scenery in this area is potentially the most beautiful terrain along this route. The train travels in stride with the river where immense fjords are viewed in the south and the stately Balmoral Mountain is seen in the background. Captain George Vancouver was the first European explorer to discover this area in 1793. Look north and try to decipher the silhouette of the Tsimshain Chief Tyee in Skip Mountain.

(40) Mile 81: North Pacific Cannery Village Museum
The North Pacific Cannery Village Museum was originally a salmon cannery operating between 1889 to 1972. The cannery employed approximately 700 workers during the apex of its success. Most employees were First Nations, Japanese and Chinese. Declared a national site in 1985, the cannery has since been preserved and converted into a museum. Visitors can get information materials on the history of the Skeena River, and attend live performances and special events.

⭐ Kermode Bears

The Kermode bear, or the Great White Spirit Bear, is found only in the rain forests of the north coast of B.C.

Kermode bears are commonly mistaken as albinos or polar bears. In fact, they happen to be sub-species of the ubiquitous black bear. Black bears are chiefly black; however, they do come in several shades including blonde, grey, brown, auburn, cinnamon and white.

It is not strange for black bears to be born of different coloured offspring. White Spirit Bears are produced by an uncommon recessive gene carried by both parents.

Today, these rare bears are considered endangered.

180 | The Skeena

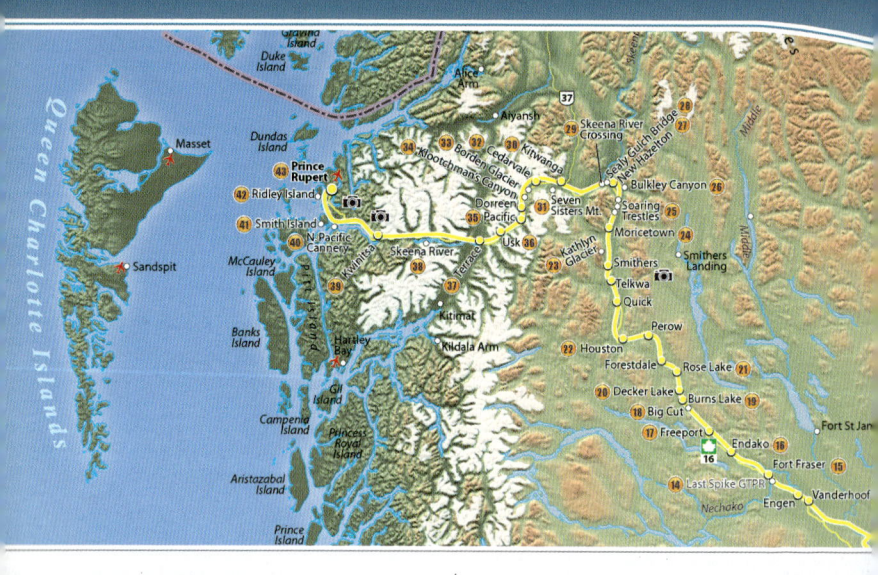

(41) Mile 83: Smith Island
This small town is home to Osland, a small Icelandic settlement established in the 1920's. Since then, the residents have migrated to Gimli, Manitoba, Canada's largest Icelandic enclave.

(42) Mile 87.3: Ridley Island

Trains transporting coal and grain empty cargoes here. Ocean freights load up the material and ship it oversea. Most massive terminals were built in 1980's.

(43) Mile 94: Prince Rupert

If passengers arrive at Prince Rupert on a clear day, they are extremely fortunate. Prince Rupert is the wettest, darkest and gloomiest city in Canada. Because of its location in the north, days are much longer in winter months. The city experiences approximately 2,552 mm of rain annually. Do not let this dissuade you from visiting Prince Rupert. It is an extremely beautiful city surrounded by old growth rain forests, coastal mountains, and remote north pacific seascapes. Visit Prince Rupert's picturesque Cow Bay filled with quaint bed & breakfasts, English style pubs, and boutiques. Most buildings in Cow Bay are built on stilts.

This city of over 14,000 was established by the vision of Charles Hays, president of the Grand Trunk Pacific Railway. He wanted Prince Rupert to be the terminus for the second transcontinental railway. He wanted to build a port that would rival the port in Vancouver. Prince Rupert was an ideal location because it was essentially closer to Asia. Unfortunately, Mr. Hays never saw his vision realized because he was aboard the Titanic when it sank.

Today, paper, fishing, forestry, and fish processing maintains Prince Rupert's economy. Its port also welcomes hundreds of cruise ships annually.

The Malahat

The Malahat at Victoria station before departure.

The Malahat

In the Gitskan language, the term 'Skeena' translates as 'river of mists.' Also referred to as the Rupert Rocket, the Skeena follows alongside this unspoiled river for the most part of the journey.

The Skeena is arguably the most scenic train routes in North America, consisting of a two-day 1,160-kilometre (725-mile) daylight journey to Northern British Columbia's wild beauty. Make contact with native culture, experience thrilling views of magnificent mountains, plus take in all the other attractions of the region. The remote landscapes and untouched forests make for a safe habitat for bears, moose, elk and wolves. The spectacles of colossal mountain ranges coupled with vistas of pristine glacial lakes are both impressive and humbling. The Skeena passes through several picturesque towns including First Nations communities. This rail route was completed in 1914 by the Grand Trunk Pacific Railway. The intention was to have a terminus at the coastal town of Prince Rupert because it was a premium location to transport goods to Asia. Along the way, several industry towns were established specializing in forestry, agriculture, fishing and mining. Today, this is the engine route used by CN rail to transport goods like grain, timber and paper to the ports ready for exporting overseas.

ROUTE GUIDE | 183

TRAIN AT A GLANCE				
Route	Distance	Travel Time	Lowest Available Fare	Classes of Service
Victoria – Courtenay	225 km	4.5 hrs	$28	Comfort

⭐ Useful Facts

» No meal service is provided on board.

» This "railiner" has no baggage car, and so there is no checked baggage service. The Canadian offers passengers many ways to save – or spend – based on factors like travel class, distance covered, and the season.

» Silver & Blue is 'deluxe' first class only available on the 'Canadian.' All meals are included.

» Ferries provide fast service between Vancouver, the arrival point of the Canadian, and Nanaimo or Victoria. Reservations are encouraged during peak season as the ferries tend to sell out.

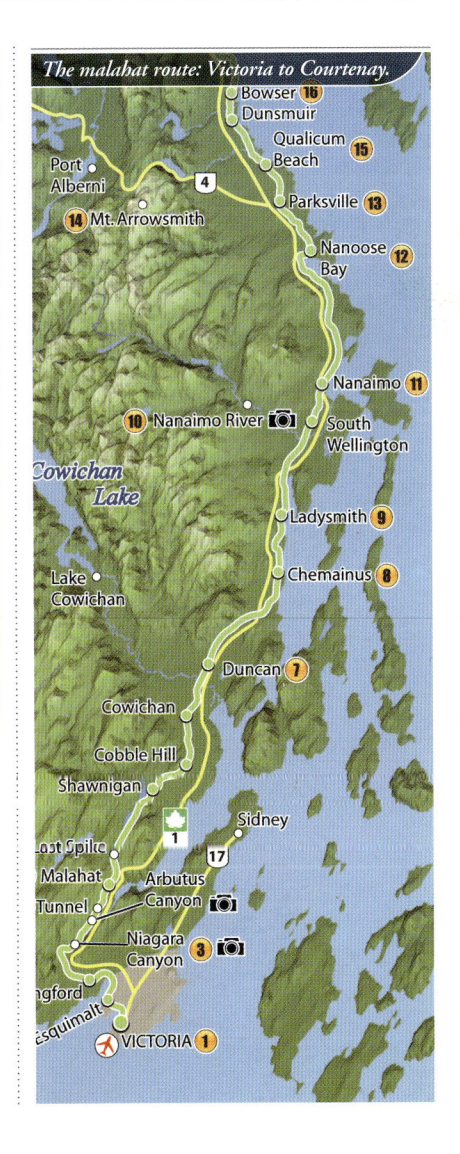

MAP SYMBOLOGY

─●─	The Malahat Route
▯	Trans Canada Highway
▭	Major Road
▬	Rivers
📷	Photo Opportunity
⊙	City/Town
---	Provincial Border
✈	Major Airport

The malahat route: Victoria to Courtenay.

- Bowser (16)
- Dunsmuir
- Qualicum Beach (15)
- Port Alberni
- Parksville (13)
- Mt. Arrowsmith (14)
- Nanoose Bay (12)
- Nanaimo (11)
- Nanaimo River (10) 📷
- South Wellington
- Cowichan Lake
- Ladysmith (9)
- Chemainus (8)
- Lake Cowichan
- Duncan (7)
- Cowichan
- Cobble Hill
- Shawnigan
- Sidney
- Lost Spike
- Malahat
- Arbutus Canyon 📷
- Tunnel
- Niagara Canyon (3) 📷
- ngford
- squimalt
- ✈ VICTORIA (1)

Victoria Subdivision
Victoria to Courtenay

1 Mile 0: Victoria:
As the Capital of British Columbia, this charming distinguished city is inhabited by 312,000 citizens. Victoria was named in honour of Queen Victoria in 1852 and the city maintains a strong British flair. Residential homes are ornamented with fragrant, radiant gardens tended with utmost pride. Victoria is home to the internationally renowned Butchart Gardens, a rare display of flowers organized in a resplendent manner, bemusing to the eye. Make sure to take a day trip to the impressive Museum of British Columbia.

2 Mile 3.7: Esquimalt
Historically, Esquimalt gains its reputation as being a military post. In 1865, the town was a bustling shipyard, because the west coast was a homeport to the British Royal Navy. Years later, it became Canadian Forces Base Esquimalt. The small homes are a tell-tale sign that this town has had a history as a military post.

3 Mile 14: Niagara Canyon
Passing through the expansive Niagara Canyon, the train crosses over a 529- foot-long bridge. This bridge had a particularly interesting history. It was originally erected at Cisco where it traversed the Fraser River. In 1912, it was carefully disassembled and shipped to the island where it was rebuilt to cross the Niagara Canyon.

4 Mile 16: Tunnel
The train goes through a 145-foot-long tunnel, the only tunnel on the E&N line.

5 Mile 20: Malahat
This is the highest point on the E&N line. Saanich Inlet can be viewed from the east of the train. 'Malahat' is a First Nations word translated as 'plenty of bait.'

6 Mile 25: The Transcontinental Last Spike
This is the most historical point in the railway where John A. Mcdonald drove the very last spike completing the transcontinental railway on August 13th, 1886. This triumphant moment was when John A. Macdonald's inconceivable dream was realized, and British Columbia joined Confederation. Enjoy the view of vineyards shooting through the earth and splashing the countryside green.

7 Mile 40: Duncan
Before this town developed into a modern city, the train station was a little whistle stop in front of William Duncan's farm. Today, Duncan is the regional area for the Cowichan First Nations band and is also referred to as the 'City of Totems.' Duncan is the gateway into some of British Columbia's old growth forests. In fact, take a small steam train ride at the B.C. Forest Museum to explore and learn more about the surrounding forests.

8 Mile 51: Chemainus
Welcome to Canada's largest outdoor

Niagara Canyon Bridge.

ROUTE GUIDE | 185

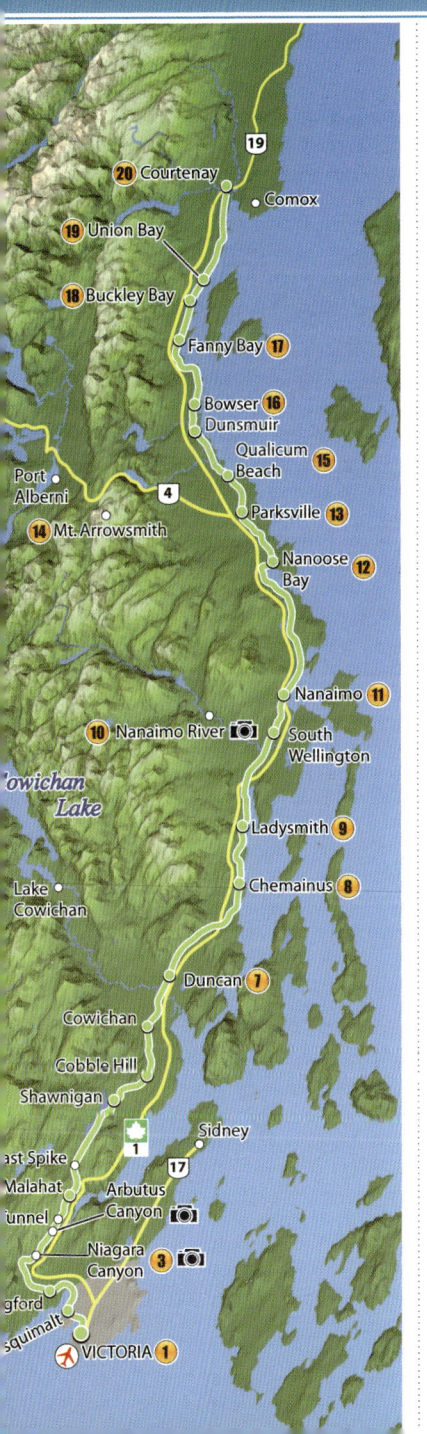

art exposition. Chemainus is renowned for the display of diverse wall murals painted by some of the most talented regional artists.

9 **Mile 58.4 Ladysmith**
Ladysmith is the point in which the train crosses the 49th parallel.

10 **Mile 65: Nanaimo River**
Relish the pleasurable view of the Nanaimo River as the Malahat crosses over the bridge. On the westside of the train, catch a glimpse of some thrill-seeking bungy jumpers. From bright coloured ropes, they fearlessly launch themselves over the bridge falling 42 metres (142 feet). These unflinching jumpers are dipped in the river head first, rebounding up again from the elasticized rope.

11 **Mile 72.5 Nanaimo**
Nanaimo was a small succession of five Coast Salish villages called Sne-Ny-Mo.

Below: Historic Nanaimo station before it was destroyed by fire in August 2007.

Passengers boarding at Qualicum Beach enroute to Victoria.

This term translates as 'where the big tribe dwells." In 1791, the Spanish explorer, Jose Narvaez, set foot on this densely forested region. Subsequently, George Vancouver, the explorer to discover Vancouver and surrounding areas, also explored the distinct area of this region. It was not until 1874 that Nanaimo was officially established, making it one of the largest port towns on the west coast. Nanaimo attracted many immigrants and settlers to mine for coal. Until the 1930s, this was Nanaimo's most prosperous industry. Since then, coal used as fuel was quickly replaced by oil and the demand for coal declined dramatically. Nanaimo is now a desired destination for retirees as it is a lovely sea-port town providing a gorgeous ocean view daily. Nanaimo is a transfer spot for those wanting to catch a ferry to Vancouver.

12 Mile 86.8: Nanoose Bay
Nanoose Bay was considered a large storage marina for gargantuan naval vessels belonging to Canada and the U.S. The ships underwent military exercises in and around Whiskey Gulf. The train crosses the island highway at Craig's Crossing and proceeds to enter the outskirts of Parksville.

13 Mile 95.2: Parksville
Catch a glimpse of an old dilapidated wooden water tank just north of the Parksville station. Prior to the 1940s, water tanks were utilized to fill train cars for fighting forest fires. Almost all water tanks along the Malahat route have been dismantled because of the replacement of diesel locomotives in 1949. Parksville borders the provincial park of Rathstrevor Beach. This area is captivatingly beautiful, comprising large old growth conifers and unspoiled beaches.

14 Mile 97.2: Mt. Arrowsmith
This is the point where Mt. Arrowsmith can be viewed. Ask an

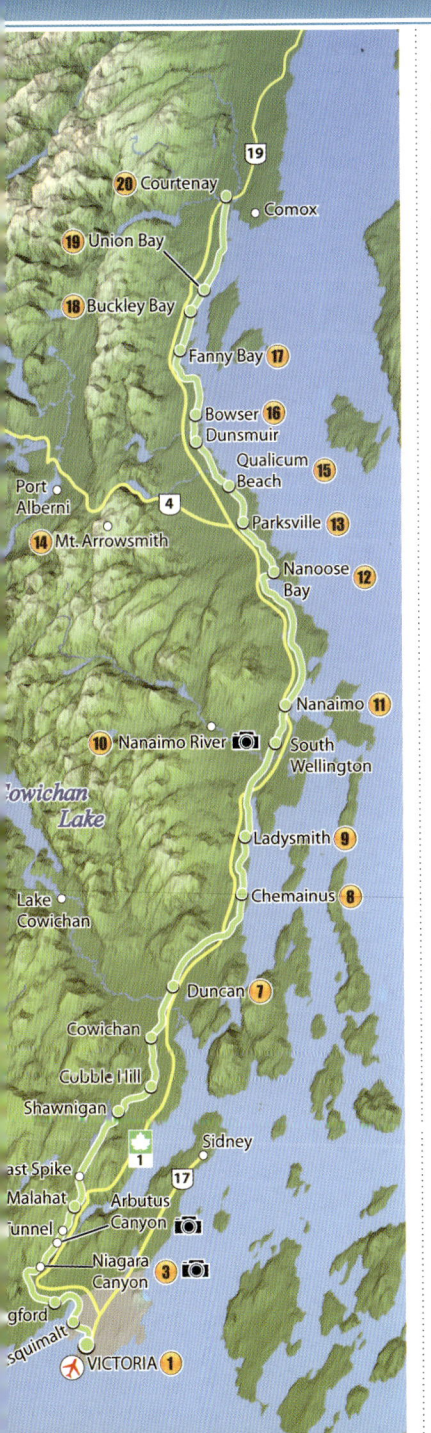

attendant for the exact time because it is easy to miss. The mountain was named after a renowned mapmaker, Mr. Aaron Arrowsmith who lived from 1750 to 1823. He designed exceptionally accurate maps based on the evidence of earlier explorations.

15 Mile 101.8: Qualicum Beach
In the Coast Salish language, 'Qualicum' Beach means, 'where the dog salmon run.'

16 Mile 114.5: Bowser
Legend has it, that in the 1930s, the Bowser Hotel provided their guests with a peculiar feature: a practicing canine bartender. Apparently, the owners of the local pub trained the dog to pour a stout, deliver it, acquire the money and return the change.

17 Mile 124.7: Fanny Bay
Fanny Bay is one of the largest oyster-processing factories on the west coast. The large white mounds hovered over by excited gulls are heaps of empty oyster shells. The remaining ramshackle of Brico, an old cable-laying ship, lays aground on the beach.

18 Mile 126.1: Buckley Bay
Buckley Bay is a lovely transfer point for travelers to catch a boat and visit surrounding islands.

Passengers detraining at Parksville station.

The Malahat

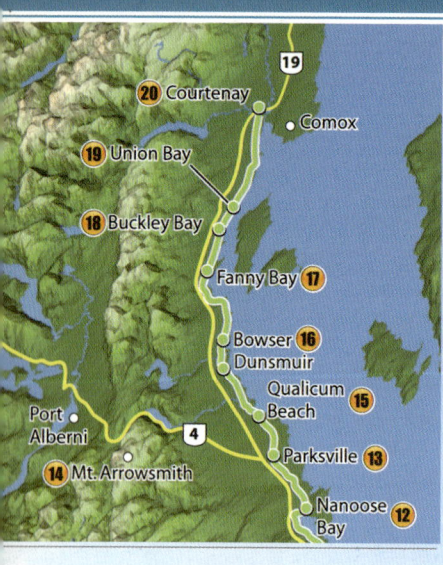

19 Mile 130.2: Union Bay
Union Bay is now an abandoned coal-shipping point where coal was transported by train and shipped off by sea. It was approximately 12 miles long.

20 Mile 140: Courtenay
The Courtenay River and Courtney town were denominated after Captain

Below: The charming Courtenay Station.

ROUTE GUIDE | 189

George Courtenay who was the captain aboard the HMS Constance. The town of Courtney was officially established in 1891. Before this, immigrants from New Zealand settled on land in 1862 with the interest of acquiring gold. The settlers excelled at fishing and farming when the search for gold proved unsuccessful.

Right: Inside the Courtenay Station.

Snow Train to Jasper's glass-enclosed Panorama cars.

Snow Train To Jasper

Enjoy the splendour of snow-capped Jasper on a winter aboard VIA Rail's Snow Train to Jasper, the corporation's route program to promote Canadian eco-tourism. Behold the sights of mammoth Alberta, from the cosmopolitan capital city of Edmonton to the quaint village of Jasper. Through glass-enclosed Panorama car that's perfect for a 360-degree viewing pleasure, travelers can join in family ski adventures, snowboarding, sledding and other fun activities on icy slopes.

Have the time of your life on your full stop to Jasper with a real snowy adventure, like exciting ski lessons and snow trekking, while enjoying the full vacation amenities of the famous Fairmount Jasper Park Lodge. Free Internet connections are available in both city stations and complimentary weekend parking in the Edmonton station.

Edson Subdivision
Edmonton to Jasper

Note: The Snow Train to Jasper and the Canadian follow the same track between Edmonton and Jasper from mile 0-235. The route is covered on pages 155-157.

ROUTE GUIDE | 191

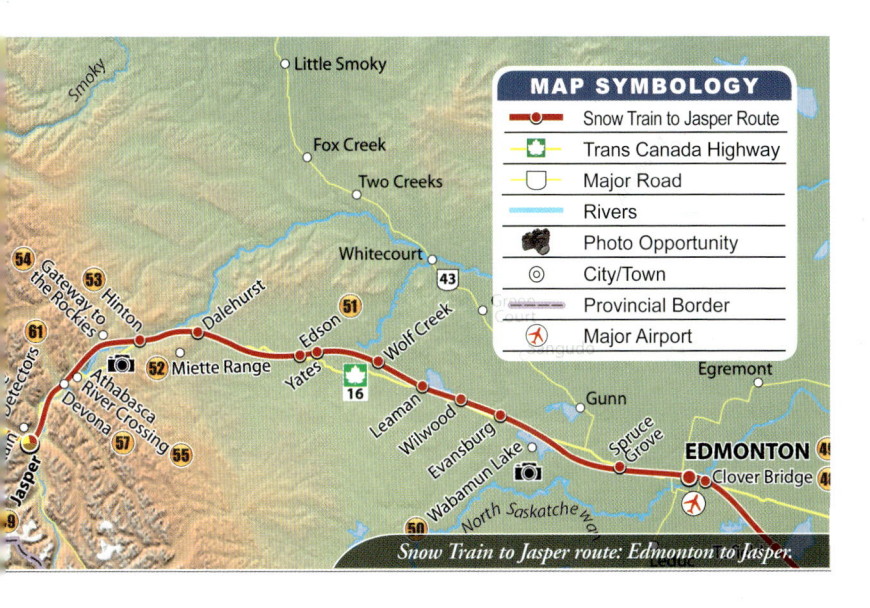

TRAIN AT A GLANCE

Route	Distance	Travel Time	Lowest Available Fare	Classes of Service
Edmonton – Jasper	379 km	6 hrs	$109	Comfort

Useful Facts

» For $109, avail of a Jasper-rific snow escapade aboard the Snow Train to Jasper from mid-December to end of March.

» The express departs from Edmonton at 4:00 pm every Friday while it leaves Jasper at 4:30 pm every Sunday.

» The route provides complimentary return shuttle bus service between the Jasper train station and your hotel. Shuttle bus service between your hotel and Marmot Basin, however, is $12 per person, per day (round trip).

» Travel light. There are no overhead compartments or coat racks onboard.

» All ski equipment and other bulky items should be registered as checked baggage.

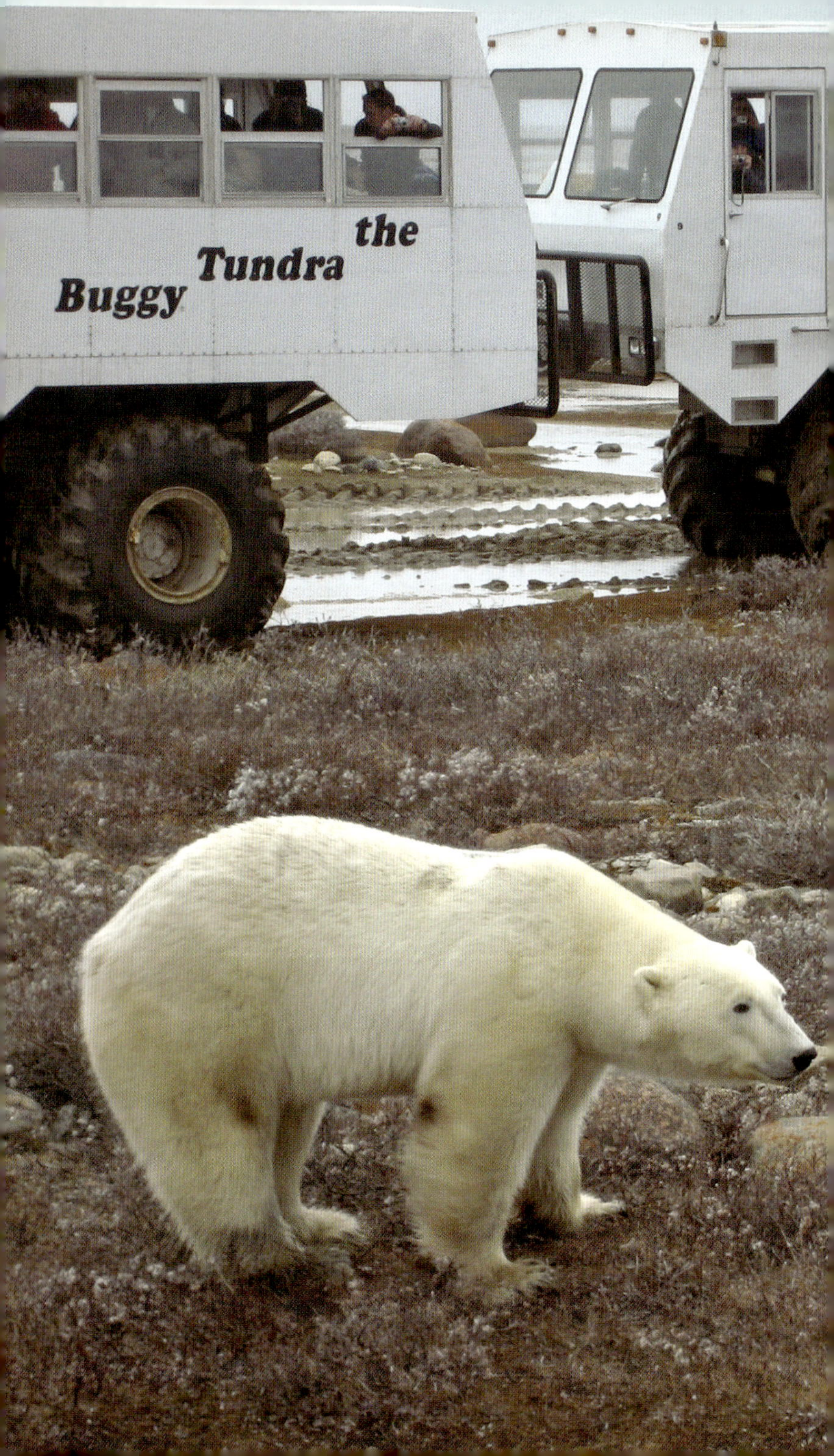
the
Tundra
Buggy

PRAIRIES & CENTRAL ARCTIC

VIA Rail can escort you to the Polar Bear Capital of the World. Churchill, the final destination from Winnipeg, is a remote northern community in the Province of Manitoba. Enjoy the peculiar sights of tundra landscapes, beluga whales, Northern lights, and indigenous fauna of Canada's north.

Be sure to try to catch a glimpse of the wild display of Northern lights arching across the nighttime sky. In summer months, watch for belugas and other whale species. This 1,700-km journey assures the passenger a comfortable accommodation.

The Park Car is attached to the Hudson Bay during the polar bear viewing season.

The Hudson Bay

Juourneying three times a week, VIA Rail's Hudson Bay route remains the most accessible way for the general public to get to communities along the Manitoba-Hudson Bay coast. The ride kicks off in Manitoba's capital city of Winnipeg, and traverses more than a thousand miles of tracks rich in refreshing views of the prairie fields, all the way to the sub-arctic Churchill regions on the coast of Hudson Bay.

The Polar Bear season in October offers a number of enhancements for travelers to Churchill, where you can see these furry friends in their natural habitat. Midway stops include The Pas, Thompson and Pukatawagan. As an added treat, passengers can arrange for special stops along the trail for some exploration of the great outdoors. Enjoy a "bird's-eye view" of the Arctic from VIA Rail's 360-degree dome observation car while enjoying delectable meals inclusive in the fare.

MAP SYMBOLOGY	
	The Hudson Bay Route
	Trans Canada Highway
	Major Road
	Rivers
	Photo Opportunity
	City/Town
	Provincial Border
	Major Airport

ROUTE GUIDE | 195

The Hudson Bay route: Winnipeg to Churchill.

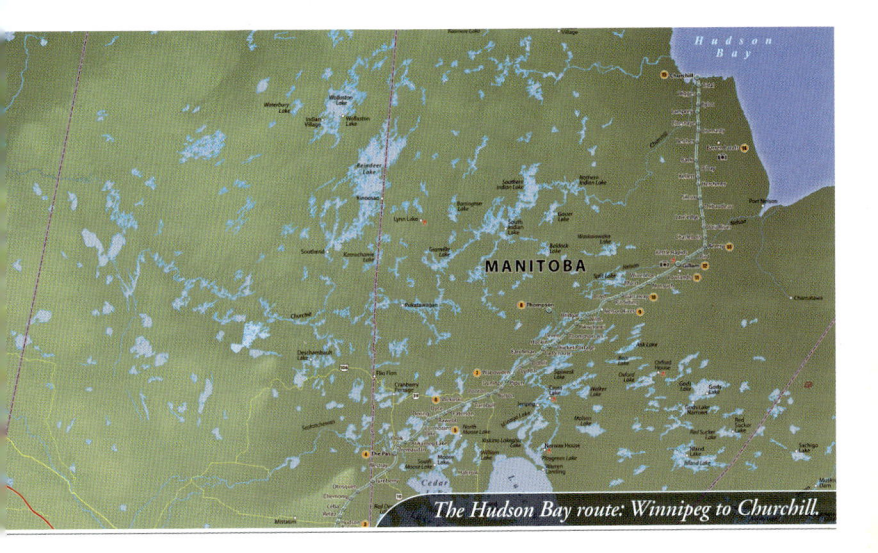

TRAIN AT A GLANCE

Route	Distance	Travel Time	Lowest Available Fare	Classes of Service	
Winnipeg - Churchill	1697 km	36 hrs	$154	Comfort	Comfort Sleeper

⭐ Useful Facts

» Train # 693 departs Winnipeg and travels by The Pas and Wabowden to Churchill. Southern travelers hop on for a trip up north to visit Churchill.

» Train #692 makes the return voyage.

» Trains #290 and 291 carry passengers between The Pas and Pukatawagan. Connections with Trains #692 and 693 are frequent.

» Winnipeg, at the southern end of the Hudson Bay connection, is on the route of the Canadian, which crosses the whole of western Canada.

» Leaving Winnipeg on Tuesday, Thursday and Sunday evenings, the Hudson Bay arrives in Churchill two days later. The train departs on the same schedule.

» Make allowance for late train arrivals and departures, which are frequent due to the unstable nature of the ground and track condition and the presence of permafrost ice.

The Hudson Bay

Dauphin station built in 1923, is one of Manitoba's finest examples of railway architecture.

Togo Subdivision
Dauphin to Canora

1. Mile 55: Portage La Prairie
Portage La Prairie is a quaint city with rows of residential character homes. The Hudson Bay and the Canadian use the same track until Portage La Prairie where the Hudson Bay makes a loop westward dipping into the Province of Saskatchewan. The train heads back into Manitoba, continuing westward. The train fringes the Riding Mountain National Park, spanning close to 3,000 kilometres and carrying several animal species including bison. This region holds one of the world's most substantial waterfowl staging areas in North America.

2. Mile 121: Dauphin
Thanks to the influx of Russian Ukrainian immigrants between the years 1896 and 1925, Dauphin has become the largest Ukrainian settlement in Canada. Ukrainian agricultural practices continue to be significant with the cultivation of the prairies. Dauphin has approximately 8,000 inhabitants residing along the banks of the Vermillion River.

Assiniboine Subdivision
Canora to Hudson Bay

3. Mile 93: Hudson Bay
This small Saskatchewan town takes pride in its affiliation and connection with the fur traders between their port and the trapping lands. The train must travel 1,000 km before passengers can bear witness to the icy waters of the Hudson Bay.

4. Mile 88: The Pas
This town is where the Saskatchewan and the Pasquia Rivers intersect. Currently, the train is 777 km north of Winnipeg and is located on the southern bank of the Saskatchewan River. The name 'The Pas' has two potential meanings.

ROUTE GUIDE | 197

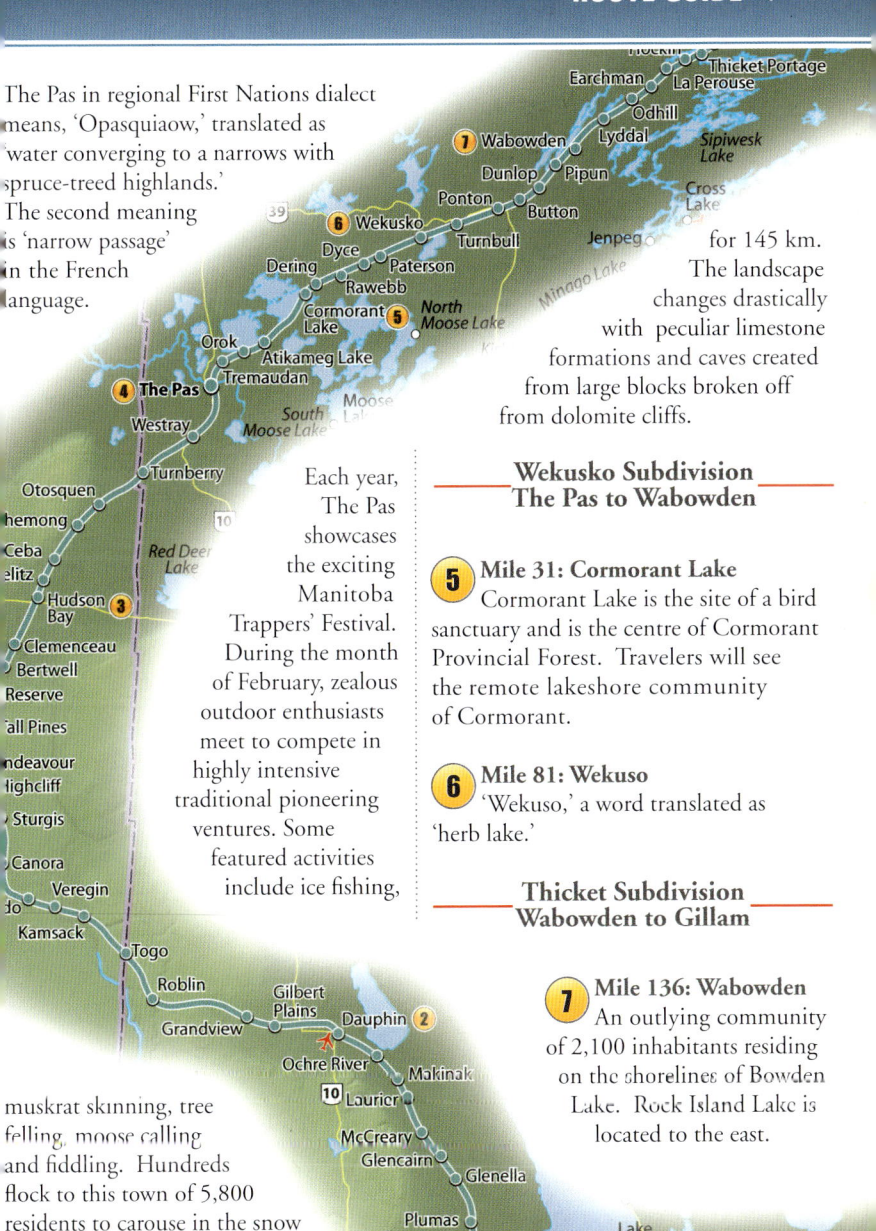

The Pas in regional First Nations dialect means, 'Opasquiaow,' translated as 'water converging to a narrows with spruce-treed highlands.' The second meaning is 'narrow passage' in the French language.

Each year, The Pas showcases the exciting Manitoba Trappers' Festival. During the month of February, zealous outdoor enthusiasts meet to compete in highly intensive traditional pioneering ventures. Some featured activities include ice fishing, muskrat skinning, tree felling, moose calling and fiddling. Hundreds flock to this town of 5,800 residents to carouse in the snow and watch the infamous World Championship Dog Sled Race.

Upon leaving the pass, the train travels through Clearwater Lake Provincial Park for 145 km. The landscape changes drastically with peculiar limestone formations and caves created from large blocks broken off from dolomite cliffs.

Wekusko Subdivision
The Pas to Wabowden

(5) Mile 31: Cormorant Lake
Cormorant Lake is the site of a bird sanctuary and is the centre of Cormorant Provincial Forest. Travelers will see the remote lakeshore community of Cormorant.

(6) Mile 81: Wekuso
'Wekuso,' a word translated as 'herb lake.'

Thicket Subdivision
Wabowden to Gillam

(7) Mile 136: Wabowden
An outlying community of 2,100 inhabitants residing on the shorelines of Bowden Lake. Rock Island Lake is located to the east.

198 | The Hudson Bay

8) Mile 191: Thompson

Thompson is home to the second-largest nickel deposit in the world. After this discovery, the INCO nickel mine was built in the 1950s raising employment and attracting more people to this community. The Hudson Bay stops here temporarily before proceeding on the journey.

9) Mile 240: Nelson River and Manitou Rapids

Only dare-devil canoeists and whitewater rafters have the courage to ride these waters. 'Manitou' means 'Devil Rapids' in Cree because these whitewaters are immensely dangerous. These rapids are the narrow passageway since the beginnings of the English–Winnipeg, Red, Assiniboine, North and South Saskatchewan Rivers.

10) Mile 259: Garraway

It is strange that this outlying North Manitoban town was named after the Garraway's Coffee House in London. This is also the location of the first fur sale by the Hudson's Bay Company in 1671.

11) Mile 319: Lowlands

The frigid and wet coastal plains of the Hudson's Bay Lowlands come into view consisting of permafrost soil 12 metres thick (36 feet). Frozen terrain has made it impossible for communication lines to be embedded in the earth, therefore, they must be supported onto tripods above ground.

Herchmer Subdivision
Gillam to Churchill

12) Mile 326: Gillam

You have officially arrived into the remote north. To date, Gillam marks the spot where roads stop and no longer extend north. The only way to get to a northern destination beyond this point is by plane or train. The 1,200 residents are mostly employed by the large

Aurora Borealis

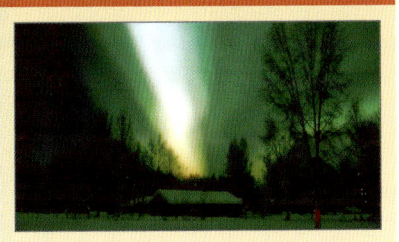

The cosmic phenomenon Aurora Borealis (or Northern Lights) occurring in the northern regions of the world can be seen while aboard the train at night.

The Aurora comprises electrically charged particles that explode into prismatic spectrums of light once they hit the upper atmosphere. Undulating shards of colour spear across the sky. The Earth's magnetic field magnetizes electrically-charged particles to the north and south poles of the earth.

A counterpart phenomenon on the south is the Aurora Australias (or Southern Lights). Pull up your blinds and bear witness to this amphitheatre of shifting colour and electric soundscapes.

hydroelectric plant positioned between three generating stations: Long Spruce, Kettle and Limestone. Stephens Lake was created from the construction of the large dam.

13 Mile 355: Amery

To the right of the train, passengers see a dilapidated 17-span, 2,600-foot-long bridge that was constructed before World War 1. This large bridge was part of the unfinished Port Nelson rail line. The project was perhaps abandoned due to the over saturation of Canadian railway lines, and the impending world war. The train takes a sharp turn northbound directly towards Churchill.

14 Mile 440: Barren Lands

The Barren Land is the tundra terrain just north of the tree line. It has the appearance of being a stark inhabitable landscape; however, it provides life for many species. Dear River and the expansive Churchill River join together and flow into Hudson Bay. The immense force of Hudson Bay lunges into the river pushing the tides in the opposite direction. There is a distinct visible difference where salt water and fresh water collide.

15 Mile 509.8: Churchill

Welcome to Churchill, where the landscapes are strikingly bare, infinite and peculiar. Churchill was initially discovered by a Dane named Jens Munk in 1619. Four-and-a-half miles up the harbour, Munk and his men stayed for the winter and unfortunately caught scurvy. Only three men were left alive by the time the ice broke the next spring. The Hudson's Bay Company were the next settlers to establish a post in this region. The first fort built by the Company was wiped out by an unfortunate fire. After replacing the fort with the Prince of Wales Fort in 1733, it was consequently seized by the French within one hour.

Thompson residents enroute to a nearby town for a funeral.

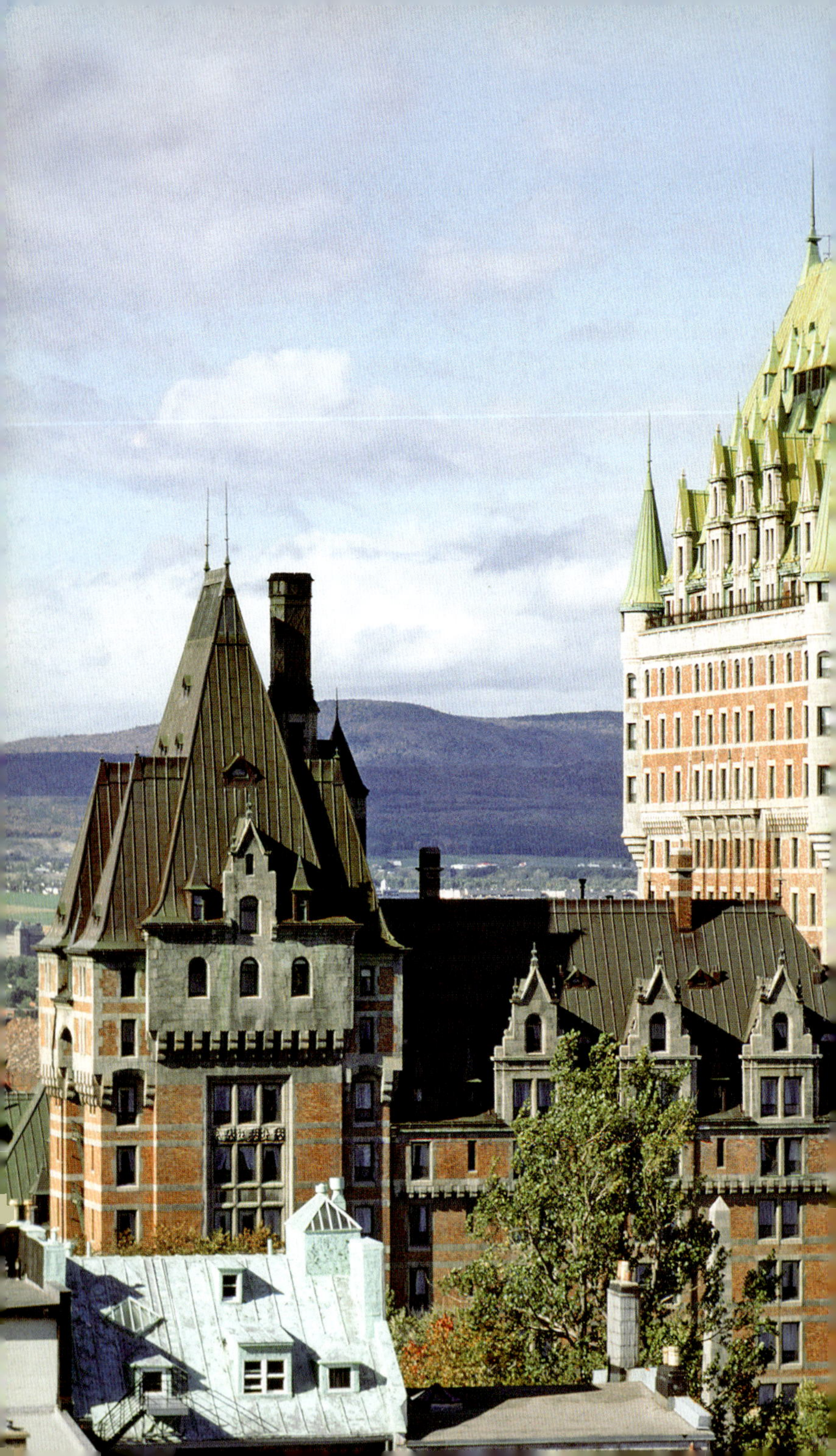

ONTARIO AND QUÉBEC

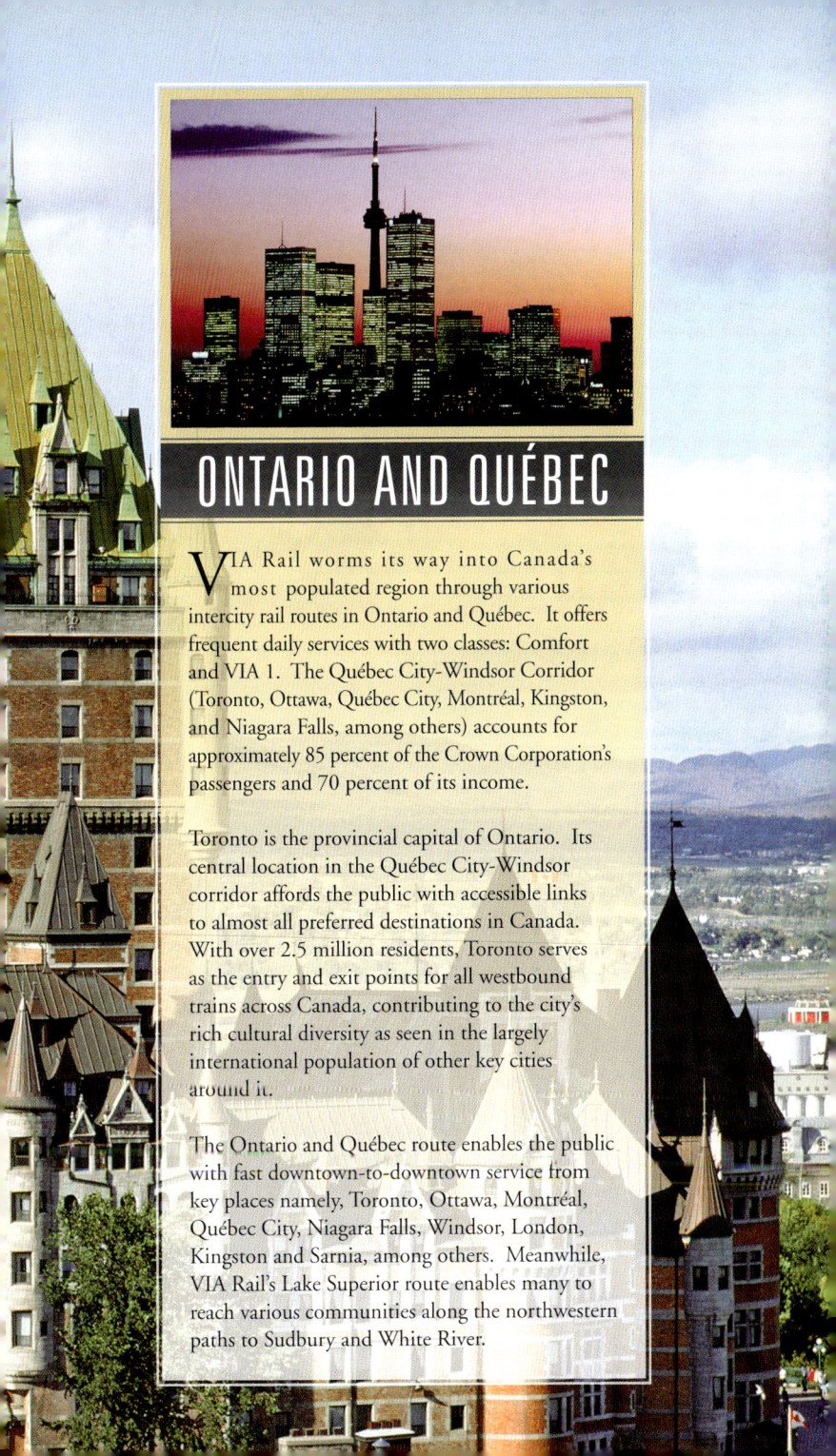

VIA Rail worms its way into Canada's most populated region through various intercity rail routes in Ontario and Québec. It offers frequent daily services with two classes: Comfort and VIA 1. The Québec City-Windsor Corridor (Toronto, Ottawa, Québec City, Montréal, Kingston, and Niagara Falls, among others) accounts for approximately 85 percent of the Crown Corporation's passengers and 70 percent of its income.

Toronto is the provincial capital of Ontario. Its central location in the Québec City-Windsor corridor affords the public with accessible links to almost all preferred destinations in Canada. With over 2.5 million residents, Toronto serves as the entry and exit points for all westbound trains across Canada, contributing to the city's rich cultural diversity as seen in the largely international population of other key cities around it.

The Ontario and Québec route enables the public with fast downtown-to-downtown service from key places namely, Toronto, Ottawa, Montréal, Québec City, Niagara Falls, Windsor, London, Kingston and Sarnia, among others. Meanwhile, VIA Rail's Lake Superior route enables many to reach various communities along the northwestern paths to Sudbury and White River.

The departure and arrivals board inside the Montréal Station.

Montréal to Toronto

Toronto and Montréal rail stations are conveniently located in downtown areas near popular hotels and the best restaurants, cutting off traffic downtime.

Convenient train schedules make planning for trips easy and flexible. Have a peaceful journey to any choice destinations in Montréal and Toronto - Cornwall, Brockville, Kingston, Belleville, Oshawa and as far as Oakville, where a train stops by nighttime except Saturdays, and departs every morning except Sundays. Take in all the awe-inspiring sceneries carved by nature and the various colours of unique village life along the way, all in the safety and comfort of various types of railcars that suit your preference. You can even mix work and leisure with the functional comforts of the train.

⭐ Useful Facts

» Passengers departing from the Dorval station can avail of the complimentary AirConnect rail service, a free shuttle service to and from the Pierre Elliott Trudeau International Airport.

» The Montréal-Toronto route and vice versa offers a choice of about 50 departures every week, with each full trip lasting five hours. For a four-hour journey, be sure to catch the express train service which departs from each city's major station daily at 5 pm.

ROUTE GUIDE | 203

The Corridor Route: Montréal to Toronto.

TRAIN AT A GLANCE				
Route	Distance	Travel Time	Lowest Available Fare	Classes of Service
Montréal - Toronto	539 km	5 hrs	$77	Comfort / VIA 1

Montréal Subdivision
Montréal to Dorval

1 Mile 0: Montréal

Montréal, the largest city of Québec, is literally the home of VIA Rail's rail network, with its headquarters located in Place Ville Marie in Montréal. All VIA Rail trains in Québec pull over in the Montréal Central Station as their arrival or departure point, a strategic location that plays a part in Montréal's massive economic growth alongside traffic congestion and urban settlement.

In this premiere city branched several railtracks that protrude to other amazing destinations especially in Ontario and Québec. One can head eastward to the Gaspé peninsula aboard the Chaleur, explore northern Québec with the Abitibi that winds to Senneterre, and go all the way to Jonquiere through the Saguenay trains.

Kingston Subdivision
Dorval to Toronto

2 Mile 10: Dorval
The train makes a temporary stop,

Montréal to Toronto

⭐ Saint Lawrence Seaway

The 3,769-km Saint Lawrence Seaway is a complex waterway system of canals, dams and locks connecting the St. Lawrence River to the Great Lakes, and was built to improve the efficiency of sea routes for international trade.

Inaugurated in 1959, the construction of the waterway did not commence until 1954 due to the immensity of this project.

New towns were constructed for some 6,500 people, mostly from riverside settle-ments who were dislodged from their homes because it was compulsory to flood areas to create appropriate depths and power pools.

unloading passengers wishing to catch a free shuttle to the Pierre Elliot Trudeau airport. This airport is one of two international airports in Montréal.

3. Mile 21-24: Ottawa River
The train crosses over the Ottawa River twice, first at mile 21, and second at mile 24. After the train finally exits the island of Montréal, the urban landscape transforms into a succession of pastoral fields dotted with old-growth deciduous trees.

4. Mile 38: Coteau
This is the junction where the railway branches off towards Ottawa, Canada's capital city.

5. Mile 45: Québec-Ontario Border
A small white and red sign marking the provincial boundary between Québec and Ontario can be seen north of the train.

6. Mile 49-51: Adirondack Mountains
The resplendent display of the Adirondack Mountains is seen to the south of the train.

7. Mile 65: Saint Lawrence Seaway
Look to the south and notice the spur line through Cornwall, Ontario. This is a part of the line that was consequently flooded by the construction of the seaway. Approximately 40 miles of track and seven stations were submerged.

8. Mile 80.5: Ingleside
This is the town of Ingleside, established for the citizens who were displaced from Aultsville, Frarran's Point, Woodland's, Nickinson's Landing and Wales because of the flooding of the St. Lawrence Seaway.

9. Mile 111: The International Bridge
The International Bridge connecting Canada and Ogdensburg, NY is to the south.

10. Mile 112.5: Prescott and Bytown Railway
The original tracks of the Prescott and Bytown Railway are passed beneath the train.

11. Mile 125: Brockville
Canada's oldest railway tunnel built in 1859 can be seen to the south. It was the first tunnel to build doors to prevent ice from developing on its roof. The tunnel closed in 1960.

ROUTE GUIDE | 205

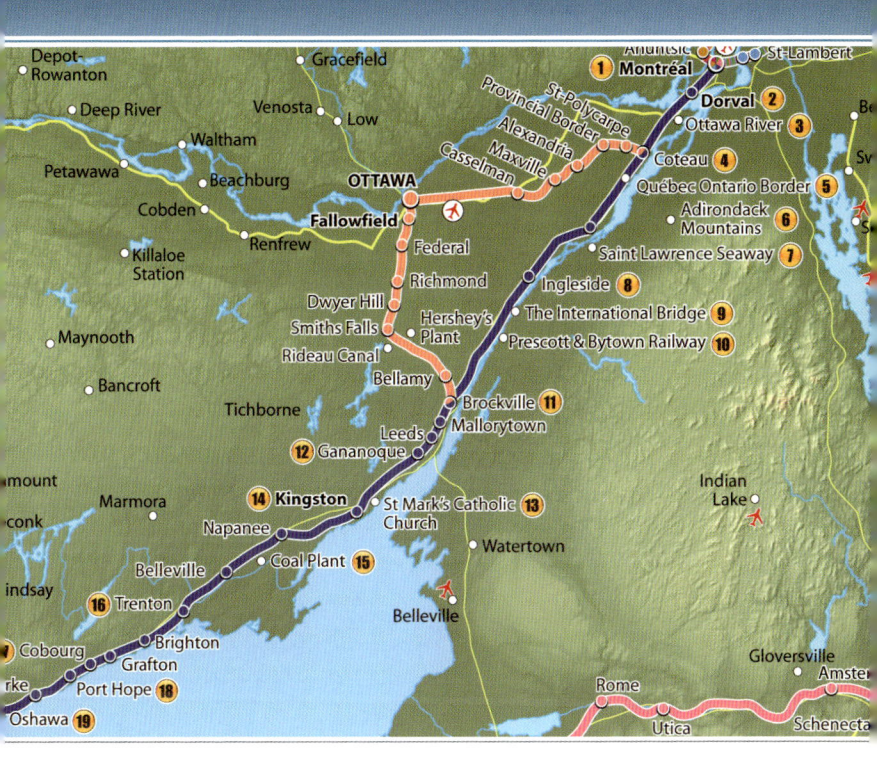

(12) Mile 154: Gananoque

This region is home to the 1,000 Islands, a tourist destination renowned for its incomparable beauty. These islands are scattered along the St. Lawrence River for approximately 60 miles. Several of the islands are made up of pink granite and lime stone, revealing an alluring and peculiar appearance. The St. Lawrence is the artery of Canada's rivers. The river commences its meandering journey from Lake Ontario and eventually flushes out into the Atlantic. It stretches across 1,247 kilometres (775 miles) and drains the largest fresh water source in the world.

(13) Mile 172: St Mark's Catholic Church

St. Mark's Gothic-style church built in 1844 can be seen to the south, along with the Great Cataraqui River.

(14) Mile 176.1: Kingston

Kingston is an important Canadian city brimming with history. Initially, this region was a First Nations village and proceeded to become a French fortress. It was subsequently transformed into a British Citadel and then became the prized capital of Canada. Sir John A. Macdonald referred to Kingston as 'home.' Today, Kingston is renowned for being a quaint and pretty university town home to Alcan, Queen's University and the Royal Military College.

(15) Mile 191: Coal Plant

The tall structures viewed from the train are a coal-fired generating plant close to Bath.

(16) Mile 232.2: Trenton

A 240-mile waterway system of

Montréal to Toronto

locks and canals linking Lake Ontario and Georgian Bay can be seen in the north on Trent River. The building of this complex system commenced in 1835. Look south and see Lake Ontario. The train follows the shorelines straight into Toronto.

Mile 264: Cobourg
Cobourg originated in 1798 when the Loyalists established this area calling it Amherst. This small community excelled as a business location for farming. In 1819, the town's name changed to Cobourg and it grew to be one of the most significant cities in Upper Canada. Victoria Hall was erected to celebrate the success of this lucrative town. Cobourg almost collapsed, however, with the failure of the railway. The town picked up pace again when affluent American tourists sought out this location as a lovely place to build their mansions. Today, Cobourg owes its economy to a sundry of industries.

Mile 270: Port Hope
Port Hope is the most well-preserved city in Canada. It has managed to maintain a sturdy and clean 19th-century streetscape adorned with over 250 perfectly preserved heritage buildings. The station stops a little ways out of town but it provides a suitable indication of what the rest of the city must look like. Aesthetically pleasing to the eye!

Mile 302: Oshawa
This city is where General Motors of Canada is centred. GM was the most principled employer for this town and after years of repressive working conditions, the workers revolted by spurring a major strike. GM workers solidified ties with the United Automobile Workers (UAW), a union allied with the Committee for Industrial Organization (CIO), an American-based organization. The workers won the strike and became a leading force in Canadian labour.

Mile 313: Nuclear Power Station
One of the world's largest natural uranium nuclear plants, Pickering Nuclear Generating Station can be seen across from Frenchman Bay.

Mile 333: Toronto
Home to approximately five million people, Toronto is the largest Canadian city, and the nation's epicentre for most Canadian corporations. Toronto's suburbs sprawl for miles, supporting the city's position as the industrial headquarters for the country. The 1970s underwent a dramatic growth in the population when English-speaking people and corporations fled the province of Québec after numerous heated situations involving the language and culture debate.

Right: Toronto Union Station main entrance.

ROUTE GUIDE | 207

Toronto to Ottawa

The Ottawa Valley Route: Brockville to Ottawa.

Toronto to Ottawa

The Toronto to Ottawa route offers a quick, seamless link to Canada's capital city of Ottawa, the political seat, to the nation's economic capital city, Toronto.

One of its heaviest rail traffics, VIA Rail deploys over 25 schedules per week to service this route, passengers of which are mostly business travelers and tourist types setting out for some cosmopolitan leisure.

Majority of trains on the Toronto-Kingston-Ottawa pause along important stations that include Fallowfield, Guildwood, Oshawa, Brockville and Belleville, among others, with one train extending all the way to Oakville and departs every morning.

Useful Facts

» Trains depart in the morning, midday and in the evening, departing from Toronto to Ottawa.

For a comprehensive route guide per mile between Toronto to Brockville, refer to the Montréal to Toronto route guide on pages 204-206. Before Mile 125 in Brockville, the train to Ottawa will turn north.

Brockville Subdivision
Brockville to Smiths Falls

1 Mile 27.6: Brockville
Also referred to as the City of Thousand Islands, Brockville thrives

ROUTE GUIDE | 209

TRAIN AT A GLANCE

Route	Distance	Travel Time	Lowest Available Fare	Classes of Service	
Toronto – Ottawa	446 km	4.5 hrs	$71	Comfort	VIA 1

on a riverside industry, courtesy of the St. Lawrence River, where down under, sunken shops provide an unusual tourist attraction. Year-round river tour boats take tourists on a riverside coasting. For the daring pack, embark on an underwater adventure to see numerous sunken ships below the river, an exciting itinerary offered by some diving operators in the area.

② Mile 1.2: Rideau Canal

The Rideau Canal is the oldest canal system in North America which opened in 1832 and is continually in use up to this day. Originally conceived to be a Canadian stronghold from the threats of the United States, the British government commissioned Liuetenant Colonel John By (after whom the old name Bytown was named) to build a waterway linking Upper and Lower Canada.

From the thick wilderness and marshes of Kingston and Ottawa, By and his men laid the waterway system on a 126-mile stretch and came up with one of the strongest and most efficient canals in the world, with 23 stations and 47 locks. Recently, in 2007, the Canal was proclaimed as a UNESCO World Heritage Site.

③ Mile 1: Hershey's Plant

Look east to see the Hershey factory. Built in 1963, the factory in the Smith town is the first to be built outside the town of Hershey in Philadelphia. Tourists can have their fill of all the chocolatey goodness while inside a viewing area where they can watch popular Hershey's chocolates being made. Then, have a bite of those mouth-watering products from the Hershey's Chocolate Shoppe and grab a bagful to bring home as delectable souvenirs.

Smiths Falls Subdivision
Smiths Falls to Federal

④ Mile 0: Smiths Falls East

The Smiths Falls is a bustling town for industries like electronics, machines, food and beverage. It was named after loyalist Major Thomas Smith, but it was not until 1826 when settlement and expansion of the area began under Abel Russel Ward. This period marked the construction of the Rideau Canal, now a historical site and a major tourist attraction.

Brockville station, Ontario.

The Toronto to Windsor Train passing by the CN Tower.

Toronto to Windsor

The Toronto-London-Windsor route is a popular choice for business trips as well as a brief visit to Toronto, given the city's dense traffic spawned by the influx of commercial activities, notably finance, telecommunications, transportation, tourism, sports, arts and media, among others. The Toronto Film Festival brings large tourist traffic every season.

The trains run southwest along Toronto up to the Ontario peninsula through major stations in Oakville and Aldershot. Other connecting tracks include Brantford, London and Chatham. Access to the U.S. border is facilitated in Windsor.

Useful Facts

» Travelers crossing the Canada-U.S. border must purchase their tickets at least nine (9) hours before departure to ensure they are included in the Customs list of passengers bound for the U.S.

Oakville Subdivision
Toronto to Bayview

① Mile 1.1: Fort York
Look south to see historic Fort York. To the south is the scene of a bitter battle on April 27, 1813, between the defending garrison and 1,700 American invaders.

This site was built in 1793 as a fortress for the provincial capital of York town from imminent American attacks. Eventually, York was attacked on several occasions, the most destructive of which was on April 27, 1813, when British

ROUTE GUIDE | 211

The Tecumseh Route: Toronto to Windsor.

TRAIN AT A GLANCE				
Route	Distance	Travel Time	Lowest Available Fare	Classes of Service
Toronto – Windsor	359 km	3.5 hrs	$57	Comfort VIA 1

retaliation caused the death of many American soldiers and destroyed the fort. In 1814, the site was rebuilt and has since withstood the test of time.

② Miles 2-3: Canadian National Exhibition

We pass the Canadian National Exhibition, the world's largest annual fair, which has attracted millions of visitors since it began in 1879. It is held in Toronto in late August and early September.

③ Mile 5: Grenadier Pond

The water is Grenadier Pond, a well-stocked, big-city fishing hole, after crossing the Humber River at Mile 5.

④ Mile 7: GO Trasit

This mile is home to the provincial commute network GO Transit since 1967, providing passengers with a smooth

Branford Station, Ontario.

transfer to and from Toronto and Oakville in its bi-level cars.

5 **Mile 13.3: Credit River**
Watch for many activities on the river including fishing and racing sculls.

6 **Mile 16: Sixteen Mile Creek**
Anticipate an exciting train ride over a 49-metre bridge built above Sixteen Mile (or Oakville) Creek.

7 **Mile 25.9: Twelve Mile Creek**
Get a grip as the train crosses a towering bridge 550 feet tall at a height of 75 feet below. Along the stretch, one can see the Hamilton Harbour with various vessels dotting the ocean. More interesting landmarks are in store for passengers bound to Niagara Falls. Refer to page 220.

Dundas Subdivision
Bayview to London

8 **Mile 0-19: Royal Botanical Gardens**
Revel in acres of lushness as the train passes the Royal Botanical Gardens. Tilt on the south for a view of the Desjardins Canal. The train gathers momentum to crawl up the Niagara Escarpment, a challenging section of tracks that was once a pit of marshes. Getting through it, the train reaches Dundas town and its valleys reflecting the vast skyline.

9 **Mile 18.6: Fairchild Creek**
Fairchild Creek is crossed on a 594-foot trestle running 65 feet above the valley floor.

10 **Mile 23: Brantford**
Brantford is famous as the place where Alexander Graham Bell worked on his invention, the telephone, in 1874, and made the first long-distance call in 1876. Bell's home is now a museum. Other Brantford attractions include the

ROUTE GUIDE | 213

Chapel of the Mohawks and Chiefswood, birthplace of Indian poet Pauline Johnson. Meantime, the imposing, high-ceilinged Brantford station built in 1904 is thought to give birth to the first sleeping car designed by Thomas Burnley in 1859 and used by the Prince of Wales in his 1860 tour. Burnley's claim, though, was never formalized as he was unable to patent his design.

Mile 29: Photo Opportunity
A sweeping curve between miles 29 and 31 affords superb views of Paris and the Grand River.

Mile 30: Photo Opportunity
The train crosses the Grand River 100 feet below through a sturdy bridge. A waterfalls on the south breaks the sweeping view. Take note of sulphur springs and deposits of paris, where the town of Paris got its name.

Mile 34: Woodstock Station
After crossing the Nith River, the train comes to several interesting buildings, including St. Paul's Church with its ominous bell tower, the nearby courthouse decorated with carvings of monkeys and a revered statue of a cow, and the two-storey Woodstock station built in 1853. A little farther is the old Ingersoll station. The cheese town of Ingersoll is best remembered for exporting a huge 7,300 pounds of cheese to England in 1866. The train then crosses the Waubuno River with villages whose streets and structures are reminiscent of English and Irish names.

Strathroy Subdivision
London to Komoka

Mile 0: London
Nestled between Lake Erie and Lake Huron lies London town, a bustling business centre that is also the seat of trade and politics.

214 | Toronto to Windsor

Many educational and medical institutions are also found here. Balancing the modern city pace is a backdrop of productive farmlands on the northern and southern parts, including Canada's tobacco and other main crops. The train passes a bridge at miles 0.4 and 1.4 across the Thames River.

13 **Mile 27: Glencoe**
The Glencoe station, with its 1890s-inspired architecture, is also the stopping point of Canada's Air Line Railway. It made its mark as the unfortunate site where Jumbo, the 13,000-pound elephant of P.T. Barnum,

Below: London Station, Ontario.

crashed with a locomotive in September 1885. From here, the train makes its final crossing of the Thames River at Mile 47.6.

14 **Mile 60: Chantam**
Chantam served a lofty purpose known as the Underground Railroad where American slaves were transported to freedom by abolitionists. The place thrives in agriculture, marred occasionally by heat waves. In July 1936, a fatal heat wave struck Chantam, with temperature reaching a scorching 45 degrees.

15 **Mile 76: Lake St. Clair**
The Lake St. Clair is a paradise in its own right, blessed with the longest growing season in Canada. Fragrant wheat and corn fields, vegetable crops, precious vineyards and tracks of fruit orchards thrive alongside the peaceful terrains of this land, also aptly called the Sun Parlour Country. On the south, the Jack Miner Sanctuary provides shelter for migratory birds while various greenhouses are abuzz with exotic plant culture.

16 **Mile 76: Windsor Station**
The Windsor Station is built on the distillery town of Walkerville, on the busy Detroit River which is a major international shipping hub then and now. The station played a major role in the peak of the Canadian liquor trade, after the U.S. imposed sanction on liquor shipment. The original station was built on what is now the Dieppe Gardens, where one can still see the old steam locomotive 5588, the Spirit of Windsor. On this site, the trains hulled to Detroit via the Lansdowne ferry, which can also be seen today as part of a dining complex in the area.

216 | Toronto to Sarnia

The International Route: Toronto to Sarnia.

Toronto to Sarnia

The Toronto to Sarnia line is a swift and comfortable journey through Toronto's southern suburbs and surrounding areas all the way to scenic Sarnia, the famed city in southwestern Ontario popular for summer outdoor entertainment.

\multicolumn{5}{c}{**TRAIN AT A GLANCE**}
Route	Distance	Travel Time	Lowest Available Fare	Classes of Service
Toronto – Sarnia	290 km	2.5 hrs	$49	Comfort

Weston Subdivision
Toronto to Halwest

1 Mile 9.6: Humber River
The train crosses the Humber River. Look south here for views of the Weston Golf and Country Club.

2 Mile 13.5: Woodbine Racetrack
Home to the best-loved English royal sport, the Woodbine Racetrack continues to hold the annual Queen's Plate since its first run in 1860. A quick change of pace and you can see Canada's Lester B. Pearson Airport. The journey takes on

busy industrial villages then pulls into Mile 14, the Halwest junction.

Halton Subdivision
Bramalea to Silver

3 Mile 15: Brampton Station
Brampton lives up to its name as the "Flower Town," with a flora variety growing from large greenhouses as vast as 24 football stadiums. The Brampton station retains its old-world charm with 18th-century architectural features like turrets and arches.

4 Mile 22.5: Credit River
This time, the train crosses an old limestone bridge over the Credit River. The Limehouse quarry was the source of limestone for tough structures, like the bridge built in 1857 as well as the Georgetown station itself. At this point, passengers are advised to grip to their seats tighter as the route to Toronto could be a challenging test of endurance.

Guelph Subdivision
Silver to London Junction

Mile 33: Photo Opportunity
Welcome to the picturesque Credit Valley and revel in the place's bevy of colours akin to fall season.

5 Mile 41: Eramosa River Valley
Here, the train crosses a 532-foot bridge over the Eramosa River Valley. Attractions include the boarding school Rockwood Academy for boys and on the south, the original Canadian National (CN) station.

6 Mile 48.5: Guelph
At this point, the train moves forward to Guelph, a city of Scottish and English immigrants, by crossing a 493-foot bridge over the Speed River. Don't miss the recharging site of a power dam on the north, as well as a park where the old CN locomotive 6167 is grounded.

7 Mile 58: Grand River Crossing
The Grand River is crossed on a 413-foot bridge.

8 Mile 62: Kitchener
Kitchener is famous for the annual Oktoberfest celebration, with overflowing beers and music lasting for several days. It is also home to delectable sausages and pies from the popular Kitchener farmers' market. On the road, one may also sight an Old Order Mennonite, whose ancestors founded the town in 1799, wearing their old costumes and going about their daily tasks in horse-drawn carts. The Kitchener station retains its red brick structure from 1897.

9 Mile 69: Petersburg
Interesting landmarks include Baden, where Sir Adam Beck who was credited for the idea of electric-powered railways, was born; and the Amish community of New Hamburg, where each year, a Mennonite Relief Sale is held. Pass along the Punkeydoodles Corners, a community of a mere 14 people but turns alive one special day in June when thousands of visitors participate in frog jumping competitions, and join a unique Post office festivity to mail letters stamped with odd postmarks.

10 Mile 75: Nith River Crossing
The highest milk-cow-producing region in North America, the Nith River Crossing is a fertile dairy and agricultural region. Don't miss a hillside tunnel where delectable cheeses are aged.

Toronto to Sarnia

11) Mile 88: Stratford
The old brick station on Shakespeare Street is an introduction to the theatrical air that permeates Stratford. A short distance away is the Shakespearean Festival Theatre, nestled on the shore of picturesque Lake Victoria, where in 1952, the first Shakespearean production, Richard III, starring Sir Alec Guinness, was held.

12) Mile 99: St. Mary's Junction
The old limestone station at St. Mary's Junction was where Thomas Alva Edison conceived some of his greatest inventions while working as a night operator in 1863. He was eventually given the pink slip when, immersed in thought perhaps, two trains nearly collided while he was on duty.

At this point, the train turns southward to Mile 119, Dundas Subdivision and passes through London.

Strathroy Subdivision
London to Sarnia

13) Mile 9.8: Komoka
The train enters the Komoka Station located in the Community Centre, home of the Komoka Railway Museum

14) Mile 11: Trout Creek Crossing
The train crosses an 805-foot bridge below Trout Creek, then heads to St. Mary's Station, on a land owned by the town butcher whose name was, incidentally, Mr. Bone. The town came to life when the railway was erected in 1858. One of the villagers' first pursuits was the construction of a limestone opera house where a lavish production of "Ben-Hur" was staged.

15) Mile 26: Fanshaw Lake
Fanshaw Lake and on its shores, Fanshaw Pioneer Village, containing many restored pioneer buildings.

16) Mile 46.3: Petrolia
This point marks the birth placae of Canada's rich oil depot in Ontario. Oil yields in the area spurred interest among capitalists who financed the construction of a railway spanning five miles. In 1858, the first commercial well in North America was explored in Oil Springs. Measuring a mere 14 feet deep, the well yielded 60 barrels of oil a day. Bigger oil explorations soon followed.

17) Mile 59: Sarnia
Around the 1830s, Sarnia was called The Rapids and was predominantly a centre of forestry merchandise. By 1858, when a railway was constructed and the oil explorations peaked, Sarnia's economic pace stirred and is now home to various big petrochemical companies.

The Sarnia to Toronto route is where Thomas Alva Edison sold newspapers to passengers before he worked as one of the rail's night operators. Not to be missed is the St. Clair Tunnel on the western side, considered as among the longest submarine links in the world. Measuring 6,025 feet, it links Canada to the United States.

ROUTE GUIDE | 219

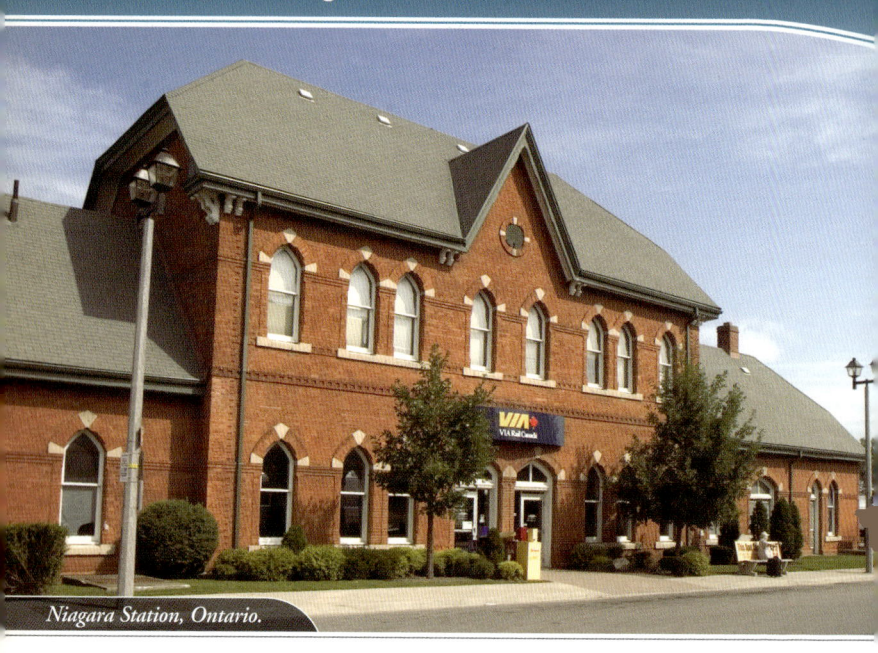

Niagara Station, Ontario.

Toronto to Niagara Falls

This route takes passengers from Canada's largest metropolis city, Toronto, to the country's most acclaimed tourist destination, the majestic Niagara Falls. This route also travels through Oakville, Aldershot, Grimsby and St. Catharines. Morning and late-afternoon departures run from each destination daily.

Be advised that the morning train departing Toronto carries on to the U.S., traveling through Buffalo and into New York. Returning from New York, the train leaves in the morning and arrives into Toronto by early evening.

Useful Facts

» The train leaves Toronto and Niagara Falls three times a day during the summer months.

TRAIN AT A GLANCE

Route	Distance	Travel Time	Lowest Available Fare	Classes of Service
Toronto - Niagara Falls	132 km	2 hrs	$21	Comfort

ROUTE GUIDE | 221

Map Symbology
- The Maple Leaf Route
- Trans Canada Highway
- Major Road
- Rivers
- Photo Opportunity
- City/Town
- Provincial Border
- Major Airport

The Maple Leaf Route: Toronto to Niagara Falls.

The train sets pace in Union Station in Oakville Subdivision, Toronto. Refer to pages 210-212 for route details. The route turns southward after passing Bayview Junction and heads to Grimsby Subdivision.

Grimsby Subdivision
Hamilton to Niagara

Mile 37.6: Photo Opportunity
Look east here for a sweeping view of Hamilton Harbour.

① Mile 38: Dundurn Castle
Set your view on the imposing Dundurn Castle, a testament to the frivolous lifestyle of the former president of the Great Western Railway, Sir Allan Napier Macnab. Completed in 1835 and covering 18,000 square feet, the castle in its heyday boasted of convenient innovations like pipeline water system and gas-powered lights in its 72 rooms. Today, the City of Hamilton owns the estate and has spent millions in dollars and years of meticulous restoration to bring back the old glory of the mansion, which is now an interesting tourist attraction.

② Mile 37: The Niagara Peninsula
Welcome to Niagara Peninsula, the heartland of Ontario's wine industry and a major fruit-producing zone. Treat your eyes to sights of bounty with heavily-laden vineyards and orchards along the way. Modern agricultural methods in Grimsby, which used to be a resort haven with its strategic lakeside location, spurred productive industries like packing, canning and winery.

Dundurn Castle.

Toronto to Niagara Falls

③ Mile 17.7: Twenty Mile Creek Crossing

The train takes a turn for the Twenty Mile Creek over a bridge measuring 1,170 feet erected above 75 feet of water. On the north, a lake view of the CN Tower can be seen. Farther is the Sixteen Mile Creek at mile 15.8, with a waiting bridge standing 57 feet high.

④ Mile 11: St. Catharines

A 512-foot bridge carries trains 94 feet above Twelve Mile Creek, with views of the city to the north.

Each year, wine enthusiasts and bohemian types flock to St. Catharines in the Niagara region to take part in three wine festivals held every major season of the year – winter, summer and fall. Just ask the locals simply where the "Grape and Wine" festival is and you are sure to join in the frolicking in no time.

⑤ Mile 9.9: Welland Canal Crossing

The Welland Canal is a series of canal systems spanning a total of 43.5 kilometres and crosses over the stretch of the Niagara Peninsula, bypassing both Niagara River and Niagara Falls, from Lake Ontario to Lake Erie. The first section was eight feet deep, made from timber locks and was completed in 1829. Improvements like larger locks and stronger materials were incorporated in the second canal which opened in 1845, on the third segment which opened in 1887, and the fourth canal which opened in 1973. These canals can be fully viewed upon crossing.

⑥ Mile 8.5: Lock Four

The train crosses the Welland Canal on lock four over a draw-bridge. Watch out for colourful sails and ships down below.

⑦ Mile 7.7: 3rd Canal Crossing

The train crosses the 1842 canal on a 540-foot bridge.

Mile 5: Photo Opportunity

Look north between Miles 5 and 3.5 for views of Lake Ontario.

⑧ Mile 2: Queenstown Power Plant

Pay respect to the 8-and-½-mile Queenstown Power Canal which transported water from the Upper Niagara River to power the town's generating plant and spurring industries. On this town, a railway station stood as legacy of dependable electric locomotives that worked nonstop to build the structure. These machines still serve their purpose to this day in a nearby ore smelter.

⑨ Mile 0: Niagara Falls Station

Prepare to meet face-to-face with the fabled Niagara Falls. At this point, the train crosses the 1,082-foot bridge some 250 feet below the swift currents of the Whirlpool Rapids. Turn your sight to the south and there in all its glory is the 176-foot-high and 2,200-foot-wide Niagara Falls. This is the site of the world's first suspension bridge built in 1848. Over the years, the bridge was modified to accommodate heavier trains and frequent routes. The Niagara Falls is prone to dare-devil jumping acts of the likes of Sam Patch, who tried in 1829 to conquer the height by jumping, and circus mainstay Blondin who crossed the Niagara Gorge on a tightrope in 1859. Both survived and inspired offshoot performers, until 1912, when such acts were prohibited by law.

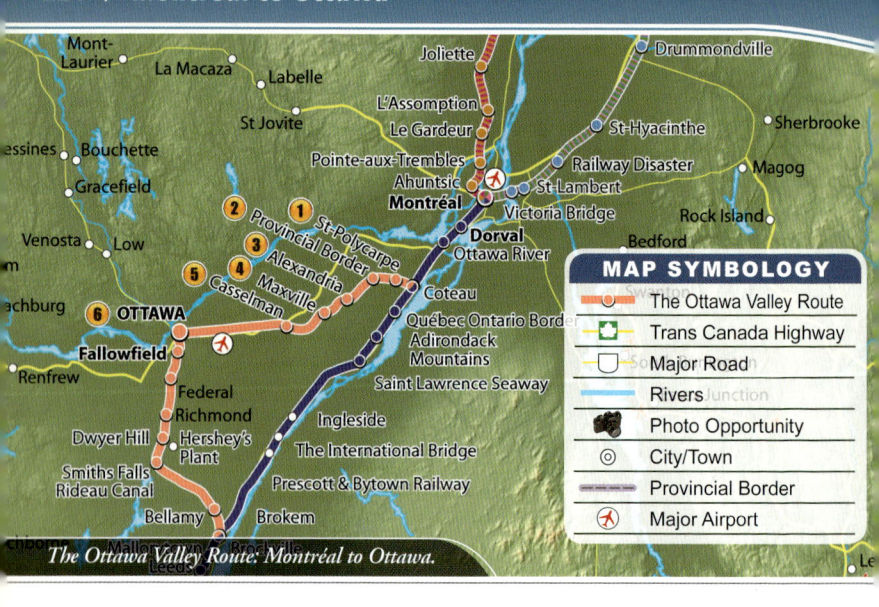

Montréal to Ottawa

VIA Rail's Montréal-to-Ottawa route is easily the smartest and most convenient way to reach Montréal, Dorval, Alexandra and Ottawa, as train travel spares the passenger from relentless bottlenecks along the busy circuits. It also provides the best protection against severe cold in the winter and the muggy heat of summer. An added treat is the complimentary shuttle bus service going to the Pierre Elliot Trudeau airport.

TRAIN AT A GLANCE					
Route	Distance	Travel Time	Lowest Available Fare	Classes of Service	
Ottawa - Montréal	187 km	2 hrs	$29	Comfort	VIA 1

Useful Facts

» The voyage takes approximately two hours with up to 30 departures leaving either destination weekly.

From the Coteau Junction, the train travels northwest en route to Ottawa. A comprehensive guide by routes from Montréal to Coteau Junction is found in the Montréal to Toronto route guide on pages 203-204.

Alexandria Subdivision
Coteau Junction to Ottawa

1. Mile 4: St-Polycarpe

Look west to see the stone church and the town of St. Polycarpe. A parish town in the 18th century, the present-day St. Polycarpe is situated in Route 340 and now occupies a stretch in Autoroute 20, making it a quaint landmark dividing Montréal and Toronto.

2. Mile 13: Provincial Border

Mile 13 marks the Québec-Ontario border.

3. Mile 23: Alexandria

Alexandria is home to some interesting religious architecture like the Bishop's Palace, Monastery of the Precious Blood and St. Finnan's Cathedral. The priest Alexander Macdonell was credited for founding the town by starting a mill which spurred manufacturing. For a time, the Roman Catholic diocese resided in Alexandria before it was transferred to Cornwall.

After the Depression and the war years, Alexandria regained its economic hold with flourishing agricultural and manufacturing industries like dairy, textile and machinery, sustaining many farm communities around it. In 1998, Alexandria became a part of the North Glengarry township, populated in part with many French Canadians.

4. Mile 34: Maxville

Maxville, so named due to the proliferation of "Macs" in Scottish highlands surrounding it, began as a quiet town in 1869. In 1881, it was awakened by the construction of a railway station that spurred small industries. However, things did not stir much and up to this day, Maxville provides nearby farm communities with merchandise and services.

Maxville officially became a part of the North Glengarry township in 1998, and is the place where valued Scottish practices are held like the annual Glengarry Highland Games. About 20,000 visitors converge in Maxville every summer for this event, which began in 1948.

5. Mile 47: Casselman

The town of Casselman can be seen as the train crosses a four-span bridge over the South Nation River. The place boasts of an early sawmill built in an adjacent area by Martin Casselman, after whom

⭐ Largest Skating Rink

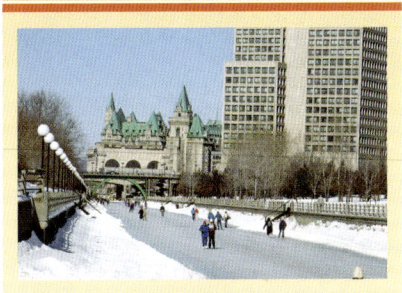

A long stretch of the Rideau Canal transforms into the world's largest skating rink during wintertime, where tourists can sashay in a massive snow rink equivalent to 90 Olympic-size hockey rinks. The spot runs from Carlton University in Hartwell all the way to the Chateau Laurier, stretching some 7.8 kilometres.

This area becomes alive with the annual Ottawa Winterlude Festival, where people can go food-tripping on various kiosks along the snowy playground.

226 | Montréal to Ottawa

the town was named. A water and sewerage system soon followed.

6 Mile 76.5: Ottawa Station
Take a breather in Ottawa Station, built in 1966 and was awarded a Massey Medal for Architecture in 1967 for its exceptional design. Originally, trains in Ottawa would traverse Union Station, but this stopped with track changes built to accommodate the scenic Colonel By

Drive. Today, Ottawa station is a busy hub of passengers aboard VIA Rail's inter-city trains plying Toronto and Montréal. Foot traffic combines in an adjoining structure, the OC Transpo's Trains station. There are no trains though, but buses stopping on transit for passengers bound for the suburbs on the east or on the city centre.

Below: Canadian Museum of Civilization.

Montréal skyline.

Montréal to Québec City

Swiftly, the Montréal-Charny-Québec City train transports passengers from downtown Montréal to central Québec City. If detraining destination is Charny station, the Montréal-Percé-Gaspé or Montréal-Halifax trains can be taken. This train ride is a perfect way to bear witness to Canada's rich French-Canadian culture.

TRAIN AT A GLANCE					
Route	Distance	Travel Time	Lowest Available Fare	Classes of Service	
Montréal - Québec City	272 km	3.5 hrs	$42	Comfort	VIA 1

⭐ Useful Facts

» Travelers will enjoy a smooth ride of approximately three hours, with the choice of up to three or four departures a day in either direction.

Note: The Montreal-Quebec train and the Ocean follow the same track between Montreal and Charny. The route is covered on pages 259-261.

ROUTE GUIDE | 229

The Québec City Route: Montréal to Québec City.

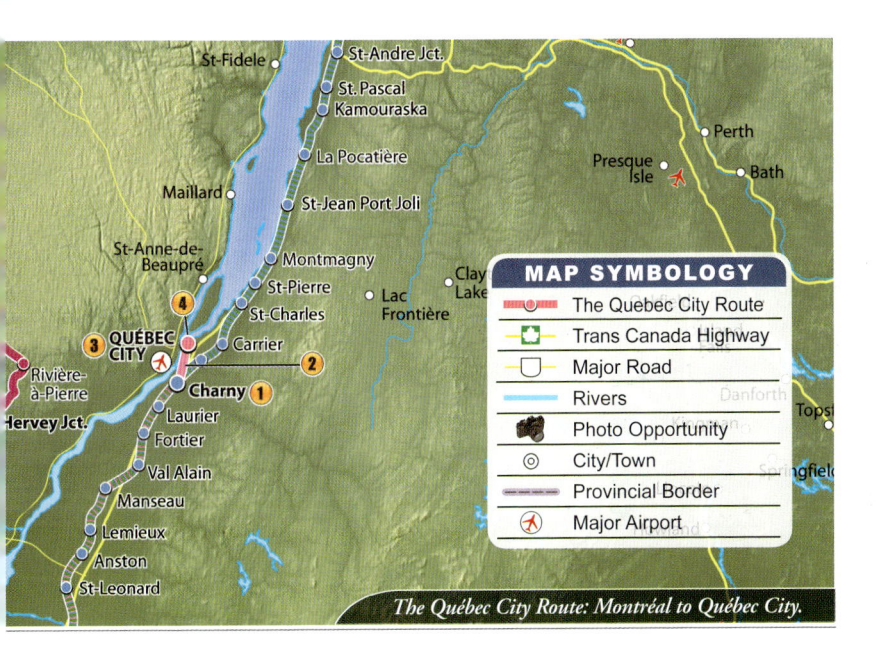

① Mile 0.3: Charny Station
The train pulls from the station to Charny town, signaling a shorter journey toward Québec City.

② Mile 1: Québec Bridge
Get another dose of bridge ride, this time on the picturesque Québec Bridge and towards the east side, a glimpse of Québec City not too far away. After crossing the bridge, the train heads west along the river path and pulls off at Mile 3.6, the Sainte-Foy station.

③ Mile 11: Québec City
The air gathers historical mist as everyone prepares to enter the old walled Québec City.

④ Mile 15: Gare du Palais
The train takes another cut to the St. Charles River en route to the Gare du Palais station.

⭐ Québec City

Québec City, the capital of Québec Province and seat of politics and commerce, was founded in 1608 and is considered one of the oldest cities in North America.

Rich in history with its fortification preserved to this day, the walled Old Town of Québec City takes pride in being declared a UNESCO World Heritage Site in 1985.

The Chaleur crossing a bridge enroute to Gaspé.

The Chaleur

The Chaleur is undoubtedly a beautiful rail route along the Gaspésie. Leaving Montréal by evening, the train unassumingly passes through several small towns and faithfully arrives at the Baie des Chaleurs by morning. The Chaleur reaches Gaspé the next afternoon after traveling 1,041 km. Traveling together, the Chaleur and the Ocean pass through the south shores of the St. Lawrence, the Matapédia Valley and finally to Baie des Chaleurs where they fork away to complete their independent routes.

The Gaspé Peninsula was a bustling area before Europeans established their towns. For 6,000 years prior to Jacques Cartier's supposed discovery of the New World, the Micmac natives lived in this region. The arrival of Basque whale hunters and Viking seafarers preceded the arrival of Jacques Cartier who declared that the uncharted territory of the peninsula belonged to him. Eventually, the British claimed this area in 1763 and an influx of Irish, Scottish and American settlers soon followed. These were the beginning stages of developing a multicultural nation.

It was surprising that this route was constructed at all. The remote terrain without the opportunity for industry provided this rail route with no benefits. The run was referred to as "the railway to nowhere." Gaspé was its terminus and it also proved to be an unprofitable port. Fortunately, tourism resuscitated this route from disaster. The Baie des Chaleurs became one of the most spectacular vistas in all of Atlantic Canada.

ROUTE GUIDE | 231

The Chaleur Route: Montréal to Gaspé.

MAP SYMBOLOGY
- The Chaleur Route
- Trans Canada Highway
- Major Road
- Rivers
- Photo Opportunity
- City/Town
- Provincial Border
- Major Airport

TRAIN AT A GLANCE					
Route	Distance	Travel Time	Lowest Available Fare	Classes of Service		
Montréal - Gaspé	1041 km	16 hrs	$96	Comfort	Comfort Sleeper	Romance by Rail

Useful Facts

» The Chaleur leaves Montréal on Wednesdays, Fridays and Sundays. From Gaspé, the train leaves on Mondays, Thursdays and Saturdays, taking up to 16 hours.

» It passes through dozens of small communities including the attractive village of Percé.

» The train arches along the south shorelines of the St. Lawrence River and into the pristine Matapédia valley, reaching the Baie des Chaleurs by early morning.

After reaching Matapédia, the Chaleur continues north beside the Gaspé Peninsula. The route from Montréal to Matapédia can be referred on The Ocean's route, on pages 255-261.

Cascapedia Subdivisionn
Matapedia to Newcastle

① Mile 35: Nouvelle
Welcome to the world's second largest fossil site! The Miguasha National

The Chaleur

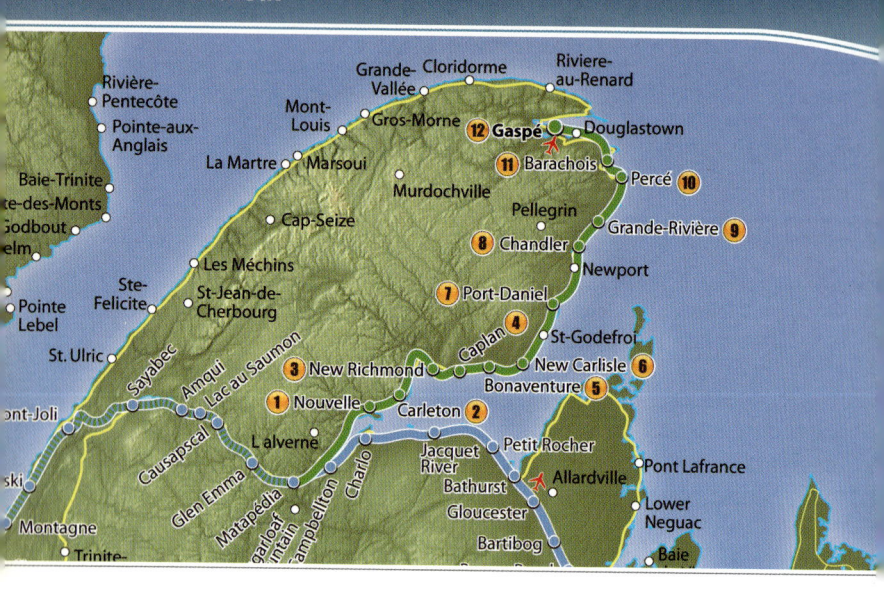

Park encompasses one of the most significant palaeontological sites in the world. The coast of the Gaspé Peninsula discloses an appropriate indication of what life may have been during the Devonian period. Approximately 370 million years ago, the Gaspé Peninsula was an exceptionally sultry habitat bearing life to primitive fauna, spiders, scorpions and fish. Several fish specimens were preserved and fossilized including the lobe-finned fish. The lobe-finned fish is particularly important because this species is suspected to have evolved as amphibians, giving rise to the first four-legged land creatures. UNESCO recognized this area as being a world heritage site in November 1999.

② Mile 26: Carleton

Victims of the Acadian expulsion in 1755 established this town in 1756. It attracted other Acadians and remains to possess a strong Acadian kinship today. This lovely town of 4,200 inhabitants is stretched along calm waters and exquisite sandy beaches.

③ Mile 0-22: New Richmond

The name of this town reveals its strong ties with the English. After the Conquest, English settlers started to trickle into this desirable region. United Empire Loyalists, Scottish, British and Irish immigrants gravitated to this ideal region to develop a solid Anglo-Saxon community. This is evident in the architecture and the quaint Protestant churches. This well-kept municipality has 4,000 inhabitants.

④ Mile 0-78: Caplan

Travelers interested in observing marine bird species will be delighted by this quaint sea village. Caplan is a vacation hot spot for locals and travelers up from the U.S. Resorts are dotted along the pristine clean beaches. This small town of 2,100

The Chaleur making its way through the verdant plain of the Maritimes.

residents was founded on the north shore of Baie des Chaleurs in 1875. Legend has it, that Caplan was denominated after a small fish.

5. Mile 87: Bonaventure

Predominantly Acadian, this small town of 2,900 residents has a sundry of charming waterfront resorts and bed & breakfasts. The Musée Acadien du Québec and the Bioparc is also located here.

6. Mile 98: New Carlisle

After the Versailles Treaty in 1783 declaring America as an independent state, United Empire Loyalists migrated to this region to establish New Carlisle. René Lévesque, a previous Québec Premier, was born in this small sea town. New Carlisle is home to 1,500 residents.

West Chandler Subdivision
New Carlisle to Chandler East

7. Mile 0-22 Port-Daniel

Port-Daniel is a typical Canadian sea-side town of 2,900 residents. Renowned for its long, sandy, smooth shores, locals and vacationers alike flock to these beaches to enjoy a delightful family picnic followed by a refreshing swim. Railway buffs have the option to see the Cap de L'Enfer (Cape Hell), a railway tunnel passing through 190-metres of rock.

East Chandler Subdivision
Chandler East to Gaspe

8. Mile 44: Chandler

Chandler is a port town whose industry is predominantly paper. It exports blank newspaper used for distribution in North America and Europe. Chandler has 3,360 inhabitants.

9. Mile 54: Grand Rivière

Located in the centre of the Gaspé region, Grand Rivière is the largest town within this region. The 3,800 residents admire the pristine vista overlooking Baie des Chaleurs.

234 | The Chaleur

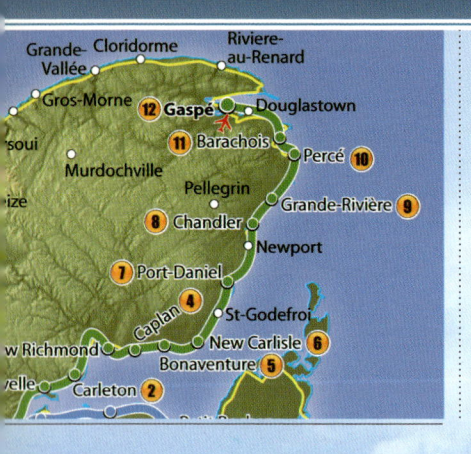

10. Mile 65: Percé

Percé is a premium location for aspiring ornithologists. Home to a bird reserve, visitors can bear witness to the homestead of at least 200,000 birds of various species. A venture into the Parc d'Ile-Bonaventure-et-du-rocher-Percé for a nature excursion is a preferred pastime of the locals. Percé is an enchanting sea-side village, revealing rustic abodes festooned with elaburate well-kept gardens. The infamous Percé Rock is a must see!

Below: Percé Rock is one of the largest natural arches in the world.

⑪ Mile 79: Barachois

Pockets of small villages dot the coastlines leading up to Gaspé. Barachois is one such small town founded by small Loyalist or British immigrant enclaves. Its name which originated from 'barre à choir' means a 'sand bar where ships were beached ashore.' The charm of this town is dimpled by St. Mary's Church built in 1895. This quaint community amalgamated with Percé and has 381 residents.

⑫ Mile 104: Gaspé

At the tip of the Gaspé Peninsula, Jacques Cartier declared possession of Canada in the name of Francois I, the King of France in 1534. There is a statue commemorating Jacques Cartier at the Musée de la Gaspésie. Gaspé, the largest urban centre along the Peninsula, is within close proximity to the Forillon National Park. Outdoor admirers are enthralled with the hikes offered alongside the coastline, and the spectacular vistas from the tops of cliffs. "Harmony between land, man and sea" is the motif representing the mountainous National Park. Amidst the isolation of the forests, a small succession of buildings is erected at Grande-Grave. The buildings are in excellent condition as they originally belonged to Anglo-Norman immigrants. Gaspé is a small finger of land encompassed by serene and rugged Atlantic waters. The Micmac, who inhabited these regions for thousands of years before the Europeans settled in the area, named the peninsula Gaspé, meaning 'land's end.' Some 6,000 people reside here.

The Saguenay

Enjoy a small quaint train voyage into Québec's northern districts. The train winds its way through forests, lakes, bed & breakfasts and inns. The terminal destination point is Jonquière, a mid-sized city approximately 500 km north of Montréal.

This train route is the most natural way to discover rural Québec. The special stop request applies to passengers desiring to be let off at an unscheduled stop, a quintessential feature for nature lovers who want to explore the Canadian wild. It also takes the passengers over the country's most elevated trestle bridges and through the second longest tunnel in Canada.

The train travels 510 km between Montréal and Jonquière. This adventure displays cascading waterfalls, whitewater rapids and countryside cottages tucked under sheltering woods. It traverses the metropolitan area of Montréal and streams through the St. Lawrence River Valley to Lauaudiére. The train then proceeds to La Mauricie, Haute Mauricie, Lac St. Jean and towards the Saguenay region.

⭐ Useful Facts

» The Saguenay leaves three times a week, leaving Montréal on Monday, Wednesday, and Friday mornings, arriving in Jonquière in the late afternoon.

» Trains departing Jonquière leave on Tuesdays, Thursdays, and Sundays.

ROUTE GUIDE | 237

Route	Distance	Travel Time	Lowest Available Fare	Classes of Service
Montréal – Jonquière	510 km	9 hrs	$50	Comfort

The Saguenay and the Abitibi travel on mutual tracks between Montréal and Hervey Junction before the Abitibi continues west to Senneterre, visiting La Tuque and Parent along the way.

St. Laurent Subdivision
Taschereau Yard to Pointe-aux-Trembles

1) Mile 127.8: Point-aux-Trembles
This delightful Montréal suburb was established in 1905 and amalgamated with Montréal in 1982. Primarily a residential town, Pointe-aux-Trembles is located on the eastern tip of Montréal. When Jacques Cartier set foot onto the New World, he was ultimately enamoured with the resplendent display of this region's conifers. Consequently, he named this area 'Point-Aux-Trembles,' translated as 'points of aspen' in 1535. Upon departing the metropolis of Montréal, passengers witness Le Gardeur Bridge on the east side of Rivière des Prairies. The train proceeds into the district of Lanaudière where the internationally acclaimed singer, Céline Dion, grew up.

Joliette Subdivision
Pointe-aux-Trembles to Garneau

2) Mile 122.3- Le Gardeur
Le Gardeur is the last concentrated urban area before traveling through Québec's fertile landscapes. This town was established in 1857 and was referred to as Saint-Paul L'Ermite. In 1978, the town was denominated as Le Gardeur and now has 18,000 residents. Le Gardeur is home to SNC Industrial Technologies specializing in manufacturing arms.

3) Mile 117.4: L'Assomption
The First Nations initially utilized this region as a portage trail. Then in 1724, the Seigneurie Saint-Pierre-du-Portage-del' Assomption was established. Sir Wilfrid Laurier, the lionized Prime Minister on the $5 bill, attended college in this town before becoming one of Canada's most well-loved leaders. This town of 16,000 residents is located on a curve of the L'Assomption River.

4) Mile 101.9: Joliette
Established by Barthélémy Joliette in 1864, this town inaugurated the second extension of the Canadian railway. Currently, with 18,000 residents, Joliette is home to Québec's longest natural skating rink stretching nine kilometres along the L'Assomption River. Annually, Joliette hosts an esteemed festival of classical music. Live performances by internationally-acclaimed musicians play on Joliette's open-air amphitheatre. The acoustics are breath-taking, ethereal and pristine. A must-see for classical music lovers!

5) Mile 49.5: Shawinigan
This city founded in 1901 has

The Saguenay

earned the reputation of being the 'City of Lights' or the 'City of Energy.' This is the hydro-electric spearhead for the entire region. The St. Maurice River is the world's most yoked river equipped with nine hydroelectric dams stretching a distance of 523 km in length. These towering hydroelectric dams are approximately 115 metres tall, the equivalent height of a 38-storey apartment complex. Shawinigan has 53,000 residents and attracts thousands of visitors each year who come to marvel at the colossal man-made dams. This city was originated in 1901, and acquired its name from the Algonquin term for 'portage on the crest.' This name makes reference to the several waterfalls here before the construction of the dams. Shawinigan is also home to one of Canada's most respected Prime Ministers, Jean Chrétien.

Mile 44: Grand-Mère
Thanks to the presence of a rock shaped as an old woman's head, this town acquired its name. The Algonquin appreciated this peculiar phenomenon and named the rock 'kokomis,' meaning 'old lady.' This town was established in 1898 and the French admired this natural wonder and continued the tradition by naming the town 'Grand-Mère,' translated as 'grandmother.' Since then, the rock has been moved and is now conserved in a city park. Grand-Mère is also home to Canada's first suspension bridge. Owing much of its economy to the pulp and paper mill located here, the town continues to flourish.

Lac St. Jean Subdivision
Garneau Yard to Jonquiere

Mile 7.3: Saint-Tite
Renowned for its Western Festival, this town attracts 400,000 visitors, approximately 100 times its population every year in September. Its rodeo, parade, savoury food, and "cowboy-related" activities prove to be an adventurous experience for pleasure-seekers of all ages.

Mile 18.7: Hervey-Jonction
This tiny town of 300 inhabitants is the point in which the Abitibi and the Saguenay part ways to continue on their independent journeys. The station, constructed in 1905, is the track junction for trains traveling from Montréal on their way to Québec City, and Lac St. Jean for the Saguenay route and towards Haut-Saint-Maurice for the Abitibi route. Shortly after departure, passengers are released into the remote areas of Québec's wildlife.

Mile 39.9: Rivière-À-Pierre
Outdoor thrill-seekers will probably want to be let off in this small town. Rivière-À-Pierre is a desired destination for advanced white water rafting. Intermediate white water rafters have

called this region 'Hell's Gates.' After an invigorating day of being tossed about on the rapids, cyclists can hop on a bicycle and follow the 68-km Jacques-Cartier/Portneuf bicycle trail. The terrain follows alongside Québec's most sublime white water rivers. The voyage is both exciting and demanding; don't forget to secure your safety helmets. This small village fringing the entranceway to the Portneuf Wildlife Reserve engages in one of the most lucrative granite exports in the world.

10 Mile 59:1 Miquick

Renowned for exciting kayak and canoe excursions, this town means 'Bear' in Algonquin. Beware!

11 Mile 61.9: Linton

Linton was once a dominant railway transfer spot from La Tuque to Québec City. It is now considered an abandoned railway ghost town. On the southwest side of Batiscan, passengers can peer at the dilapidated remains of an old railway bridge. While traveling alongside the river, rock climbers may be seen scaling the steep cliffs above the swirling, perilous rapids of the river.

12 Mile 69.9: Pont-Beaudet

Pont-Beaudet was the initial command post for the construction of the railway in 1886. The Windsor Loghouse was the meeting place for railway innovators, entrepreneurs and suppliers to meet and discuss efficient methods of building the railway. Pont-Beaudet had a small general store, one farm and the necessary equipment needed to get the job done. The town was simple; it meant business.

13 Mile 90.7: Club Triton

A.L. Light, the leading engineer of the railway construction, established the Triton Fish and Game Club in 1893. Renowned politicians such as Winston Churchill and various U.S. presidents frequented this spot as a brief getaway from their demanding positions. Currently, it is one of the most prestigious fishing destinations in the world, attracting affluent sport fishers. Remote, private and safe lodging is available in a 50-room five-star hotel located in the dense brush. Arrival to this vacation destination is by boat only. Travelers may also enjoy a visit to the Innusit Village offering overnight accommodation in authentic teepees.

14 Mile 95.3: Lac Éduoard

This serene lake is the headwaters for the Batiscan and Jeannotte Rivers. When tuberculosis was a rampant disease in the late 1800s and early 1900s, Lac Éduoard institutionalized a sanatorium for those suffering with the disease. Those with the disease were quarantined and segregated from the rest of society. Today, however, this region is riddled with vacation resorts and lodgings for travelers wanting to experience the remote outdoors.

15 Mile 106.2: Summit Club and Summit

Welcome to the resort country! Resorts are erected at an altitude of 446 metres. The view of the lake and wooded area from the large bay windows of these resorts are stunning. Three water basins are located in this area: the St. Maurice River (Bostonnais), Lac St. Jean (Métabetchouane River) and the St. Lawrence (Batiscan River).

16 Mile 143: Lac Bouchette

This small town of 1,500 residents was founded in 1882. Since 1907, the lake has been a renewal and pilgrimage centre

The Saguenay

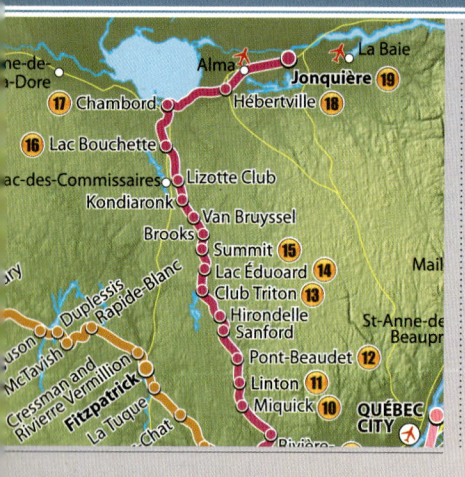

where people can go on cleansing retreats. The establishment called L'Ermitage Saint-Antoine-de-Padoue also offers lodging. Also located on the lake is Centre Vacances-Nature (The Nature-Vacation Centre).

Mile 159.5: Chambord
Established in 1857, this small town located on the entrance to Lac St. Jean has a small population of 1,800. Chambord attracts geological enthusiasts who are free to explore 11 caverns filled with diverse fossils and hydrologic wonders.

These caverns comprise 700 metres of passageways zigzagging through the earth.

18 Mile 181.4: Hébertville
With a small population of 3,900, this town became the spearhead for agriculture and colonization for the Lac St. Jean region after it was established along the fur trade passage.

19 Mile 201.5: Jonquière
After its establishment in 1847, Jonquière merged with Chicoutimi, becoming the city of Saguenay with a population of 153,000 people in 2002. This is the Saguenay train terminus. The economy remains strong, thanks to its industries of paper mills and aluminum smelter. This lively northern city boasts of an exciting nightlife. Saguenay is famous for showcasing events continuously throughout the year. Saguenay is the entertainment haven for those excited by festivals and huge productions.

242 | The Abitibi

The Abitibi Route: Montréal to Senneterre.

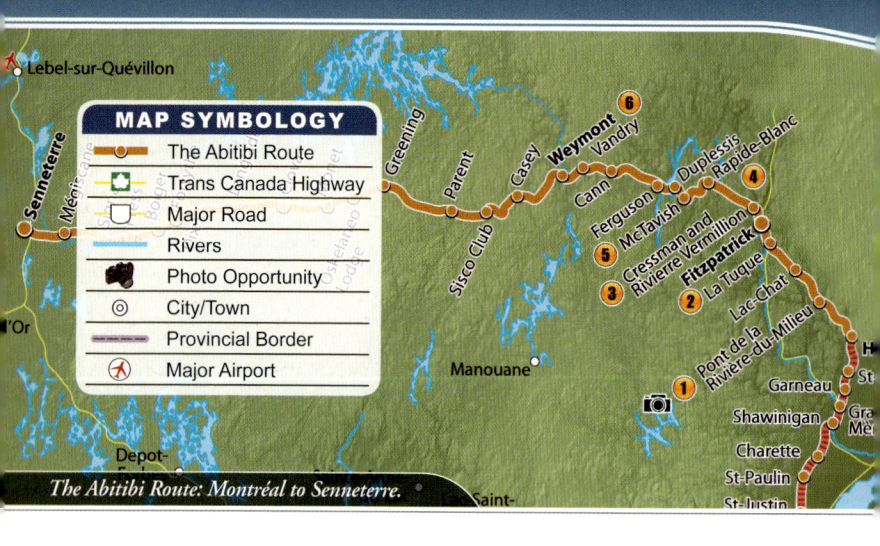

The Abitibi

The Abitibi is another train exploring the picturesque charm of northern Québec. Traversing through La Tuque, Sanmaur, Parent, Clova and Senneterre, the passenger is certain to admire the charming layouts of northern Québec communities. The request of an unscheduled stop is a privilege for passengers who prefer to step off and explore unfamiliar Canadian terrain.

The Abitibi share the same tracks with the Saguenay until it forks off to continue its northbound journey to Haute Mauricie and Abitibi. This route takes the passengers through charming towns with densely wooded areas, remote lakes and character cottages. The Abitibi is the ideal journey to explore the authentic lifestyle of French-Canadian culture.

⭐ Useful Facts

» The Abitibi departs Montréal on Monday, Wednesday and Friday mornings, arriving in Senneterre by early evening. It leaves Senneterre on Tuesdays, Thursdays, and Sundays.

TRAIN AT A GLANCE				
Route	Distance	Travel Time	Lowest Available Fare	Classes of Service
Montréal - Senneterre	717 km	11.5 hrs	$74	Comfort

The Abitibi and the Saguenay utilize the same tracks between Montréal and Hervey Junction. The Saguenay continues north to Jonquière/Chcoutimi and the Abitibi carries on east to Senneterre. Prior to 1996, these trains were night trains. Now, the lovely rustic ambience of East Coast culture is accessible to observe and enjoy.

Reference to the Abitibi train route from Montréal to Hervey Junction is also covered in The Saguenay route guide on page 237-238.

La Tuque Subdivision
Hervey Junction to Fitzpatrick

1 Mile 96: Pont de la Rivière-du-Milieu
Discover Québec's highest railway bridge. Pont de la Rivière-du-Milieu translates as 'middle river bridge' in English. The bridge is over 60 metres high and stretches across 121 metres. Be advised: Those suffering from fear of heights should close their blinds. It crosses the Milieu River and enters the Haut-Saint-Maurice district.

2 Mile 122.2: La Tuque
La Tuque was established in 1911 because of a hill that uncannily resembled a fluffy woolen hat. Sadly, in 1940 this hill was somewhat obliterated by dynamite explosion during the construction of the Tuque Dam. This town initially attracted several families because of its large pulp and paper mill established by the Brown brothers from New Hampshire. The pulp mill continues to be a prosperous industry as it currently employs 800 people. La Tuque is the gateway to several premium hunting, fishing and outdoor locations, and it hosts "Classique Internationale de Canots de la Mauricie," an internationally renowned canoe race. Originally, this region was a fur processing post. La Tuque was an ideal location as it was situated at the base of four waterways channeling in different directions.

3 Mile 12.9: Cressman and Rivierre Vermillion
Here, the train crosses a distinguished bridge. Look to the south and bear witness to a waterfall spilling from the source. According to First Nations history, this waterfall marks the spot where several Iroquois drowned after pillaging the Algonquin.

4 Mile 20.4: Rapide-Blanc
Rapide-Blanc is a particularly small village that was a makeshift community for the men constructing the Rapide-Blanc Dam in 1934. Today, the nearly abandoned town has a few chalets for travelers wanting to vacation in remote areas.

5 Mile 38.7: McTavish
The town of McTavish was almost completely wiped out from the flooding caused by the construction of the Rapide-Blanc Dam. After departing, the train travels down the middle of the river on a raised bridge made of rock. It gives the passengers the sensation of skimming across the water.

6 Mile 67.9: Weymont
This town is a small Atikamekw community of Algonquin roots residing on the side of the mountain. The name of this town of 1,150 inhabitants translates as 'mountain vantage point' in the regional language. In 1997, the residents of Weymontachie were forced to evacuate because of an impending forest fire. Fortunately, the fire changed its direction to the northwest only a few metres before the flames licked the first homes.

244 | The Lake Superior

The Lake Superior Route: Sudbury to White River

MAP SYMBOLOGY
- The Lake Superior Route
- Trans Canada Highway
- Major Road
- Rivers
- Photo Opportunity
- City/Town
- Provincial Border
- Major Airport

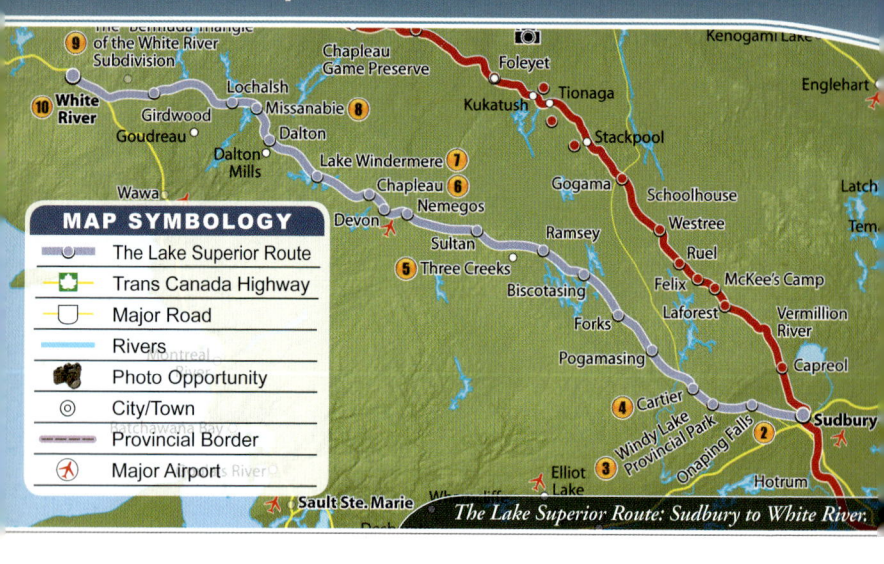

The Lake Superior

Take a break from Ontario's urban landscapes and ride the Lake Superior. Yes, Ontario does have isolated regions brimming with nature!

Usually a precarious region to travel through during Ontario's arduous winter months, the Lake Superior safely carries passengers through thick forests and over meandering rivers to Sudbury and White River. Stopping in Cartier and Franz, the Lake Superior also encourages outdoor enthusiasts to request special stops wherever desired.

Useful Facts

» The trains leave Sudbury on Tuesday, Thursdays, and Saturday mornings at 9:40 a.m. arriving in White River at 18:00.

» The Lake Superior departs from White River on Wednesday, Friday, and Sunday mornings at 9:30 a.m. arriving in Sudbury at 19:00.

Cartier Subdivision
Sudbury to Cartier

1. Mile 79: Sudbury
Greater Sudbury is now considered the biggest city in northeastern Ontario and the seat of government and business. Many professional services thrive in the area including medicine, education and media. Turn your view to the north as the train moves on for a glimpse of the Sudbury Arena, while over the south is the INCO smokestack, the tallest smokestack in the world, towering at 1,250 feet high.

2. Mile 101: Onaping Falls
Catch a view of the Onaping Falls, where the refreshing sight of white water compensates for the rugged terrains on the way.

ROUTE GUIDE | 245

TRAIN AT A GLANCE				
Route	Distance	Travel Time	Lowest Available Fare	Classes of Service
Sudbury - White River	494 km	9 hrs	$53	Comfort

3 Mile 103-105: Windy Lake Provincial Park
South between Mile 103-105 is Windy Lake Provincial Park.

4 Mile 113: Cartier
Thank God for the Cartier landmark, where the train is a salvation to the isolated communities in far-flung areas along the railway.

Nemegos Subdivision
Cartier to Chapleau

5 Mile 77-94: Three Creeks
Refresh your eyes with the sights of three creeks along the way, beginning with Bowen Creek (Mile 77), the Woman River (Mile 86) and further along at Mile 94, the Walkami River.

6 Mile 136: Chapleau
Time for some fresh air as the train pulls over to Chapleau Station, where passengers can do some leg stretching in the Centennial Park right behind the station; and admire the old CPR steam locomotive 5433 exhibited here.

White River Subdivision
Chapleau to White River

7 Mile 15-27: Lake Windermere
The train moves on toward the stirring sights of Lake Windermere, coasting along Miles 15 to 27.

8 Mile 57: Missanabie
Set trail in Missanabie, an old community where quaint cottages on Dog Lake shore served as a resting place for trail adventurers bound for James Bay. Some of these cottages are still in use today.

9 Mile 107: The "Bermuda Triangle" of the White River Subdivision
This mile is of interest as site of a few infamous incidents that earned it the monicker 'Bermuda Triangle' of the White River Subdivision.

In the 1950s, a man named Buddy Weedon mysteriously disappeared while on his way to close his cabin. Only his wallet was found since. A decade earlier, camp owner Jack Hargass was found murdered in this area by two men who were overheard discussing the crime they committed. Justice was served when a watch certified to be owned by Hargass was found in the criminal's possession. Bid adieu to this eerie site at Mile 110 at Negwazu Lake.

10 Mile 129: White River
Welcome to White River, the home of Winnie The Pooh, the popular bear cartoon character in books and television. Inspiration for the famous bear began in 1914 when a White River resident Captain Harry Colebourne bought a trapped bear cub which he named after his hometown of Winnipeg. On the economic front, White River thrives on forestry and logging, where most of the locales work in timber sites for spruce, fir, pine, birch and other trees.

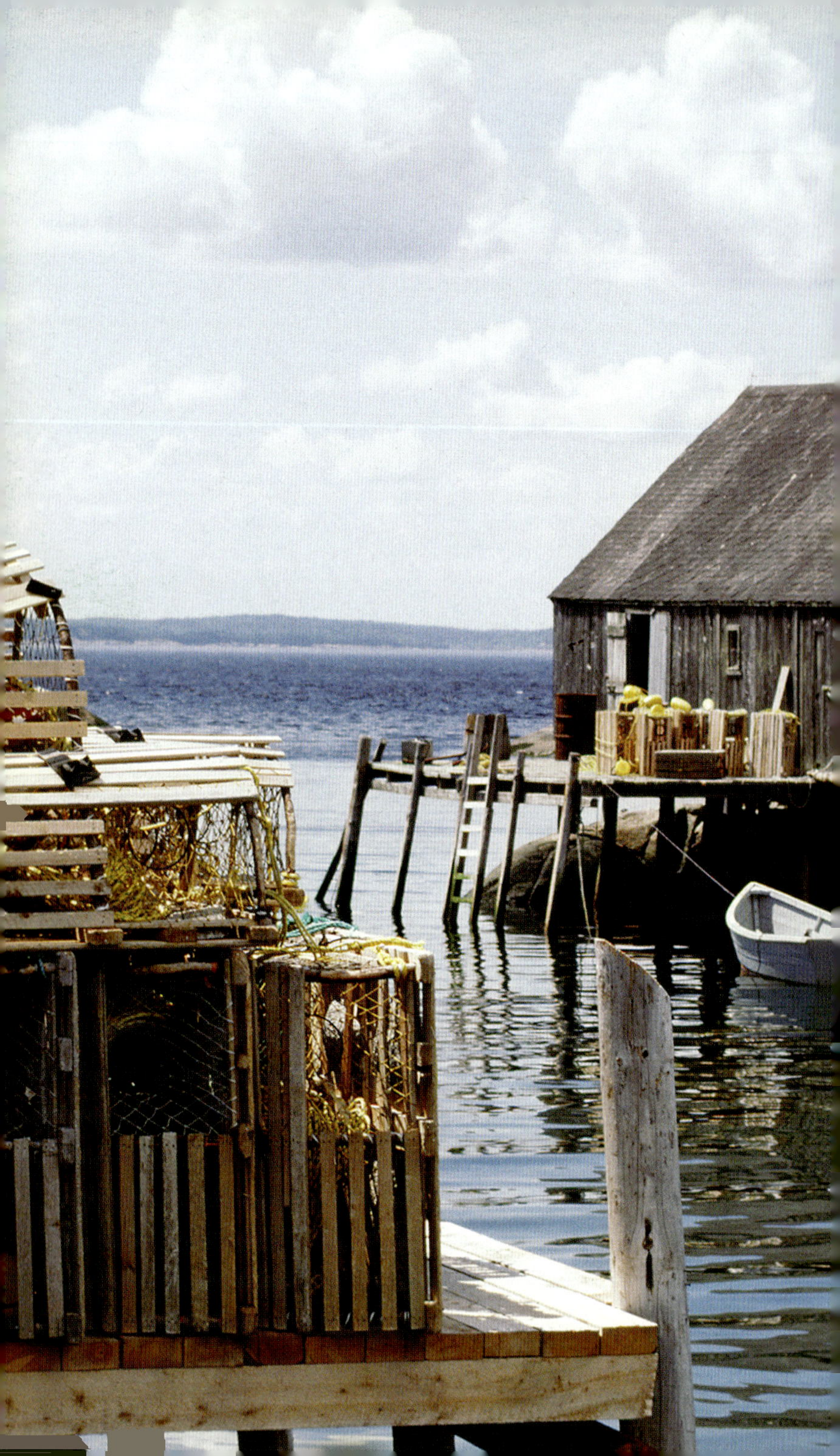

ATLANTIC CANADA

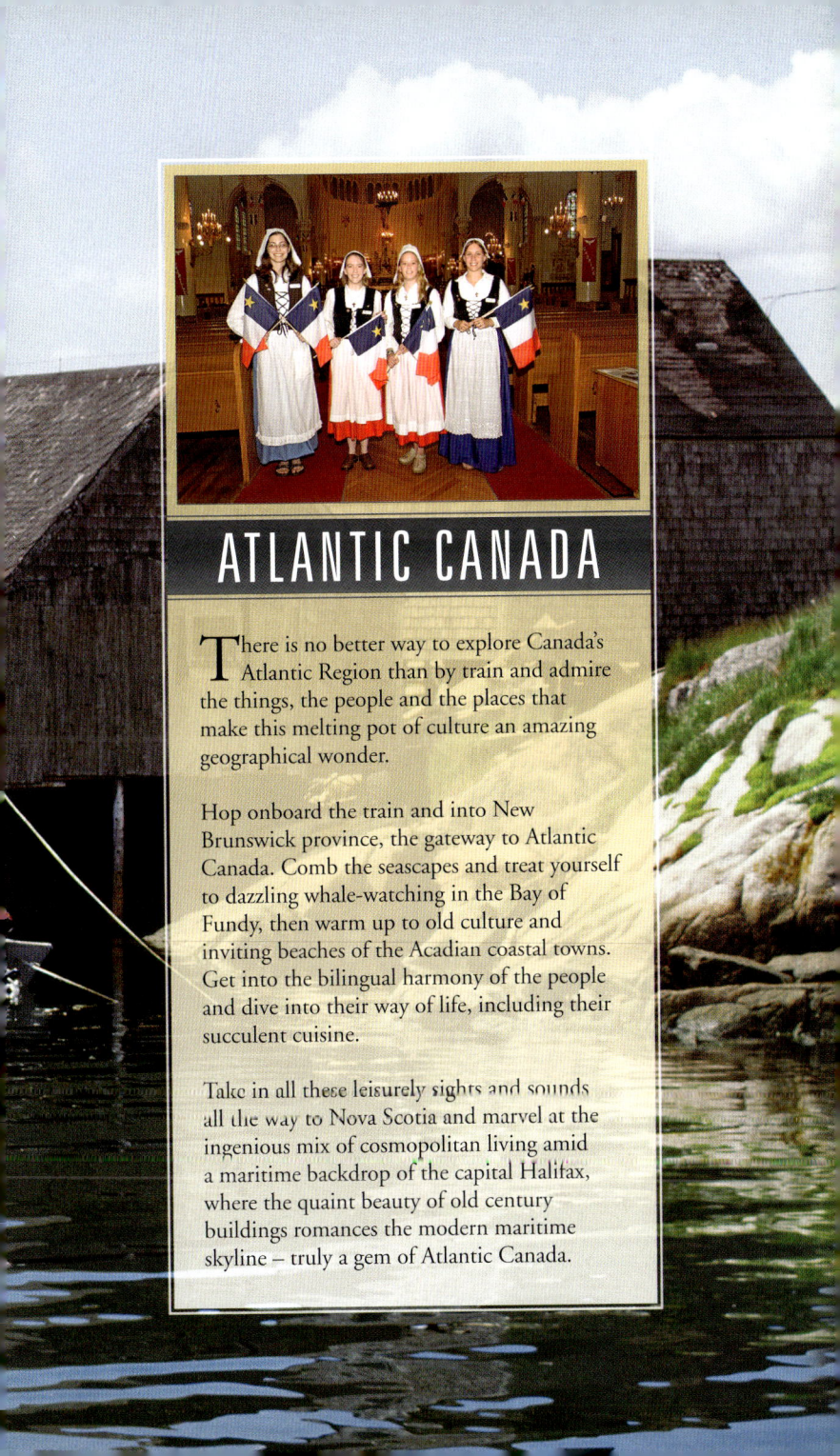

There is no better way to explore Canada's Atlantic Region than by train and admire the things, the people and the places that make this melting pot of culture an amazing geographical wonder.

Hop onboard the train and into New Brunswick province, the gateway to Atlantic Canada. Comb the seascapes and treat yourself to dazzling whale-watching in the Bay of Fundy, then warm up to old culture and inviting beaches of the Acadian coastal towns. Get into the bilingual harmony of the people and dive into their way of life, including their succulent cuisine.

Take in all these leisurely sights and sounds all the way to Nova Scotia and marvel at the ingenious mix of cosmopolitan living amid a maritime backdrop of the capital Halifax, where the quaint beauty of old century buildings romances the modern maritime skyline – truly a gem of Atlantic Canada.

The Ocean travelling through beautiful autumn coulours of eastern Canada.

The Ocean

The second longest-running train in Canada, the Ocean was named for the run that followed from Montréal to Halifax. The rail line following the St. Lawrence River and the Gulf of St. Lawrence to the Atlantic was built by the Intercolonial Railway.

Maritimers were not especially keen on having the railway because they felt it was an inducement to join Confederation. Canadian railways at this time were saturated and unprofitable. Therefore, Maritimers believed the route would not pay its way. Nonetheless, the rail line was built in 1904 and has been operating ever since.

Halifax rail yards were the busiest in Canada during World War II. This was the terminus for troops and military equipment to be transferred onto ships to cross the Atlantic. The route commences in Montréal and travels 1,346 km (836 miles) through quaint communities along the Lower Saint Lawrence, down the Matapédia Valley, traversing New Brunswick and on to Nova Scotia.

TRAIN AT A GLANCE						
Route	Distance	Travel Time	Lowest Available Fare	Classes of Service		
Montréal – Halifax	1346 km	20 hrs	$120	Comfort	Comfort Sleeper	Easterly

ROUTE GUIDE | 249

The Ocean Route: Montréal to Halifax.

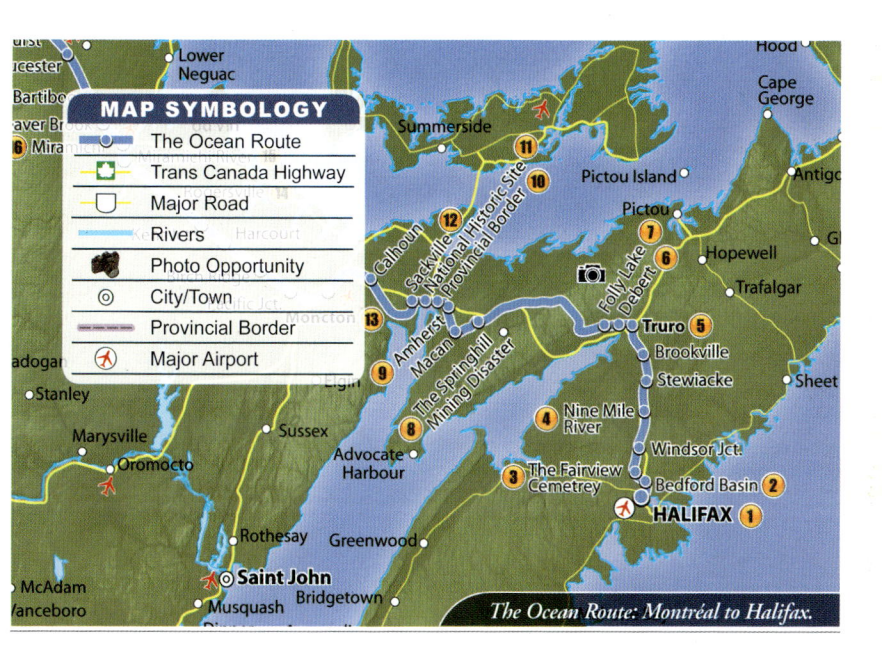

⭐ Useful Facts

» The Ocean departs Montréal in the evening and traverses along the southern shores of the St. Lawrence River. Passengers are greeted by the exquisite sight of the Baie des Chaleurs in the morning.

» The Chaleur and the Ocean share the same tracks until The Ocean breaks away south across New Brunswick to the city of Moncton by noon.

» The train arrives in Halifax by mid-afternoon. It arrives in Montréal Central Station the following morning.

Bedford Subdivision
Truro to Moncton

① Mile 0: Halifax

Welcome to the birthplace of Canada's English heritage. Halifax is a charming city located along the Atlantic's rugged coastline of Nova Scotia. This city is heralded as the most pristine colonial city established in the North Americas. Founded by Britain in 1749, Halifax was the inaugural city for Canada's first parliament. This was ideal because Halifax was home to the world's second most lucrative port. A star-shaped citadel enclosed by Victorian gardens still stands as a reflection of the once regal imperial harbour.

Today, Halifax maintains the position of

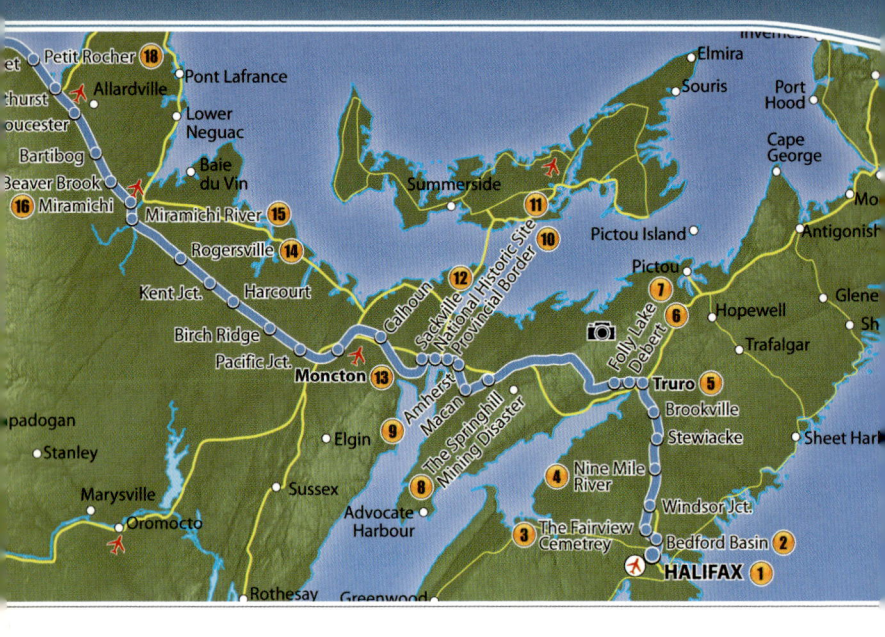

250 | The Ocean

being Canada's largest and busiest port in Atlantic Canada. Home to Dalhousie, one of the most prestigious universities in Canada, Halifax holds the reputation of being a highly-esteemed hospitable city. Halifax has an array of renowned restaurants dotted along the coastlines. Distinguished in the arts, Halifax offers superb live theatre, exciting jazz shows and elegant art galleries. Don't forget to make a trip to the lively pub district after a day of seaside shopping. Stroll down to the piers and take North America's oldest saltwater ferry ride to Canada's Afro-American Culture Museum.

Halifax Station, Nova Scotia.

② Mile 2: Bedford Basin

On December 6, 1917, the world's second largest man-made explosion occurred before the detonation of the first atomic bomb. This tragic accident involved a Norwegian vessel Imo, transporting Belgian supplies, colliding into a French munitions ship, Mont Blanc. The French ship was carrying 5,000 tons of fatal explosives including, benzenes and acids. The crew swiftly jumped onto lifeboats and descended onto the sea, furiously rowing to shore before the explosion occurred. Unfortunately, this did not save the crew members.

The explosion obliterated a whole suburb killing approximately 1,600 people. The impact of the explosion completely leveled the train station and freight trains were shorn apart, traveling up to two miles away. Debris caused serious injuries for residents living four miles away from the devastating eruption. A dreadful blizzard struck that evening, making it difficult for victims to receive emergency help.

3 Mile 4: The Fairview Cemetery

Approximately 125 victims from the tragic 1912 sinking of the Titanic rest peacefully in this cemetery The Fairview Cemetery is also home to hundreds of unidentified victims of the Halifax explosion.

4 Mile 32.4: Nine Mile River

This is home to North America's first iron railway bridge. The durability of this bridge replaced wooden bridges across the country. It was built in 1877

5 Mile 64: Truro

An ideal place for outdoor enthusiasts, Truro offers white water rafting atop the Bay of Fundy, home to the world's highest tides. The Bay of Fundy, around the Salmon River, displays a resplendent show of its tidal shore. Also, twice daily, a strong wave of water from the Bay of Fundy forces upstream on the Salmon River reversing its flow. The famous Stanfield Underwear Company, renowned for inventing cotton stretch knitwear, is located in Truro. This town of 42,000 occupants is referred to as the 'hub of Nova Scotia' because of its reputation as being the central industrial, commercial and shopping area. Offering a variety of delightful restaurants and old heritage colonial buildings, Truro is a perfect town to experience Maritime culture.

Museums of paleontology and geology from the Jurassic and Triassic periods are found in Parrsboro, a town close by.

New Castle Subdivision
Moncton to Campbellton

6 Mile 11-24: Debert

Debert is home to one of the most integral archeological excavation sights in North America. Objects dating older than 11,000 years have been found providing essential information on the life of early Paleo-Indian settlement. Debert was also a significant military base during World War 1.

7 Mile 23: Folly Lake

Watch for wildlife in this area. It is not uncommon to see a bear or moose feeding along the tracks. Folly Lake is a natural phenomenon, created by a melting glacier blocking both ends of a narrow pass. Enjoy the passing forests of beech, birch and maple.

Mile 25-30: Photo Opportunity

This five-mile stretch bears some of Nova Scotia's resplendent beauty. The train zigzags through Wentworth Valley and travels high above the perimetre of Wallace River.

8 Mile 59: The Springhill Mining Disaster

Springhill is home to several unfortunate coal mining accidents. Since 1872, Springhill had been the site of three fatal mining tragedies occurring in 1891, 1956 and 1958. DOSCO forced the mines to shut down in 1958. Many jobs were lost forever because the mines were never reopened. Today the mines are filled with water that provides Springhill's industrial park with geothermal heat.

252 | The Ocean

9 Mile 76: Amherst

Amherst is renowned for its tasteful Victorian mansions and elaborate murals displayed in the business district. Once the railway rolled in, the quiet town of Amherst experienced an industrial boom between 1880 and 1914, bringing prosperity. The land of Amherst, located on the Chignecto Isthmus, was initially established by the Acadians in 1672. This town is in close proximity to the Joggins dinosaur fossil museum. Pack a Maritime picnic and enjoy the warm beaches of the Northumberland Strait. Amherst currently has a population of 12,000.

10 Mile 80: Provincial Border

Nova Scotia and New Brunswick are separated by Missaquash River.

11 Mile 81: National Historic Site

Fort Beauséjour is a historical sight where the French and British battled over the territory. The French built Fort Beauséjour in 1751 as protection against the British who were close by at Fort Lawrence. Fort Beauséjour became rather dilapidated by 1755 when the British and the Massachusetts volunteers invaded it. The French surrendered after two weeks of perpetual attack. The British seized the area, naming it Fort Cumberland, and revitalized the fort.

12 Mile 86: Sackville

Home to 5,393 inhabitants, Sackville is a picturesque colonial town taking pride in its heritage. The town is tastefully designed with arching trees lining the streets, and well-kept yards belonging to charming domiciles. The town attracts several students because of the prestigious Mount Allison University, a reputable post-secondary educational institution. Radio Canada International is also broadcast from Sackville. In seven languages and eight shortwave emitters, this radio station broadcasts the voice of Canada to the world.

13 Mile 125: Moncton

Moncton, with 59,313 citizens, is acclaimed for being one of Canada's bilingual cities. Before the expulsion of the French from Fort Beauséjour in 1755, the Acadians resided along the Petitcodiac River. Shortly after, American settlers established the city in the mid-19th century. Moncton was a flourishing ship-building port and the Intercolonial Railway saw potential for prosperity and constructed a rail route ending in Moncton's ports. This was ideal for importing and exporting goods overseas. Today, Moncton is the second largest city in New Brunswick where Acadians make up approximately 35 percent of its population. Moncton is the epicentre for Acadian culture, and social institutions such as Université de Moncton maintain its predominantly French nature.

New Castle Subdivision
Moncton to Campbellton

14 Mile 44: Rogersville

Rogersville consists of a long stretch of predominantly flat land. The First Nations Algonquin band lived in this territory for several years. In Micmac, the official Algonquin language, this area is named 'Kouchibouguac' which means 'river of long tides.' Tides flow

Amherst Station, Nova Scotia.

ROUTE GUIDE | 253

into the flatlands for several kilometres. Rogersville is home to the Kouchibouguac National Park, founded in 1969. The diverse wildlife and distinguished landscapes are now safely protected from development of any kind. This town is inhabited by 1,340 and provides a tourist information booth for visitors.

15 Mile 62: Miramichi River.

Approximately 217 kilometres long, this river has sustained the people who have lived along the shorelines for hundreds of years. Most renowned for its logging and fishing, the river maintains employment for people living in this region. The Acadian fishermen established their roots in the mid-1700s. English loggers and shipbuilders settled soon after. The Great Miramichi Fire of 1825 swept through this region, demolishing most of the forests. Fortunately, the logging industry survived.

The river was reputable for its abundance of Atlantic salmon. Sadly, the river was over-fished resulting in its drastic decline. The river weaves through the forests of Northeastern New Brunswick and forks west of Newcastle. The chief river flushes out into the Gulf of St. Lawrence.

16 Mile 66: Miramichi

With the union between Newcastle, Chatham and three villages, it is no wonder that Miramachi is home to several ethnic groups. Basque fishermen initially established Newcastle. Soon thereafter, the Scottish and the Irish arrived in droves as shipwrights and lumbermen. In fact, Joseph Cunard, the creator of the Cunard Steamship line, resided here. Each July, Miramichi celebrates its Irish heritage with a festive celebration. The city has

Sackville Station, New Brunswick.

The Ocean

19,240 inhabitants and its resources are primarily fishing and forestry.

(17) Mile 110: Bathurst
Home to 12, 924 citizens, Bathurst is the northern entrance to the Acadian Peninsula located at the mouth of the Nepisiquit River. This area is a common destination for outdoor lovers because of its close proximity to natural sites. Bathurst is the largest city in Northeast New Brunswick and offers services to surrounding towns.

(18) Mile 121: Petit-Rocher
Acadians were the first settlers who were displaced in the 1755 Acadian expulsion. A new settlement was established by Jean Boudreau and Pierre Laplanate in 1797. The new community flourished with farming, fishing and logging as the major resources. The fishing industry supported the economy until the 1960's. Today, employment is located outside of Petit-Rocher and most residents must commute to work. Surrounding mines and paper mills are the major sources of employment for the locals. The Mines and Minerals Interpretation Centre of New Brunswick is found here. Petit-Rocher acquired its French name alluding to a small rock off a headland that sculpts a cove for the town. Every year on August 15th, the Acadians celebrate their national holiday here. Petit-Rocher is home to only 1,966 residents.

(19) Mile 138: Jaquet River
Another charming Maritime community, Jaquet River rests on the Baie des Chaleurs and has only 1, 060 inhabitants. Visitors enjoy the view of scintillating seascapes from bluffs towering from the exquisite clean and remote beaches. Camping in a fully-serviced campground at Belledune is a pastime favourite for locals. Jaquet River is adjacent to the Québec towns of Maria and Carelton.

(20) Mile 154: Charlo
Heralded as one of New Brunswick's

favoured tourist destinations, this town is located on the shores of Baie des Chaleurs. Fringing Des Chaleurs Provincial Park, this quaint village of 1,449 residents offers an array of year-round outdoor activities. Cozy bed & breakfasts and resorts are spread along the boundless beaches, verdant hills, rivers and lagoons. Specializing specifically in tourism, Charlo does not have any major industries. The small town has a regional airport.

21 Mile 173: Campbellton

Campbellton started off as an industrial town shortly after the arrival of the railway. With the establishment of the McLennan Engineering workshops in 1988 and the construction of the Alexander Mill in 1891, this town attracted residents in search of employment. Since then, the town has continued to grow. Today, Campbellton celebrates its long-time relationship with Salmon. Located on the estuary of the Restigouche River, salmon fishing has been a major economic resource for the town. Every year in late June and early July, the town puts on a Salmon festival to celebrate its heritage. Campbelltown has 7,798 inhabitants

Mont Joli Subdivision
Campbellton to Rivière du Loup

22 Mile 0-12: Sugarloaf Mountain

Sugarloaf Mountain may be seen when departing Campbelltown station. Admirers of the outdoors enjoy the year-round activities offered in the Sugar Mountain National Park. During the summer months, hikers can climb the summit of the mountain (1000 ft) and enjoy the panoramic vistas of the Baie-des-Chaleurs, and the Restigouche River. The undulating hills of a far-off Gaspé Peninsula of Québec can also be seen.

23 Mile 12: Matapédia

The Matapédia River, a tributary of the Restigouche River, sculpted a canyon defining the western perimetre of the Gaspé Peninsula. Home to 800 residents, Matapédia is a historic landmark defining the location where the Battle of the Restigouche occurred. In 1760, a French fleet sailing from France to vindicate New France was seized by the English.

Only three ships survived making it to the Baie des Chaleurs. A small museum to commemorate this battle displays an audio-visual representation of the siege.

Saint-André-de-Restigouche, is the location of Fort Listuguj. The fort was used as a dwelling for deported Acadians, French colonists and Micmac to harmoniously live together and fight against English invaders. Today, Saint-André-de-Restigouche is the largest First Nations enclave in the Gaspé area.

24 Mile 47: Causapscal

With 2, 080 residents lumber and salmon fishing are the engines of the town's economy. Causapscal is distinguished for providing some of the best salmon fishing in the world.

25 Mile 55: Lac au Saumon

This area of large open water, referred to as 'Lac au Saumon' is actually a broadening in the Matapédia River. This small district of 1,553 inhabitants was given its name for the vast supply of salmon found in this area. Historic Acadian stylized houses fringe along the banks revealing the homesteads of the first settlers.

26 Mile 60: Amqui

Thanks to the surrounding area of forests and oceans, Amqui acquires most of its income from lumber and fish. This town of 6,473 is internationally-acclaimed as being one of the hottest salmon and trout spots on the Atlantic. Take the chance to peak inside Amqui's tourist centre. The actual building emulates the architecture of the old railway station. Inside, murals showing Amqui's historical heritage are displayed.

Before its harmonious state today, Amqui underwent several conflicts to try to become an independent community. In 1907, the village centre separated from the parish municipality of Saint-Benoit-Joseph-Labre, and selected the name Amqui in 1948. It was not until 1961 that the town was given status and once again joined the parish municipality. Amqui is a Micmac word meaning 'into where one has fun.'

27 Mile 76: Sayabec

Relying predominantly on the forest industry, tourism also provides income into this small town of 2,000 inhabitants. Located between the head of Lac Matapédia and Matapédia Valley, this town provides excellent fishing locations. Sayabec is incredibly self-sustaining, not relying much on surrounding urban centres.

28 Mile 105: Mont-Joli

Mont-Joli is another infamous Canadian town developed because of the railway. The Intercolonial Railway established a run traveling along Mont-Joli in this area fixed on the perimetre of the Lower St. Lawrence and Gaspé regions. It is worth taking a trip to Grand-Métis to discover the radiant Jardins de Métis botanical gardens. Lord Mount Stephen, who acquired his earnings by investing in the transcontinental Canadian Pacific Railway, bequeathed his estate to his niece in 1927. The following year, Elsie Stephen Meighen Reford grew a fertile English-styled garden. She tended and expanded the beautiful gardens until 1959. The government of Québec subsequently inherited the land and divided it into eight distinct styled gardens for public viewing. The gardens have been repurchased and are now tended by Elsie's grandson.

29 Mile 123: Rimouski

Home to 42,000 residents, Rimouski is a Micmac name meaning 'land of the moose.' On May 29, 1914, over 1000 people were killed in the terrible sinking of the Empress of Ireland in the St. Lawrence River. This Canadian Pacific vessel ran between England and Québec City. At Pointe-au-Père, located next to Rimouski, a monument was erected commemorating those who lost their lives. Visit the Musée de la Mer and witness an authentic collection of artifacts recovered from the shipwreck. Close by, a lighthouse is situated at the exact location where the river formally becomes the Gulf of St. Lawrence.

30 Mile 161: Trois Pistoles

According to folklore, a French sailor in the 17th century, was sailing along the river and lost his goblet. The goblet was worth three pistols and was accidentally dropped in the river. This is how Trois Pistoles acquired its peculiar name. This community of only 3,635 is home to a gargantuan church called the Notre-Dame-des-Neiges. The church, completed in 1887, is adorned with three silver-plated bell towers. Visitors enjoy an excursion to L'Ile aux Basques, who in the 15th century discovered this region.

ROUTE GUIDE | 257

Recent archaeological excavation sites disclosed artifacts indicating that Basque fishermen came to this island hunting for whales each year. Remains of ovens were uncovered revealing how the Basque melted whale oil. The Basque made way over the Atlantic 100 years before Jacques Cartier 'discovered' the New World. Today, Trois Pistoles survives by agriculture, forestry and tourism.

(31) Mile 161: Rivière-du-Loup

Locals boast that Rivière-du-Loup displays the second most resplendent sunsets in the world after Hawaii. Visitors are provided with two sunsets per evening. One sun set sinks between two crisscrossing mountains and the other is an exact replication of the first reflecting from the pristine St. Lawrence River. The River is bridged over a 372-foot edifice. This structure is also a spot from where one can see the sublime display of eight waterfalls stretching for over a mile and falling over 300 feet. Coupled with its beauty, Rivière-du-Loup is an urban oasis. This town of 18,000 residents was the epicentre for communications between Atlantic Canada and Québec and home to the most eastern terminus before the Maritimes. Currently, Rivère-du-Loup is the leaving place for the ferry to Saint-Siméon and the entrance for the highway bound for New Brunswick.

Montmagny Subdivision
Riviere-du-Loup to Diamond Junction

(32) Mile 41: La Pocatière

La Pocatière has a national park called 'Montagne du Royaume' located at the centre of the city. The tallest hill ascends 122m and is a perfect destination for exercise enthusiasts. Currently, this town of 5,000 inhabitants is the home to the world-renowned multinational company Bombardier. This enterprise employs hundreds of residents to help manufacture transportation equipment. Bombardier produces subway cars that are distributed to subway systems all over the world. Agriculture is closely associated with the town's history. In 1859, this town inaugurated Canada's first agricultural school and currently has the L'Institut de Technologie Agricole. Visitors may go to the Musée Francois-Pilote, an ethnological museum revealing the rural decline of the 19th century.

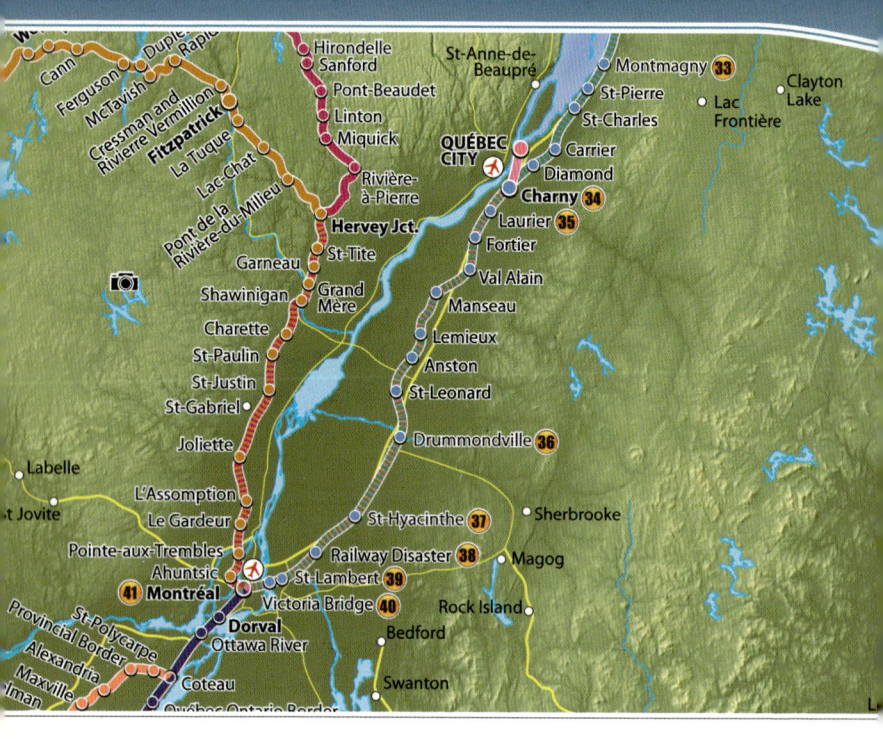

33 Mile 78: Montmagny

Montmagny is a vacation spot for snow geese during their long-winded migration journeys. Bi-annually, these birds fly down and loiter on Montmagny's higher riverbeds. In fall, they fly down from the arctic and stop in Montmagny where there is a bountiful source of food along the riverbeds. Again, the birds settle along the riversides before whisking away up north for the summer. Each year the locals extol the snow goose with the Festival de L'Oie Blanche. Activities includes the observation, interpretation and appreciation of the heritage related to this bird.

Montmagny is not far away from the Irish Memorial in Grosse-Ile. This was the area where immigrants were quarantined to lessen the spread of cholera, typhus and tuberculosis. Between the years of 1830 and 1850, several Irish immigrants fled their nation to escape from disease and famine. Officials forced approximately four million immigrants from 42 differing countries to be quarantined before the Port of Quèbec between the years of 1832 and 1937.

Diamond Subdivision
Charny

34 **Mile 0: Charny**
Thanks to the railway, Charny is another city founded along the tracks. Currently, it is an integral rail centre serving as a confluence point for surrounding destinations. Positioned on the bank of the Chaudière River, the train departs Charny by traversing the river on a 1,000-foot-long bridge. Québec's largest railway hangar is located here. On January 1, 2002, Charny amalgamated with the city of Lévis. The Charny district has 10,661 occupants.

Drummondville Subdivision
Charny to Ste Rosalie

35 **Mile 28: Laurier**
This town was named after one of the most intriguing, gregarious Canadian Prime ministers, Sir Wilfred Laurier. Laurier, Canada's first French-Canadian Prime Minister, worked hard to promote an example of moderate liberalism and understanding. He fervently believed in the importance of national unity and economic growth. He was in office between the years 1886 until 1911. Take a look at a $5 bill; Laurier's profile is determined and focused.

36 **Mile 98: Drummondville**
Each year, the 47,000 residents of this city participate in the July festival Le Mondial des Cultures, celebrating and promoting the diveristy of ethnicities around the world. This spot was a military town on the Saint-Francois River before 1812. After the war between Canada and the U.S., the town of Drummondville was established. Initially a booming town of industry, the innovation of hydroelectric power contributed to the decline in agriculture. Gunpowder and silk fabrication became the leading force for Drummondville's industrial progress. The 1920s proved to be a lucrative decade for Drummondville despite the Great Depression. The textile industry boomed with the founding of Dominion Textile and Celanese. Textiles remained the dominant contributor to this region's economy, ensuring employment for years to come.

St. Hyacinthe Subdivision
Ste Rosalie to Montréal

37 **Mile 41: Saint-Hyacinthe**
This city is the agricultural hub of this region. Settlers discovered the fine quality of the soil in this area and commenced to establish farms. Founded in the late 18th century, this area flourished rapidly, enticing commercial, religious and business organizations. Currently, it is an economic powerhouse in regards to packaging, converting and distributing food. Annually, Saint-Hyacinthe holds an agricultural fair, inviting local and surrounding area farmers to explore and celebrate the joys of cultivation. In 1993, Saint-Hyacinthe became the first Canadian city to be initiated as a member of the International Association of Science Parks.

The Saint-Hyacinthe Seminary is a lovely building heralded for its beautiful stained glass windows. This building holds expositions promoting the religious traditions of the diocese.

38 **Mile 55: Railway Disaster**
One of the most tragic Canadian train accidents occurred on June 29,

1864. After briefly stopping in St. Hilaire Station, the train carrying 475 passengers proceeded forth. The passengers were predominantly immigrants traveling from Québec to Montréal. Most were anticipating going west to start new lives. The train reached a swing bridge one mile ahead and a red light signaled the engineers to stop. The bridge was opened to allow five barges and a steamship to pass. The train continued on and tragically plummeted down the breach and into the water. Ninety-nine people were killed and several were injured.

39 Mile 70: Saint-Lambert
Saint-Lambert is a quiet suburb of Montréal with a somewhat British flair. Anglophones were attracted to this area because of the construction of the beautifully-crafted Victoria Bridge. In 1959, the Saint-Lambert Lock was established, a direct seaway guiding large ships safely along the St. Lawrence River and straight to the engine of North America's industrial capital. This stretch of water starts in Saint-Lambert and follows the river for 3,700km towards the head of the Great Lakes. Approximately 21,051 inhabitants live in Saint-Lambert.

40 Mile 71: Victoria Bridge
Shortly after the train departs from Saint-Lambert station, the train travels over the Victoria Jubilee Bridge. Inaugurated in 1859, the bridge was named in honour of Queen Victoria. Currently, the bridge is referred to as the Victoria Bridge. This was the first bridge constructed to cross over the St. Lawrence River. Crossing the river before this innovation was arduous and trying.

During winter months, depending on the strength of the ice, people had to cross by sleigh. In the summertime, the river was crossed by boats. During the fall and spring months, the river was impossible to cross. During springtime, the ice would break apart causing too many obstructions for boats to pass. In the fall, it was impossible to determine the strength of ice. People had to wait for temperatures to drop well below freezing point. Built between 1854 and 1859, the bridge was officially opened by the

ROUTE GUIDE | 261

Prince of Wales on August 25, 1860. The Victoria Bridge became the longest bridge in the world.

41 **Mile 74: Montréal**
Welcome to Canada's heartland of the arts! This city is brimming with culture, music, art theatre and life. Art is a way of life in Montréal, as opposed to a luxury that appeases the tired mind after a day in the bustling city. Montréal holds 3,300,000 residents and is the meeting place for Québecois, North Americans, Latin Americans and Europeans. Montréal has turned into a cosmopolitan city in the last 100 years. The influx of immigrants from other parts in the world has supplied Montréal with several distinct enclaves of exquisite food and culture. The Italian, Greek, Portuguese and Chinese districts are well worth visiting.

When in Montréal, be sure to revel in the nightlife. Live jazz venues, comedy acts, theatre and dance shows are provided year round. Don't let the cold dissuade you from coming to Montréal; the heat of exciting entertainment will warm the traveler, imbuing them with utmost pleasure. Two exquisite art galleries to attend are La Musée D'Art Contemporain (Museum of Contemporary Art) and The Museum of Fine Arts. There are other Montréal landmark sights: McCord Museum of Canadian History, Mont-Royal Park, the Olympic Stadium and the Montréal Botanical Gardens. Marvel at Montréal's distinct charisma and absorb her youthful charm.

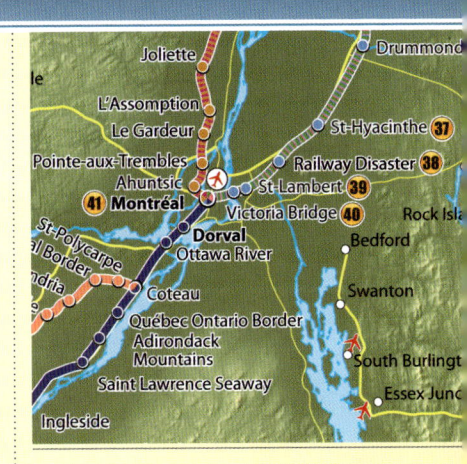

DESTINATION		REMARKS / REMARQUES
*********	PLEASE	
MONTREAL		
OTTAWA		
WINDSOR	PRESENT YOUR TICKET	SOLD OUT/COMPLET
CHECKED BAGGAGE		VIA BRANTFORD LO
MONTREAL	SERVICE PRIOR TO 15	
LONDON		
OTTAWA		
*********	WELCOME TO UNION STATION	*****

APPENDIX

Appendix A: Timetable 262-301
   How to Use The Timetable 264-265
   Western Canada 266-275
   Prairies and Central Arctic 276-277
   Ontario and Québec 278-299
   Atlantic Canada **300-301**

Appendix B: Suggested Itineraries 302-307

Appendix C: Travel Tour Operators 308-309

Appendix D: Overseas Travel Agents 310-311

Appendix E: Railway Lingo 312-315

How to Use The Timetable

The Timetable is a key tool to access comprehensive information per route. Passengers track their trip with reader-friendly train-by-train details: departure time, distance, stopping stations and guide to connecting terminals. Handy signs and symbols steer passengers into a safe trip even before the journey begins.

LEGEND	
🧳	Checked Baggage
★	Stop on Request
◐	Station Opening Hours
✈	AirConnect
NT	Newfoundland Time
AT	Atlantic Time
ET	Eastern Time
CT	Central Time
MT	Mountain Time
PT	Pacific Time

DAYS OF OPERATION	
1	Monday
2	Tuesday
3	Wednesday
4	Thursday
5	Friday
6	Saturday
7	Sunday
x	Except
x6,7	Except Saturday and Sunday
BLANK	Daily

Checked Baggage

Select trains are equipped with baggage cars depending on the route (see Timetable for reference). Passengers are advised to check in big luggage and hand-carry only essential items like purse or briefcase. Baggage check-in procedure is done at the station's check-in counters at least one hour before departure time.

Checked-in baggage is free, provided it complies with the weight limit of 23 kg (50lbs) and size limit of 120 cm (48inches). Surcharge is imposed on items exceeding the limits for each train, but must not go over the maximum restriction of 32 kg (70lbs) weight or 180 cm (72inches) size, except for skis. More information about baggage policy are available at *www.viarail.ca/baggage*.

Stop on Request

Station Opening Hours
Stations open at least half an hour before a scheduled train arrives.

AirConnect
A free shuttle service for VIA Rail passengers needing quick transport to and from the Dorval station and the Pierre Elliott Trudeau International Airport.

JASPER • VANCOUVER

TRAIN		KM	1	
NAME			Canadian	
DAYS			3, 5, 7	
Winnipeg, MB CT		1943	1655	DP
Portage la Prairie	42	2032	1805	
Brandon North	42	2150	1915	
Rivers, MB	42	2173	1940	
Melville, SK		2394	2230	
Watrous	★	2602	0040	
Saskatoon		2702	0205 / 0230	AR / DP
Biggar		2792	0345 🛄	
Unity, SK CT	42	2885	0446	
Wainwright, AB MT	42	3017	0517	
Viking	★	3089	0606	
Edmonton		3221	0805 / 0855	
Evansburg	42	3331	1010	
Edson	★	3430	1124	
Hinton ◐	42	3518	1234	
Jasper, AB MT		3600	1405 / 1530	AR / DP
Valemount, BC PT	★	3721	1634	
Blue River	42	3814	1802	
Clearwater	42	3923	1959	
Kamloops North		4038	2210 / 2245	
Ashcroft (CN Station)	42	4117	0016	
Boston Bar	42	4240	0243	
Hope	42	4305	0402	
Chilliwack	42	4355	0442	
Abbotsford ✈	42	4380	0504	
Vancouver, BC PT (Pacific Central Station)		4466	0750	AR

* The above schedule is only an example.
* Schedules are subject to change.
* **42** Train offers a stop on request upon a 48-hour advance notice.

266 | Western Canada

■ The Canadian

TORONTO • WINNIPEG			
TRAIN			1
NAME			Canadian
DAYS		KM	2,4,6
Toronto, ON ET (Union Station)		0	0900	DP
Washago	42	143	1108
Parry Sound (CP station)	42	241	1258
Sudbury Jct.*	42	422	1558
Capreol		444	1635 / 1700	AR / DP
Laforest	42	493	1752
McKee's Camp	42	494	1800
Felix	42	521	1816
Ruel	42	527	1827
Westree	42	547	1840
Gogama	42	583	1920
Foleyet	42	683	2040
Elsas	42	739	2128
Oba	42	859	2258
Hornepayne		921	0025 / 0100	AR / DP
Hillsport	42	989	0151
Caramat	42	1046	0245
Longlac	42	1084	0315
Nakina	42	1133	0349
Auden	42	1222	0454
Ferland	42	1265	0532
Mud River	42	1273	0545
Armstrong ET	42	1314	0650
Collins CT	42	1348	0625
Allanwater Bridge	42	1401	0703
Savant Lake	42	1440	1440
Sioux Lookout		1537	0905 / 0925	AR / DP
Red Lake Road	42	1652	1054
Redditt	42	1735	1213
Minaki	42	1758	1237
Ottermere	42	1780	1259
Malachi	42	1784	1302
Copeland's Landing	42	1788	1303
Rice Lake, ON	42	1796	1311
Winnitoba, MB	42	1801	1316
Ophir	42	1806	1321
Brereton Lake	42	1826	1336
Elma	42	1854	1416
Winnipeg, MB CT		1943	1545	AR

APPENDIX A | 267

JASPER • VANCOUVER

TRAIN			1	
NAME			Canadian	
DAYS		KM	3,5,7	
Winnipeg, MB CT		1943	1655	DP
Portage la Prairie	42	2032	1805	
Brandon North	42	2150	1915	
Rivers, MB	42	2173	1940	
Melville, SK		2394	2230	
Watrous	42	2602	0040	
Saskatoon		2702	0205 / 0230	AR / DP
Biggar		2792	0345	
Unity, SK CT	42	2885	0446	
Wainwright, AB MT	42	3017	0517	
Viking	42	3089	0606	
Edmonton		3221	0805 / 0855	AR / DP
Evansburg	42	3331	1010	
Edson	42	3430	1124	
Hinton	42	3518	1234	
Jasper, AB MT		3600	1405 / 1530	
Valemount, BC PT	42	3721	1634	
Blue River	42	3814	1802	
Clearwater	42	3923	1959	
Kamloops North		4038	2210 / 2245	AR / DP
Ashcroft (CN Station)	42	4117	0016	
Boston Bar	42	4240	0243	
Hope	42	4305	0402	
Chilliwack	42	4355	0442	
Abbotsford	42	4380	0504	
Vancouver, BC PT (Pacific Central Station)		4466	0750	AR

42 Train offers a stop on request upon a 48-hour advance notice.

* There is a 10 km distance from Sudbury, ON to Sudbury Jct., ON. Shuttle service is not available.

The Canadian

VANCOUVER • JASPER

		TRAIN	2	
		NAME	Canadian	
		DAYS	2,5,7	
		KM		
Vancouver, BC PT (Pacific Central Station)		0	1730	DP
Mission	42	61	1915	
Agassiz	42	106	1952	
Katz	42	128	2010	
North Bend	42	201	2130	
Ashcroft (CN Station)	42	349	2357	
Kamloops North		428	0150 / 0225	AR / DP
Clearwater	42	543	0414	
Blue River	42	652	0608	
Valemount, BC PT	42	745	0749	
Jasper, AB MT		866	1100 / 1220	
Hinton	42	948	1335	
Edson	42	1036	1438	
Evansburg	42	1135	1550	
Edmonton		1245	1730 / 1820	AR / DP
Viking	42	1377	2000	
Wainwright, AB MT	42	1449	2045	
Unity, SK CT	42	1581	2302	
Biggar		1674	0030	
Saskatoon		1764	0145 / 0210	AR / DP
Watrous	42	1864	0323	
Melville, SK		2072	0550	
Rivers, MB	42	2293	0823	
Brandon North	42	2316	0835	
Portage la Prairie	42	2434	0956	
Winnipeg, MB CT		2523	1120	AR

42 Train offers a stop on request upon a 48-hour advance notice.

* There is a 10 km distance from Sudbury, ON to Sudbury Jct., ON. Shuttle service is not available.

APPENDIX A | 269

WINNIPEG - TORONTO

TRAIN			2	
NAME			Canadian	
DAYS		KM	4,7,2	
Winnipeg, MB CT		2535	1225	DP
Elma	42	2612	1327	
Bereton Lake	42	2640	1346	
Ophir	42	2660	1402	
Winnitoba, MB	42	2665	1407	
Rice Lake, ON	42	2670	1413	
Copeland's Landing	42	2678	1423	
Malachi	42	2682	1426	
Ottermere	42	2686	1431	
Minaki	42	2708	1449	
Redditt	42	2731	1511	
Red Lake Road	42	2814	1633	
Sioux Lookout		2929	1835 / 1855	AR / DP
Savant Lake	42	3026	2017	
Allanwater Bridge	42	3065	2042	
Collins CT	42	3118	2129	
Armstrong ET	42	3152	2305	
Mud River	42	3193	2341	
Ferland	42	3201	2350	
Auden	42	3244	0024	
Nakina	42	3333	0124	
Longlac	42	3382	0159	
Caramat	42	3420	0231	
Hillsport	42	3477	0319	
Horepayne		3545	0430 / 0505	AR / DP
Oba	42	3607	0558	
Elsas	42	3727	0732	
Foleyet	42	3783	0819	
Gogama	42	3883	0944	
Westree	42	3919	1014	
Ruel	42	3939	1037	
Felix	42	3945	1041	
MoKoo'o Camp	42	3972	1057	
Laforest	42	3983	1111	
Capreol		4022	1230	
Sudbury Jct.*	42	4044	1321	
Parry Sound (CP Station)	42	4225	1617	
Washago	42	4323	1749	
Toronto, ON ET (Union Station)		4466	2000	AR

The Skeena

JASPER • PRINCE GEORGE • PRINCE RUPERT

TRAIN			5	
NAME			Skeena	
DAYS		KM	3,5,7	
Jasper, AB MT		0	1245	DP
Harvey, BC PT	★	106	1338	
Dunster	★	142	1412	
McBride		174	1444	
Goat River	★	217	1541	
Loos	★	232	1558	
Dome Creek	★	262	1632	
Bend	★	265	1636	
Penny	★	285	1656	
Longworth	★	301	1711	
Hutton	★	314	1724	
Sinclair Mills	★	319	1730	
McGregor	★	331	1743	
Upper Fraser	★	341	1752	
Aleza Lake	★	349	1801	
Willow River	★	378	1831	
Prince George (VIA Station)		409	1908	AR
DAYS		KM	4,6,1	
Prince George (VIA Station)		409	0800	DP
Vanderhoof		520	0955	
Fort Fraser	★	560	1032	
Endako		594	1050	
Burns Lake		650	1158	
Houston		734	1308	
Telkwa	★	780	1352	
Smithers		795	1420	
New Hazelton	★	869	1537	
Kitwanga	★	912	1627	
Cedarvale	★	933	1651	
Dorreen	★	957	1712	
Pacific	★	967	1721	
Usk	★	988	1740	
Terrace (Kitimat)		1007	1805	
Kwinitsa	★	1084	1909	
Prince Rupert, BC PT		1160	2025	AR

★ Stop on request.

APPENDIX A | 271

PRINCE RUPERT • PRINCE GEORGE • JASPER

TRAIN			6	
NAME			Skeena	
DAYS		KM	3,5,7	
Prince Rupert, BC PT		0	0800	DP
Kwinitsa	★	76	0917	
Terrace (Kitimat)		153	1025	
Usk	★	172	1048	
Pacific	★	193	1107	
Dorreen	★	203	1119	
Cedarvale	★	227	1144	
Kitwanga	★	248	1208	
New Hazelton	★	291	1230	
Smithers		365	1424	
Telkwa	★	380	1437	
Houston		426	1522	
Burns Lake		510	1632	
Endako		566	1725	
Fort Fraser	★	600	1757	
Vanderhoof		640	1835	↓
Prince George (VIA Station)		751	2029	AR

DAYS		KM	4,6,1	
Prince George (VIA Station)		751	0730	DP
Willow River	★	782	0808	
Alez Lake	★	811	0838	
Upper Fraser	★	819	0847	
McGregor	★	829	0856	
Sinclair Mills	★	841	0909	
Hutton	★	846	0915	
Longworth	★	859	0929	
Penny	★	875	0945	
Bend	★	895	1006	
Domo Crook	★	898	1010	
Loos	★	928	1045	
Goat River	★	943	1102	
McBride		986	1203	
Dunster	★	1018	1235	
Harvey, BC PT	★	1054	1309	↓
Jasper, AB MT		1160	1600	AR

Western Canada

The Malahat

VICTORIA • NANAIMO • COURTENAY					
TRAIN			199	299	
NAME			Malahat	Malahat	
DAYS		KM	x7	7	
Victoria, BC PT (450 Pandora Ave.)		0	0800	1000	DP
Esquimalt	★	6	0807	1007	
Palmet (Ft. Victoria)		10	★	★	
Langford	★	13	0819	1019	
Malahat	★	32	0848	1048	
Cliffside		40	★	★	
Strathcona Lodge		42	★	★	
Shawnigan	★	45	0908	1108	
Cobble Hill	★	50	0917	1117	
Hillbank		55	★	★	
Cowichan	★	58	0927	1127	
Duncan		64	0935	1135	
Hayward (Drinkwater Rd.)		68	★	★	
Chemainus	★	82	0956	1156	
Ladysmith	★	93	1008	1208	
Cassidy	★	105	1018	1208	
South Wellington		108	★	★	
Starks		111	★	★	
Nanaimo		117	1035 1050	1235 1250	AR DP
Wellington	★	124	1058	1258	
Nanoose Bay		142	★	★	
Parksville		153	1127	1327	
Qualicum Beach	★	164	1138	1338	
Dunsmuir	★	177	1151	1351	
Deep Bay (Gainsberg Rd.)		190	★	★	
Buckley Bay		203	★	★	
Union Bay	★	211	1221	1421	
Courtenay, BC PT		225	1245	1445	AR

★ Stop on request.

COURTENAY • NANAIMO • COURTENAY

TRAIN			198	298	
NAME			Malahat	Malahat	
DAYS		KM	x7	7	
Courtenay, BC PT	★	0	1315	1515	DP
Union Bay		14	1339	1539	
Buckley Bay		22	★	★	
Deep Bay (Gainsberg Rd.)		35	★	★	
Dunsmuir	★	48	1409	1609	
Qualicum Beach	★	61	1422	1622	
Parksville		72	1433	1633	
Nanoose Bay		83	★	★	
Wellington	★	101	1502	1702	
Nanaimo		108	1510 / 1525	1710 / 1725	AR / DP
Starks		114	★	★	
South Wellington		117	★	★	
Cassidy	★	120	1542	1742	
Ladysmith	★	132	1552	1752	
Chemainus	★	143	1604	1804	
Hayward (Drinkwater Rd.)		157	★	★	
Duncan		161	1625	1825	
Cowichan	★	167	1633	1833	
Hillbank		170	★	★	
Cobble Hill	★	175	1643	1843	
Shawnigan	★	180	1652	1852	
Strathcona Lodge		183	★	★	
Cliffside		185	★	★	
Malahat	★	193	1712	1912	
Langford	★	212	1741	1941	
Palmer (Ft. Victoria)		215	★	★	
Esquimalt	★	219	1753	1953	
Victoria, BC PT (450 Pandora Ave.)		225	1800	2000	AR

274 | Prairies and Central Arctic

The Hudson Bay

WINNIPEG • THE PAS				
TRAIN			693	
NAME			Hudson Bay	
DAYS		KM	3,5,1	
Winnipeg, MB CT		0	2013	DP
Portage la Prairie		88	2116	
Gladstone	47	148	2203	
Plumas	47	169	2236	
Glenella	47	191	2305	
McCreary	47	224	2342	
Laurier	47	238	2356	
Ochre River	47	262	0015	
Dauphin		283	0043	
Gilbert Plains	★	315	0114	
Grandview	★	331	0130	
Roblin, MB		385	0223	
Togo, SK	★	412	0251	
Kamsack		446	0327	
Veregin	48	459	0340	
Mikado	48	473	0352	
Canora		484	0416	
Sturgis		520	0457	
Endeavour		549	0527	
Reserve	★	586	0603	
Hudson Bay, SK		636	0655	
The Pas, MB		777	0850 0930	AR DP
Tremaudan		790	★	
Orok		798	★	
Atikameg Lake		804	★	
Budd		825	★	
Halcrow		837	★	
Cormorant		843	1044	
Dering		850	★	
Rawebb		864	★	
Paterson		890	★	
Wekusko		907	★	
Turnbull		927	★	
Ponton		949	★	
Dunlop		973	★	
Pipun		985	★	
Wabowden		996	1310	
Odhill		1031	★	
Hockin		1064	★	
Leven		1066	★	
Thompson, MB CT		1149	1625	AR

APPENDIX A | 275

CHURCHILL

TRAIN		693	
NAME		Hudson Bay	
DAYS	KM	3,5,1	
Thompson, MB CT	1149	1755	DP
Sipiwesk	1199	★	
Pikwitonei	1220	1940	
Bridgar	1229	★	
Wilde	1249	★	
Arnot	1257	★	
Mile 238.3	1260	★	
Boyd	1279	★	
Pit Siding	1289	★	
Munk	1310	★	
Mile 278.6	1326	★	
Ilford	1337	2210	
Nonsuch	1353	★	
Wivenhoe	1366	★	
Luke	1390	★	
Gillam (Nelson River)	1401	2320 / 2350	AR / DP
Kettle Rapids	1414	★	
Bird	1435	★	
Amery	1448	★	
Charlebois	1463	★	
Weir River	1477	0205	
Lawledge	1492	★	
Thibaudeau	1508	★	
Silcox	1520	★	
Herchmer	1540	0355	
Kellet	1548	★	
O'Day	1562	★	
Back	1575	★	
M'Clintock	1588	★	
Belcher	1603	0544	
Cromarty	1617	★	
Chesnaye	1632	★	
Lamprey	1646	★	
Bylot	1659	★	
Digges	1670	★	
Tidal	1685	★	
Churchill, MB CT	1697	0830	AR

Left margin brackets: 3,5,1 (Thompson to Gillam); 4,6,2 (Gillam to Churchill)

★ Stop on request.

47 Train stops to detrain, and entrains passengers with advance notice.

48 Train stops to entrain passengers in locations beyond the Hudson Bay.

Prairies and Central Arctic

■ The Hudson Bay

CHURCHILL • THE PAS				
TRAIN			692	
NAME			Hudson Bay	
DAYS		KM	2,4,6	
Churchill, MB CT		0	2030	DP
Tidal		12	★	
Digges		27	★	
Bylot		38	★	
Lamprey		51	★	
Chesnaye		65	★	
Cromarty		80	★	
Belcher	★	94	2321	
M'Clintock		109	★	
Back		122	★	
O'Day		135	★	
Kellett		149	★	
Herchmer		157	0105	
Silcox		177	★	
Thibaudeau		189	★	
Lawledge		205	★	
Weir River		220	0300	
Charlebois		234	★	
Amery		249	★	
Bird		262	★	
Kettle Rapids		283	★	
Gillam (Nelson River)		296	0515 / 0545	AR / DP
Luke		307	★	
Wivenhoe		331	★	
Nonsuch		344	★	
Ilford		360	0655	
Mile 278.6		371	★	
Munk		387	★	
Pit Siding		408	★	
Boyd		418	★	
Mile 238.3		437	★	
Arnot		440	★	
Wilde		448	★	
Bridgar		468	★	
Pikwitonei		477	0920	
Sipiwesk		498	★	
Thompson, MB CT		548	1105	AR

★ Stop on request.
47 Train stops to detrain, and entrains passengers with advance notice.
48 Train stops to entrain passengers in locations beyond the Hudson Bay.

WINNIPEG

		KM		
TRAIN			692	
NAME			Hudson Bay	
DAYS		KM	3,5,7	
Thompson, MB CT		548	1235	DP
Leven		611	★	
Thicket Portage		624	1425	
Hockin		633	★	
La Perouse		645	★	
Earchman		656	★	
Lyddal		680	★	
Wabowden		701	1545	
Pipun		712	★	
Dunlop		724	★	
Button		736	★	
Turnbull		770	★	
Wekusko		790	★	
Paterson		807	★	
Dyce		820	★	
Dering		847	★	
Cormorant		854	1805	
Halcrow		860	★	
Budd		872	★	
Atikameg Lake		893	★	
Tremaudan		907	★	
The Pas, MB		920	1920 / 2000	AR / DP
Hudson Bay, SK		1061	2155	
Reserve	★	1111	2236	
Sturgis		1177	2353	
Canora		1213	0043	
Mikado		1224	0055	
Veregin	48	1238	0107	
Kamsack		1251	0121	
Togo, SK	★	1285	0156	
Roblin, MB		1312	0225	
Grandview	★	1366	0317	
Gilbert Plains	★	1382	0333	
Ochre River	47	1435	0434	
McCreary	47	1473	0506	
Plumas	47	1528	0612	
Gladstone	47	1549	0645	
Portage la Prairie		1609	0736	
Winnipeg, MB CT		1697	0838	AR

Ontario and Québec

■ Montréal to Toronto

MONTRÉAL • KINGSTON

TRAIN		651	655	53	43	
DAYS	KM	x6,7	6	x7	x6,7	
Montréal, QC	0			0645		DP
Dorval, QC ✈	19			0711		
Cornwall, ON	111			0801	From Ottawa	
Brockville	204					↓
Gananoque ◐	249					
Kingston	285	0530	0650	0923	1041	AR
				0926		DP
Napanee ◐	322		0712		1105	
Belleville	357	0614	0732			
Trenton Jct. ◐	377	0627	0744			
Cobourg	426	0659	0816			
Port Hope ◐	438	0711	0826		1207	↓
Oshawa	488	0743	0854	1109		
Guildwood	518	0800	0912		1252	
Toronto	539	0820	0929	1140	1309	AR
Oakville						
Aldershot, ON						

TORONTO • ALDERSHOT

TRAIN		57	61	45	65	47	67	69	
DAYS	KM		x6			x6	x6		
Montréal, QC	0	0940 🛄	1145		1540		1700	1820	DP
Dorval, QC ✈	19	1007 🛄	1211		1606		1726	1847	
Cornwall, ON	111	1103 🛄	1301	From Ottawa	1656	From Ottawa		1941	↓
Brockville	204	1153 🛄						2029	
Gananoque ◐	249								
Kingston	285	1239 🛄	1423	1445	1818	1903		2114	AR
		1243 🛄	1427		1822			2117	DP
Napanee ◐	322								
Belleville	357	1330 🛄		1526				2202	
Trenton Jct. ◐	377								
Cobourg	426	1413 🛄				2014		2243	
Port Hope ◐	438								
Oshawa	488	1451 🛄		1637	2005	2054	2114	2320	↓
Guildwood	518	1513	1625	1655				2340	
Toronto	539	1532 🛄	1642	1712	2036	2125	2145	2358	AR
							2155		DP
Oakville							2220		↓
Aldershot, ON							2232		AR

* No available local service between Montréal and Dorval or Guildwood and Toronto.
* The train stops at Napanee only for advance reservations made before 06:10 of the departure day.

APPENDIX A | 279

ALDERSHOT • TORONTO

TRAIN	KM	52	652	56	60	
DAYS		x6,7	6	x6		
Aldershot, ON		0600	0625			DP
Oakville		0613	0639			
Toronto	0	0635	0705			AR
		0655	0725	0930	1135	DP
Guildwood	21	0717	0745	0950	1158	
Oshawa	51	0736	0805	1009	1219	
Port Hope ◐	101					
Cobourg	113	0813	0839	1043	1256	
Trenton Jct. ◐	163					
Belleville	182	0851	0918	1121	1337	
Napanee ◐	217					
Kingston	254	0929	0955	1159	1417	AR
		0933	0959	1203	1421	DP
Gananoque ◐	290					
Brockville	335	1026	1053	1302	1511	
Cornwall, ON	428	1114	1139	1348	1603	
Dorval, QC ✈	520	1204	1228	1437	1656	
Montreal, QC	530	1223	1246	1456	1717	AR

KINGSTON • MONTRÉAL

TRAIN	KM	64	66	48	68	668	650	
DAYS			x6	x6,7	x6,7	6,7	x6,7	
Aldershot, ON								
Oakville								
Toronto	0	1510	1700	1730	1835	1835	2200	DP
Guildwood	21			1749	1856	1855	2220	
Oshawa	51	1544	1734	1809	1917	1914	2238	
Port Hope ◐	101			1836	1946	1943	2304	
Cobourg	113			1848	1955	1952	2312	
Trenton Jct. ◐	163			1914		2020		
Belleville	182	1651		1931		2036	2350	
Napanee ◐	217			1951		2056		
Kingston	254	1726		2009	2110	2117	0027	AR
		1730			2113	2121		DP
Gananoque ◐	290				2136	2143		
Brockville	335			To Ottawa	2204	2216		
Cornwall, ON	428	1856			2254	2306		
Dorval, QC ✈	520	1946	2121		2346	2358		
Montreal, QC	530	2005	2140		0006	0018		AR

✈ AirConnect: A free shuttle service for VIA Rail passengers needing quick transport to and from the Dorval station and the Pierre Elliott Trudeau International Airport.

Toronto to Ottawa

OTTAWA • KINGSTON

TRAIN	KM	71	41	641	43	
DAYS						
Ottawa, ON	0		0545	0700	0835	DP
Fallowfield (Barrhaven)	16		0607	0720	0858	↓
Smiths Falls ◐	66		0636	0749	0928	
Brockville	111		0705	0819	0957	↓
Gananoque ◐	156	To Windsor				
Kingston	191		0746 / 0749	0900 / 0903	1037 / 1041	AR / DP
Napanee ◐	228				1105	
Belleville	264		0829	0943		
Trenton Jct. ◐	283					
Cobourg	333		0909	1022	1200	
Port Hope ◐	344				1207	
Oshawa	394	0645	0945	1058		↓
Guildwood	425			1116	1252	
Toronto	446	0725 / 0750	1016	1133	1309	AR / DP
Oakville		0816				↓
Aldershot, ON		0829				AR

TORONTO • ALDERSHOT

TRAIN	KM	57	643	45	47	67	49	69	
DAYS			7		x6	x6			
Ottawa, ON	0		0850	1235	1700		1815		DP
Fallowfield (Barrhaven)	16		0909	1255	1720		1834		↓
Smiths Falls ◐	66	From Montréal	0939				1904	From Montréal	
Brockville	111		1008	1357	1818		1938		↓
Gananoque ◐	156			1421					
Kingston	191	1243	1048 / 1051	1441 / 1445	1859 / 1903	From Montréal	2018 / 2021	2117	AR / DP
Napanee ◐	228		1112						
Belleville	264	1330	1135	1526			2101	2117	
Trenton Jct. ◐	283						2115		
Cobourg	333	1413	1212		2014			2243	
Port Hope ◐	344		1219						
Oshawa	394	1451		1637	2054		2214	2320	↓
Guildwood	425	1513	1308	1655			2237	2340	
Toronto	446	1532	1325	1712	2125	2155	2254	2358	AR / DP
Oakville						2220			↓
Aldershot, ON						2232			AR

* No local service between Ottawa and Fallowfield or Guildwood and Toronto.

APPENDIX A | 281

ALDERSHOT • TORONTO

TRAIN		40	640	42	60	
DAYS	KM	x6,7	6	x6		
Aldershot, ON		0600	0625			DP
Oakville		0613	0639			
Toronto	0	0635 / 0655	0705 / 0725	0930	1135 🍴	AR / DP
Guildwood	21	0717	0745	0950	1158	
Oshawa	51	0736	0805	1009	1219 🍴	
Port Hope ◐	101					
Cobourg	113	0813	0839	1043	1256 🍴	
Trenton Jct. ◐	163					
Belleville	182	0851	0918	1121	1337 🍴	
Napanee ◐	217					
Kingston	254	0929 / 0933	0955 / 0959	1159 / 1203	1417 🍴	AR / DP
Gananoque ◐	290					
Brockville	335	1031	1058	1257		
Smiths Falls ◐	380	1100	1127		To Montréal	
Fallowfield (Barrhaven)	430	1131	1157	1400		
Ottawa, ON	446	1147	1214	1416		AR

KINGSTON • OTTAWA

TRAIN		40	64	46	48	648	
DAYS	KM			x6	x6,7	6,7	
Aldershot, ON							
Oakville							
Toronto	0	1220	1510	1530	1730	1835	DP
Guildwood	21				1749	1855	
Oshawa	51	1254	1544	1604	1809	1914	
Port Hope ◐	101				1836	1943	
Cobourg	113			1639	1848	1952	
Trenton Jct. ◐	163				1914	2020	
Belleville	182		1651		1931	2038	
Napanee ◐	217				1951	2056	
Kingston	254	1434 / 1438	1726	1747 / 1751	2009 / 2012	2117 / 2121	AR / DP
Gananoque ◐	290				2033	2143	
Brockville	335	1524		1837	2100	2221	
Smiths Falls ◐	380	1553	To Montréal		2129	2250	
Fallowfield (Barrhaven)	430	1623		1940	2159	2321	
Ottawa, ON	446	1639		1956	2215	2338	AR

Ontario and Québec

Toronto to Windsor

TORONTO • LONDON

TRAIN		71	671	73	75	
DAYS	KM	x6,7	6,7		x6,7	
Montréal, QC						
Oshawa, ON		0645				
Toronto	0	0725 0750	0750	1210	1625	DP
Oakville	34	0816	0816	1237	1659	
Aldershot	56	0829	0829	1251		
Brantford	97	0859	0859	1321	1743	
Woodstock	140	0926	0926	1349	1813	
Ingersoll ☾	154	0940	0940			
London	185	0959 1002	0959 1002	1420 1425	1845 1851	AR DP
Glencoe ☾	235	1030	1030			
Chatham	290	1118	1118	1541	2010	
Windsor, ON	359	1159	1159	1623	2055	AR

WINDSOR

TRAIN		675	83	79	67	
DAYS	KM	6,7	x6,7		x6	
Montréal, QC					1700	DP
Oshawa, ON					2114	
Toronto	0	1625	1715	1915	2145 2155	AR DP
Oakville	34	1654		1941	2220	
Aldershot	56	1709	1753	1953	2232	
Brantford	97	1742	1824	2022		
Woodstock	140	1812	1855	2049		
Ingersoll ☾	154			2103		
London	185	1844 1850	1926	2121 2126		AR DP
Glencoe ☾	235			2154		
Chatham	290	2009		2236		
Windsor, ON	359	2054		2318		AR

WINDSOR • LONDON

TRAIN		40	52	640	652	
DAYS	KM	x6,7	x6,7	6	6	
Windsor, ON	0					
Chatham	69					
Glencoe ◐	124					
London	174					
Ingersoll ◐	205					
Woodstock	219					
Brantford	262					
Aldershot	303	0600	0600	0625	0625	DP
Oakville	325	0613	0613	0639	0639	
Toronto	359	0635	0635	0705	0705	AR
		0655	0655	0725	0725	DP
Oshawa		0736	0736	0805	0805	↓
Ottawa, ON		1147		1214		↓
Montréal, QC			1223		1246	AR

TORONTO

TRAIN		82	70	72	76	78	686	
DAYS	KM	x6,7					5	
Windsor, ON	0		0555 🧳	1005	1335	1800		DP
Chatham	69		0642 🧳	1049	1419	1845		↓
Glencoe ◐	124			1133		1929		↓
London	174		0753 🧳	1204	1533	2001		AR
		0620	0758 🧳	1210	1539	2007	2045	DP
Ingersoll ◐	205		0819			2026		↓
Woodstock	219	0648	0833 🧳	1240		2039		↓
Brantford	262	0720	0907 🧳	1312	1637	2112		↓
Aldershot	303		0939 🧳	1341	1706	2142		↓
Oakville	325		0954 🧳	1354	1719	2155	2223	↓
Toronto	359	0820	1019 🧳	1418	1745	2219	2250	AR
Oshawa								
Ottawa, ON								
Montréal, QC								

Ontario and Québec

■ Toronto to Sarnia

TORONTO • LONDON • SARNIA					
TRAIN		85	87	89	
DAYS	KM			x6	
Toronto, ON	0	1050	1740	2200	DP
Brampton	34	1133	1820	2237 ☽	
Georgetown ☽	47	1146	1833	2248	
Guelph	79	1211	1858	2312	
Kitchener	101	1235	1922	2335	
Stratford	143	1308	1955	0007	
St. Marys	161	1328	2019	0025 ☽	
London	195	1404 / 1409	2056 / 2101	0101	AR / DP
Strathroy ☽	227	1430	2129		
Wyoming ☽	267		2202		
Sarnia, ON	290	1511	2217		AR

■ Toronto to Niagara Falls

TORONTO • NIAGARA FALLS • NEW YORK						
TRAIN		97-64	93*	95		
DAYS	KM					
Toronto, ON	0	0830	1000	1745	DP	
Oakville	34	0857	1024	1810		VIA
Aldershot	56	0913	1039	1825		
Grimsby ☽	90	0949		1903		
St. Catharines	114	1009	1133	1925		
Niagara Falls, ON	132	1032	1155	1948	AR	
Niagara Falls, NY	135	1235			DP	
Buffalo (Exchange)	172	1310				
Buffalo (Depew)	182	1325				
Rochester	280	1427				
Syracuse	417	1550				
Rome	473	1635				AMTRAK
Utica	494	1657				
Amsterdam	590	1755				
Schenectady	619	1815				
Albany-Rensselaer	648	1905				
Hudson	692	1930				
Rhinecliff	734	1951				
Poughkeepsie	758	2006				
Croton-Harmon	824	2045				
Yonkers	853	2104				
New York, NY	875	2135			AR	

* No local service between Poughkeepsie, Croton-Harmon, or Yonkers.
* Schedules of Amtrak trains are subject to change.

SARNIA • LONDON • TORONTO

TRAIN		86	84	88	
DAYS	KM	x6,7			
Sarnia, ON	0		0655	0900	DP
Wyoming ☽	22		0711		
Strathroy ☽	63		0742	0944	
London	95	0520	0809	2007	AR
			0814	2012	DP
St. Marys	130	0553	0844	2052	
Stratford	147	0612	0903	2111	
Kitchener	189	0644	0932	2143	
Guelph	211	0707	1006	2210	
Georgetown ☽	243	0738	1030	2234	
Brampton	256	0749	1040	2244 ☽	
Toronto, ON	290	0824	1113	2316	AR

NEW YORK • NIAGARA FALLS • TORONTO

TRAIN		90	92	94*	694*	98-63	
DAYS	KM						
New York, NY	0					0715	DP
Yonkers	22					0739	
Croton-Harmon	51					0758	
Poughkeepsie	117					0842	
Rhinecliff	141					0857	
Hudson	183					0920	
Albany-Rensselaer	227					1005	
Schenectady	256					1028	AMTRAK
Amsterdam	285					1045	
Utica	381					1144	
Rome	402					1158	
Syracuse	458					1245	
Rochester	595					1403	
Buffalo (Depew)	693					1501	
Buffalo (Exchange)	703					1514	
Niagara Falls, NY	740					1615	AR
Niagara Falls, ON	743	0635	1415	1415	1700	1745	DP
St. Catharines	761	0701	1440	1440	1725	1811	
Grimsby ☽	785	0719	1459			1829	VIA
Aldershot	819	0757	1535	1532	1817	1905	
Oakville	841	0810	1548	1545	1830	1920	
Toronto, ON	875	0835	1613	1610	1855	1947	AR

* Seasonal services are available from June 27, 2008 up to September 29, 2008.

Montréal to Ottawa

MONTRÉAL • ALEXANDRIA						
TRAIN		31	631	33	
DAYS	KM	x6,7	6		
Montréal, QC	0	0635	0735	1000	DP
Dorval ✈	19	0700	0801	1026	
Coteau, QC	63				
Alexandria, ON	100	0752	0849	1110	
Casselman ◐	140			1132 ★	
Ottawa	187	0836	0936	1157	
Fallowfield, ON (Barrhaven)	203				AR

OTTAWA • FOLLOWFIELD							
TRAIN		635*	35	37	639	39	
DAYS	KM		x6	x6,7	6,7	x6,7	
Montréal, QC	0	1250	1510	1645	1800	1805	DP
Dorval ✈	19	1317	1536	1711	1826	1839	
Coteau, QC	63				1851	1904	
Alexandria, ON	100	1407	1626	1755	1917	1925	
Casselman ◐	140	1431 ★					
Ottawa	187	1457	1719	1840	2002	2010	
Fallowfield, ON (Barrhaven)	203			1907		2037	AR

* No local service between Montréal and Dorval or Ottawa and Fallowfield.

✈ AirConnect: A free shuttle service for VIA Rail passengers needing quick transport to and from the Dorval station and the Pierre Elliott Trudeau International Airport.

FALLOWFIELD • OTTAWA

TRAIN		30	630	32	
DAYS	KM	x6,7	6	x6,7	
Fallowfield, ON (Barrhaven)	0	0612		0903	DP
Ottawa	16	0636	0730	0927	
Casselman ◐	63				
Alexandria, ON	103	0720	0813	1009	
Coteau, QC	140	0746	0844		
Dorval ✈	184	0812	0909	1059	
Montréal, QC	203	0832	0929	1119	AR

ALEXANDRIA • MONTRÉAL

TRAIN		632	634*	34	36	38	638	
DAYS	KM	6,7		x6	x6,7	x6,7	6,7	
Fallowfield, ON (Barrhaven)	0							DP
Ottawa	16	0950	1245	1510	1625	1750	1800	
Casselman ◐	63		1311 ★			1815 ★	1823 ★	
Alexandria, ON	103	1032	1332	1552		1842	1845	
Coteau, QC	140			1621[5]				
Dorval ✈	184	1127	1429	1647	1757	1929	1939	
Montréal, QC	203	1147	1450	1707	1817	1949	1959	AR

5 Train stops on Fridays to detrain.

★ Stop on request.

* Avail of the checked baggage service on train 634 except on Sundays and on train 635 except on Saturdays. Please note there is no checked baggage service at Casselman station.

Montréal to Québec City

QUÉBEC • CHARNY

TRAIN		615	15	17	617	
DAYS	KM	1,4,6	1,4,6	2,5,7	2,5,7	
OPERATES		16 Jun 18 13 Oct 18	14 Jun 08 16 Oct 08	15 Jun 08 17 Oct 08	17 Jun 08 14 Oct 08	
Québec, QC	0					DP
Sainte-Foy	21					
Charny	26	0423	0455	0455	0523	
Drummondville	172	0604	0633	0633	0704	
Saint-Hyacinthe[2]	19	0710	0710	0710	0748	
Saint-Lambert	265	0745	0748	0748	0823	
Montréal, QC	272	0757	0815	0830	0835	AR

MONTRÉAL • CHARNY

TRAIN		20	620	22	622	
DAYS	KM	x6,7	6,7	x6	6	
Montréal, QC	0	0700	0820	1255	1330	DP
Saint-Lambert	6	0713	0833	1308	1343	
Saint-Hyacinthe	53	0742	0902			
Drummondville	100	0818	0931	1403	1438	
Charny	246			1546	1613	
Sainte-Foy	251	0953	1106	1553	1621	
Québec, QC	272	1017	1130	1617	1645	AR

* No local service between Québec City, Sainte-Foy and Charny or Saint-Lambert and Montréal.

* Shuttle service operates to and from Charny and Québec City (Gare du Palais). Make appropriate reservations before departure.

3 Train stops on Wednesdays to entrain.

MONTRÉAL

TRAIN		21	23	25	27	
DAYS	KM	x6,7				
Québec, QC	0	0600	0750	1300	1735	DP
Sainte-Foy	21	0623	0813	1323	1758	
Charny	26		0819			
Drummondville	172	0756	0946	1503	1944	
Saint-Hyacinthe[2]	19	0831[3]	1023		2015	↓
Saint-Lambert	265	0859	1100	1559	2045	
Montréal, QC	272	0914	1115	1614	2100	AR

QUÉBEC

TRAIN		24	26	16	616	14	614	
DAYS	KM	x6,7		3,5,7	3,5,7	1,4,6	1,4,6	
OPERATES				13 Jun 08 15 Oct 08	15 Jun 08 12 Oct 08	14 Jun 08 13 Oct 08	16 Jun 08 11 Oct 08	
Montréal, QC	0	1615	1755	1815	1825	1830	1845	DP
Saint-Lambert	6	1628	1808	1854	1843	1854	1905	
Saint-Hyacinthe	53		1836	1928	1915	1928	1939	
Drummondville	100	1729	1905	2018	1952	2018	2020	
Charny	246			2152	2127	2152	2202	↓
Sainte-Foy	251	1905	2041					
Québec, QC	272	1929	2105	*	*	*	*	AR

The Chaleur

		GASPÉ · MONTRÉAL			
TRAIN			17	617	
NAME			Chaleur	Chaleur	
DAYS		KM	1,4,6	1,4,6	
OPERATES			14 Jun 08 16 Oct 08	16 Jun 08 13 Oct 08	
Gaspé, QC ET		0	1430	1505	DP
Barachois		40	1518	1554	
Percé		63	1548	1626	
Grande-Rivière		80	1610	1649	
Chandler		97	1633	1716	
Port-Daniel		130	1727	1811	
New Carlisle		167	1816	1900	
Bonaventure		182	1830	1915	
Caplan		200	1846	1932	
New Richmond		214	1908	1958	
Carleton		254	1953	2044	
Nouvelle	★	269	2010	2104	
Matapédia		325	2140	2215	
Causapscal	★	382	2228	2302	
Amqui		404	2250	2324	
Sayabec	★	428	2311	2344	
Mont-Joli		475	2359	0032	
Rimouski		504	0031	0104	
Trois-Pistoles		565	0141	0221	
Rivière-du-Loup		608	0232	0301	
La Pocatière		676	0315	0344	
Montmagny	★	736	0348	0417	
Charny		800	0440 0455	0508 0523	AR DP
Drummondville		947	0633	0704	
Saint-Hyacinthe		993	0710	0748	
Saint-Lambert		1040	0748	0823	
Montréal, QC ET (Central Station)		1047	0830	0835	AR

* No local service between Saint-Lambert and Montréal.

★ Stop on request.

MONTRÉAL · GASPÉ

TRAIN			16	616	
NAME			Chaleur	Chaleur	
DAYS		KM	3,5,7	3,5,7	
OPERATES			13 Jun 08 15 Oct 08	15 Jun 08 12 Oct 08	
Montréal, QC ET (Central Station)		0	1815	1825	DP
Saint-Lambert		7	1854	1843	↓
Saint-Hyacinthe		54	1928	1915	
Drummondville		100	2018	1952	
Charny		247	2152 2207	2127 2142	AR DP
Montmagny	★	311	2303	2237	
La Pocatière		371	2337	2311	
Rivière-du-Loup		439	0023	2355	
Trois-Pistoles	★	482	0052	0033	
Rimouski		543	0211	0201	
Mont-Joli		572	0248	0231	
Sayabec	★	619	0333	0323	
Amqui		643	0355	0345	
Causapscal	★	665	0415	0405	
Matapédia		722	0535	0500	
Nouvelle	★	778	0632	0602	
Carleton		793	0652	0627	
New Richmond		833	0737	0717	
Caplan		847	0754	0735	
Bonaventure		865	0810	0755	
New Carlisle		880	0834	0819	
Port-Daniel		917	0914	0901	
Chandler		950	1012	1003	
Grande-Rivière		967	1034	1027	
Percé		984	1054	1053	↓
Barachois		1007	1131	1128	
Gaspé, QC ET		1047	1212	1214	AR

*Shuttle service operates to and from Charny and Québec City (Gare du Palais). Make appropriate reservations before departure.

The Saguenay

MONTRÉAL · JONQUIÈRE				
TRAIN			601	
NAME			Saguenay	
DAYS		KM	1,3,5	
Montréal, QC ET (Central Station)		0	0830	DP
Ahuntsic		25	0908	
Pointe-aux-Trembles		45	0924	
Le Gardeur	★	54	0930	
L'Assomption	★	62	0934	
Joliette		86	0953	
Saint-Justin	★	125	1020	
Saint-Paulin	★	138	1029	
Charette	★	151	1039	
Shawinigan		170	1058	
Grand-Mère	★	180	1106	
Garneau	★	185	1114	
Saint-Tite	★	197	1126	
Hervey		217	1155	
Rousseau	42	238	1227	
Rivière-à-Pierre		251	1249	
Miquick	42	281	1321	
Jacques-Cartier Club	★	294	1332	
Pont Beaudet	42	299	1336	
Saint-Hilarie	★	300	1337	
Lac-Malouin	42	304	1342	
Iroquois Club	★	307	1345	
Stadacona	★	310	1348	
Sanford	42	316	1355	
Pearl Lake	★	323	1402	
Club Nicol	★	328	1410	
Triton Club	42	333	1415	
Lac-Édouard		341	1423	
Cherokee	42	349	1430	
Caribou	42	350	1432	
Club Grégoire	42	353	1434	
Summit	42	358	1444	
Brooks	★	366	1450	
Kiskissink	★	374	1501	
Van Bruyssels	★	376	1503	
Lac des Roches	42	384	1511	
Kondiaronk	★	386	1514	
Lizotte Club	42	396	1531	
Lac-Bouchette	★	416	1549	
Chambord		444	1620	
Hébertville (Alma)		477	1655	
Jonquière, QC ET		510	1725	AR

JONQUIÈRE • MONTRÉAL

TRAIN			600	602	
NAME			Saguenay	Saguenay	
DAYS		KM	2,4	7	
Jonquière, QC ET		0	0810	1110	DP
Hébertville (Alma)		33	0839	1139	
Lac-Bouchette	★	94	0941	1241	
Lizotte Club	42	114	1003	1303	
Kondiaronk	★	124	1015	1315	
Lac des Roches	42	126	1017	1317	
Van Bruyssels		134	1025	1325	
Kiskissink	★	136	1027	1327	
Brooks	★	144	1038	1338	
Summit	42	152	1044	1344	
Club Grégoire	42	160	1055	1355	
Caribou	42	160	1055	1355	
Cherokee	42	161	1057	1357	
Triton Club	42	177	1113	1413	
Club Nicol	★	182	1117	1417	
Pearl Lake	★	187	1124	1424	
Sanford	42	194	1130	1430	
Stadacona	★	200	1137	1437	
Iroquois Club	★	203	1140	1440	
Lac-Malouin	42	206	1143	1443	
Saint-Hilaire	★	210	1147	1447	
Pont Beaudet	42	211	1148	1448	
Jacques-Cartier Club	★	216	1152	1452	
Miquick	42	229	1209	1509	
Rivière-à-Pierre		259	1240	1540	
Rousseau	42	272	1300	1600	
Hervey		293	1400	1700	
Saint-Tite	★	313	1419	1719	
Garneau	★	325	1431	1731	
Grand'Mère	★	330	1439	1739	
Shawinigan		340	1448	1748	
Charette	★	359	1506	1806	
Saint-Paulin	★	372	1513	1813	
Saint-Justin	★	385	1525	1825	
Joilette		424	1554	1854	
L'Assomption	★	448	1611	1911	
Le Gardeur	★	456	1615	1915	
Pointe-aux-Trembles		465	1623	1923	
Montréal, QC ET (Central Station)		510	1715	2015	AR

★ Stop on request.
42 Train offers a stop on request upon a 48-hour advance notice.

The Abitibi

MONTRÉAL • LA TUQUE				
TRAIN			603	
NAME			Abitibi	
DAYS		KM	1,3,5	
Montréal, QC ET (Central Station)		0	0830	DP
Ahuntsic		25	0908	
Pointe-aux-Trembles		45	0924	
Le Gardeur	★	54	0930	
L'Assomption	★	62	0934	
Joliette		86	0953	
Saint-Justin	★	125	1020	
Saint-Paulin	★	138	1029	
Charette	★	151	1039	
Shawinigan		170	1058	
Grand'Mère	★	180	1106	
Garneau	★	185	1114	
Saint-Tite	★	197	1126	
Hervey		217	1215	
La Tuque		297	1331 1333	
Fitzpatrick		302	1336	
Cressman	★	326	1358	
Club Vermillion	★	333	1407	
Rapide-Blanc	★	335	1410	
Lac-Darey	★	349	1423	
Duplessis	★	358	1433	
McTavis	★	371	1439	
Windigo	★	373	1446	
Ferguson	★	381	1454	
Club Wigwam	★	387	1458	
Vandry	★	395	1506	
Dessane	★	402	1511	
Saint-Maurice Riv. Boom	★	410	1516	
Weymont, QC ET	★	413	1519	AR

★ Stop on request.

SENNETERRE

TRAIN			603	
NAME			Abitibi	
DAYS		KM	1,3,5	
Weymont, QC ET		413	1519	DP
Sanmaur	★	416	1523	
Cann	★	423	1529	
Club Bélanger	★	428	1539	
Hibbard	★	440	1545	
Casey	★	455	1557	
McCarthy	★	471	1611	
Sisco Club	★	474	1613	
Manjobagues	★	482	1619	
Parent		495	1640	
Timbrell	★	508	1652	
Club Rita Inc.	★	516	1657	
Strachan	★	519	1700	
Maniwawa Club	★	524	1704	
Greening	★	532	1711	
Oskelaneo Lodge	★	539	1716	
Oskelaneo River	★	550	1728	
Clova		561	1736	
Coquar	★	571	1744	
Money	★	585	1755	
Consolidated Bathurst	★	595	1801	
Kapitachuan Club	★	598	1806	
Bourmont	★	600	1808	
Club Beaudin Inc.	★	604	1813	
Langlade	★	613	1817	
Da-Rou-Lac Lodge	★	614	1819	
Gagnon	★	624	1825	
Dix	★	627	1828	
Bolger	★	640	1836	
Forsythe	★	650	1846	
Press	★	672	1905	
Signai	★	682	1913	
Mégiscane	★	703	1930	
Senneterre, QC ET	★	717	1955	AR

The Abitibi

SENNETERRE • LA TUQUE

TRAIN			604	606	
NAME			Abitibi	Abitibi	
DAYS		KM	2,4	7	
Senneterre, QC ET		0	0545	0845	DP
Mégiscane	★	14	0558	0858	
Signai	★	35	0615	0915	
Press	★	45	0623	0923	
Forsythe	★	67	0641	0941	
Bolger	★	77	0656	0956	
Dix	★	90	0659	0959	
Gagnon	★	93	0702	1002	
Da-Rou-Lac Lodge	★	103	0707	1007	
Langlade	★	104	0709	1009	
Club Beaudin Inc.	★	113	0712	1012	
Bourmont	★	117	0714	1014	
Kapitachuan Club	★	119	0717	1017	
Consolidated Bathurst	★	122	0722	1022	
Monet	★	132	0731	1031	
Coquar	★	146	0742	1042	
Clova		156	0750	1050	
Oskelaneo River	★	167	0800	1100	
Oskelaneo Lodge	★	178	0807	1107	
Greening	★	185	0813	1113	
Maniwawa Club	★	193	0827	1127	
Strachan	★	198	0830	1130	
Club Rita Inc.	★	201	0832	1132	
Timbrell	★	209	0834	1134	
Parent		222	0850	1150	
Manjobagues	★	235	0903	1203	
Sisco Club	★	243	0908	1208	
Mc Carthy	★	246	0910	1210	
Casey	★	262	0925	1225	
Hibbard	★	277	0937	1237	
Club Bélanger	★	289	0944	1244	
Cann	★	294	0952	1252	
Sanmaur	★	301	0958	1258	
Weymont, QC ET	★	304	1001	1301	AR

MONTRÉAL

TRAIN			604	606	
NAME			Abitibi	Abitibi	
DAYS		KM	2,4	7	
Weymont, QC ET	★	304	1001	1301	DP
Saint-Maurice Riv. Boom	★	307	1004	1304	
Dessane	★	315	1010	1310	
Vandry	★	322	1015	1315	
Club Wigwam	★	330	1023	1323	
Ferguson	★	336	1027	1327	
Windigo	★	344	1034	1334	
McTavis	★	346	1041	1341	
Duplessis	★	359	1048	1348	
Lac-Darey	★	368	1058	1358	
Rapide-Blanc	★	382	1110	1410	
Club Vermillion	★	384	1113	1413	
Cressman	★	391	1122	1422	
Fitzpatrick		415	1143	1443	
La Tuque, QC		420	1151 1153	1451 1453	AR DP
Hervey		500	1400	1700	
Saint-Tite	★	520	1419	1719	
Garneau	★	532	1431	1731	
Grand'Mère	★	537	1439	1739	
Shawinigan		547	1448	1748	
Charette	★	566	1506	1806	
Saint-Paulin	★	579	1513	1813	
Saint-Justin	★	592	1525	1825	
Joliette		631	1554	1854	
L'Assomption	★	655	1611	1911	
Le Gardeur	★	663	1615	1915	
Pointe-aux-Trembles		672	1623	1923	
Ahuntsic		692	1637	1937	
Montréal, QC ET (Central Station)		717	1715	2015	AR

★ Stop on request.

The Lake Superior

_	SUDBURY • WHITE RIVER		
TRAIN			185
NAME			Lake Superior
DAYS		KM	2,4,6
Sudbury, ON ET		0	0900	DP
Azilda	★	11	0910
Chelmsford	★	19	0915
Larchwood	★	26	0919
Levack	★	39	0930
Cartier		55	1000
Benny	★	68	1015
Stralak	★	74	1022
Pogamasing	★	87	1035
Sheahan	★	92	1040
Metagama	★	114	1100
Biscotasing	★	143	1130
Roberts	★	153	1140
Ramsey		169	1155
Woman River	★	193	1215
Sultan	★	211	1230
Kormak	★	228	1245
Kinogama	★	232	1250
Nemegos	★	249	1305
Devon	★	264	1315
Chapleau		275	1415
Esher	★	288	1430
Musk	★	304	1440
Nicholson	★	311	1450
Bolkow	★	331	1510
Dalton		344	1525
Missanabie		367	1550
Lochalsh	★	385	1610
Franz		405	1630
Girdwood	★	436	1705
O'Brien	★	468	1730
White River, ON ET		484	1745	AR

* There is a 10 km distance from Sudbury, ON to Sudbury Jct., ON.

No shuttle service.

WHITE RIVER • SUDBURY

TRAIN			186	
NAME			Lake Superior	
DAYS		KM	2,4,6	
White River, ON ET		0	0900	DP
O'Brien	★	16	0915	
Girdwood	★	48	0945	
Franz		79	1020	
Lochalsh	★	99	1040	
Missanabie		117	1100	
Dalton		140	1120	
Bolkow	★	153	1135	
Nicholson	★	173	1155	
Musk	★	180	1202	
Esher	★	196	1215	
Chapleau		209	1315	
Devon	★	220	1330	
Nemegos	★	235	1345	
Kinogama	★	252	1359	
Kormak	★	256	1401	
Sultan	★	273	1420	
Woman River	★	291	1435	
Ramsey		315	1450	
Roberts	★	331	1507	
Biscotasing		341	1515	
Metagama	★	370	1545	
Sheahan	★	392	1610	
Pogamasing	★	397	1615	
Stralak	★	410	1633	
Benny	★	416	1640	
Cartier		429	1710	
Levack	★	445	1725	
Larchwood	★	458	1736	
Chelmsford	★	465	1740	
Azilda	★	473	1745	
Sudbury, ON ET		484	1830	AR

The Ocean

HALIFAX • MONTRÉAL				
TRAIN			15	615
NAME			Ocean	Ocean
DAYS		KM	x2	x2
OPERATES			14 Jun 08 15 Oct 08	15 Jun 08 12 Oct 08
Halifax, NS AT		0	1235	1235	DP
Truro		103	1411	1411
Springhill Jct.	★	200	1528	1526
Amherst, NS		227	1553	1551
Sackville, NB		243	1610	1608
Moncton		304	1700 1720	1659 1719
Rogersville	★	397	1822	1821
Miramichi		433	1858	1857
Bathurst		504	2009	2008
Petit Rocher	★	521	2025	2024
Jacquet River	★	549	2045	2044
Charlo	★	574	2103	2102
Campbelton, NB AT		605	2150	2149
Matapédia, QC ET		624	2140	2119
Causapscal	★	681	2228	2206
Amqui		703	2250	2227
Sayabec	★	727	2311	2247
Mont-Joli		774	2359	2335
Rimouski		803	0031	0007
Trois-Pistoles		864	0141	0104
Rivière-du-Loup		907	0232	0201
La Pocatière		975	0315	0244
Montmagny	★	1035	0348	0317
Charny		1099	0440 0455	0408 0423	AR DP
Drummondville		1246	0633	0604
Saint-Hyacinthe		1292	0710	0710
Saint-Lambert		1339	0748	0745
Montréal, QC ET (Central Station)		1346	0815	0757	AR

★ Stop on request.

* No local service between Saint-Lambert and Montréal.

MONTRÉAL · HALIFAX

TRAIN			14	614	
NAME			Ocean	Ocean	
DAYS		KM	x2	x2	
OPERATES			14 Jun 08 13 Oct 08	15 Jun 08 12 Oct 08	
Montréal, QC ET (Central Station)		0	1830	1845	DP
Saint-Lambert		7	1854	1905	
Saint-Hyacinthe		54	1928	1939	
Drummondville		100	2018	2020	
Charny		247	2152 2207	2202 2217	AR DP
Montmagny	★	311	2303	2312	
La Pocatière		371	2337	2346	
Rivière-du-Loup		439	0023	0032	
Trois-Pistoles	★	482	0052	0151	
Rimouski		543	0211	0251	
Mont-Joli		572	0248	0328	
Sayabec	★	619	0333	0413	
Amqui		643	0355	0435	
Causapscal	★	665	0415	0455	
Matapédia, QC ET		722	0502	0542	
Campbelton, NB AT		741	0716	0725	
Charlo	★	772	0748	0757	
Jacquet River	★	797	0807	0816	
Petit Rocher	★	825	0829	0838	
Bathurst		842	0854	0903	
Miramichi		913	1010	1020	
Rogersville	★	949	1044	1054	
Moncton		1042	1144 1159	1154 1209	
Sackville, NB		1103	1246	1257	
Amherst, NS		1119	1302	1313	
Springhill Jct.	★	1146	1324	1335	
Truro		1243	1448	1522	
Halifax, NS AT		1346	1620	1656	AR

* Shuttle service operates to and from Charny and Québec City (Gare du Palais). Make appropriate reservations before departure.

Classic Cross Canada

Discover Canada's varied geography and fantastic scenery from the bustling commercial centre of the country, Toronto, Ontario to the west coast's beautiful port city, Vancouver, British Columbia. Enjoy the journey on board VIA Rail's legendary Canadian travelling through Ontario's rugged north and across the peaceful prairies into Alberta, with a stopover in the magnificent Rocky Mountain National Parks. Explore the charming towns of Jasper and Banff and visit stunning Lake Louise, and then continue across B.C.'s varied landscapes to Vancouver, B.C., nestled between soaring mountains and sparkling ocean. See why people from around the world choose to see Canada by train!

Useful Facts

» This tour departs from Toronto, ending in Vancouver (east/west) OR from Vancouver, ending in Toronto (west to east). Described below is the east to west itinerary: please reverse for the Vancouver departure or call the Tour Operators listed in Appendix D for the Classic Cross Canada - West to East details.

» 10-day Fully Independent Tour.

» Sightseeing and meal inclusions may vary.

Day 1 - Toronto, ON
Your tour begins with a transfer within Greater Toronto, including Pearson International Airport, to your downtown hotel.
• Overnight Toronto

Day 2 - Toronto / VIA Rail
An assisted transfer is provided to Union Station for a morning departure aboard VIA Rail's Canadian. As the train heads into Ontario's cottage country and around the spectacular Great Lakes, settle down in your cozy Silver & Blue class sleeping car accommodations or visit the train's lounges. All meals are served in the Art Deco dining car by VIA Rail's friendly, professional staff.
• Overnight VIA Rail
• Breakfast, Lunch and Dinner on the Train Included

Day 3 - VIA Rail
Relax today in comfort as you journey westward into Canada's wide-open prairies, through the gently rolling patchwork of wheat fields dotted with colourful clusters of grain elevators. Complimentary tea and coffee are available in the Park car, a pleasant spot to get acquainted with your fellow travellers.
• Overnight VIA Rail
• Breakfast, Lunch and Dinner on the Train Included

Day 4 - VIA Rail / Jasper, AB
Today the Canadian takes you to the magnificent Rocky Mountains with an early afternoon arrival in charming Jasper, located in the heart of Canada's largest national park. After a transfer to your hotel, the remainder of the day is yours to explore in this captivating mountain resort.
• Overnight Jasper
• Breakfast, Lunch and Dinner Included

Brewster's exhilarating SnoCoach ride onto the surface of the Athabasca Glacier.

Day 5 - Jasper / Columbia Icefields / Banff, AB

The drive from Jasper to Banff is along one of Canada's most famous scenic routes, the Icefields Parkway. Rushing waterfalls, crystal-clear rivers, emerald lakes, alpine meadows and snowcapped peaks provide ever-changing views of the mountain wilderness. Watch for wildlife, as bears, bighorn sheep, elk, moose and mountain goats inhabit this area. Enjoy an exhilarating SnoCoach ride on the frozen Athabasca Glacier, one of the largest bodies of ice south of the Arctic Circle.
- Overnight Banff

Day 6 - Banff / Lake Louise, AB

See the strange formations known as hoodoos, tour Tunnel Mountain Drive overlooking the splendid Bow River Valley and ride the gondola to the top of Sulphur Mountain for panoramic vistas on the Discover Banff Tour. In the afternoon, enjoy the picturesque drive from Banff, past Vermillion Lakes with the striking background setting of Mt. Rundle, to beautiful Lake Louise. Transfer to your hotel.
- Overnight Lake Louise

Day 7 - Lake Louise / Jasper

This afternoon, return along the scenic Icefields Parkway, which winds along the shoulder of the Great Divide following the headwaters of three major rivers, to the town of Jasper. Transfer to your hotel.
- Overnight Jasper

Day 8 - Jasper

Visit the picturesque Pyramid and Patricia Lakes and Maligne Canyon, one of the most spectacular gorges in the Canadian Rockies on the Discover Jasper Tour. Also, explore the incredible disappearing Medicine Lake and stop at Maligne Lake for a leisurely lake cruise, where you'll encounter dense green forests, mighty glacial peaks and emerald-blue waters.
- Overnight Jasper

Day 9 - Jasper / VIA Rail

With an assisted afternoon transfer to the VIA Rail station, depart Jasper aboard the Canadian and head west through British Columbia to the beautiful west coast city of Vancouver. Enjoy the impressive and diverse scenery en route and the friendly ambiance of the Park Car's lounges and panoramic dome.
- Overnight VIA Rail
- Dinner on the Train Included

Day 10 - VIA Rail / Vancouver, BC

Travel through BC's lush Fraser Valley before your early morning arrival at Vancouver's Pacific Central Station. The tour concludes with a transfer within Greater Vancouver, including Vancouver International Airport.
- Continental Breakfast on the Train Included

Atlantic Adventure

You're off on an adventure into Québec and Canada's Maritimes! Your first stop is Montréal and then VIA Rail's Corridor whisks you to charming Québec City. Enjoy a relaxing journey aboard VIA Rail's Ocean as we travel to beautiful Nova Scotia; tour historic Halifax, romantic Peggy's Cove, the picturesque Annapolis Valley and New Brunswick's Reversing Falls and Hopewell Cape. Then a trip along the impressive Confederation Bridge takes us to Prince Edward Island with stops at Charlottetown and Green Gables.

Few regions of the world are fortunate enough to experience the beauty of autumn's foliage and when travelling in the autumn, the Maritimes offer a wonderful opportunity to witness the fall colours. Explore the unique history, natural beauty and hospitality of Canada's eastern provinces!

Day 1 - Montréal, QC
Your tour begins in Québec's cosmopolitan city of Montréal. A transfer from the airport to the hotel is provided.
- Overnight Fairmont Queen Elizabeth Hotel

Day 2 - Montréal
Today on the Deluxe Montréal Tour, relive the history of the city founded in 1642, with a visit to Old Montréal. The excursion's highlights include Notre-Dame Basilica, Mount Royal, St. Joseph's Oratory, Montréal Harbour, Chinatown and Montréal's grand residential districts. Ride a cable car and visit the Olympic Tower. At the Biodome you'll see the flora and fauna of four diverse eco-systems and the Botanical Gardens. As well, the Insectarium, the only one of its kind in North America, is home to several thousand insects from all over the world.
- Overnight Fairmont Queen Elizabeth Hotel

Day 3 - Montréal / VIA Rail / Québec City / VIA Rail / Montréal
This morning board VIA Rail's Corridor train, in VIA 1 class, bound for Québec City. Enjoy breakfast at your seat and arrive late morning for the Québec City Tour. The city's old quarter is North America's only walled city north of Mexico and has been identified as a UNESCO World Heritage Site. In the early evening return to Montréal on the Corridor and enjoy a delicious VIA Rail dinner served at your seat.
- Overnight Fairmont Queen Elizabeth Hotel
- Breakfast and Dinner Included

Day 4 - Montréal / VIA Rail
Have a day at leisure in this cosmopolitan town that blends the excitement of a bustling commercial city with the quaintness of the old and new. Montréal, the metropolis of the province of Quebec and the second largest French-speaking city in the world, is a dynamic and modern city that still preserves its architectural heritage. Contributing to the charm of this city are the various multi-ethnic neighborhoods and the parks. Lafontaine Park and Mount-Royal Park are two. Transfer from the hotel to Montréal's rail station, Gare Centrale

Re-enactment of British military life in the 1800s at the Halifax Citadel.

for an early evening departure aboard VIA Rail's Ocean, in Easterly class.
- Overnight VIA Rail
- Dinner on the Train Included

Day 5 - VIA Rail / Halifax, NS
Breakfast is served in the dining car as our journey aboard the Ocean continues into the Maritimes; through the charming province of New Brunswick and into scenic Nova Scotia. Today's destination is this province's historic port capital, Halifax, which is situated on the Atlantic shore and has the world's second largest natural harbour.
- Overnight Delta Halifax
- Breakfast on the Train Included

Day 6 - Halifax / Atlantic Tours / Digby, NS
Today you explore more of Canada's Ocean Playground on a driving tour that takes us along the Lighthouse Trail to the most recognized lighthouse of all at Peggy's Cove. Mail a postcard home from the only lighthouse in North America with a post office! Visit Grand Pré National Historic Park in the Annapolis Valley and the Port Royal National Historic Park and continue on to Digby with Atlantic Tours. Digby is a treasure trove of Nova Scotia heritage settled in 1783 by United Empire Loyalists, led by the British Admiral, Sir Robert Digby.
- Overnight Old Orchard Inn
- Breakfast and Dinner Included

Day 7 - Digby / Atlantic Tours / Saint John, NB
This afternoon, cruise the Bay of Fundy to New Brunswick. In Saint John, visit Reversing Falls Rapids. The phenomenon is caused by the tremendous rise and fall of the tides of the Bay of Fundy, which are the highest in the world and are a result of the tidal action originating in the Southern Indian Ocean sweeping around the Cape of Good Hope and then northward into the Bay of Fundy. They are also affected by the distance of the moon from the earth at this longitude. In Saint John, the bay tides rise 28 ½ feet.
- Overnight Delta Brunswick Hotel
- Breakfast Included

Day 8 - Saint John, NB / Atlantic Tours / Charlottetown, PE
Your tour continues through Fundy National Park to Hopewell Cape. Fundy

National Park of Canada encompasses some of the last remaining wilderness in southern New Brunswick. After lunch, cross to Prince Edward Island on the Confederation Bridge, a 12.9-kilometre (8-mile) span—the longest bridge over ice-covered waters in the world! Tour Canada's birthplace, Charlottetown.
- Overnight Charlottetown (with Atlantic Tours)
- Breakfast and Lunch Included

Day 9 - Charlottetown
Enjoy a morning at leisure in Charlottetown before visiting the diverse habitats of Prince Edward Island National Park, which provides homes for a variety of plants and animals; sand dunes, barrier islands and sand pits, beaches, sandstone cliffs, wetlands and forests. The National Park also features cultural resources, notably Green Gables. This attraction, which has become famous around the world, was the inspiration for the setting in Lucy Maud Montgomery's classic tale of fiction, "Anne of Green Gables." This evening, enjoy a delicious lobster dinner!
- Overnight Charlottetown (with Atlantic Tours)
- Breakfast and Dinner Included

Day 10 - Charlottetown / Atlantic Tours / Halifax
Today you return to Halifax and take a scenic cruise, crossing from PEI to Nova Scotia on the ferry. The tour concludes with a mid-afternoon arrival in Halifax.

■ Churchill Northern Adventure

Come along for an adventure in Manitoba's northern sub-Arctic region where you'll become acquainted with the Lords of the Arctic Canada's polar bears! In late fall, ice forms along the western coast of Hudson Bay and just before the bay freezes, large numbers of polar bears gather together along the coast until they can move out onto the frozen ice. Your destination is Churchill and your journey is aboard VIA Rail's Hudson Bay. You'll discover the fascinating diversity of mammals and human cultures found in the tundra region. Ride in a Tundra Buggy®, explore the area from above in a helicopter and experience dog sledding. An adventure awaits you in Manitoba's North!

Day 1 - Winnipeg, Manitoba / VIA Rail
Welcome to bustling Winnipeg, Manitoba. Transfer from the Winnipeg airport to the VIA Rail station for an evening departure aboard VIA Rail's Hudson Bay in sleeping car accommodations. As the train heads into the night, relax in your sleeping car accommodations or in the lounge. Meet over dinner with the rest of the group before leaving.
- Overnight VIA Rail
- Dinner Included

Day 2 - VIA Rail
View remote Canada from the comfort of your train as you travel Manitoba for 1,700 kilometres (1,055 miles), into the

province's vast, northern countryside.
- Overnight VIA Rail
- Breakfast, Lunch and Dinner Included

Day 3 - VIA Rail / Churchill, Manitoba
Rise early as you arrive at your destination the accessible arctic town, Churchill. Tour this historic town and the striking tundra region surrounding it. Later this evening, perhaps catch a show of the spectacular Northern Lights!
- Overnight Churchill
- Continental Breakfast Included

Day 4 - Churchill
It's an all-day close-up view of the accessible Arctic from a Tundra Buggy®. It's a great opportunity to photograph or just sit back and watch the wild life go about their daily lives.
- Overnight Churchill
- Box Lunch Included

Day 5 - Churchill
A full day tour of the area is included today with some spare time left to take an optional heli-tour for a "bird's-eye-view" of the accessible arctic. Later take some free time to shop for local crafts!!
- Overnight Churchill

Day 6 - Churchill / VIA Rail
Before we leave we will experience another form of arctic transportation, the dog sled! Then we will meet for a farewell to Churchill dinner and transfer to the train station for the departure off the Hudson Bay.
- Overnight VIA Rail
- Dinner Included

Day 7 - VIA Rail
Spend a relaxing day onboard, enjoying the passing scenery and friendly ambiance of the Hudson Bay and a time to reflect on your amazing experience.
- Overnight VIA Rail
- Breakfast, Lunch and Dinner Included

Day 8 - VIA Rail / Winnipeg
Rise early for a continental breakfast and your morning arrival in vibrant Winnipeg and the wide open prairies. Tour concludes with transfer within the Greater Winnipeg area, including the Winnipeg International Airport. Thank you for travelling with John Steel Rail Tours.
- Continental Breakfast Included

The King of Arctic Canada.

Travel Tour Operators

Your dream Canadian trip is just a click of a mouse or a phone call away, thanks to select tour and travel operators that offer all-in-one travel assistance to Canada. We have listed down the best of the lot and we are happy to recommend them to travelers anywhere.

Choose any or combinations of airline ticketing, hotel accommodations, car rentals, entertainment tickets and reservations to popular shows and attractions, and exciting sightseeing packages. Itineraries can be personalized to suit your interests and schedule, be it a romantic getaway for two, a group adventure or a weeklong family fun. These tour operators will save you half the time preparing for your trip, sending you right to where your real journey starts – VIA Rail trains.

America By Rail
5000 Northwind Drive, Suite 226
East Lansing, Michigan 48823 USA
Toll free: 1-888-777-6605
Website: www.americabyrail.net

Atlantic Tours Gray Line
1660 Hollis Street, Suite 211
Halifax, NS B3J 1V7 Canada
Toll free: 1-800-565-7173
Website: www.ambassatours.com

Brennan Vacations
Joseph Vance Building
1402 3rd Avenue, Suite 717
Seattle, WA 98101 USA
Toll free: 1-800-237-7249
Website: www.brennanvacations.com

Brendan Worldwide Vacations
21625 Prairie Street
Chatsworth, CA 91311-5833 USA
Toll free: 1- 800-421-8446
Website: www.brendanvacations.com

Brewster Tours
100 Gopher Street, Box 1140
Banff, AB T1L 1J3 Canada
Toll free: 1-800-661-1152
Website: www.brewster.ca

Canada a la Carte
1402 3rd Avenue, Suite 717
Seattle, WA 98101 USA
Toll free: 1-877-977-6500
Website: www.canadaalacarte.com

Cartan Tours
3033 Ogden Avenue
Lisle, IL 60532 USA
Toll free: 1-800-422-7826
Website: www.cartantours.com

Clipper Vacations
2701 Alaskan Way, Pier 69
Seattle, WA 98121-1199 USA
Toll free: 800-888-2535
Website: www.clippervacations.com

Collettte Vacations
162 Middle Street
Pawtucket, Rhode Island 02860 USA
Toll Free: 1-800-340-5158
Website: www.collettevacations.com

Discover Holidays
Suite 905, 850 West Hastings St.
Vancouver, BC V6C 1E1 Canada
Toll Free: 1-800-243-0129
Website: www.discoverholidays.ca

Exclusively Canada
Suite 229, 998 Harbourside Drive
North Vancouver, BC V7P 3T2 Canada
Toll Free: 1.888.730.9500
Website: www.exclusivelycanada.travel

Globus & Cosmos
5301 South Federal Circle
Littleton, CO 80123-2980 USA

GLOBUS Toll free: 1-866-755-8581
Website: www.globusjourneys.com

COSMOS Toll free: 1-800-276-1241
Website: www.cosmosvacations.com

Grand Circle Travel
347 Congress Street
Boston, MA, 02210 USA
Toll free: 1-800-321-2835
Website: www.gct.com

John Steel Rail Tours
RR 8, 825 Gibsons Way
Gibsons Landing, BC V0N 1V8 Canada
Toll free: 1-800-988-5778
Website: www.johnsteel.com

Jonview Canada
1300 Yonge Street
Toronto, Ontario M4T 1X3 Canada
Tel: (416) 323-9090
Website: http://www.jonview.com

Maupintours
10650 West Charleston Blvd.
Summerlin, NV 89135-1014 USA
Toll free: 1-800-255-4266
Website: www.maupintour.com/

Odyssey Learning Adventures
182 Princess Street
Kingston, ON K7L 1B1 Canada
Toll free: 1-800-263-0050
Website: www.ambassatours.com

Rail Travel Center
125 Main Street, P.O. Box 206
Putney, VT 05346 USA
Toll Free: 1-800-458-5394
Website: www.ambassatours.com

Rail Travel Tours
Box 44, 123 Main Street
Winnipeg, MB R3C 1A3 Canada
Toll Free: 1-866-704-3528
Website: www.railtraveltours.com

Tauck World Discovery
10 Norden Place
Norwalk, CT 06880 USA
Toll free: 1-800-788-7885
Website: www.tauck.com

Trafalgar Tours
801 E. Katella Ave. 3rd Floor
Anaheim, CA 92805 USA
Toll free : 800-854-0103
Website: www.trafalgartours.com

Travelsphere
Compass House, Rockingham Road,
Market Harborough, Leicestershire,
LE16 7QD United Kingdom
Tel: 0870-240-2426
Website: www.travelsphere.co.uk

Vantage Deluxe World Travel
90 Canal Street
Boston, MA 02114-2031 USA
Toll free: 1-617-878-6000
Website: www.vantagetravel.com

Yankee Holidays
100 Cummings Center, Ste. 120B
Beverly, MA 01915 USA
Toll free: 1-800-225-2550
Website: www.yankee-holidays.com

Overseas Travel Agents

If you live in a country other than Canada or the United States, you may purchase your tickets through one of these overseas travel agents. Their names and addresses are listed on this page.

People with speech or hearing problems may communicate through telecommunication devices for the hearing-impaired.
(TTY: 1-800-268-9503)

Argentina

Vanguard Marketing SA
Juncal 840 6ºA
Buenos Aires, C1062ABF Argentina
Tel.: 54 11 4322 5100
Fax: 54 11 4328 2563
Website: www.vanguardmarketing.com.ar

Australia

Asia Pacific Travel Marketing Services
10 Tudor Street
Surry Hills, Sydney, NSW2010 Australia
Tel.: 61 2 9319 6624
Fax: 61 2 9319 4151
Website: www.aptms.com.au

Austria

Canada Reisen
Buchberggasse 34
A-3400 Klosterneuburg
Tel.: 011 43 2243 / 25994
Fax: 011 43 2243 / 26198
Website: www.canadareisen.at / www.amerikareisen.at

Brazil

South Marketing International
Franklin Roosevelt Ave.
194 GR505
20021 120 Rio de Janeiro,
RJ - Brasil
Tel.: 55 21 2517-4800
Fax: 55 21 2517-4808
Website: www.southmarketing.com.br

Denmark

My Planet
Noerregade 51
DK 7500 Holstebro, Denmark
Tel.: 97 42 50 00
Fax: 96 10 02 50
Website: www.benns.com

France

Express Conseil
5 bis, rue du Louvre
75001 Paris, France
Tel.: 1 44 77 87 94
Fax: 1 42 60 05 45
Website: www.ecltd.com

Germany

Canada Reise Dienst
CRD International Stadthausbruecke 1-3
20355 Hamburg, Germany
 Tel.: 49 40 3006160
Fax: 49 40 30061655
Web: www.crd.de

Hong Kong

Japan Travel Bureau, Inc.
Room UG305, UG 3rd Floor,
Chinachem Golden Plaza
77 Mody Road,
Tsimshatsui East Kowloon, Hong Kong
Tel.: 852 2734 9288
Fax: 852 2722 7300
Email: jtb@jtb.com.hk

Japan

Japan Travel Bureau Inc.
1-6-4 Marunouchi
Chiyoda - ku, Tokyo 100 005
Tel.: 03 3820 8011
Fax: 03 3820 6380

Korea

Seoul Travel Service, Ltd.
5th Fl. Jaencung Bldg
192-11, 1-Ka Ulchiro,
Chung-Ku, Seoul, Korea 100-191
Tel.: 02 755-1144
Fax: 02 753-9076
Website: www.seoultravel.co.kr
Tour Marketing Korea
5th Fl. Hanmi Building, # 1
Kongpyong-Dong, Chongro-Gu, Seoul
Tel.: 02 732-7700

Mexico

Trenes Y Otros Servicios
S de RL e CV
Praga 27 Co. Juarez, Mexico 06600 DF
Tel.: (5255) 5207-2258
Fax: (5255) 5207-7154
Email: mexico@viarail.ca

Netherlands

Incento B.V.
P.O. Box 1067
1400 BB Bussum, Netherlands
Tel.: 035 69 55111
Fax: 035 69 55155
Website: www.incento.nl

New Zealand

The Canada & Alaska Holiday Book
101 Great South Road Remuera
PO Box 74551, Market Road
Auckland, New Zealand
Tel.: 64 9 522 5975
Fax: 64 9 524 8248

United Kingdom

1st Rail
Trafford House
Chester Road, Old Trafford
Manchester, M32 ORS England
Tel.: 0845 644 3553 (local call)
Fax: 0845 644 3552 (local call)
Email: mail@1stRail.com
Website: www.1strail.com/

Railway Lingo

A

Air Brake – An important mechanism in the standard safety of trains, air brakes are installed on both freight and passenger cars as the standard braking system. Each car on the train is equipped with an air brake, and the whole braking system is managed by an engineer onboard. Air brakes consist of compressed air. During emergency, these brakes are automatically released by reducing the air pressure, slowing down and stopping the train to safety.

Activity Coordinator – The Activity Coordinator is one of the most popular crew members on the train. Approachable and charismatic, this person leads fun and engaging activities for passengers like interactive games and entertainment in the train's Activity car.

Alerter – Another safety device installed on the train, the alerter ensures the brakes are turned on during an emergency. This device sounds off a horn alarm if the brake, whistle or any of the control components is not tapped within the required time duration. The brakes are automatically turned on after five minutes. This device is especially handy if the engineer on the train's central brake control is unable to respond to an emergency situation for some reason.

Axle – The metal hinge supporting the railcar wheels as base. In general transport, wheels are usually just suspended on the axle as they spin. In train mechanism, the axle is permanently fused to the railcar wheels and rolls around with it. The welded design ensures that the wheels stay on the rails. It also shifts the mass of the car to the journal bearings for prolonged car efficiency.

B

Ballast – The ground foundation that serves as a roadbed when laying down the train tracks. It is usually made of gravel or rock and stone pieces.

Box Car – Generally referred to as a freight car, the fully-enclosed box car has sliding doors on either side. It is used to carry cargo that cannot be exposed to weather elements.

C

Caboose – The car at the tail end of a freight train usually thought of as private area for crew members. The caboose is actually an observatory post for engineers and the crew to check the train's condition, detect potential problems and alert others on a perceived danger on tracks. Today, the caboose is considered obsolete with the coming of automatic detectors installed on tracks, and is sadly relegated to train nostalgia especially by pioneering crew members.

Coach – Refers to the individual car segment that comprises a train, and is used to transport passengers to a destination. A coach layout is normally two rows of seats, with a walking aisle in the middle of each row.

Comfort Class – The best way to travel VIA Rail on a budget. Comfort Class affords passengers with an economically-priced ticket but with the comforts of stretch-out reclining seats and the same panoramic viewing windows as in the other classes. Ticket price does not include meals, but an onboard food take-out service is available.

Consist – A railway lingo referring to

all the car segments of an entire train. Simply put, the total number of a train's cars and all its attachments including the locomotives.

Container – Generally refers to huge stackable square vessels usually made of steel and used to carry all kinds of products and commodities for long-distance transport. They are either hauled on ships, trucks or flatcars using cranes and industrial rollers.

Coupler – Attached at the rear of all railcars to clasp the cars in line together. The cars are automatically connected by a coupler, but an authorized rail worker fastens the hoses and cables to ensure solid power and brake connections. Disengaging the cars (uncoupling) is also done manually as a safety precaution to ensure no clasped units are left.

D

Derailment – An incident when the wheels of a car come off the rail track, causing a train to stop. Trains are well equipped with safety fixtures to prevent derailment, but for safety precautions, an engineer may deliberately derail a train. Small 'derail' signs are planted in some sections of rail yards where unattended cars are stopped to prevent collision with trains on the main track.

Diaphragm – A protective shield made of ridged material extended between adjacent cars meant to shelter passengers especially from the rains and snow as they make their way from car to car.

Dispatcher – The rail crew manning the direction and movement of all trains and directs the general rail traffic from a central location within an area.

Dome Car – Also called the Skyline car, a glass-enclosed car with upper level viewing deck where passengers can go for a full view of the rolling landscapes or simply hang out to relax with a drink and engage in conversation with other passengers.

Drawing Room (Triple Bedroom) – The best sleeping compartment among all VIA Rail facilities and is available only in the premier coaches, the Park car and Chateu car. Elegant and spacious, it comfortably accommodates three persons with an upper bed and two bunk beds decked with comfy mattresses. It also features a walk-in private washroom, shower room, closets, luggage area and air-conditioning.

E

Engineer – The main person responsible for running the train's locomotive. Train engineers must posses rigid training certifications, specifically safety and troubleshooting to ensure a smooth and pleasant experience for all passengers.

F

Flag Stop – Refers to a station where a train is forced to make a stop in response to a signal. A flag stop may occur in an emergency or procedural check and is not always listed in the Timetable.

Flange – A one-inch fold on the innermost rim of a railcar's wheel that prevents it from slipping off the track, keeping the entire train on track.

Foamer – The railway slang for a person who is obsessed with the rail system, hooked both on the travel mode and in the physical sense of train assembly. The rail fan supposedly foams at the mouth at the sight of a train, hence the term "foamer."

RAILWAY LINGO

G

Gauge – Refers to the standard distance between the rails of a track, which is set at 4 feet, 8.5 inches since the 1880s for North American railways, paving the way for stronger tracks.

Grade – A change in the elevation of a track's section, measured in percent to feet scale over a certain distance. For instance, a 4 percent grade means the track either shifts up or down 4 feet in a distance of 200 feet.

Green Eye – The railroad term for a clear signal indicating the train may proceed at normal speed.

H

Highball – Slang for a commonly understood signal or plain verbal order that allows a train engineer to drive the locomotive at the fastest legal speed. The word came from an old railway practice of lifting a coloured ball atop a high pole to mean a clear, unobstructed track beyond.

Hot Box Detector – The modern alternative to caboose observation posts, these heat-sensitive devices are positioned in strategic corners of the main tracks. Once they come in contact with so-called hot boxes (overheated journal bearings), an alarm is immediately sent to the crew through automatic signals or recorded warnings.

J

Journal Bearing – Box-shaped components attached to the axle and a standard to railcar systems. Each axle is paired with two journal bearings, which takes on the weight of the car and distributes the mass evenly over the axels hinged on it. Journal bearings are important in trouble detection, with engineers and crew on constant alert for signs of a "hot box" or overheated journal bearings on trains in motion.

L

Locomotive – The central "vein" of a train system, also called the engine. The train's locomotive is equipped with cables and leads, and propels itself to pull the railcars. A rail consist may be composed of two or more locomotives, with the first one referred to as the A or lead locomotive, and the other unmanned units are called the B locomotives.

M

Milepost (mile marker) – Rectangular white boards visible on every mile along the tracks imprinted with black numbers that indicate the miles the train will travel from a certain point of reference, allowing passengers to anticipate an interesting landmark and get ready with their cameras.

N

Narrow Gauge – A rail gauge that measures less than the prescribed standard gauge of 4' 8 ½", usually those older, short rail tracks that were unable to bear the weight of general cargo.

P

Panorama Car – A glass-enclosed dome car that affords passengers with a 360-degree view of lush Canadian sceneries. This single-level car is a special feature of the Skeena and the seasonal Snow Train to Jasper.

R

RDC Car – Used in VIA Rail's Malahat and Lake Superior routes, the Rail Diesel Cars (RDC) inspired the design for modern bi-directional rail cars that can advance on either end. From multiple diesel engine power and military-type design, today's RDCs are a joy to ride on with faster engine and well-appointed interiors.

Red Eye – The railroad term for a red signal indicating stop.

Roomette – A single-bed sanctuary perfect for the lonesome traveler needing a private space for some quick work update or simply wishing to savour a memorable trip alone. Compact yet features the basic amenities like power outlet, a washroom, toilet and vanity. The comfortable bed transforms into a relaxing seat beside the window by day.

S

Service Manager – The head of the train attendants and crew responsible for the general operation and activities inside the train, and to whom passenger concerns regarding the trip are directed for immediate resolution.

Siding – An adjacent track fixed to the main track that enables a train to divert in its direction to allow another train to pass, avoiding derailment or collision.

Signal – A communications device that transmits signs and instructions used by the train crew in assessing the train's movement, particularly on a specific track condition or rail traffic.

Slide Fence – A safety device planted along mountainous rail tracks. Once they are knocked down or crushed over by rocks or snow, slide fences automatically sends off signals to alert the train crew of track obstructions along the way.

Switch – A movable segment of a track directed by a remote control that allows a train to switch from one track to another.

T

Take Out – An onboard meal service where passengers of Comfort class and those without food inclusions in their ticket can purchase meals, snacks and beverage.

Terminal – The term "terminal" encompasses not just the train station, but the entire railway hub where passengers converge, cargoes are handled, and all other train-related activities take place.

Throttle – A grip that acts as a kind of switch to regulate the flow of fuel or electricity that goes into the train engine, affecting its speed and velocity depending on the amount of fuel injected.

Tie – Refers to the fixture of concrete or wooden slabs or sticks implanted in the gravel and where the rails are secured. Also known as "cross tie."

Timetable – A printed reference for both passengers and freight trains containing important trip details like schedule and direction, including stops and connections.

Turntable – A hauling device used in rail terminals for easily carting and turning around heavy engines and massive cars.

V

Vestibule – A kind of an enclosed foyer at the end of each car where passengers can pass underneath.

Y

Yard – A general section of a rail business that serves as a centre specifically for mechanical maintenance and where general train works are done.

Index

A

A Brief History of Canada, pp. 11, 36
Abitibi, pp. 9, 237, 242, 243, 294-297
Acadian (s), pp. 232, 247, 254, 255
Accommodation & Seat Configuration, p. 9, 84
Activity Car, pp. 72, 106, 107, 128, 312
Activity Coordinator, pp. 4, 72, 312
Advance discounts, p. 99
Air Brake, p. 312
AirConnect, pp. 202, 264, 279, 286
Alberta, pp. 12, 26, 28, 38, 154, 158, 189
Albreda Subdivision, p. 158
Aldershot, pp. 209, 210, 219, 278-285
Alerter, p. 312
Alexandria Subdivision, p. 225
Amtrak, pp. 99, 284, 285
Appalachian Region, p. 29
Appendix, pp. 9, 262-315
Armstrong to Sioux Lookout, p. 148
Arts and Cultures, pp. 9, 11, 18
Ashcroft Subdivision, p. 163
Assiniboine River, pp. 150, 151
Athabasca River, p, 156
Atlantic Adventure, p. 304
Atlantic Canada, pp.139, 230, 247, 250, 257, 263, 300
Aurora Borealis (or Northern Lights), p. 199
Automobile Car, p. 120
Avalanche Zone, p. 126
Axle, pp. 127, 312

B

Baggage Car, pp. 76, 80, 102
Baggage Policy, pp. 97, 102, 264
Baie des Chaleurs, pp. 230, 231, 233, 249, 254, 255
Bald eagle, pp. 31, 171, 179,
Ballast, pp. 60, 118, 312
Battle Bluff Tunnel, p. 163
Bayview Junction, p. 221
Bears, pp. 30, 31, 34, 303, 306
Beaver, p. 32
Bedford Subdivision, p. 248
Bell, Alexander Graham, p. 212
Belleville, pp. 208, 278, 280, 281
Belugas, pp. 30,193
Berth (s), pp. 68, 74, 84, 88, 112
Big horn sheep, p. 32
Biggar to Edmonton, p. 154
Black bears, pp. 28, 30,31,179
Bloc Québécois, pp. 17, 24
Block, pp. 124, 126
Blue River to Kamloops, p. 162
Bombardier Transportation, p. 81
Bonaventure, pp. 233, 290, 291
Boreal Forest, pp. 30, 148
Boston Bar, p. 163, 164
Box Car, p. 120, 312
Bramalea to Silver, p. 217
Brantford, p. 209
British Columbia Railway, p. 64
British culture, p. 36
British Isles, pp. 23, 37
British North American Act, p.46
British Royalty, p. 59
British settlers, p. 118
Brockville, pp. 202, 208, 278-281
Brule Lake, p, 157
Budd Company, p. 82
Buffalo, pp. 220, 284, 285
Bulkley Subdivision, p. 176
Bullet Lounge, p. 110
Burns Lake, pp. 174, 175, 270, 271
Butchart Gardens, p. 184
Bytown and Prescott Railway, p. 60

C

Caboose, pp. 121, 312, 314
Campbellton to Riviere-du-Loup, p. 255
Canada pp. 3, 4, 5, 8, 12, 15, 22, 23, 24, 204
Canadian National Railway, pp. 4, 44, 45, 47, 54, 63, 165
Canadian Northern Ontario Railway, p. 147
Canadian Northern Railway, pp. 43, 46, 54, 63
Canadian Pacific Railway, pp. 43,45, 58, 145, 165
Canadian route, p. 101
Canadian Shield, pp. 28, 29, 43, 145
Canadian, pp. 13,142, 169, 195, 196
Canadians, pp. 36-43, 48, 156
Canora to Hudson Bay, p. 196
Canrailpass, p. 99
Capreol, p. 63
Captain George Vanvouver, p. 179
Car or Service Attendants, p. 108
Cariboo Mountains, p. 160
Cartier Subdivision, p. 244
Cascade Mountain Range, pp. 165, 166
Cascapedia Subdivision, p. 231,
Centre Beam Car, p. 121
Chaleur, pp. 230, 231, 232, 249, 290, 291
Champlain and Saint Lawrence Railroad Company, pp. 43, 56, 60
Chandler East to Gaspe, p.233
Chapleau Game Preserve, p. 147
Chapleau to White River, p. 245
Charny, pp. 228, 258, 288-291,300
Chateau Car, pp. 75, 84, 86
Chatham, p. 209
Check-In Time, p. 100
Cherrett, Liane, p. 128
Chinese, pp. 150, 179
Chinook, p. 178
Chronology, p. 60
Churchill Northern Adventure, p. 306
Churchill, p. 63, 193
Cisco, p. 164, 184
Classic Cross Canada, p. 302
Clearwater Subdivision, p. 162
Clova, pp. 242, 295, 296
CN tower, p. 144
Coach Car, pp. 74, 77, 78, 87, 88, 90, 91, 312
Collenette, David, p. 49
Comfort Class, pp. 68, 99, 100, 106, 109, 312,315
Comfort Sleeper Class, pp. 68, 71
Confederation, pp. 160, 184
Connaught Tunnel, p. 47
Conservative Party, p. 17
Consist, p. 312
Container, p. 313
Coo, Bill p. 64
Copper Creek Tunnel, p. 163
Coquitlam, p. 166
Cordilleran Region, p. 28
Cornwall, pp. 202, 225
Corridor and Ocean routes, p. 78
Coteau Junction, p. 224
Cougar (s), pp. 30, 33
Coupler, p. 313
Coyotes, p. 28
Craigellachie, BC, p. 46
Cutarm Potash Mine p, 152
Cylindrical Hopper Car, p. 122

D

Dauphin, pp. 63, 196, 274
Deadman's Island, p. 174
Deluxe Double Bedrooms, p. 90
Democratic Party (NDP), p. 17
Derail Signs, p. 126
Derailment, p. 313
Diamond Subdivision, p. 258
Diaphragm, p. 313
Diefenbaker, John, Prime Minister, pp. 59, 64, 160
Dining Car, pp. 70, 79, 87, 91
Discounts, p. 99
Dispacher, p. 313
Dome Car, pp. 108, 313
Dome Creek, pp. 171, 270, 271
Dorval, pp. 69, 98, 203, 224, 264, 278, 279, 286, 287
Double bedroom, pp. 68, 74, 85
Double Bridge Crossing, p. 164
Drawing Room, pp. 86, 313
Drummondville Subdivision, p. 258
Dundas Subdivision, p. 212
Dundurn Castle, p. 221

INDEX | 317

E

East Chandler Subdivision, p.233
East Indian, p. 150
Easterly Class, pp. 49, 65, 70, 107
Easterly Learning Coordinator, p. 70
Edmonton, pp. 4, 26, 47, 60, 63, 80, 141, 154, 189
Edson Subdivision, pp. 154, 189
Elk, pp. 31, 34
Endako to Smithers, p. 174, 175
Engineer, p. 313
English Canada, p. 37
Equality rights, p. 16
Esquimalt and Nanaimo Railway, p. 64
Europeans, pp. 12, 36, 144
Exchange or refund, p. 96

F

Fairmount Jasper Park Lodge, p. 189
Fallowfield, p. 208
Fares and Reservations, pp. 96, 98, 99
Federal government, pp. 13, 47, 48
First Class, pp. 56, 99, 100, 109
First Nations, pp. 22, 23, 36, 144, 177, 179
Flag Stop, p. 313
Flanger Boards, p. 126
Flatcar, p. 121
Foamer, p. 313
Followfield, p. 96
Forest Fires, p. 162
Forillon National Park, p. 235
Forks, p. 150
Fort Mcmurry, Alberta, p. 156
Fox, Terry, p. 161
Fraser Canyon, p. 160, 166
Fraser River at Hell's Gate, p. 165
Fraser River, p. 159, 160, 164, 166, 167, 172, 184
Freight trains, p. 119
French, pp. 16, 23, 144, 225
Funeral Trains, p. 59

G

Garneau Yard to Jonquiere, p. 238
Gaspé, pp. 203, 230, 231, 232, 235
Gauge, p. 53, 314
General Electric P42-DC model, p. 83
General Motors F40PH-2D model, p. 83
Get To Know Canada p. 9
Gillam to Churchill, p. 198
Glen Fraser Car, pp. 83, 94
Global Economic Model, pp. 11, 20
GO Transit, pp. 46, 64, 144
Goat, p. 34
Gondola Car, p. 123
Gourmet meals, p.87
Government and Politics, pp. 11, 12,
Grade, p. 314
Grain Elevator, p. 153
Grand Trunk Pacific Railroad, pp. 152, 171
Grand Trunk Pacific Railway Company, pp. 43, 44, 54, 152, 155, 168, 173, 174, 177, 181
Grand Trunk Railway, pp. 42, 43, 44, 45, 60
Great Canadian Links, p.42
Great Canadian Railtour Company, p. 64
Great Depression, pp. 55, 58
Great Lakes, p. 204
Great Lakes-St. Lawrence Lowlands region, pp. 29, 43
Great Western Railway, p. 60, 221
Green Eye, p. 314
Green Signal, p. 124
Grimsby, p. 219, 221
Grizzly bear, pp. 28, 32
Guelph Subdivision, p. 217

H

Halifax, pp. 49, 62, 99, 246, 247, 249
Hamilton, p. 64, 212, 217, 221
Hanus, Chris, 4
Hawes, Jasper, p. 157
Hays, Charles Melville pp. 45, 62, 152, 181
Head End Power (HEP 1) cars, p. 74
Henry Rider Haggard, p. 171
HEP 1 Cars, p. 84, 87
HEP 2 Cars, pp. 77, 88
Herchmer Subdivision, p. 198
Hervey Junction to Fitzpatrick, p. 243
Higball, p. 314
Hobos, p. 58
Hopper Car, p. 123
Hot Box Detector p. 127, 314
House of Commons, p. 13
How to Use The Timetable, p. 264
How To Use This Guide, p. 6
Hudson Bay and the Gaspé routes, p. 74
Hudson Bay, pp. 37, 38, 47, 60, 63, 163, 176, 194, 195, 196

I

Immigration recruitment, p. 53
Immigration, p. 14
Indian immigrants, p. 26
Indo-Canadian centres, p. 26
Innuitian belt, p. 29
Interior Plains, p. 28
International travelers, p. 96
Internet, p. 96
Interpretation of Railway Signal Lights, p. 124
Inuit, pp. 22, 23
Ireland, pp. 16, 23
Irish settlers, p. 23
ISIC card, p. 99
Italian, p. 24, 150

J

Jackfish, p. 57, 148
Jamaican, p. 150
Japanese, p. 179
Jasper House Hawes, p. 157
Jasper National Park, pp. 156, 157, 158
Jasper- Prince Rupert (The Skeena), p. 105, 180
Jasper Tramway, p. 158
Jasper, pp. 60, 63, 72, 142, 169
John Steel Rail Tours, p. 4
Joliette Subdivision, p. 237
Jonquière, pp. 105, 201, 236, 238, 241-243, 292, 293
Journal Bearing, p. 314

K

Kamloops, pp. 64, 142, 163, 164, 167
Kanata, p. 36
Kapuskasing Lake, p. 147
Kelowna, p. 64
Kempenfelt Bay, p. 144
Kermode Bears, p. 179
Kicking Horse Pass, p. 56
Killer Whale, p. 33
King Edward VII, p. 60
King George V, p. 59
Kingston, pp. 29, 69, 96, 201, 202, 203
Kitchener, p. 26
Kitselas, p. 178
Komoka Railway Museum, p. 218
Kwinitsa, p. 179

L

La Prairie, pp. 43, 56, 60
La Tuque, p. 242, 243
Lac St. Jean Subdivision, p. 238
Laflamme, Joe, p. 146
Lake Athabasca, p. 156
Lake Couchiching, p. 145
Lake Erie, pp. 29, 213
Lake Huron, pp. 29, 213
Lake Manitoba, p. 62, 151
Lake Ontario, pp. 29, 205, 206, 222
Lake Superior, pp. 29, 58, 244
Lake Winnipeg, p. 28
Late Stops in Major Station, p. 114
Laurentian Plateau, pp. 29, 43
Laurier, Wilfred, p. 160
Leacock, Stephen, p. 144
Lester B. Pearson Airport, p. 216
Liberals, p. 17

Index

Locomotive, p. 314
London, pp. 69, 96, 209, 213, 218
Loons, p. 30
Lost or stolen ticket, p. 99
Lower Canada (Québec), p. 37
LRC cars, pp. 69, 81, 91, 93

M

Macdonald, John A., pp. 45, 50, 184
Mackenzie, William, p. 46, 147
Malahat, pp. 82, 141, 182
Manitoba Lake Railway and Canal Co., p. 46
Manitoba, pp. 12, 26, 38, 60, 196
Manitou Lake, pp. 152, 153
Manor Car, p. 75, 84
Maritimes, pp. 17, 65, 70, 248
Matapédia, p. 231, 230
McBride to Prince George, p. 171
McLure and Barrière, p. 162
Melville, p. 63, 152
Métis, pp. 22, 51
Miette Range, p. 155, 157
Mile-by-mile route guides, p. 6, 7
Milepost(s), p. 125, 314
Miner, Billy, p. 167
Mining Disaster, p. 251
Missing Connecting Trips, p. 114
Mission p. 167
Monashee, p. 161, 170
Mont Joli Subdivision, p. 255
Montmagny Subdivision, p. 257
Montréal- Jonquière (The Saguenay), p. 105
Montréal Subdivision, p. 203
Montréal to Ottawa route, p. 224
Montréal to Québec City, p. 228
Montréal to Toronto route, pp. 202, 208, 224
Montréal-Senneterre (The Abitibi), p. 105
Montréal-Toronto route, p. 202
Moose, pp. 32, 34
Mount Borden, p. 177
Mount Robson, p. 73, 107
Mountain goats, pp. 30, 33
Mountain Pine Beetle Epidemic, pp. 173
Mountain Pose (Tadasana), p. 128
Mountain Time, p, 154
Mt. Fitzwilliam, p. 158
Mt. Rockingham, p. 158
Multiculturalism, p. 11, 22
Mural Lounge, pp. 72, 86, 109

N

Nanaimo, p. 60, 185
Narrow Gauge, p. 314
Nation that the Railway Built, 50
Natural Regions, p. 11, 28
Nechako Subdivision, p. 172
Nemegos Subdivision, p. 245
New Brunswick, pp. 12, 37, 38
New Castle Subdivision, pp. 251, 252
New France, p. 24
New Westminster, p. 166, 167
Newcastle, p. 118
Newfoundland, pp. 12, 23, 38, 63
Niagara Falls, pp. 165, 201, 212, 219, 220, 222, 223
Niagara Gorge Railroad Company, p. 54
North America Rail Pass, p. 99
North American Free Trade Agreement, p. 21
North American Rail Pass, p. 99
North and South Thompson Rivers, p. 162, 163
North Saskatchewan River, p, 154
Northwest Company, p. 163
Northwest Rebellion, p. 57
Northwest Territories, p. 12
Nova Scotia, pp. 12, 26, 37, 38, 47, 246
Nunavut, p. 12, 15, 22

O

Oakville, p. 64, 202, 209, 219, 221
Ocean's route, p. 231,
Ogdensburg, NY, p. 204
Ojibway, p. 22, 144
Okanagan Valley Railway, p. 64
Okanagan Wine Train, P. 83
Onboard and Overnight, p. 112
Ondatjee, Michael, p. 18
Ontario and Québec route, p. 201
Ontario, pp. 12, 60, 64, 200, 201, 203, 204, 216
Orca, p. 33
Oshawa, pp. 202, 208
Ottawa and Prescott Railway Company, p. 60
Ottawa, pp. 55, 63, 64, 69, 96, 201, 204, 208, 224
Overseas Travel Agents, p. 310

P

Pacific Scandal, p. 46
Pack light, p. 101
Panorama car, pp. 80, 93, 189, 314
Panorama Lounge, p. 69
Park Car, pp. 70, 72, 75, 76, 88, 109
Parliament, p. 13, 15
Parry Sound, p. 145
Percé Rock, p.234
Percé, p. 234, p. 231,
Phone reservation, p. 96
Pickering, p. 64
Pointe-aux-Trembles to Garneau, p. 237
Polar Bear, p. 28, 30, 194
Port Alberni, p. 64

Port Moody, pp. 56, 62
Prairies & Central Arctic, pp. 192, 193
Pre-Boarding Checklist, p. 100
Prince Edward Island, pp. 12, 53, 61
Prince George, pp. 63, 141, 169, 172
Prince Rupert, pp. 45, 63, 141, 169, 179
PRIVA custom car service, P. 83
Propane Tanks, p. 127
Prospector Cariboo, p. 65
Provincial governments, p. 14
Public Address System, p. 107
Pukatawagan, p. 194

Q

Qu'Appelle River Valley p. 152
Québec City, pp. 69, 96, 201, 229
Québec City-Windsor Corridor, pp. 48, 201
Québec Reservoirs, p. 28
Québec, pp. 12, 24, 60, 200, 204, 236-239, 242, 243, 255-260, 278, 280, 282, 284, 286, 288-292, 294, 296, 298, 301, 304, 316
Queen Charlotte Islands, p. 169
Queen Elizabeth, pp. 64, 12, 59
Queen Victoria, pp. 60, 184
Quest for Independence, p. 38

R

Rail America Inc., p. 64
Rail Gauge System, p. 118
Rail Travel Tips, 5
Railway construction, p. 43
Railway Full of Freight Cars, p. 120
Railway Lingo, p. 6, 312
Railway Yoga, p. 6, 128
RDC 1, p. 82, 94, 314
Red Eye, p. 315
Red River Floodway, p. 149
Red Signal, p. 124
Redpass Junction, p. 108, 159, 170
Refrigerator Car, p. 122
Refund, p. 96
Regina, p. 55
Renaissance bedrooms, pp. 89, 90
Renaissance Cars, pp. 78, 89
Renaissance Dining cars, p. 91
Renaissance Service car, p. 91
Reporting Lost or Stolen Item, p. 102
Rideau Canal, p. 209
Rivière du Loup, p. 60, 257
Robson Subdivision, p. 170
Rocky Mountain goats, p. 32
Rocky Mountaineer, p. 64
Rocky Mountains, pp. 28, 73, 106, 142, 156, 158, 163
Rogers, Albert Bowman, Major p. 56
Romance by Rail, p. 71
Room Service, p. 113

INDEX | 319

Roomette, p. 315
Royal Hudsons, p. 59
Royal Tours, p. 59
Royal Train, p. 64
Rupert Rocket, pp. 168, 182

S

Safety Measures Onboard, p. 102
Saguenay, pp. 9, 105, 236-238, 240, 241, 243, 292, 293
Saint-Jean, Québec, pp. 43, 56
Salmon Life Cycle, p. 165
Sandford Fleming, pp. 46, 52
Sarnia, p. 44, 216, 218
Saskatchewan Rivers, pp. 28, 196
Saskatchewan, pp. 12, 26, 38, 196
Saskatoon, pp. 59, 60, 64, 142, 153
School train, p. 63
Self-service ticketing kiosks, p. 96
Senneterre, p. 242
Servers or Service Attendants, p. 108
Service Manager, p. 315
Seven Sisters Mountain Range, p. 177
Shaske, John, p. 4
Shower, pp. 88, 113
Shuswap, p. 163
Siding, p. 315
Signal, p. 315
Signs and Symbols, p. 126
Silver & Blue pp. 64, 73, 101, 107, 143
Silver to London Junction, p. 217
Simon Fraser, p. 160
Single Bedroom, pp. 68, 74, 85
Sioux Lookout, pp. 147, 149
Skeena River, pp. 178, 179
Skeena, pp. 16, 80, 141, 159, 169, 172, 182
Skyline cars, pp. 72, 75, 76, 106, 107
Sleeping Car (s), pp. 56, 75, 79, 84, 88
Slide Detectors, p. 127
Slide Fence, p. 315
Smithers to Terrace, p. 176
Smiths Falls Subdivision, p. 209
Snow Train to Jasper, pp. 141, 189, 190
Special Stops, p. 105
Speed Limit Signs, p. 126
St. Catharines, p. 219
St. Hyacinthe Subdivision, p. 258
St. John's Newfoundland, p. 161
St. Laurent Subdivision, p. 237
St. Lawrence River, pp. 29, 60, 204, 205, 209, 231, 236, 248, 249, 256, 257, 260
Standard gauge, pp. 53, 118
Station Name Boards, p. 127
Station stops, p. 43
Ste Rosalie to Montréal, p. 258

Stephenson, George, p. 118
Strathroy Subdivision, pp. 213, 218
Student Discounts, p. 99
Sudbury, pp. 29, 43, 102, 142, 146
Suggested Itineraries, p. 302
Supreme Court, pp. 15, 39
Switch, p. 315

T

Table Mountain, p. 174
Take Out, p. 315
Tank Car, p. 122
Taverna to McBride, p. 170
Telkwa Subdivision, p. 174
Terrace, p. 178, 179
Territorial Governments p. 15
Tete Jaune, p. 158, 170,
The Continental Divide, p. 158
The Pas, pp. 194, 196
Thicket Subdivision, p. 197
Throttle, p. 315
Thunder Bay, p. 161
Tie, p. 315
Timetable, pp. 6, 263, 264, 315
Tipping Guideline, p. 109
Togo Subdivision, p. 196
Toronto to Montréal, p. 227
Toronto to Bayview, p. 209
Toronto to Brockville, p. 208
Toronto to Capreol, p. 144
Toronto to Halwest, p. 216
Toronto to Niagara Falls, p. 219
Toronto to Ottawa route, p. 208
Toronto to Sarnia, p. 216
Toronto to Sarnia, p. 81
Toronto to Windsor, p. 209
Toronto, pp. 47, 60, 64, 69, 72, 96, 202, 201, 20, 208, 219
Toronto-Vancouver transcontinental route, p. 72
Toronto-Winnipeg-Jasper-Vancouver (The Canadian), p.105
Totem Class, p. 71
Totem Pole, pp. 176, 177
Traffic lights, p. 124
Train at a Glance, pp. 143, 169
Train Classes and Services pp. 9, 68
Travel Agency, p. 96
Travel Setbacks, 114
Travel Tips, p. 143
Travel Tour Operators, p. 308
Trent River, p. 206
Trestle Rapids, p. 147
Truro to Moncton, p. 248
Twelve Mile Creek, pp. 212, 222
Types of Railcars, 74

U

Ukrainian Canadians, p. 26

Union Station, pp. 221, 226
United Empire Loyalists, p. 37
United States of America, pp. 12, 21
University of British Columbia p. 4
Upper Canada, p. 37, 206

V

Van Horne, Cornelius, pp. 46, 47, 54, 57, 61
Vancouver Island, p. 60, 141
Vancouver, George, p. 185
Vancouver, pp. 25, 60, 72, 159, 160, 166
Vermillion River, p. 196
Vestibule, p. 315
VIA Destinations, p. 49
VIA Rail fleet, p. 78
Victoria Cross Range, p. 158
Victoria, p. 64, 184

W

Wabakimi Park, p. 148
Wabamun Lake, p, 155
Wabowden to Gillam, p. 197
Wagon wheels, p. 42
Wainwright Subdivision, p, 154
Watrous Subdivision, p, 152
Way of the Rail Publishing, p. 5
Wekusko Subdivision, p. 197
Well's Gray Provincial Park, p. 162
West Coast Express, p. 64
Whales, p. 30, 33
Wheat Boom, p. 151
Whistle Posts, p. 127
Whistle prohibited, p. 126
Whistle tunnel, p. 126
Whistler Northwind, p. 80
Whistler Mountaineer, p. 65
White River Subdivision, p. 245
Windsor, pp. 60, 69, 96, 127, 210
Windsor-Québec City Corridor, p. 96
Winnipeg Union Station, p. 150
Winnipeg, pp. 54, 60, 63, 64, 128, 142, 149, 193, 194, 195, 196
Winnipeg-Churchill (The Hudson Bay), p.105
Wolves, p. 28

Y

Yale Subdivision, p. 163
Yard, p. 315
Yellow Signal, p. 124
Yellowhead Highway, p. 171
Yellowhead Pass, p. 158, 171
Yellowhead region, p. 158
Yukon, p. 15,
Yukon Territory, p. 28

Acknowledgements

■ Photographs & Illustrations Credits

Abbreviations for the credits are as follows:
CH = Chris Hanus, CIL = Compare Infobase Limited, JIC = Jupiter Image Corporation, GT = George Triay, SI = Suzanne Ingeborg, TD = Triay Design, VRC = VIA Rail Canada, **t** (top), **b** (bottom), **c** (centre), **l** (left), **r** (right), **b/g** (background).

FRONT COVER, b/g JIC; r Alquin Reyes; c Triay Design; **SPINE**, JIC; **BACK COVER**, b/g JIC; l Alquin Reyes; bl VRC, bc Margaret Kitson; br VRC.

INTRODUCTION
1 VRC; 2-3b/g VRC, 4tl Sean Azar; 4bl Sean Azar; 5bl VRC; 6 VRC; 7r TD; 7l TD; 7br TD; 7bl TD; 8 VRC.

GET TO KNOW CANADA
10-11b/g JIC; 10r JIC; 12bl JIC; 13t JIC; 13c JIC; 14tl SI; 15br Ottawa Tourism; 16 JIC; 17l TD; 17r TD; 17rc TD; 17lc TD; 17b Ottawa Tourism; 19 SI; 20bl NASA/JPL-Caltech; 22 JIC; 23tl Library and Archives Canada; 24 Library and Archives Canada; 25tl SI; 25b Library and Archives Canada; 26tl Library and Archives Canada; 26br Library and Archives Canada; 27b/g JIC; 27c TD; 28l Alquin Reyes; 28r JIC; 29 TD; 30 TD; 31 TD; 32 TD; 33 TD; 34 TD; 35b/g Alquin Reyes; 36 JIC; 37 Library and Archives Canada; 39 Tourism Ottawa.

HISTORICAL ROOTS OF CANADA'S RAILWAY
40-41b/g Glenbow Archives; 41 Glenbow Archives; 42 Glenbow Archives; 43 Glenbow Archives; 44bl TD; 44br Glenbow Archives; 45 Glenbow Archives; 46 Glenbow Archives; 47 Glenbow Archives; 48 SI; 50 Glenbow Archives; 51 Glenbow Archives; 52 Glenbow Archives; 53tl Glenbow Archives; 53br Glenbow Archives; 54 Glenbow Archives; 55 Glenbow Archives; 56 Glenbow Archives; 57 Glenbow Archives; 58 Glenbow Archives; 59 Jasper Yellowhead Museum & Archives; 61 JIC; 62 JIC; 65 CH.

TRAIN CLASSES & SERVICES
66-67b/g N. Matsumoto; 66 VRC; 68tl SI; 68r SI; 68cr SI; 68br VRC; 69tr SI; 69c VRC; 69bl SI; 70tl VRC; 70tr VRC; 70br SI; 7tl VRC; 71bl VRC; 72tl VRC; 72l N. Matsumoto; 72r VRC; 72br CH; 73l SI; 73c N. Matsumoto; 74 TD; 75 TD; 76 TD; 77 TD; 78 VRC; 79 VRC; 80t VRC; 80b TD; 81 TD; 82 TD; 83 TD/VRC; 84t TD; 84c TD/VRC; 84bl TD; 84br VRC; 85tl SI; 85cl TD; 85cr SI; 85bl TD; 85b VRC; 86tl TD; 86c VRC; 86b TD/VRC; 87tr TD/VRC; 87b TD/VRC; 88t SI; 88cr TD; 88cl SI; 88b TD; 89t VRC; 89c VRC; 89l VRC; 89b VRC; 90tl TD; 90tr VRC; 90c VRC; 90b VRC; 91t VRC; 91c VRC; 91b VRC; 92t VRC; 92l TD/VRC; 92b SI; 93tl TD/VRC; 93r VRC; 93bl TD/VRC; 93br CH; 94tl TD; 94r CH; 94cl TD/VRC; 94b CH; 95 VRC.

TRAIN TRAVEL TIPS
96-97b/g SI; 97 SI; 98 VRC; 99l VRC; 99r VRC; 100b SI, 101tr SI; 101bc SI; 103 TD; 104bl SI; 105tr CH; 106tl SI; 107r TD/VRC; 108bl CH; 110bg VRC, 110tl VRC; 111tr VRC; 112bl SI; 113 VRC; 115 SI.

CANADIAN RAILWAY 101
116-117b/g JIC; 117 JIC; 118 TD; 119 N. Matsumoto; 120 TD; 121 TD; 122 TD; 123 TD; 124 TD; 125 TD; 126 CH; 127 CH/TD; 128 GT; 129 GT; 130 GT; 131 GT; 132 GT; 133 GT; 133 GT; 134 GT; 135 GT; 136 GT; 137 GT.

ROUTE GUIDE
Western Canada - 138b/g SI; 139 SI; 140 Alquin Reyes; 142 VRC; 143 CIL; 144tl SI; 145tl JIC; 145c CIL; 146-147 CIL; 148-149 CIL; 150-151 CIL; 150l SI; 152-153c CIL; 152br CH; 153tr CH; 154-155 CIL; 156 CIL; 157b N. Matsumoto; 158bl CH; 159t CIL; 159br CH; 160t CIL; 160l Library and Archives Canada; 161t CH; 161br CH; 162 JIC; 163t CIL; 163br CH; 164t CIL; 164bl CH; 165tl JIC; 165br CH; 166 VRC; 167t CIL; 167r RCMP Archives Canada; 168 VRC; 169 CIL; 170t CIL; 170bl VRC; 171 CH; 172 CH; 173t CIL; 173r JIC; 174 CIL; 175 CH; 176tl CH; 176bl CH; 177t CIL; 177br CH; 178t CIL; 178bl CH; 181b/g CH; 182 CH; 183r CII; 184br CH; 185l CIL; 185br CIL; 186 CH; 187l CIL; 187br CH; 188-189bg CH; 188tl CIL; 189tr CH; 190 N. Matsumoto; 191 CIL; **Prairies & Central Arctic** - 192-193b/g Margaret Kitson; 194t Margaret Kitson; 195 CIL; 196 CH; 197 CIL; 198 CIL; 199r JIC; 199cr CH; 199br CH. **Ontario & Québec** – 200-201b/g JIC; 201 JIC; 202 VRC; 203 CIL; 204tl JIC; 205 CIL; 206 CIL; 207 VRC; 208 CIL; 209br SI; 210 VRC; 211 CIL; 212 VRC; 213 CIL; 214 CIL; 214-215b/g VRC; 216 CIL; 218 CIL; 219 VRC; 220 SI; 221 CIL; 221br Rick Cordeiro; 222 CIL; 223 JIC; 224 CIL; 225 JIC; 226tl CIL; 226-227b/g Tourism Ottawa; 228 VRC; 229t CIL; 229br CH; 230 VRC; 231 CIL; 232 CIL; 233 VRC; 234tl CIL; 234-235b/g JIC; 236 CIL; 238 CIL; 240tl CIL; 240-241b/g VRC; 242 CIL; 244 CIL. **Atlantic Canada** – 246-247b/g JIC; 247 Tourism Nova Scotia; 248 VRC; 249 CIL; 250tr CIL; 250r Nova Scotia Archives and Records Management; 250br VRC; 252bl CH; 253t CIL; 253bl SI; 254 CIL; 257 CIL; 258 CIL; 260-261b/g VRC; 261tr CIL.

APPENDIX
262-263b/g VRC; 263 VRC; 264-301 Armon Invento; 303 CIL; 305 CIL; 307 CIL; 310 TD; 311 TD; 303 Brewster Inc.; 305 Suzanne Ingeborg; 307 Jupiter Image Corporation.

www.railwaymapguide.com

Bridges *Tunnels* *Majestic Peaks*

RAILWAY MAP GUIDE

WAY OF THE RAIL PUBLISHING is proud to introduce these beautifully crafted and highly detailed maps of one of the world's longest and most awe-inspiring train routes—Canada. Our Railway Map Guide series is your ticket to Canada's most exotic regions, accessible only by train. But don't take our word for it! Look inside and unfold one of the greatest rail adventures on earth.

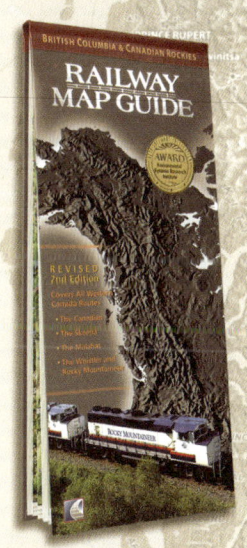

Rocky Mountaineer Edition

Accross Canada

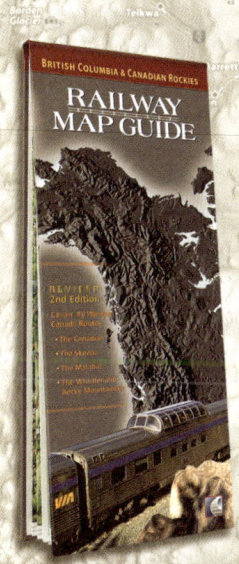

British Columbia & Canadian Rockies

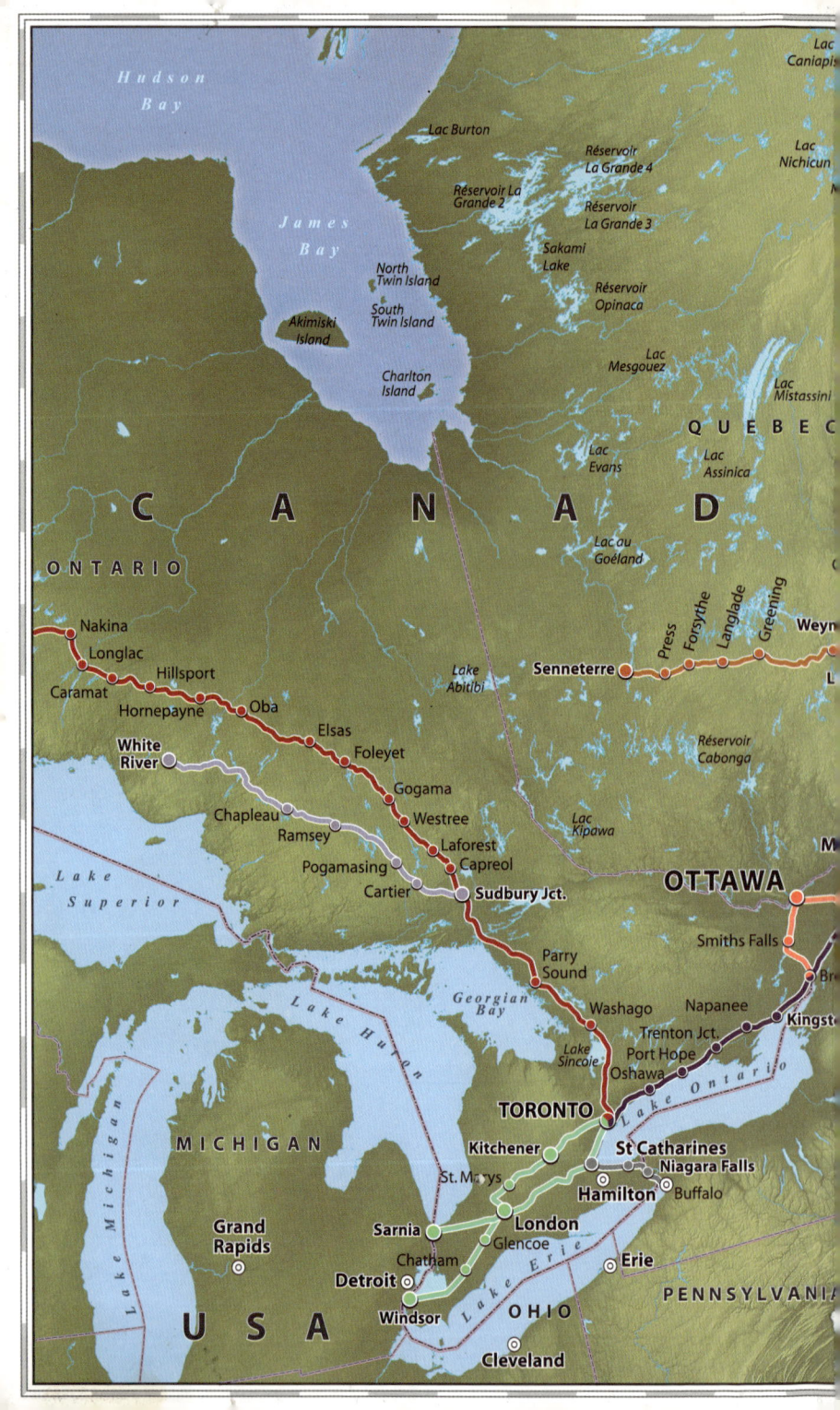